Threatening Property

Columbia Studies in the History of U.S. Capitalism

Columbia Studies in the History of U.S. Capitalism
Series Editors: Devin Fergus, Louis Hyman, Bethany Moreton, and Julia Ott

Capitalism has served as an engine of growth, a source of inequality, and a catalyst for conflict in American history. While remaking our material world, capitalism's myriad forms have altered—and been shaped by—our most fundamental experiences of race, gender, sexuality, nation, and citizenship. This series takes the full measure of the complexity and significance of capitalism, placing it squarely back at the center of the American experience. By drawing insight and inspiration from a range of disciplines and alloying novel methods of social and cultural analysis with the traditions of labor and business history, our authors take history "from the bottom up" all the way to the top.

Threatening Property

Race, Class, and Campaigns to
Legislate Jim Crow Neighborhoods

Elizabeth A. Herbin-Triant

Columbia University Press   New York

Columbia University Press
Publishers Since 1893
New York   Chichester, West Sussex
cup.columbia.edu

Library of Congress Cataloging-in-Publication Data
Names: Herbin-Triant, Elizabeth A., author.
Title: Threatening property : race, class, and campaigns to legislate Jim Crow
    neighborhoods / Elizabeth A. Herbin-Triant.
Description: New York : Columbia University Press, [2019] | Series: Columbia studies in
    the history of U.S. capitalism | Includes bibliographical references and index.
Identifiers: LCCN 2018044278 (print) | LCCN 2018045069 (ebook) |
    ISBN 9780231548472 (e-book) | ISBN 9780231189705 (cloth) |
    ISBN 9780231189712 (pbk.)
Subjects: LCSH: African Americans—Segregation—North Carolina—History—
    20th century. | Discrimination in housing—North Carolina—History—20th century. |
    North Carolina—Race relations—History—20th century. | Social classes—North
    Carolina—History—20th century.
Classification: LCC E185.61 (ebook) | LCC E185.61 .H495 2019 (print) |
    DDC 305.8009756/0904—dc23
LC record available at https://lccn.loc.gov/2018044278

Cover design: Chang Jae Lee

Cover images: Photo: Undated photograph of housing for black workers in east Winston.
Courtesy of the Forsyth County Public Library Photograph Collection. Map: Insurance
Maps of Winston-Salem, North Carolina, Sanborn Map Company, 1912. North Carolina
Maps, https://web.lic.unc.edu/nc-maps/.

For my father, Robert Russell Herbin

One right after another is being taken away from the colored people, one injustice after another being perpetrated. . . . There has developed in North Carolina the greatest menace yet, a movement . . . which will undoubtedly result in legislation, segregating the Negro on the farm lands, thus giving the lie to [Booker T.] Washington's advice to his people that if they will only be good and buy land they will be let alone and will flourish.

—Oswald Garrison Villard, letter to Robert Russo Moton, 1914

Our Neighbors

To love my neighbor as myself
I've always longed to do,
And yet I never can succeed:
My neighbor is a Jew.

To love my neighbor as myself
I've struggled week by week,
I cannot keep this great command:
My neighbor is a Greek.

To love my neighbor as myself,
And not a duty shirk,
I've prayed, but have completely failed:
My neighbor is a Turk.

To love my neighbor as myself
I've toiled with all my soul,
But I know why I missed the mark—
My neighbor is a Pole.

To love my neighbor as myself
And help him in his need,
I cannot do, though hard I've tried:
My neighbor is a Swede.

To love my neighbor as myself
I said, "I know I can!"
I failed, but I've a good excuse:
He is a colored man.

—H. Pearson, published in *The Crisis*, 1913

Contents

Acknowledgments

I suppose this book began more than three decades ago at my parents' dining room table, where my father, Robert Russell Herbin, would lean back in his chair—so far back that he seemed about to topple over—and tell vivid tales about our family and his childhood in Greensboro, North Carolina. His father, Robert Lee Herbin, worked on the farm of a well-to-do white man, Russell Hall, caring for milch cows and growing tobacco. My grandmother, Laura Tonkins Herbin ("Mama" Herbin), ran a small grocery store. While my grandparents (born in 1905 and 1908) did not own their own farm when my father was young, Mama Herbin's father, Isaac "Pap" Tonkins (born in 1870), owned a fairly large one. Along with property, Pap enjoyed considerable influence in his community. Both white and black people would come to him for help with their problems. Often, African American men accused of misdemeanors were released to him, with the understanding that he would keep an eye on them. The influence that Pap wielded had something to do with his being a farm owner. This affected how he viewed himself as well as how others viewed him. The effects of Pap's status as a landowner also lasted generations, influencing the ambitions and sense of self of his descendants.

My father spent his childhood in an area that people referred to as Red Hill (named for the color of its soil) curing tobacco, caring for milch cows, and attending services at the Celia Phelps United Methodist Church, of which Pap Tonkins had been one of the founders. He also found ways to entertain himself by, for example, bumping the school bus that his district hired him to drive to Dudley High into buses driven by his classmates, also on their way to school. He attended North Carolina A&T and was president of the school's NAACP. Though he scored high enough to attend the University of North Carolina's dental school, the school was not "ready" to integrate, and the state subsidized his graduate education at Meharry Medical College in Nashville. Determined to get away from Jim Crow, he moved north.

My father's stories sparked an interest in the South that stayed with me through the years. Circling back to these stories now, after finishing this book, I realize that I've been trying to make sense for years of how, after Pap Tonkins's successes, the next generation (my grandparents and their siblings) worked someone else's farm. I did not intend to study the area that my family came from—and this book is in no sense a family history—but the story of middling white backlash against the successes of black southerners somehow brought me back to the North Carolina Piedmont. It has been, in a sense, a homecoming, and one of its pleasures has been getting to visit the final resting places of my relatives when I'm in town on research trips. For introducing me to stories about the South, for his deep love of history, and for so much else, I dedicate this book to my father.

As an undergraduate at Harvard University, I had many professors who made history exciting to me. Evelyn Brooks Higginbotham in particular did so; I also spent a wonderful year after college working for and learning from her. Eric Foner, Barbara Fields, Betsy Blackmar, Richard Bushman, and William Leach at Columbia University, where I did my graduate work, encouraged me to think more deeply about class and a number of other issues. In doing so, they helped shape my worldview and research interests. This book is influenced in important ways by these scholars and their ideas. Thanks especially to Eric, a kind and supportive mentor. I appreciate the financial support provided by Columbia University, including fellowships granted through the History Department and the Graduate School of Arts and

Sciences, and the Mrs. Giles Whiting Foundation, which granted me a Whiting Fellowship in the Humanities. I also thank Yale University for financial support and Jim Scott, K. Sivaramakrishnan, and Glenda Gilmore for guidance during my year as a postdoctoral fellow in the Program in Agrarian Studies.

I was fascinated to discover through the work of Jack Temple Kirby that Clarence Poe, editor of the *Progressive Farmer*, believed one of the most essential ways to improve life on the farm for small white farmers was to remove black farmers from their communities, after the model of South Africa's Natives Land Act. I met Jack Kirby after he agreed to serve as commentator for a panel that I was putting together, and we had lunch. For a couple of years—until his untimely death—I enjoyed a friendship with Jack. He sent chatty emails about books and his adventures in retirement exploring Florida's natural world. This book comes out too late to thank him, but I wish to acknowledge Jack's influence on this project. This book takes a discovery presented by Jack Kirby in a 1969 article and elaborated on years later by Jeffrey J. Crow—that segregation efforts were not limited to cities, that in fact there was a campaign to segregate the southern countryside in the years before World War I, and that this campaign was presented not as hateful and backward but as progressive—and seeks to explain and contextualize it.

I'd like to acknowledge, too, the historians I've met over the last several years at conferences and elsewhere working in African American, southern, agricultural, or environmental history (or some combination of these) who have spoken with me about this project and, in many cases, offered advice: Andrew C. Baker, Karen Benjamin, Gretchen Boger, Jeffrey Crow, Pete Daniel, Brian Donahue, Kendra Field, Jim Giesen, Michele Gillespie, Paige Glotzer, Jeff Gonda, Steven Hahn, Mark Hersey, LeeAnn Lands, Connie Lester, Liz Lundeen, Robert Nelson, Sarah Phillips, Mark Schultz, Claire Strom, Conevery Bolton Valencius, Jason Ward, Bert Way, and Jeannie Whayne. I've appreciated the collegiality of these historians and admire their work. Adriane Lentz-Smith and Christian Lentz opened their home in Durham to me and took me to a dinner party with Kat Charron, Stephen Kantrowitz, and Tim Tyson, who seemed enthusiastic about this project at a time when I needed encouragement.

M. Ruth Little took me on a personal tour of Longview Gardens in Raleigh. Fam Brownlee, at the Forsyth County Public Library in Winston-Salem, gave texture to the city's history with his long and detailed stories. Ken Badgett helped me locate sources on C. H. Jones and S. J. Bennett, and Todd Kesselring helped locate data for the maps. I appreciate the help of numerous archivists and librarians as I conducted research and gathered images.

I'd like to thank St. John's University for granting me teaching reductions to allow me more time to write and the members of the St. John's history department for their encouragement and friendship: Dolores Augustine, Fran Balla, Mauricio Borrero, Elaine Carey, Tracey-Anne Cooper, Susan Schmidt Horning, Tim Milford, Susie Pak, Phil Misevich, Alejandro Quintana, Kristin Szylvian, Nerina Rustomji, Konrad Tuchsherer, and Lara Vapnek. It was a great pleasure to work with such a collegial, warm, and smart group of people. Thanks, too, to everyone who has welcomed me at the University of Massachusetts Lowell. I appreciate the support and friendship of my history colleagues, Chris Carlsmith, Abby Chandler, Shehong Chen, Andrew Drenas, Lisa Edwards, Lauren Fogle, Bob Forrant, Katie Gill, Paul Keen, Jonathan Liebowitz, Chad Montrie, Michael Pierson, Fletcher Smith, Christoph Strobel, Elizabeth Williams, Patrick Young, and colleagues in other departments, especially Tony Szczesiul, Kirsten Swenson, Sue Kim, Keith Mitchell, and Jonathan Silverman. Thank you to Dean Luis Falcón for supporting this project through a semester-long sabbatical and teaching reductions. I've had many students at St. John's and UMass Lowell who have been a joy to teach. Seeing them encounter primary sources in southern and African American history has helped keep this material fresh for me.

Special thanks to Claire Strom, former editor of *Agricultural History*; Randal Hall, editor of the *Journal of Southern History*; and Bethany Johnson, managing editor of the *JSH*, for providing me the opportunity to test out my ideas and to the anonymous reviewers of my articles in these journals, who provided immensely helpful suggestions. Thank you to the History of Capitalism series editors, especially Devin Fergus, and to Bridget Flannery-McCoy at Columbia University Press for their enthusiasm about this project and valuable feedback; to Bridget, Christian Winting, and Michael Haskell for shepherding this book through production; and to

Rob Fellman for helpful copyediting. Deepest thanks to the press's reviewers, whose detailed comments made this book much stronger and whose faith in the project lifted my spirits: Margaret Garb, Mark Schultz, and an anonymous third reviewer. Many thanks, too, to Kellie Carter Jackson and Tony Szczesiul for reading parts of the manuscript, and to James Beeby, Jeff Gonda, Chad Montrie, and Adrienne Petty for reading the entire thing; these readers offered excellent suggestions.

I'd like to acknowledge friends who shared the trials and tribulations of graduate school, especially Zaheer Ali, Victoria Cain, Jeremy Derfner, Jim Downs, Lisa Ford, Monica Gisolfi, Sara Gregg, Reiko Hillyer, Thea Hunter, Kellie Carter Jackson, Nancy Kwak, Tim McCarthy, Adrienne Petty, Lisa Ramos, Janice Traflet, Karine Walther, and Ashli White (I'm no doubt leaving people out, unintentionally), and Elena Schneider, a friend from college and fellow historian who brought her joie de vivre to even the AHA. Thanks too to Heidi Barrett-Model, Amber Ramage, and many other dear friends outside the field of history who have followed my progress on this project and enriched time spent away from it.

I wish to express my gratitude to my family members for their support of this project. Thanks to everyone on the Triant-Speare side of the family, especially Diane Triant (a writer herself, and a loving grandmother who provided child care on many occasions when I needed it), Jeanne Triant, Craig Estes, and Peter Canellos. I've enjoyed talking with Craig and Pete over the years about many of the themes that animate this book. I wish to acknowledge all my relatives on the Sterry-Herbin side, especially the late Marvin Sterry, who was eager to read my "book" long before it was a book, and Doris Herbin Tarpley and the late Laura Tonkins Herbin, who housed and entertained me with family stories while I conducted research at the National Archives and the Library of Congress. Deepest thanks to my mother, Carole Sterry Herbin, who made a home for us, full of love and creativity and home-grown food, and who has nurtured and cared for me, my kids, and my father. I appreciate the patience of Phoebe, George, and Laurel Triant, my dear and delightful children, who have been competing with this book for attention their entire lives. The person who deserves the most thanks for seeing this book through is William Speare Triant, my sweetheart, my joy, my love.

Introduction

Fifty years after the Civil War began, African Americans were making measurable economic progress in North Carolina. Formerly enslaved people and their children scraped together meager earnings from hours bent under the sun, tending cotton, tobacco, and other crops, to purchase farm land—which they did at higher rates than white farmers. Urban workers labored in hot tobacco factories and used their savings to buy modest homes. They put money into churches and into schools, producing black teachers, lawyers, doctors, and business owners. Their rise took place slowly, as they faced significant hurdles, but steadily. W. E. B. Du Bois, discussing the successes of African Americans in Durham, noted that unlike white entrepreneurs, who were able to look to wealthy investors and expert advisors, "the Negro gathers capital by pennies from people unused to investing; he has no experts whom he may hire and small chance to train experts; and he must literally grope for success through repeated failure."[1]

In parts of the state, middling white people—above poor whites financially but perpetually in danger of losing economic and social status—met the successes of African Americans in gaining property with a vicious backlash. In both the countryside and some cities, they worked to limit the areas where African Americans could purchase property, hoping to keep for themselves access to valuable farmland and urban real estate, along with the better standard of living available in neighborhoods that received municipal services. These people worked to sort property by race in the neighborhoods occupied by the middling classes (elite neighborhoods were already sorted by race as their only black residents were employees living with their employers), and in doing so, to create an unequal system in which African Americans had a harder time acquiring property and in which the property they did acquire was less valuable simply because it was in a black neighborhood.

White elites rarely led this backlash, and in some cases, they worked to contain it. Indeed, white southerners were a varied group made up of people who did not experience the world they inhabited in the same way. From farmers who competed with African Americans over the purchasing of land to planters who hired African Americans to work their soil, from laborers struggling to make do in urban mills to factory owners whose fortunes were built on textiles and tobacco, white southerners' economic and social situations played an important role in shaping their perspectives.

White southerners generally supported a set of policies that fit under the banner of white supremacy in the late nineteenth and early twentieth centuries (policies including the segregation of public spaces), but we must be careful not to overstate the extent of their agreement with one another. When it came to policies that affected their own economic opportunity— including access to property ownership, decent wages, and cheap workers— the things that separated white southerners from one another led to bitter disagreement. White supremacy did not mean the same thing to different groups of white southerners; a shared "whiteness" did not overcome the divisions between and among white people in the South.[2]

The historical record does not always easily reveal divisions among white southerners, who are often lumped together—as white people, as white supremacists, as Democrats (particularly after many former Populists joined the Democratic Party). The illiterate poor, for example, left few records of their thoughts. The story of how some white people worked to bring about residential segregation in North Carolina starting around 1912, along with the story of how other white people undermined those efforts, offers an unusual opportunity to observe these divisions—divisions that often line up with class (though not always, as examples in the coming chapters illustrate). This book tells these two stories. It also tells the story of some African Americans who—in spite of all the things working against them in Jim Crow North Carolina—were acquiring property, thus provoking anxiety on the part of middling whites and fueling a campaign for residential segregation.

At the behest of their middling white residents, a number of southern cities enacted ordinances establishing separate residential areas for their white and black inhabitants. Baltimore's city council passed such an ordinance in 1910. Several cities in Virginia—Ashland, Norfolk, Portsmouth, Richmond, Roanoke—did the same between 1911 and 1913, as did Greenville, South Carolina, and Mooresville and Winston-Salem, North Carolina, in 1912. Atlanta passed a residential segregation ordinance in 1913, Greensboro, North Carolina, passed one in 1914, Spartanburg, South Carolina, in 1915, and by 1916, so had Louisville, St. Louis, Oklahoma City, and New Orleans.[3] Segregationists justified these laws with rhetoric about "prevent[ing] conflict" between black and white people and promoting "the public peace."[4]

These laws were short-lived. In North Carolina, one of a few states to nullify its ordinances through state courts (*State v. Darnell*, 1914), the ruling of the state supreme court stood. In other states that nullified their ordinances, such as Maryland and Georgia, residential segregation became legal again either because legislators passed new legislation that addressed the court's issues with the ordinance or because the court's decision was later reversed. Residential segregation ordinances upheld by state courts lost their legal footing when the U.S. Supreme Court declared them unconstitutional in 1917 in *Buchanan v. Warley*. The opinion of the court in *Buchanan*, written by Justice William R. Day, argued that the Louisville ordinance deprived owners of a right protected by the Constitution: "The Fourteenth Amendment protects life, liberty, and property from invasion by the States without due process of law. Property is more than the mere thing which a person owns. It is elementary that it includes the right to acquire, use, and dispose of it." According to the court, both white and black citizens had a right to buy, use, and sell property.[5]

After *Buchanan* declared residential segregation laws unconstitutional, segregationists tried to achieve similar ends through other means, including the use of restrictive covenants, which were contracts signed by owners agreeing not to sell or lease their property to African Americans. In *Shelley v. Kraemer*, the Supreme Court declared restrictive covenants, common in the United States between 1910 and 1948, not unconstitutional but unenforceable through legal methods. In any case, as the legal historian Mark Tushnet points out, "private agreements" such as restrictive covenants were "less effective than public statutes" as it was not easy to stop a property owner who had signed such a covenant from breaking it. After *Buchanan*, white supremacists also used violence and intimidation as well as zoning and urban renewal to segregate neighborhoods by race, enforcing themselves what the criminal justice system would not enforce for them.[6]

Some segregationists envisioned Jim Crow extending beyond the cities into the countryside. Clarence Poe led a campaign for rural residential segregation from his perch as editor of the *Progressive Farmer*, a farm journal widely read among small white farmers with an interest in learning the latest scientific agricultural techniques in order to maximize efficiency. Poe, because he articulated and influenced the agrarianism of small white farmers, is a uniquely useful route to understanding the aspirations and anxieties of small white farmers in the early twentieth century and how those aspirations and anxieties were directed away from class-based interracial efforts to limit the power of merchants and landlords and toward race-based efforts to limit the access of African Americans to land.[7]

Poe and his readers wanted not a return to slave-run plantations but a new model of smaller farms run by educated, forward-looking white farmers. A participant in a transnational exchange of ideas about segregation, Poe took inspiration from South Africa, where laws prohibited black people from owning land outside of designated areas. Poe's campaign encouraged moderates on the so-called race question to turn to a program that sharply limited opportunity for African Americans—and led to an upswing in racism as, according to Du Bois, "a growing mass of white farmers" demanded residential segregation.[8]

While the idea of residential segregation for the countryside made some progress, it was never put into action. Poe organized a political convention with a rural residential segregation platform to meet in Raleigh in 1914. To his chagrin, rural segregation was removed from the platform. After this setback, Poe began to advocate on behalf of an amendment to the North Carolina state constitution that would allow the members of a community to limit future land sales to members of a particular "race," another mechanism for promoting rural segregation. It received real consideration but did not pass, and the possibility of enacting a law that divided rural North Carolina into separate black and white sections had died by 1915, two years before *Buchanan*, which would have made the program null had it been put into law.[9]

While historians have generally examined the urban and rural campaigns separately, *Threatening Property* tells their stories together.[10] Proponents of residential segregation in Winston and the countryside watched one another's efforts and weighed in on them. They did not work toward residential segregation in isolation but in conversation. Observers at the time drew comparisons between the two programs, too. Examining these efforts as connected reveals an agenda shared by middling white people in parts of the state that had relatively high black populations, namely the Coastal Plain and Piedmont. These white people shared the goal of limiting African Americans' access to property to help their own efforts to gain and protect investments in property. A group that faced farm loss and relocation to industrializing cities (which offered wage-paying jobs with little chance for advancement), middling whites in the Piedmont and the coastal region viewed property ownership as the best route to stability and prosperity for their families in an insecure world, and they were willing to embrace the tool of segregation policy to achieve this.

In pursuing their own interests, at least as they understood them, middling white people challenged the elites who traditionally set policy. Thus the campaigns for residential segregation law in North Carolina show an approach to white supremacy that prioritized the interests of certain middling whites—who did not want African Americans living near them because they thought that black neighbors would lower their property values and jeopardize their social status—over those of elite North Carolinians. This challenge was quashed, and a paternalistic and progressive approach to "race relations" prevailed—one that allowed its adherents (generally elites) to think of themselves as supporting fairness and economic opportunity for African Americans even as they made sure to maintain access to their black workers and continued to pay these workers a pittance for their labor.

A large part of what made someone "middling" or "elite" was where the person resided. The middling whites discussed in this book lived on small farms in the North Carolina countryside or residences in the eastern part of the city of Winston, as did African Americans. Elite whites in the countryside, meanwhile, owned larger farms than did middling farm owners, and they hired croppers to work their land. Some of them were absentee owners. Winston's elites owned homes in the tony West End, which was somewhat distant from black neighborhoods. Social and professional networks and institutions connected these elites to one another. A person's job, too, helped define his or her class. Middling white workers were employed as grocers and salesmen, tradesmen, and foremen in tobacco companies; elites worked as lawyers, bank owners, and factory owners.

While poor white people sometimes appear in this story (and in some ways, their experiences overlapped with those of middling whites), they are not the focus of this story. They lived near middling whites and African Americans, and they labored near them as croppers or tobacco workers. But because they did not own property, they did not concern themselves with property values in the same way that middling whites did.

Middling whites were precariously in the middle class, and material things mattered to them as a way of maintaining their status. For them, segregation was motivated by more than symbolism; it was not just a way of asserting their superior status over African Americans (though this was an important secondary motivation).[11] Middling whites—some but not all of whom had pulled themselves out of the class of renters to own their own property—wanted their residences to be separate from those of African Americans so that they could hold on to the wealth that had accrued in their homes and farms and, thus, hold on to their social status. For these people, segregation was about maintaining economic opportunity and status in addition to displaying power. Even the segregation of public accommodations had economic implications. This type of segregation, which helped middle-class whites categorize individuals by race (an increasingly confusing job in anonymous cities where well-to-do mixed-race people entered white spaces), ensured that what was accessible to white people was better than what was available to black people, whatever their class, and reserved certain taxpayer-funded resources, such as libraries, for the sole use of white people.[12]

While some middling white individuals did work toward a more egalitarian society through the Republican or Populist parties, it was usually the case that middling white peoples' vision of egalitarianism included themselves but not African Americans. Middling whites were excluded by elites from taking leadership positions in what was supposed to be a democracy, but they too sought to exclude the people whom they considered beneath them. Middling whites sought not a broad justice but a place at the table for themselves.[13]

Scholars have acknowledged the existence of conflicting viewpoints among white southerners during many historical periods.[14] For example, as historians explain it, different perspectives and interests were a big part of why in the 1890s some white farmers turned to a new political party, the Populist Party. They believed that the Democratic Party, which catered to the interests of elites, did not address their perspectives or meet their needs.[15] Scholarly analysis should also be applied to investigating the different perspectives of white southerners on segregation and disfranchisement during the age of Jim Crow. I disagree with William Cohen that "solidarity existed" between different classes of white southerners "when it came to segregation and, to a somewhat lesser extent, political exclusion" and with Joel Williamson, who, though he differentiates between radical and conservative strains of racism (ideological rather than class-interest-based differences), still sees a "white unanimity against blackness, molded rigid in a white culture, monolithic, total, and tight."[16] The story is more nuanced than this. Class helped shape the interests of different groups of white people.[17] Elite and middling whites did not see eye to eye when it came to residential segregation, just as they did not on other matters.

An investigation into the campaigns for residential segregation law helps explain what prompted middling whites to embrace residential restriction by 1912 or 1913 as a route to protecting their social and economic status. It explores what the idea of residential segregation meant in the countryside (where, according to the sociologist T. J. Woofter, who began studying the problems of the South in the 1920s, "personal contacts" connected white and black people "in farming and in small town life") and in the modern city (where "contacts . . . are impersonal and corporate").[18] It considers how the version of white supremacy embraced by middling whites differed from that of elites—where the perceived interests of middling and elite whites converged regarding policy toward African Americans and where they split. (This last point helps us understand why other types of segregation law— for example, the segregation of public accommodations—succeeded while residential segregation, which came later, just as the most active period of crafting segregation law was ending, failed.)[19] An examination of these campaigns would not be complete without exploring how African Americans in North Carolina responded and why their response was not as robust as, for example, that of black residents of Louisville, whose work against the segregation ordinance in their city led to victory in the *Buchanan* case.

Through examining campaigns to segregate private property, *Threatening Property* illuminates relationships of different classes of white people to one another and to African Americans in early-twentieth-century North Carolina—relationships that are often misunderstood. The bonds that linked different groups of whites together were, at times, tenuous. Middling whites understood that they viewed certain (but not all) aspects of the so-called race problem differently from elites, and they considered it essential that their solution to this "problem" prevail in order that their vision of prosperity and democracy might take hold. A number of these white people understood that the white supremacy championed by elites offered middling whites very little.

The segregation that middling whites wanted did not come to fruition in North Carolina partly because residential segregation laws were perceived—by some elites, at least—as unconstitutional and un-American in denying people the right to dispose of their property as they wished. But—perhaps more importantly—this type of segregation would have benefited a group that did not wield real political power, middling whites, at the expense of elites. Residential segregation of the countryside was not enacted. Residential segregation in Winston proved more successful, with an ordinance passed, but the state supreme court declared the ordinance invalid when it undermined the economic interests of elites. The failed

l segregation thus reveals the position of middling
led by elites.

l residential segregation either kept silent, not wishing
........; whites who were still an important part of their economy (R. J. Reynolds needed someone to buy his cigarettes, after all), or they
claimed the moral high road, citing principle. Segregation that limited the
ability of blacks to associate with whites was acceptable, they claimed, while
segregation limiting African Americans' right to buy property (along with
the right of whites to sell property to blacks) was not. The people who
blocked residential segregation law did not oppose segregation per se—
instead, they opposed a type of segregation that they argued was unconstitutional for limiting the most essential category of rights, property rights,
and mean-spirited for limiting the opportunities of blacks. There was, they
claimed, a line past which segregation should not go. The financial situation
of elites—one that favored keeping black workers close enough that they
could continue laboring in their fields and factories—allowed them to claim
moral authority, to present themselves as the region's "best men," who had
the interests of both whites and blacks at heart. It was certainly convenient
for elites that their economic interests aligned with their perception of themselves as paternalists.

For white elites, black people were not competitors but valued workers,
ones more easily exploitable than white workers. Elites' vision for their region
differed from that of middling whites, too. Small farmers and those who
sympathized with them hoped that the South might become a land of independent yeoman farmers who participated in their government, and middling whites in cities hoped to climb up the ladder of success. Meanwhile,
elites generally wished to maintain the status quo, wherein their class held
the reins of economic and political power. The successes of some African
Americans in gaining property were not impeding this; elites still found
black labor to be available and compliant. It may be, in fact, that they considered black workers more willing to work within an exploitative system
when they saw that it was not impossible to rise up the economic ladder
to a modest prosperity. White elites in North Carolina did not actively
support black property ownership beyond the individual level, but neither

did they work to prevent African Americans from buying property laboring and middling white neighborhoods.

The divide between middling and elite white people explains why this particular type of segregation stalled. Segregation of public spaces—such as streetcars and theaters—was perceived as benefiting both middling and elite whites. Middling whites gained better resources than African Americans as well as a boost to their self-esteem in a feeling of superiority. It was important to elite whites—including paternalists, who liked to think of themselves as caring about the needs of black people—that the hierarchy established during slavery be maintained. But residential segregation was different. It affected people's financial interests—and it affected the financial interests of these two groups of white people differently.

As Barbara Jeanne Fields and others have argued, looking at an earlier historical period, racism in the American colonies and the United States developed hand in hand with the enterprise of growing cash crops using slave labor, an enterprise central to the colonies' and the nation's economies. Racism took form as white elites tried to justify exploiting the labor of African Americans. During slavery, poor and yeoman whites were largely protected from becoming exploited labor, but after Emancipation they had to compete against black people for resources and low-paying work. Racism evolved after Emancipation as elite whites controlled black labor through new systems such as sharecropping and the convict lease system and as poor and middling whites, no longer able to get by as yeomen, tried to keep themselves above African Americans.[20] This book explores the changing contours of racism in the long aftermath of slavery, showing how the racism of elites differed from that of nonelites. These two groups lived and operated in distinct economic contexts, which meant that they viewed African Americans—and how the presence of African Americans affected their own economic situations—differently.[21]

Animosity toward black people ebbed and flowed depending on circumstance. As perspectives changed, so too did policies, and as policies changed, the civil rights of African Americans expanded or contracted. Racism toward African Americans was heightened among poor and middling white people in the South in the decades after Populism's demise (stoked by Democrats who wished to break up the political alliance between Republicans and Populists). It was particularly fierce around 1910 to 1915—not coincidentally, a time of increasing black landownership.[22] Between 1870 and 1910, African American farmers in the Upper South gained a significant amount of property, even though this was a period of economic depression—and at the same time, white farm owners lost land. The gains of African Americans were most dramatic in Virginia, but in North Carolina, too, black and white farmers noticed the change. Clarence Poe published articles that pointed out this trend and expressed anxiety about black farmers owning what he considered to be too much land. Poe and his readers feared that white farmers would not be able to get the land they needed to prosper. The antagonism that white farmers felt toward African Americans came with them as they migrated to cities and adapted to an urban setting in which African Americans who could afford to do so entered middle-class spaces (public spaces, until these were segregated, but also neighborhoods, as residents), discomfiting urban whites. In cities, white homeowners fixated on property values, worrying that their homes would be rendered less valuable if African Americans lived near them, as more and more were able to do.[23]

Even as economic context plays an important role in shaping racism, it cannot explain all of the contours that racism takes. As David Roediger puts it in his study of the racial consciousness of white workers, "Racism is not a matter of bread alone, but is in addition a way in which white workers have come to look at the world." This helps explain why white people, driven by their fears of what they imagine African Americans to be, make decisions against their economic interests. Racism is often irrational. Roediger borrows the term "wage" from W. E. B. Du Bois to describe a type of "compensat[ion]" for the low pay white workers received for their labor: "status and privileges conferred by race could be used to make up for alienating and exploitative class relationships."[24] Racial exclusion offered the white working class more than protection from economic competition; it offered them a psychological boost, an increase in status. It also, no doubt, allowed them to release some of the anger they felt about their own situation more safely than if they had directed this anger toward the people who kept them from attaining the economic lives they wanted—that is, white elites.

In the end, the advantages of white supremacy accrued in different ways to different classes of white southerners, and the advantages available to poor and middling white people pale in comparison to those enjoyed by elites. White supremacy allowed poor and middling white southerners to think of themselves as better than black people, to release pent-up anger, and to enjoy certain economic privileges, such as less expensive housing than that in black neighborhoods. It did not help them gain decent wages or hold onto their farms.[25] Elites tried to distract the people below them from the unequal distribution of privileges through racist rhetoric.

Racist rhetoric can be deployed by people who use it consciously to further particular ends (such as elites wishing to end or control the voting of African Americans); it can also be internalized (at which point it is ideology). This story will include elites who chose certain rhetoric intentionally in order to stoke the racism of poor and middling whites for political gain; it will also include people of all classes whose fears of African Americans were strong and visceral, their concerns expanding beyond economic interest. This is partly a story of elites influencing the less educated white people around them, but it is also a story of elites, too, internalizing rhetoric and developing real aversion to African Americans. White North Carolinians expressed their aversion through complaints about matters beyond their own economic marginalization, including interracial sex. Of course, racism as driven by economic interest and racism as driven by fears of interracial sex are connected. In North Carolina, racism began as justification for economic exploitation, but as it developed into a worldview, it expanded into other areas, including fear of threats to whites people's "racial purity."

Jim Crow, a system through which white southerners excluded African Americans from certain spaces and found ways to prevent them from voting, was kept in place through law, convention, and violence. It was not right after the Civil War but in the last decades of the nineteenth century and first decade of the twentieth that segregation came to shape where and how black and white southerners interacted, and it took a while to hammer out the various Jim Crow policies.[26] There is a tendency to think of Jim Crow as a set of rigid laws, as sharply defined and fixed. But this is not exactly right, as Jim Crow defined human relationships. Jane Dailey, Glenda Elizabeth Gilmore, and Bryant Simon describe Jim Crow as "a precarious balancing act, pulled in all directions by class, gender, and racial tensions" and as "a social relationship, a dance in which the wary partners matched their steps, bent, and whirled in an unending series of deadly serious improvisations."[27] Recent books examine the negotiations that took place as white southerners made Jim Crow fit their needs, which varied over time and space, and as African Americans tried to carve out room within the strictures of Jim Crow for opportunity and personhood.[28] In his investigation of how Jim Crow operated in rural Hancock County, Georgia, Mark Schultz finds nuance and variety rather than a "Solid South" with only one approach to dealing with African Americans. Relations between black and white inhabitants of this part of Georgia were characterized by intimacy and "personalism," as the white elites who dominated the county did not need a formal system of segregation in order to maintain power.[29] My book emphasizes the experimentalism and dynamism of Jim Crow, too, and shows one type of segregation to have been deeply contested.

This book examines efforts to enact de jure segregation. Historians have not all found the focus on de jure segregation or even the distinction between de jure and de facto segregation to be useful.[30] There is value to studying de jure segregation, however, and there is also an important distinction between the two types of segregation. As Mary White Ovington, one of the founders of the NAACP, pointed out, "it is one thing for an individual or a group of individuals to dictate a Negro policy, and it is a different and more serious thing when this policy becomes a law." According to Ovington, "In the first case, the oppressed race has a fighting chance; but when the discrimination is legalized, to combat it becomes a crime."[31] Like Ovington, I see a meaningful difference here, but it is not the only reason I focus on campaigns for de jure segregation. The work of trying to put residential segregation into law (and of fighting against this) created some types of evidence, such as aldermen's records and newspaper accounts of public hearings, that were not produced through private methods of segregating where people live, evidence that allows me to grapple with the question of who wanted this type of segregation and who did not.

This book relies on previous scholarship on the successes of African Americans in purchasing property, including some excellent studies on North Carolina.[32] This scholarship investigates how African Americans used household production, or "rural entrepreneurship," as well as skilled jobs producing bright-leaf tobacco and off-farm jobs like stemming in tobacco factories to earn money to purchase land and support their schools. It also explores why African Americans were able to acquire more property in cities, where white owners were less concerned with keeping property in the family, than in the countryside.[33] The success of African Americans in North Carolina in increasing their property holdings in the decades after Emancipation is an essential part of the story of residential segregation, as opposition often met those who purchased property near white people.

Threatening Property also builds on scholarship that investigates ideas about race and property, particularly property values—ideas that drove the opposition facing black property owners in North Carolina and throughout the nation. In Atlanta, for example, home owners came to favor the single-family home and the "park-neighborhood" in the early twentieth century as these two particular spaces came to, in LeeAnn Lands's words, "signal white-ness."[34] In post–World War II metropolitan Detroit, white property owners spun exclusion as driven not by racism but by the need to protect property values; according to David M. P. Freund, they "treated race as one of several objective and measurable land-use variables, seldom making distinctions between the threat posed by apartments or overcrowding or even industrial development, on the one hand, and racial integration or 'Negro housing,' on the other."[35]

Indeed, the assumption that African Americans lower property values is a common one; as N. D. B. Connolly, focusing on Miami, explains it, "Real estate was not a blank slate onto which people simply scratched their own meaning. . . . Through the burden of history, real estate carried an inherent racial politics—a white supremacist politics—that made white Americans, immigrants, Native Americans, and even black Americans themselves understand black people—and . . . the black poor, especially—as potential threats to property values."[36] It was in this context, where whites assumed that black neighbors would harm their property values, that middling whites, fearful of slipping in status and resources, pushed for segregation ordinances.[37]

Middling whites feared that as black farmers and industrial workers advanced, there would be less room for white people to do the same. Indeed, they worried that some small white farmers and industrial workers were doing the opposite of advancing. These whites were not models of Anglo-Saxon accomplishment, and, to some observers, they seemed to lean more toward savagery than civilization (a depiction that would meet its apogee years later in Erskine Caldwell's *Tobacco Road*). While anxiety about racial decline focused on poor, propertyless whites, not middling whites, it reveals a belief that, in the words of Natalie Ring, "whiteness was an unstable racial category that had to be reinforced and redefined continually," that economic and social status had to be protected for the good of not just the individual but the entire "race."[38]

Property in real estate was not the only property at stake for white southerners who felt threatened economically or socially. As Cheryl I. Harris has argued, their whiteness was a form of property, too, and they wished to protect the advantages they gained from it. The political theorist C. B. MacPherson defines property as "a man-made institution which creates and maintains certain relations between people"—not a "thing" but a "right," including the right to exclude others from a thing (a right enforced by the state). Whiteness gave those who could claim it access to benefits—distributed unequally among white people—that Jim Crow laws denied African Americans.[39] White southerners felt entitled to state protection of these benefits; as Du Bois put it, they believed that "whiteness is the ownership of the earth forever and ever."[40]

White people realized economic benefits from their whiteness by accessing real estate and other opportunities denied to African Americans; they also expropriated wealth from African Americans and kept it for themselves.[41] In the example of residential segregation, landlords enriched themselves by forcing black people to pay high rents to live in inferior housing stock, and white residents of segregated neighborhoods kept the better resources for themselves (including paved and well-lit streets), even though these resources were partially funded by black taxpayers.

The exploitation of African American labor and property has been essential to the operation of the engine of American capitalism; as Manning Marable explains, "Capitalist development has occurred not in spite of the exclusion of Blacks, but *because* of the brutal exploitation of Blacks as workers and consumers."[42] Certainly, white Americans have benefited by gaining African American–owned property (through eminent domain and other measures) and excluding African Americans from participating in the free market. Segregation also stimulated and fortified capitalism by creating separate classes of devalued and underpaid workers, white and black. Employers benefited greatly from a system that paid different (but in both cases, low) wages for black and white workers, and they also benefited from having their workers at hand. Segregation, of course, was not the only tool used to control black labor during Jim Crow (disfranchisement and racial violence were also vital), but it was an essential one.

Threatening Property explores two different approaches to extracting wealth from African Americans: excluding them from property with better municipal services that their taxes helped fund (the approach of middling whites) and undercompensating them for their labor (the approach of white elites). The approach that prevailed—that of elites—richly rewarded anyone who hired black workers.

North Carolina, though one of several states that sought to enact urban residential segregation at the behest of middling whites, found itself at the center of the campaign for rural residential segregation. Historians may well ask why it was North Carolina that held this dubious privilege. Small white farmers played an important role in the state. These farmers, who operated much farmland, especially in the mountains and Piedmont, came from a tradition of independent thought that went even further back than 1857, when Hinton Helper, as one historian put it, "seemingly rejected his heritage and culture" by publishing a scathing critique of slavery from the perspective of the state's nonslaveholding whites. Helper based his opposition to slavery on its economic effects on white small farmers; like many other antislavery thinkers, he did not concern himself with its effects on African Americans.[43] North Carolina's small white farmers—more so than the small white farmers of other states—also had a voice, which they expressed in venues such as the *Progressive Farmer,* the most important farm journal of its day. While small white farmers in other parts of the South may have seen the world (including the question of rural segregation) as North Carolina's small white farmers did, they lacked the opportunity to put forward their vision.[44]

This story starts with the transformation of North Carolina's countryside. Chapter 1 examines North Carolina's small white farmers: what challenges they faced after the Civil War, what they aspired to, why many of these farmers started moving to nearby cities in the late nineteenth century, and what work they found in these cities. It also tells the life story of Clarence Poe, the champion of these farmers. It looks to explain something essential to the campaign for residential segregation in the state: why small white farmers felt beleaguered and how Poe captured the sense of discontent among these farmers to become their leading spokesman. Chapter 2 examines the political contest between the Populists and Democrats, which caused the replacement of a more rational—though still racist—perspective on African Americans with irrational rhetoric and fearmongering in the popular consciousness. North Carolina's political leadership in the 1890s and early 1900s, both Populist and Democratic, stoked racial animus in the state, using racist rhetoric with the goal of winning the political support of poor and middling white people. The world shaped by these politicians was one in which middling white people came to reject the idea of working alongside African Americans to meet common goals and instead embraced the idea that segregation was the best route to their own success.

Chapter 3 examines how other states and countries influenced the idea of residential segregation in North Carolina. Clarence Poe eagerly followed the Union of South Africa's efforts to restrict black land ownership to certain areas, for example, and his thinking was deeply influenced by that of Maurice Evans, an architect of segregation in South Africa. Proponents of residential segregation law in North Carolina also watched as other southern states passed segregation ordinances. This chapter shows events in North Carolina to have been part of broader national and global trends.

Chapters 4 and 5 explore efforts to put residential segregation into law in North Carolina. Chapter 4 examines Winston-Salem's residential segregation ordinance—who propelled it forward and who brought about its end. Middling whites in the city felt threatened as black tobacco workers moved into housing stock near the tobacco factories—housing that had not been occupied by African Americans previously. While many elite whites did not particularly care about residential segregation, since it did not directly affect them (blacks were not moving into their neighborhoods, after all), some—like Chief Justice Walter Clark of the North Carolina Supreme Court—saw residential segregation laws as driving cheap and dependable black workers out of the cities where they were needed in tobacco manufacturing and other industries. Clark did not use this term, but he protected corporate rights—the right of corporations like the Reynolds Tobacco Company to access and retain workers—over the rights of middling white people to block African Americans from their neighborhoods in his ruling on the ordinance.[45] African Americans' response to the ordinance is remarkable, when compared to that of African Americans in Louisville to their city's ordinance, for its silence.

Chapter 5 explores how Clarence Poe deployed the agrarianism of small white farmers in favor of rural segregation—how he sought to convince these farmers that their chance for success as small farm owners would come only if they lived and worked separately from black farmers. Small white farmers, who watched with increasing bitterness and desperation as black farmers acquired farmland, came to believe they needed help from the state in the form of segregation policy in order to hold onto economic opportunity. White elites and African Americans objected to the idea of rural segregation for various reasons, including its undesirable effects on the productivity of planters' farms as well as its unfairness in limiting the economic opportunities of African Americans.

Woven into all of these chapters are examples of African American success—data showing black farmers acquiring farmland at a higher rate than white farmers, black Republicans gaining political offices (such as Congressman George White), and black families moving into rural communities and urban neighborhoods near white families. In the reactions to these gains, some but not all of which were particular to North Carolina, we see a broader national story: that of middling whites lashing out against the political, economic, and social accomplishments of African Americans, few as these accomplishments might be. Middling whites would tolerate little progress for black people—whether it was a black politician appointed to the board of directors of an institution that cared for blind white people (James H. Young), a black editor who presented white women as no more precious than black women (Alexander Manly), or a black tobacco worker moving onto a formerly all-white block (William Darnell). Elites were willing to accept some of this (a degree of economic progress for African Americans) but not all of it (political success, for example, or the criticism of a system that protected white women but not black women).

Throughout the nation, white people met examples of black success with lynchings and whitecapping, political silencing, and attempts at residential segregation. They did this because they understood that a person's role in society is determined by the value of that person's property, along with the influence wielded by the group within which that person belongs. People who lack economic and political power are liable to be cast as different and separate, and a world will be imagined to explain why they deserve a subordinate position. Middling white people wanted more than this for themselves.

I

Middling Whites in Postbellum North Carolina

Growing up in a world of flailing small farmers, witnessing his family's struggles to succeed in agriculture, Clarence Poe developed an interest early in life in helping white croppers and small landowners gain stability and prosperity. Poe described the community he grew up in as "barely middle-class."[1] He considered his own family typical of the type of farm family he wished to help. As was the case for most white southerners, Poe's ancestors came from France, Scotland, England, and Ireland, facts in which he took great pride because he believed that in Europe "the spirit and ideals of the civilization we enjoy today were gradually developed." Poe acknowledged that his family members had owned slaves before the Civil War but claimed that they were not aristocrats and "had always worked with their own hands."[2] This was probably more true for his father's people than his mother's. Poe's mother, Susan Dismukes Poe, came from a prominent Chatham County family. Her father was a planter as well as clerk of the county court, another relative was a Whig leader, and yet another was the wife of William Dorsey Pender, a major general in the Confederate army who was fatally wounded at Gettysburg. Poe's father came from somewhat humbler stock.[3]

Poe's family, once wealthy (his great-grandfather Jesse Poe owned 380 acres, worked by twenty-six enslaved people who were valued in 1859 at

$13,020), lost much of its wealth as a result of the Civil War.[4] His grand-fathers lent out money before the war and were not able to regain it, result-ing in "serious financial losses."

> As a matter of fact, this situation was so common throughout the South that a word of explanation should be helpful. I have never heard of a bank existing in my county before the Civil War. Some of the wealthiest men would make loans and, since there were no laws to pre-vent it, might charge high interest rates and ask for double security. Acceptable collateral at that time consisted mainly of slaves and land. . . . If we consider that [Confederate and state] bonds, slaves, and Confederate money—all three—were absolutely and simultaneously extinguished as sources of wealth and credit in 1865, it is easy to see that the best-intentioned men were often unable to pay the merest frac-tion of their debts.[5]

The family did not regain its economic position in the decades after the war. Clarence Poe characterized his father, William Baxter Poe, a Confed-erate veteran, as "a small farmer" (though his farm was large enough that he hired laborers to help him work it). William Baxter lost his family's home-stead in 1890 when "an unfortunate business venture, coupled with an attack of fever at a critical period, swept away all his hard-earned savings and left him resourceless with a mortgaged home." After this, he worked at other jobs, including one that brought the family to Greensboro, North Car-olina, and rented a smaller farm while saving the money needed to buy back the family farm.[6]

After losing their farm, the Poes—like so many southern and western farmers of the time—looked to the "new bright hope" of the Farmers' Alli-ance, a group that helped farmers lobby for reform in the days before the Populist Party was founded. Perhaps Poe's focus on the economic insecu-rity of small white farmers was influenced by hearing about and seeing the economic decline of his own family, especially his father's loss of the family home when Poe was at an impressionable age. Poe's experiences led him to develop a lifelong goal for the South: that the region would allow small white farmers, through hard work and cooperation, to save money and buy and hold onto land.[7]

William Baxter Poe had a paternalistic perspective on African Americans that was more typical of elites than of middling farmers. In an article he published in the *Outlook* in 1903 (a surprising accomplishment for a "small farmer"), William Baxter Poe reminisced about various African Americans he had known over the years, some of them enslaved by his father or grandfather, others tenants on his own farm. While patronizing about their morality and participation in activities like conjuring, William Baxter Poe was able to observe a diversity of personalities and levels of ability among African Americans. He also pointed out in a matter-of-fact tone that black farmers had been quite successful in gaining farmland for a time after Emancipation, when cotton prices were high. Without bitterness, he observed: "There are a considerable number of negro farmers . . . who have adopted improved methods and are winning a fair degree of success. I know one in my own neighborhood who is just now building one of the prettiest homes in the vicinity." William Baxter Poe actually wanted to see more African Americans raise their aspirations and improve their quality of life; he believed that this would prove beneficial to them and to their white neighbors.[8]

> The interests of the Southern white workman—whether farmer, mechanic, or day-laborer—are also involved in this matter. He needs protection against low-grade negro labor just as certainly as the unskilled Western man needs protection against low-grade Chinese labor. But we cannot "exclude" the negro if we wished to do so, and the South would not exclude him if it could. . . . The conviction grows on me that the only way for the unskilled Southern white man to avoid being dragged toward the economic level of the negro is to lift the negro nearer the white man's industrial ideals and standard of living.[9]

In this article, William Baxter Poe sounds like a member of the elite (with his focus on helping African Americans do better rather than on "excluding" them from opportunities). He mourns the changing relations between black and white ("Unfortunately, that friendly tie, that close personal relationship, between former master and former slave binds together a steadily diminishing number of whites and blacks") and claims to see a "permanent good feeling between the races."[10]

Clarence Poe was no stranger to elites or their outlook. But he chose as his cause small white farmers, and he rose to prominence by encouraging them and championing them, by voicing and helping shape their aspirations. This chapter follows in the years after the Civil War the class of small white farmers that Poe hoped to reach through his farm journal, as land ownership became more precarious and as some small farmers turned to industrial work in cities. Because of the experiences of these people—the difficulties they faced—Poe's message, that economic opportunities afforded to black farmers posed a direct threat to their own prospects, would resonate with them.

A STATE SHAPED BY SMALL FARMERS

North Carolina stretches over five hundred miles, from the Atlantic Ocean to the rugged Smoky Mountains in the western part of the state. Geologists divide it into three sections, each stretching north to south: Coastal Plain, Piedmont, and Mountain. Alongside the coast lies a level swath of land often called the Coastal Plain or Low Country. From there, the state slopes up to a wide submontane plateau (the Piedmont, a word derived from the French for "foothill"), around three hundred feet above sea level in the east to 1,200 to 1,500 feet above sea level in the west. The Mountain section, which is part of the Appalachian chain, reaches nearly seven thousand feet. These three sections are not unique to North Carolina; indeed, they stretch like ribbons southward from New England to the Gulf of Mexico.[11]

The Coastal Plain, fertile and flat, was a good place for farming and as a result had a higher proportion of plantations than the other sections. Depending on the composition of the soil—made up in different parts of the Coastal Plain of sand, clay loam, shells, or some combination thereof— farmers produced cotton, grasses, fruits, and vegetables. Corn and sweet potatoes were especially important to the economy. This section also had a number of swamps, which could be made suitable for cultivation with draining.[12]

Harder to farm than the Coastal Plain—one source describes its soil as "stiffer and tougher and therefore much more difficult to cultivate than the sandy loams of eastern North Carolina"—the Piedmont was less attractive to planters and thus had a higher proportion of small-scale farmers. It was

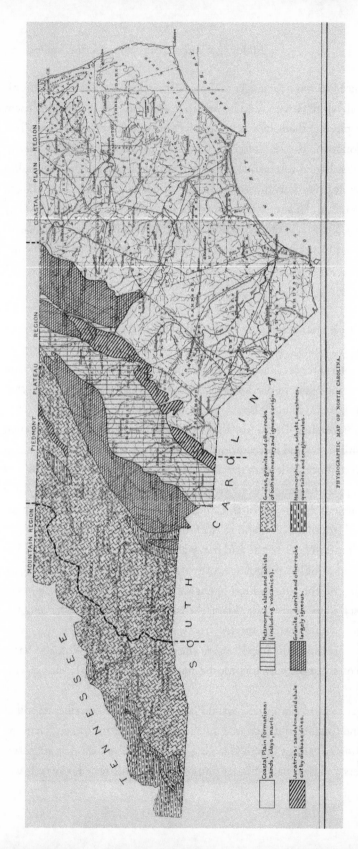

FIGURE 1.1 Physiographic map of North Carolina, 1906.
Source: Courtesy of the Outer Banks History Center, State Archives of North Carolina.

full of gentle hills and valleys and fast streams, the power of which would be harnessed for industry, and its soils were red clay—often powdery when dry and sticky when wet—and rocky. Piedmont farmers grew a wide variety of crops, including cotton and tobacco, but also grasses, fruits, and vegetables, as in the Coastal Plain.[13]

The Mountain region tended to be inhabited by subsistence farmers. Although rich in soil, the mountains were not suited to large-scale farms. These farmers grew vegetables and fruits and were particularly proud of their apples, Irish potatoes, and hay. The tillers of the mountains also produced tobacco, though generally for home consumption rather than for the market.[14]

Farmers cultivated cash crops mostly in the Piedmont and the Coastal Plain—though North Carolina, more than most other southern states, grew a variety of crops rather than focusing on a single cash crop. North Carolina was not as wedded to cotton as other parts of the South, for example; the state was eighth in cotton production in 1890. When cotton prices sank, cotton farmers tended to plant less cotton and more tobacco. The counties that grew the most cotton were in the central Coastal Plain and southern Piedmont. Tobacco, meanwhile, while grown in most of the state's counties for personal use, was produced for the market primarily in thirty counties, eleven of which produced over a million pounds per year. These eleven counties, credited with raising two-thirds of the state's tobacco crop of 1889, were mostly in the northern Piedmont. North Carolina was second in tobacco production in 1895 (after Kentucky) but was number one for the value of its tobacco crop. About six million pounds of rice per year were produced on about 12,000 acres in the lower Cape Fear and other low-lying coastal areas and then processed by Wilmington's National Rice Milling Company. Peanuts, corn, wheat, oats, sweet potatoes, and dairy were also important to the state's economy.[15]

Jonathan Daniels, a careful observer of the state and son of the famed—or infamous, depending on one's perspective—editor Josephus Daniels, described the Coastal Plain as a "conventional old agricultural plantation South of cash crops, Negro labor, and a straight Democratic ticket." While the Coastal Plain was generally characterized by plantation land rented to croppers, many of them African American, small and middling white farmers predominated in certain counties, typically in the northeast. Most of the state's African Americans remained in the eastern part of the state, even after the end of slavery (in 1860, one in twenty slave owners in the Coastal Plain had twenty or more slaves; in contrast, one in fifty Piedmont slave owners owned twenty or more enslaved people). The Piedmont did have African American inhabitants, but small white farmers and industrial workers predominated. The mountains were inhabited by small white farmers who were different culturally from those in the other two regions, influenced by a "long dwelling apart." Daniels noted that in spite of the homogeneity of ethnic background, there were different "types" of whites in North Carolina, each shaped by section.[16]

Though North Carolina, like other southern states, had a wealthy and powerful planter class, small farmers shaped the state's character, if a modern historian can indulge in such a term. State lore described white North Carolinians as turning up their noses at their aristocratic neighbors in Virginia and South Carolina and as proud of contributing proportionally fewer generals and more privates than other southern states to the Confederate war effort. An early-twentieth-century observer described the typical resident of the state as "an equalitarian individualist," someone who "believes in the possibility that he and his fellows may advance" and "is no longer humbled, if he ever was, by the aristocracy of his neighbors."[17] This generalization helps explain the fierce commitment to small farming in the state and the desire among the state's middling whites for legislation to protect their interests, at least as they understood them.[18]

Small farmers included owners of small farms and croppers who aspired to become farm owners.[19] Some farm owners inherited their land from relatives; others purchased farmland that owners had left behind to take jobs in textile manufacturing or forestland unused after turpentine production went into decline. Small farm owners usually grew subsistence crops as well as crops for the market; subsistence agriculture provided some protection during times of low production or low prices for the cash crops they grew. Croppers, meanwhile, who were paid as wages either a share of the crop they raised or proceeds from the sale of this share, were directed by their landlords on what to grow—cash crops—and how to grow them, and they went into debt purchasing food to feed their families. There was fluidity between the two groups, as sometimes croppers pulled themselves into owner-ship. Clarence Poe described tenancy—overly optimistically, as some-times owners lost their small farms and became croppers, too—as "a transi-tion stage—a necessary, wholesome, and not unhappy stage—on the way to ownership."[20] Small farm owners and croppers relied on family labor to grow their crops. It is this "household basis of cultivation"—more than the number of acres worked—that characterizes small farmers. Small farmers also supplemented family labor by swapping labor with neighbors.[21]

There may have been a preponderance of small farmers in North Caro-lina, but political power remained in the upper class, as it did in the rest of the South and had since before the Civil War. The upper class was made up of planters, merchants, factory owners, bankers, doctors, lawyers, certain members of the clergy, and politicians. These people often came from the same families, and it was not unusual for a successful planter to become a merchant or to hold political office. Property requirements limited who could vote until 1857; white men had to own at least fifty acres of land to vote for state senator, one hundred acres to run for the legislature, and more still to run for senator or governor. Even after the advent of "free suffrage," elites held the reins of political power. Slave owners were disproportionately represented in the general assembly in 1860, for example, holding 85 percent of the seats.[22] Below this class in social stature and political power was a mid-dle class made up of small businessmen and landholders, then, below them, factory workers and croppers.[23]

After the Civil War, elites continued to dominate the state legislature and to hold many of the state's seats in Congress, but their power was not with-out limit. Black and white Republicans controlled the "Black Second," for example, a district made up of ten counties mostly in the eastern part of the state, for nearly three decades. The black majority wielded political power in the second district until the disfranchisement amendment to the state constitution stripped African Americans of the right to vote in 1900. This district, which Democrats redrew in 1872 to keep black voters from influ-encing nearby districts, is an example of the vibrancy of the two-party system in North Carolina before 1900. Democrats would present the district as a symbol of "Negro misrule" in the state during the white-supremacy cam-paign at the end of the nineteenth century.[24]

The political power of elites may not have been absolute, as demonstrated by the existence of the Black Second and counties in the mountains dominated by small white farmers, but it was enough that at least one historian of the state describes North Carolina as "not democratic either in the sense of being governed by the people's will or of displaying equality and respect for the individual within the community."[25] Middling whites did not take well to the attempts of elites to dominate them, however. North Carolina—because it was a place where small white farmers were numerous and where they were able to voice their discontent (through Populism and through the *Progressive Farmer*)—was the perfect setting for an assertion of the needs of middling white people.

SLAVERY, THE CIVIL WAR, AND SMALL WHITE FARMERS

Because of the influence of its small farmers, North Carolina had not wholeheartedly supported the Confederate cause. Quakers living in the Piedmont opposed slavery on moral grounds, and many small farmers would have preferred not to be surrounded by slave labor. Hinton Rowan Helper, whose 1857 work criticizing the institution of slavery was embraced by the national Republican Party, grew up on a small farm in the state. Helper argued in *The Impending Crisis of the South* that the South as a whole—though particularly its middling whites—was harmed by slavery, made "woefully inert and inventionless." Under slavery, the South had fallen behind the North in all pursuits, including both agricultural and industrial production. Slavery enriched "an inflated oligarchy" at the cost of the many. Helper expressed great bitterness on the part of the smallholding class against the slaveholding aristocracy. The gentry not only denied small white farmers social and political equality; they also made them unfit for the exercise of these things. It was not vague forces responsible for this but rather the gentry, who "purposely and fiendishly perpetuated" the "unparalleled illiteracy and degradation" of small whites. Indeed, Helper argued, "never were the poorer classes of a people, and those classes so largely in the majority, and all inhabiting the same country, so basely duped, so adroitly swindled, or so damnably outraged."[26]

In 1896, Helper noted that *The Impending Crisis* had taken a "prowhite" (rather than a problack) antislavery perspective and declared that decades after the Civil War his allegiance remained with whites—so much so that it was his hope that the "Race Problem" would be solved in such a way that "there will . . . thenceforth remain upon the earth only white peoples." It was his earnest desire to see "the universal substitution of what is white and wise and winsome for what is black and blundering and baleful."[27]

Helper's belief that slavery hurt small whites was not an anomaly in the state. Helper argued that if the state's voters could vote to keep or remove slavery, "at least two-thirds of them would deposit the *no slavery* ticket," including "perhaps one-fourth of the slaveholders themselves."[28] His numbers may not be correct, but there is truth to the observation that many North Carolinians (including quite a few of the inhabitants of the mountains) opposed slavery and supported the Union. The state resisted joining the Confederacy for several months in 1861, though it eventually did. Especially after July 1863, however, dissatisfaction with the Confederate government and with the toll taken by the war grew among residents of the state. North Carolinians were angry because, among other reasons, the Confederacy had not prevented the Union from capturing much of the eastern part of the state, officers from other states often commanded North Carolina troops, and though the Conscription Act of 1862 had suggested that men would defend their state, they were often sent to other states. Some North Carolinians wished to see the state pull out of the Confederacy or the Confederacy surrender. A North Carolina peace movement emerged and grew in popularity.[29]

North Carolina may not have been fully on board with secession, but it did its share to support the war effort, sending 125,000 men to fight for the Confederacy (though a high number of these men deserted) and enduring much suffering as a result. The 125,000 men who served made up almost 97 percent of the population of white men between the ages of twenty and sixty, which was 128,889 in 1860. About 15,000 men from North Carolina also fought for the Union. About 40,000 North Carolinians died in the war, in action, from wounds, or of disease. The war brought hard times to North Carolina—as, indeed, it did to the rest of the South.

Union forces captured parts of the coast, from which they conducted raids and destroyed infrastructure like railroad lines, bridges, and cotton mills as well as private property like crops, houses, and barns. The death of a third of the state's adult men, the loss of property in slaves, and the inflation of currency took a heavy toll on the economy. One way the state, hoping to rebuild, sought to raise funds after the war was by raising taxes. These increased taxes, along with the ravages of war, forced many farmers to sell land or shift to cash-crop production—which was riskier than subsistence farming. As a result of these changes, the yeomanry was less stable than it had been before the Civil War. Many yeomen fell into debt and lost their farms. Plantations, meanwhile, were broken up into smaller farms that were rented out to croppers.[30]

SMALL FARMERS AFTER THE CIVIL WAR

Republicans in Congress enacted the Southern Homestead Act of 1866 to bring the benefits of homeownership to a broader swath of the population. They made 46 million acres of public land in Alabama, Arkansas, Florida, Louisiana, and Mississippi available for homesteading, meaning for these lands to go to former slaves and landless white people. They wanted to reorder economic and social relations in the region by granting property to people who lacked an economic footing. Considered a failure, the act gave away marginal lands—swampy, untillable, or far from transportation infrastructure—and relatively few of the homesteaders were former slaves. Congress repealed the act after ten years. But through this act and the Homestead Act of 1862, which gave away lands in the West, tens of thousands (or more) of white southerners gained land.[31]

Even as some white southerners gained land after the Civil War, the situation of other small farmers in the region grew worse. A shortage of cash in the South meant that few individuals had the capital to run large plantations. Large landholders had lost their slaves, and they could not pay cash wages. Meanwhile, yeoman farmers, too, had generally lost their financial assets, and the newly freed slaves lacked the money they needed to set themselves up as independent farmers. Sharecropping and tenancy allowed landowners to grow cotton and other cash crops without having to pay cash wages while also allowing freed slaves and poor whites to maintain some autonomy in their day-to-day working lives.[32]

The difference between tenancy and sharecropping was a degree of independence. Neither tenants nor sharecroppers owned the land they worked, but tenants usually owned one or two mules or farm equipment. Tenants rented land, paying cash or a share of their crop as rent; tenants technically owned their crops. Sharecroppers owned neither the farm equipment they used nor the crops they grew; landlords owned the crops and paid sharecroppers proceeds from the sale of part of the crop as wages. Landowners controlled sharecroppers' work more than tenants' because the sharecroppers were working on the landlords' crops and the landlords had an interest in seeing that these crops were as large and profitable as possible.[33] Sharecroppers and tenants had to grow cash crops in order to qualify for loans from merchants or planters (their future crops were used as security for their loans) or to purchase supplies on credit. Called the crop lien system, this credit came at extremely high rates of interest.[34]

Tenancy and sharecropping benefited landlords in a few ways. The two systems required little capital (as workers were paid part of the crop they grew), and they ensured that the workforce stayed through the harvest because that was when they received their pay. There were many problems with sharecropping and tenancy for the worker. For one, workers were not paid when crops failed. Different states had different laws on who had first right to a crop, a landlord owed his rent or a merchant with a lien on the crop. Generally, if a landowner was in debt, his creditor could lay claim to the crop, leaving nothing to the person who had grown the crop. Also, if a sharecropper owed both a landlord and a merchant, the crop would go toward paying the creditors, even if nothing was left over for the sharecropper. The system also allowed room for landlords to cheat their workers. For these reasons, the people who worked as tenants and sharecroppers were desperately impoverished.[35]

Republicans in power in North Carolina generally sought to protect vulnerable farmers after the Civil War. For example, Justice William Blount Rodman of North Carolina's supreme court wrote two opinions—for *Harrison v. Ricks* and *Haskins v. Royster*, both in 1874—that worked to protect sharecroppers and tenants by encouraging landlords to make written rather than oral contracts with these workers. While these cases declared share-croppers lacking in any right to the land and crop, they did draw a distinction between sharecroppers and tenants—important because it allowed for not just the worse option (sharecropping) but also a more favorable category (tenancy).[36] *Harrison* distinguished the two categories of workers: tenants were empowered in owning their crop and being the ones to divide the crop in order to pay a share to the landlord as rent; croppers did not own or divide their crops. Croppers, though they did have "in some sense, the possession of the crop, it is only the possession of a servant."[37] In *Haskins*, Rodman further explained what it meant for a cropper to be considered a servant: "as much a servant as if his wages were fixed and payable in money." The cropper's having grown the crop did not entitle him to any relationship to that crop. He was, as Marx would put it, alienated from the fruit of his labor.[38]

Starting in 1875, Democrats newly in power passed a number of amendments to the 1868 constitution that favored the landlord in questions of who owned the crop and whose lien on the crop had priority. They removed the distinctions between the different categories of workers on farms, leaving the remaining category—that of the cropper—lacking autonomy and ownership of the crop. The lien laws also favored the landlord: as Adam Jacob Wolkoff explains it, "Because he owned the crop, the landlord's lien on it was 'preferred to all other liens.' Merchants . . . could continue to provide food and supplies to tenants, but they could not cut the landlord in the payment line." Putting the landlord's lien ahead of the merchant's also led to costlier credit for croppers because merchants charged more to balance the increase in risk.[39]

As cropping became landless farmers' primary option, North Carolina's small farmers became ever more vulnerable to the vicissitudes of the market. Landlords required that croppers grow cash crops. Small farm owners, too, began to rely more on cash crops. Traditionally, yeomen had focused on growing foods for their families and livestock rather than cash crops and then had sold what they did not need. In the decades of the 1870s, they began to grow fewer sweet potatoes and less wheat and corn and to raise fewer pigs and cows; they put their effort into growing more tobacco and cotton. Cotton in particular brought farmers much heartbreak, as the British bought less of the crop—they had sources in Egypt and India now—and farmers produced too much of it. The price of cotton fell over the decades, from twenty-five cents per pound in 1868 to seven cents in the 1890s. Deflation, which the United States suffered around this time, lowered crop prices and increased the value of farmers' debts. Farmers tried to solve the problems of debt and low crop prices by growing more cash crops.[40]

Even while the options available to landless farmers became narrower, croppers found ways to assert their rights, and even under Democratic leadership, their rights actually included a type of possession of the crop. Examining "the lived experience of landlord-tenant relations," Wolkoff argues that landlord-tenant law "was never a static or hegemonic order"—that croppers (he calls them tenants) had some room to claim the fruits of their labor as their own property and from time to time did so successfully.[41]

In one case that went up to the state supreme court and was decided in 1881, a white Granville County tobacco farmer named Alexander Curtis sued Abner Veazey, his landlord. The men had divided the tobacco crop, but Veazey took Curtis's share out of the barn and smokehouse. Veazey argued that because the land and buildings on it were his, he had a right to enter and remove what he wished. Both the superior court and supreme court sided with Curtis, declaring the tobacco Curtis's property alone.

In another case, George Copeland, an African American farmer in Anson County, tossed two bags of seed cotton off of the wagon he was driving to his landlord's cotton gin, where the cotton would be ginned and divided. Later that day, he returned to pick up the two bags and kept them for himself. Charged with larceny, Copeland brought his case before the state supreme court, where Justice Thomas Ashe determined that Copeland had "actual possession" (not the same as ownership) of the cotton—which he did not give up when he tossed out the bags of cotton. Returning to pick up the cotton, he was not stealing but rather "reclaiming property that remained under his control." This property would leave his control only when it reached the cotton gin for division, and it was only at that point that he could be considered to have stolen it. Much hinged on the legal definition of "possession," and croppers legally enjoyed a joint possession with their landlords until the crop was divided and they were paid their share as a wage. As Wolkoff describes this, "the landlord's lien provided one form of possession, but the tenant or cropper's 'actual possession' constituted another form of quasi-ownership."[42]

Small farmers typically preferred ownership to cropping, but it should not be assumed that those who were able to purchase their own farms automatically did better than croppers. As Harold Woodman explains it, both small farm owners and renters generally worked "marginal farms" and were disadvantaged in the "competition" with "larger, more efficient farms."[43] While owning land may not have brought about a dramatically different situation from the one that renters found themselves in, it did come with benefits, such as the first lien on the crop. Perhaps the most important benefit of farm ownership was the autonomy it allowed the owner.

Landowners usually had to grow cash crops in order to pay off their debts, but they had more control over what they planted than croppers, who generally had little or no say over what to plant, or when, or how. Small landholders, unlike croppers, generally had the freedom to grow the subsistence crops that meant they would not have to purchase food. As a result, small farm owners produced more food for their families than did renters—producing more milk, butter, pork, lard, flour, and meal than renters—and were able to use expensive credit for "business use," investing in things like fertilizers and modern tools rather than using credit to pay living expenses.[44]

While it is difficult to separate out the different factors explaining why farm owners had an advantage over croppers, it is clear that they did. The measure of autonomy they enjoyed affected the way they worked, and the way they worked affected their working and living conditions. The 1910 census listed the average value of North Carolina farms (including "land and buildings on farms") operated by owners as $2,101, compared to $1,278 for tenants.[45] A 1923 state bulletin pointed out something that was true decades earlier, too: "landless" farmers were more likely to engage in "exhaustive" farming practices than were owners, meaning that over time their soil became degraded and their yields lower. Their poverty also shaped their living conditions.[46]

> The landless families live in poorer houses, they live under worse sanitary conditions, have poorer health, lose more of their children by death than the owners do. They are more illiterate, fail to reach as high grades in school, take less papers and magazines, have fewer books in

their homes, attend church and Sunday-school less, have fewer home amusements, attend community affairs less often.[47]

Conditions among croppers looked quite grim; among small farm owners, things looked somewhat brighter. Because farm ownership mattered, rural people paid attention to which farmers were pulling themselves into farm ownership. They noted whether new farm owners were white or black, and when black farmers purchased desirable properties, they worried that small white farmers were losing out on opportunities for advancement.

Autonomy brought farm owners psychological benefits. A farm owner, as people believed, enjoyed freedom from the supervision of others and variety in his or her work. It should be noted, though, that the autonomy of small farmers did not mean that these farmers were islands disconnected from others; in fact, the self-sufficiency of yeomen operated at the level of the community rather than the individual farm. Successful yeomen exchanged goods and counted on one another in times of hardship (those in plantation areas counted on nearby planters, too).[48]

In 1890, most residents of North Carolina still worked in agriculture, even though the state had a number of textile mills and tobacco-processing plants, primarily in the Piedmont.[49] That same year, the census counted 1,617,947 people living in North Carolina, 561,018 of them (almost 35 percent) "Negro." It also counted 178,359 farms, which were operated by owners, rented for a share of the crop, or rented for a fixed monetary value (in North Carolina, this arrangement was relatively uncommon, used for a little over ten thousand farms). By far, most farms (almost two-thirds) were operated by owners; this was the case for 117,469 farms. The yeomanry had not disappeared, even if the status of yeoman farmers seemed less stable; as some yeomen lost their farms, other farmers—croppers, or the children of yeomen—purchased farms. Just over fifty thousand farms were rented for a share of the crop, meanwhile. The 1890 census did not track the race of these farmers.[50]

Between 1900 and 1910, the total numbers of farms operated by owners and nonowners increased, among both white and black farmers (table 1.1). While the number of farms operated by white owners grew by 11 percent, the number of farms operated by black owners grew by more than twice that number.

TABLE 1.1 Number of farms operated by white and black owners and croppers, North Carolina

Year	Farms operated by whites	Farms operated by white owners	Farms operated by white tenants	
1900	169,773	111,544	55,785	
1910	188,069	123,877	63,148	

Year	Farms operated by blacks	Farms operated by black owners	Farms operated by black tenants	
1900	54,864	17,434	37,223	
1910	65,656	21,443	44,139	

Year	% change in white owners	% change in black owners	% change in white tenants	% change in black croppers
1900–1910	11	23	13	18.6

Note: The census uses the term "tenant"
Source: http://socialexplorer.com.

An increasing percentage of North Carolina's farms were operated by nonowners (42.3 percent in 1910, up from a third in 1890), and a third of white farmers were croppers. The size of farms in the state was growing smaller, too.[51] These trends help explain why small white farmers viewed themselves as beleaguered. Seeing their black neighbors increasingly coming to farm ownership, small white farmers believed that this would lead to less opportunity for themselves.

In 1913, Poe sounded the alarm on the pages of the *Progressive Farmer* about the trend of increasing black farm ownership:

If anyone is inclined to question whether what we have said in this article can be officially substantiated, he has only to consult the official census figures for the decade 1900–1910. . . . And in the South Atlantic States (the Carolinas, Virginia, Georgia, Florida, Maryland, and Delaware), the Negro acreage increased 13 per cent, while the white decreased 2 per cent.

As Booker Washington says, the Negro now owns farm lands "greater in area than the five States of Vermont, New York, Massachusetts, Rhode Island, and Connecticut. . . . [This] is largely due (1) to the Negro crowding out the small white farmer by lower standards of living, and (2) to the fact that the white farmers in many sections have moved away because of the lack of adequate white society."[52]

Poe's explanation for the success of black farmers—that they economized (or, here, accepted "lower standards of living") and that white folks sold their land to African Americans when they found themselves in the racial minority—allowed him to shift the blame away from small white farmers. Small white farmers should not be criticized for their sense of decency, he implied—they would not ask their families to put up with degradation, and they would not live where they were surrounded by black neighbors.

Most African Americans in postbellum North Carolina worked someone else's land; by 1910, over two-thirds of black farmers were still croppers. Property ownership among African Americans in the state did rise dramatically during the period of 1890 to 1910, however. In 1870, 1,628 African Americans owned $658,500 worth of real estate (an average of $404); in 1910, 20,707 owned $22,810,089 (an average of $1,102).[53] Robert Kenzer has demonstrated that much of this gain was among black people in North Carolina's cities, who were more successful than those in its countryside at acquiring property: "Despite composing only 16.6 percent of North Carolina's black population and being both younger and more likely to be female than the rural black population—factors that generally inhibit homeownership—black urbanites in 1910 composed nearly half of all black homeowners." This was the case for a few reasons, including that white farm owners often wished to hold onto their property for their children, while whites in cities were less committed to keeping property in the family.[54] Yet black farmers, too, were improving their lot.

Poe saw the trend of rising numbers of black farm owners in his hometown. Chatham County, just to the southwest of Raleigh, lies squarely in the Piedmont. In many parts of the county, black and white farmers lived and worked next to one another. While many of these black farmers rented, a number owned their land. For example, near the farm that William Poe owned and lived on in 1900 were three farms owned by African American families, headed by Rocia, Flora, and Lloyd Goldston. The Goldstons lived on their farms with their families.[55] Ten years later, African Americans continued to own farms next to white families in the area. Poe's rural

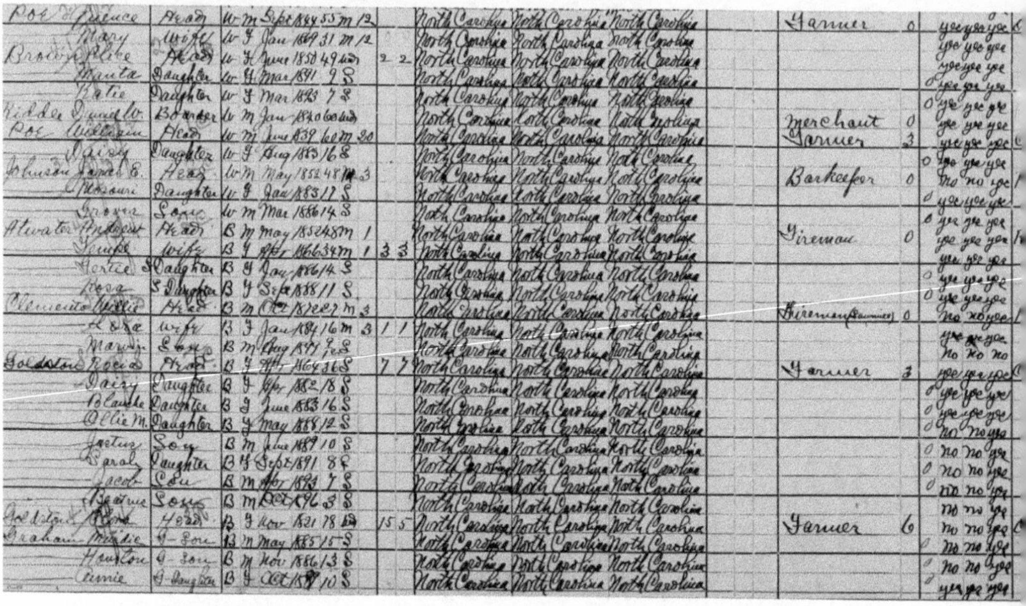

FIGURE 1.2 Census manuscript showing the Poe homestead surrounded by farms owned by African Americans in 1900.
Source: Twelfth Census of the United States, Schedule No. 1—Population, 1900, Chatham County, North Carolina, Rock Rest Township, Enumeration District 14, Sheet 3B, http://familysearch.org.

segregation campaign was not a response to an influx of black farmers (as there was no such influx) but to increasing numbers of black neighbors climbing up the economic ladder to farm ownership. It was an attempt to renegotiate relations in the countryside, where living near black renters might have been acceptable (though perhaps not ideal) to whites but where competing with black buyers for farmland was not.[56]

Poe complained in 1913 that his family farm was surrounded by African Americans, hinting that while he could find black buyers for the farm, there were no white buyers. The Poes decided to leave the farm "absolutely vacant this year, we having refused to sell to a Negro, and the white family who were there last year having left because there were not enough white neighbors in the community."[57] Poe's description of the advance of African Americans into rural communities is reminiscent of domino theory, wherein neighborhoods fell to black farmers, one after the next:

There was something epic, something tragic, about the letter we had only last week from a cousin who lives on a strip of this old farm. "It looks like sometime we will have to give up this community to the blacks," he wrote me half-despairingly, and yet with a determination to make yet other efforts before giving up—and all at once the epic significance of his struggle dawned upon us. He is a hero of the rear-guard of our ancient Anglo-Saxon civilization who still keeps the colors flying and still wages a valiant battle to hold a community for the white race and the white man's civilization, tho almost surrounded by a silent, insidious, ever-advancing opposition. And he is but a type—a type of thousands and thousands of others who are similarly fighting similar tragic battles all over the South from Virginia to Texas and whose appeals, alas! have been but voices in the wilderness, unheard and unregarded by the town-dwelling leaders of our race.[58]

Poe's military metaphors reveal that for him, this was a war. Black buyers, not renters, made up the "ever-advancing opposition," an army marching forward to get hold of the American dream for themselves.

The trend of black southerners buying land and growing wealth more rapidly than white southerners between 1890 and 1910 held true in much of the South. Neil Canaday demonstrates this trend in Calhoun County, South Carolina, for example, arguing that literate African Americans were more likely to acquire property there. That black farmers were purchasing land at higher rates than white buyers is all the more impressive considering that, in Tennessee (and in other states, too), black buyers paid significantly more than white buyers for land, even though the land they purchased tended to be less valuable.[59] Evan Bennett explores some of the strategies employed by black farmers that helped them amass property; by growing the profitable bright-leaf tobacco, a number of black farmers in Cedar Grove, North Carolina, saved enough money to purchase their own farms. As farmers realized the potential of land in the Piedmont for tobacco growing, plantation owners subdivided their land into small farms, and small operators began to farm land that had previously not been under cultivation.[60]

Certainly, black farmers faced challenges. While some of these challenges were unique to them—such as the lack of wealth coming out of slavery—others created by the Jim Crow system actually affected both black and white farmers. In *Standing Their Ground*, Adrienne Petty argues against "the enduring and mistaken assumption that the Jim Crow system had no negative impact beyond black people, and that white people in the South uniformly benefited from the systematic exclusion, exploitation, and abrogation of political rights meted out to black people."[61] The system of cropping, for example, originally meant to allow planters to continue working their fields with the labor of formerly enslaved people, also ensnared white farm workers. Residential segregation law also serves as an example of a policy that was meant to benefit white people but did not always do so, as it limited the rights of white land owners to sell property that might have been undesirable to whites (as was the Poe's family farm) to African Americans instead.

THE SMALL WHITE FARMER'S CHAMPION

Small farmers black and white purchased lands that had previously been used by the turpentine industry as it left the state. They found new opportunities in cultivating bright-leaf tobacco and in truck farming, made possible by the expansion of the railroad. Yet the yeoman's life had become a less stable proposition. Many croppers aspired to become small farm owners who grew subsistence crops, but this was a dream they had trouble achieving.[62]

North Carolina's small white farmers viewed farm ownership as an essential part of their cultural heritage, which valued independence. Many of the ideas about the value of farm ownership that circulated in late-nineteenth- and early-twentieth-century North Carolina had been articulated by Thomas Jefferson generations earlier. Jefferson presented small white farm owners as citizens and workers essential to the nation as well as to the success of local farming communities. He argued that the qualities associated with small farming (autonomy in one's work and closeness to nature) created a more independent person: small farming built character. The notion that virtuous land owners made better citizens justified property requirements for the vote. Meanwhile, this so-called democracy excluded from participation people who lacked independence, like women and slaves.

Not all of these ideas about labor and citizenship originated with Jefferson. The idea that the type of labor a person carries out shapes his character came out of eighteenth-century European philosophy. In his *Wealth of Nations* (1776), for example, Adam Smith argued that specialized labor created dull workers and bad citizens because the process of doing the same thing over and over again stifled creativity.[63] But Jefferson popularized these ideas in America, glorifying farmers as "the chosen people of God," diligent workers who cared about the public good and "whose breasts [God] has made his peculiar deposit for substantial and genuine virtue." Jefferson contrasted the virtues of farmers to the moral failings of factory workers, whom he viewed as corrupted by their dependence on "the casualties and caprice of customers."[64]

From Jefferson's day to the present, agrarianism has thrived as the nation became more and more industrialized—indeed, *because* the nation (and agriculture) was becoming industrialized. Many Americans saw industrialization's ugly side and yearned for simpler days. They viewed industrial life as corrupt and destructive of democracy. Agrarianism helped them feel better about their industrializing nation and allowed them to hope that the values forged in the countryside would be protected.[65]

Poe and other agrarians considered the stakes for maintaining a yeomanry to be high. A large and successful yeomanry would allow the South to be an agrarian oasis in an industrial nation, the only place of true democracy in a nation where the gap between rich and poor was becoming ever larger. If small farmers could not prosper in the South, the region would continue as a land of poverty, exploitation, and suffering, southern agrarians believed—a land where some landlords, merchants, and industrialists gained wealth but where most of the population endured great hardship. Attaining yeoman status was thus an end in itself, not a step on the way to grander ambitions. Those who embraced the yeoman ideal viewed large farms as antidemocratic as their owners could not work their holdings themselves and relied on laborers. As Poe explained this, "To make the rural South a great democracy of thrifty, home-owning small white farmers—this is our only hope of becoming a permanently great and forceful section."[66]

Clarence Poe articulated and influenced the agrarianism of small white farmers in North Carolina, an agrarianism that was not the same as

FIGURE 1.3   Clarence Poe as a young man in his office at the *Progressive Farmer*.
Source: Courtesy of the State Archives of North Carolina.

Jefferson's, for Poe's had evolved along with the times. Poe's life and work illuminate the connection between agrarianism and racism, showing why small white farmers believed they would have more opportunity for success apart from African Americans.

Born in 1881, Poe came of age at a time when North Carolina's public schools provided a short school term to allow children to work in the fields most of the year. He attended the one-room Rocky Branch School in Chatham County, which was open four months each year. He did not attend high school or college; his education—as his son pointed out years later—"came from many sources." These included "the teachings of his mother, herself a teacher," as well as "diligent reading of many books and good magazines." Self-conscious about his lack of formal education, Poe devoted much time to reading the classics. As an adult, Poe also learned from "extensive travel to all parts of the Eastern and Southern United States, two trips to Europe, and one trip around the world studying agricultural conditions . . . and most especially from many conversations and vigorous discussions with the leading educators, businessmen, statesmen and leaders in all walks of life."[67]

He may not have been formally educated, but Poe was not poor, and he grew up in an attractive home. He describes it in his autobiography:

> The old country home where I was born, a sturdy six-room one-and-a-half-story frame house with a tall rock chimney at each end, a separate kitchen and dining room, smokehouse, barns, carriage house, and screw cotton gin, had been built long before the Civil War. A wide porch ran the entire length of the house on the sunny south side with inviting benches along the wall. . . . My grandfather had long before planted sycamores whose gleaming white bodies, now grown quite large, bordered the picket fence that enclosed the yard. A large "horse apple" tree was nearby, also a vegetable garden, a grape arbor, and apple, peach, and pear trees.[68]

Poe moved to Raleigh as a sixteen-year-old to work at the *Progressive Farmer*, thus beginning a rise that he later presented as a Horatio Alger story.[69] He had written a letter to the editor of the journal along with an article for publication arguing in favor of an extended school term (at the time, the state provided for an eleven-week school year). The editor invited Poe to work at the *Progressive Farmer* as an office boy, and he arrived at the journal's offices in a $2.75 suit that did not cover his wrists or his ankles. Out of place—one article about Poe teased that "a more simple, gawky, awkward youth never came from country to town"—he soon learned to hold his own in the city.[70] Poe was bookish, earnest, ambitious, and hard working, and he put his attention toward improvement not only of his region but also of himself. He wrote a note to himself in 1911 promising to "take care of my body (1) by vigorous exercise, (2) eight hours sleep unbroken by serious thought, (3) frequent rest, and (4) erect bearing at the desk and away from it." Even as an adult, he took icy baths and insisted that his children sleep on an outdoor sleeping porch, believing that this was healthful.[71] His secretary described Poe as "nice enough," though overworked, and of a "nervous, irritable temperament." She observed that he "seems to be on the point of a regular nervous breakdown."[72]

When Poe was eighteen years old, in 1899, he became editor of the *Progressive Farmer*, which had about five thousand subscribers at the time. Poe bought majority control of the journal in 1903, and it blossomed under his direction, purchasing smaller agricultural newspapers and expanding through the South. A high-profile, active editor, Poe shaped the journal to reflect his experiences and values. He both influenced farmers and was influenced by them. He wrote within the bounds of what would have made sense to these farmers, and he heeded them in a way that politicians did not always bother to do, as they were a group without significant political power. Based in Raleigh, the *Progressive Farmer* was printed in different editions for the Carolinas and Virginia; Alabama and Georgia; Tennessee, Mississippi, Louisiana, and Arkansas; and Texas. Circulation grew. In 1917, the journal had a circulation of 200,000; by 1926, it had 475,000 subscribers. Four years later, after purchasing and merging with Atlanta's *Southern Ruralist*, its circulation exceeded one million. (The next most popular farm journal was Nashville's *Southern Agriculturalist*, with a circulation of 630,000.) The *Progressive Farmer* was one of a number of farm journals—white southern farmers also read the *Southern Cultivator* and the *Southern Planter*, among other publications, and black farmers read the *Negro Farmer* and the *Southern Workman*. The *Progressive Farmer* was the journal with the largest circulation by 1930, though. Poe remained at the helm of the journal until 1954.[73]

Founded by Leonidas Polk in 1886 as the organ of the Farmers' Alliance, the journal remained deeply influenced by Populist ideas under Poe's leadership, which it showed by opposing monopolies and encouraging farmers to form agricultural cooperatives. The popularity of the *Progressive Farmer* suggests that Populist ideas had not fallen out of favor along with the Populist Party. No longer expressed through politics, these ideas were articulated in places such as the press. There they came together with Progressive ideas about reform.[74]

As editor, Poe promoted what he called "two-armed farming"—that is, farming with crops and livestock. He advised farmers to diversify in order to free themselves from the grip of cotton and tobacco. His goals were broader than touting certain agricultural methods, though; one friend summed this up in a paean to Poe: "He has taught farmers how to farm, but most of all he has taught them how to live."[75] He made his case for how farmers should live on the pages of the *Progressive Farmer* and in speeches and books. While working to build the *Progressive Farmer*'s reputation and circulation, he also published *Cotton: Its Cultivation, Marketing, and Manufacture*, with C. W. Burkett (1906); *A Southerner in Europe* (1908); *Where Half the World Is Waking Up* (1912); *Life and Speeches of Charles B. Aycock*, with R. D. W. Connor (1912); and *How Farmers Cooperate and Double Profits* (1915).[76]

Poe worked hard to gain a position of influence. His son Charles Aycock Poe, a Raleigh lawyer, recalled that his father regularly sent off letters to a mailing list that included newspaper editors, state and federal politicians, and business leaders. He accompanied these letters with "an editorial he had written or speech he had given and urging their consideration and support for his views." Charles Aycock Poe believed that this, along with his father's editorial page, was responsible for his influence; he cited Albert Coates in calling Clarence Poe "a master at molding and organizing public opinion."[77] Another source described Poe as "one important reason why the word 'progressive' is so much a part of [North Carolina's] tradition." Indeed, no "editor has had as great or as prolonged an influence over the rural South as Clarence Poe. For 56 years he has called the editorial shots in *The Progressive Farmer*. . . . [From this position] Poe has had an unequalled opportunity to shape the thinking of the rural South."[78]

Poe's diligence paid off; people who were interested in southern agriculture paid attention to what he had to say. He gained recognition, receiving honorary degrees from Wake Forest College (Litt.D., 1914); the University of North Carolina (LL.D., 1928); Washington College, Maryland (LL.D., 1929); and Clemson Agricultural College (Sc.D., 1937). He was also appointed to or voted into a number of prominent positions. He was a trustee of the North Carolina State College of Agriculture and Engineering (1916–1931), a member of the executive committee of the University of North Carolina (starting in 1931), a member of the State Board of Agriculture (1913–1931), a member of a state commission authorized to draft a revision of North Carolina's state constitution (1931–1932), and the chairman of a state commission that won ratification of five amendments revising the state tax system (1936).[79] Poe's secretary observed in 1920 that Poe was "in everything here [in Raleigh], and some folks say he is likely to be the next governor." She suspected that Poe actually hoped to become secretary of agriculture.[80] In 1939, there was buzz about Poe "being groomed" as a "dark horse" candidate for the governor's office.[81] He was put forward in 1940 to fill Henry A. Wallace's term as U.S. secretary of agriculture; he was backed because he was a southerner, because he had a large following among southern farmers, and because he was an "advocate and defender of New Deal farm policies." President Roosevelt chose Claude Wickard instead, however, in spite of what he referred to as Poe's "fine qualities."[82]

Poe's situation in life was vastly different from that of the farmers who read his journal. In 1912, Poe married Alice Aycock, the daughter of Charles Aycock, the white-supremacist governor of North Carolina from 1901 to 1905. Poe and Alice had three children, Charles Aycock Poe, William Dismukes Poe, and Jean Shepperd Poe (later, Mrs. Gordon Smith Jr.). Alice Aycock Poe, described by an observer as "a small, immensely bright and cheerful woman," kept quiet when politics were discussed: "Public affairs had been a constant source of conversation around the Aycock family circle, and while Mrs. Poe had well-defined views, it was her belief that women should talk among themselves of household and family matters while the men pondered affairs of state."[83]

In spite of his connections and his stature, Poe did retain some important connections to small white farmers, including a common political transformation. Poe came from a family of Populists and gravitated toward Populist solutions to agricultural problems such as cooperative buying and selling. Influenced by the white-supremacist propaganda put out by the Democrats, he came to view the possibility that white women would be ravaged by black men as a dark cloud looming over the heads of white farmers—perhaps as threatening to rural life as the vicious system of credit of the day. He was also drawn in by the reform agenda of the Democrats; he believed that the reforms embraced by Progressive Democrats—for example, to the education system—would help small farmers revitalize their communities. It was this shared political and intellectual journey that enabled Poe to engage small white farmers as effectively as he did, to articulate their aspirations and capture their imaginations. Black farmers read the *Progressive Farmer*, too, but the journal was meant for white readers. It often referenced the editor's desire to help white farmers, and it featured mostly white people on its pages.[84]

Though inspired by Populism, Poe remained true to the Democratic Party. Indeed, one of his friends joked that Poe was "such a good Democrat he has never used his middle name [Hamilton] in public." (The friend continued the joke: "His middle name should have been Jefferson instead of Hamilton.")[85] Poe was considered, according to the *State*, part of "North Carolina's liberal tradition," broadly defined as "one that was deeply and sincerely concerned with getting a decent break for the common man."[86] He was not a liberal as we think of the term today. Poe's son noted that his father's readers would have been "horrified" to know that Poe subscribed to the *Nation* and the *New Republic*, both "liberal (and to some, radical) publications." Poe read them "to stimulate his thinking, and [because] he believed devoutly in trying to look at all sides of a question." Poe, according to his son, "deplored the ultraconservative tendency of so many in the South."[87] On the so-called race problem he was considered a "spokesman for the Southern moderates." As Poe's position on segregation makes clear, however, southern "moderates" shared some views with demagogues like Ben Tillman. Poe also "strenuously" opposed the desegregation of public schools.[88] When desegregation proceeded, Poe "advocated separate high schools for the sexes as a possible means of avoiding some of the undesirable consequences of desegregation."[89]

CLARENCE POE'S AGRARIAN DREAM

Under Poe's editorship, the *Progressive Farmer* aimed to help small farmers forge a deep commitment to a yeoman way of life, which it attempted to do by offering them an inspirational vision of farming. It was a romantic agrarian vision, full of gurgling brooks and chirping birds, fragrant fields and hearts full of satisfaction. It hailed "the psychological value, or spiritual value we might call it, that is found in the fact that the small farmer is not a mere cog in some gigantic wheel but can take a piece of land and have the satisfaction of seeing from day to day his own soil, his own crops, his own animals improving and developing through his own nurture and affection."[90] The *Progressive Farmer* insisted that there was something magical about working the land: "The man who has once caught the spirit of the farm, who has felt the deep, elemental earth-thrill in his veins, will never outgrow the old love and the old longings," the journal announced. The journal tried to explain what made for an ideal farmer, and first on the list was love for the land; the "true farmer . . . feels the lure of the soil and hears the call of the fields." Such a farmer did not focus on making money above all else; to him, farming was "more than a living"—it was also "a life, full, satisfying, fruitful and joyful."[91]

The *Progressive Farmer*'s ideal farmer enjoyed doing his work himself and putting both "soul" and "muscle" into it. "Some people seem surprised to see me wheeling manure into my garden, and doing all the garden work myself instead of hiring a darky to do it," one writer for the journal commented. But, he explained, "we have a far greater pride in the crops that our own hands have planted and tended, and I should lose much of the pleasure in my garden if some one else was doing the work for hire."[92]

The ideal farmer also took pride in caring for his land, the *Progressive Farmer* argued. Poe was deeply influenced by the ideas of Liberty Hyde Bailey, agricultural reformer and chairman of the Country Life Commission. Thus, it should not come as a surprise that the *Progressive Farmer* adopted a key belief of Bailey's: loving the land meant nurturing it. Good farmers who loved their land knew to avoid the "sin and folly of our robber methods of handling the soil."[93] They considered their work to be a privilege. "Let us indeed think of ourselves as tenants of the Almighty," Poe encouraged farmers, "caretakers of His soil, each of us with a plot of soil that we are definitely expected to keep, conserve, and beautify as were our first parents in their little Eden." Poe hoped that love for their farms would encourage farmers to husband the land, which would in turn make their farms more profitable and the region more successful.[94]

The *Progressive Farmer* tried to spread its agrarian ideals to the next generation, working to convince children that the farm was the place to spend their lives. It published articles on the value of farm life and provided passages for children to memorize, such as "The Country Boy's Creed":

I believe that the Country which God made is more beautiful than the City which man made; that life out-of-doors and in touch with the earth is the natural life of man. I believe that work is work wherever we find it, but that work with Nature is more inspiring than work with the most intricate machinery. I believe that the dignity of labor depends not on what you do, but on how you do it; that opportunity comes to a boy on the farm as often as to a boy in the city, that life is larger and freer and happier on the farm than in town, that my success depends not upon my location, but upon myself—not upon my dreams, but upon what I actually do, not upon luck, but upon pluck.[95]

The obvious resonance of this creed with the Apostles' Creed suggests that Poe saw agrarianism as like religion in shaping a worldview. Moreover, Poe's agrarianism was connected to a particular version of Christianity (the Protestant work ethic comes to mind) in which, through adopting an agrarian perspective, farm children can better appreciate God and God's work.

As the title of the creed reflects, much of the journal's interest in young people was directed toward farm boys, not farm girls. Boys would grow up to be heads of households, responsible for deciding whether their families lived in the country or the city, while girls would grow up in a subordinate role. And so the journal suggested that boys learn to love farming by taking on projects of their own, developing individual interests in raising cattle or flowers. They should prepare to run farms of their own by studying agriculture in school; they should aim to become "alert, intelligent, progressive farmer[s]," the type of farmer who could make the region "the fairest and most fruitful farming section in America."[96]

Clarence Poe aimed to mobilize farmers; he also agitated for state and local government officials to improve the opportunities available to the South's white farmers. The reforms Poe fought for included agricultural modernization, improved public education in rural areas, reforms to the crop lien system, an end to lynching (because it affected the character of whites and their reputation outside of the South), Prohibition (he considered "the ancient curse of drink" comparable to the evils of "monarchy" and slavery, and he helped make North Carolina a "dry" state), public ownership of urban utilities, clean government, and "decent" entertainment at state fairs.[97] Poe considered these reforms essential to the revitalization of rural life for white farmers.

Looking in more detail at Poe's perspective on reforms to agriculture, education, and the crop lien system and at his views on lynching show Poe to be a true southern Progressive—someone who was interested in "progress" for the region and who considered limiting the opportunities and freedoms of African Americans an essential part of that "progress."

Improving agriculture was the reform closest to Poe's heart. Poe used the *Progressive Farmer* as a platform from which to broadcast the importance of "scientific agriculture," that is, the use of scientifically tested farm techniques and equipment. Southern farmers would prosper to the extent that they used "modern" methods of working the land, Poe argued. Such methods included diversifying crops, using new equipment, and building up soils through the use of fertilizers and nitrogen-fixing plants, all techniques that had been studied by scientists at agricultural colleges and experiment stations with the goal of making agriculture more efficient. "Nobody can stop the tide of knowledge that is teaching men to get more out of their labor than ever before," announced one article in the journal. "Only a fool will be content to give two days' hard labor to do what he might learn to do in one day, or to work two acres to produce what he might learn to produce on one acre."[98] The journal publicized and praised the work of extension workers and researchers in the agricultural colleges and used the language and suggestions of agricultural reformers. The goal was for farmers to use "progressive" techniques to produce more and better crops and livestock and to use land freed up through greater efficiency to grow food crops—then to use the money they saved through scientific agriculture to pull themselves out of debt and become landowners.

Poe and his writers hoped that modern methods of working the land would help farmers live and work according to the Jeffersonian ideal. "Progress" and "modernization" did not mean that farmers should grow cash crops on large farms—they meant that modern machines and agricultural practices should be used to help farmers prosper on relatively small yeoman farms. These small farmers would grow a variety of crops, aiming to feed their families and livestock as well as produce some goods for the market. The idea that modern technologies could help farmers participate at will in the market was, in retrospect, unrealistic. As Daniel Rodgers put it in *Atlantic Crossings*, "the outward inertia of the countryside belied its increasing incorporation into a world agricultural market." Farmers were forced to participate in the market by their reliance on credit and their need to pay taxes.[99]

Poe offered the American West and China as examples supporting his case in favor of using modern farm machinery. Western farmers, according to Poe, because they had to make do with too few farmers, had learned to make farms more productive by using farm machinery; they also raised livestock, which brought in a substantial income and provided manure for crops. The efficiency and tidiness of Western farms highlighted the "shabbier houses," "neglected" lands, inferior livestock, and bad roads that covered the South. The hope was that southerners would be inspired to follow the example set by farmers in the West.[100]

Meanwhile, the low wages of Chinese workers were a result of workers' low productivity given the lack of tools and machines. "Men and women weavers doing work that machines would do at home. Grain reaped by sickles instead of horses and reapers as in America. Sixteen men at Hankow to carry baggage that one man and a one-horse dray would carry in New York. Women carrying brick, stone, and timber up the mountainside at Hong Kong"—all wasted effort, Poe believed. Because workers received so little money, they kept the merchants, banks, and other businesses poor also, according to Poe. From this, Poe drew as a lesson for the South that small farmers should embrace machines, which would allow each worker to achieve more and create a prosperity that would benefit all southerners in some way. He did not pay attention to the law of supply and demand—that increased yield would lead to lower prices.[101]

In addition to modern farm tools, Poe supported improved education. Education would help farmers understand why and how they should adopt "scientific" methods of agriculture, and it would drive farmers to work hard and seek out the best in life. The *Progressive Farmer* strongly encouraged young men and women to attend college before taking on their life's work as farmers. One article told a young man considering a career in agriculture that he should study just as hard as his brother, who was training to become a doctor.[102] Another article argued that the young woman who had been to college would find the "humdrum of every-day routine" on the farm less tiresome because "her study of poetry and art history have heightened her love of bird songs and God's great out-of-doors."[103] Yet another article claimed that a college-educated man would not be happy following a single mule through the fields all day, for "if he had been content to farm just as well as his neighbors, he would not have gone to college." This college-educated farmer, the article went on, believed in "a possibility of a finer and richer country life" and was dedicated to pursuing it.[104] That college-educated young people would return to the farm, bringing with them knowledge and potential for leadership, was a dream that went unrealized.

"More efficient public schools" were "the supreme need" of the rural South, according to the *Progressive Farmer*. The journal noted the prevalence of illiteracy in the South and the fact that the length of North and South Carolina's school terms were longer than only one other state's (New Mexico). The "inefficiency" of the school system kept the region poor and backward, "like a ball and chain holding us back in all our efforts to run forward."[105] The *Progressive Farmer* urged that the region adopt higher school taxes and lengthen the school term, among other reforms meant to improve schools. Better schools would improve rural communities both by teaching children skills and by making them eager consumers. One of the journal's writers argued that poor children would not learn to want modern technologies in homes lacking such comforts and conveniences. Thus it should be the role of schools to show children how clean and sanitary homes could be. And this, in turn, would make them better farmers because they would realize that they could not purchase stoves and toilets without efficiently run farms.[106]

Poe argued that reforms should be made on behalf of small white farmers not only to the education system but also to the credit system. Farmers needed to borrow money to purchase seeds, fertilizer, equipment, food, and clothing. Merchants, wary of farmers defaulting on their loans, gave credit to farmers only if these farmers planted cash crops and if they granted the merchants a lien on their crop. This was true not just for poor croppers but also for farmers who owned land but who still lacked cash that could be used as collateral.[107]

Poe used the harshest words available to describe the crop lien system, claiming that it kept farmers in a state of bondage akin to slavery. "The crop lien, credit system destroys manhood," he complained. "It was made to take care of slaves, or folks just out of slavery, and it breeds the slave-attitude in all who are subject to it. The farmer who gives a crop lien or mortgage is bound to do all his trading with the supply merchant who holds the mortgage. He belongs to the merchant. He lacks freedom." In addition to binding farmers to merchants who tended to charge exorbitant rates, the crop lien tied farmers to one crop, thus exposing them to the risks inherent in monoculture. It was the crop lien that prevented many farmers from following Poe's advice to diversify.[108] Poe blamed the credit system for much, including environmental problems and widespread poverty: "The gullied, barren fields and ramshackle houses, and the general evidences of disaster and decay which meet us in so many sections of the South despite all our natural advantages—these are not wholly . . . but very largely the monuments of the crop lien system, which has laid its blighting hand on every class of our rural population."[109]

Because the crop lien was such a negative force in southern farm life, Poe considered it essential to fight the system. Farmers could play a role in this fight. Small farmers should spend money more carefully, Poe insisted; they should also adopt Populist tactics such as working together to operate as a large farm would in buying and selling products. Rural segregation would become part of this effort because cooperative work among small white farmers was being undermined by "the present wholesale sandwiching of whites and Negroes in our rural districts." Cooperative work, it was thought, required tightly knit agricultural communities—and reformers like Poe assumed that racial and ethnic homogeneity enhanced the ability of people to form social bonds. Living in close proximity to African Americans endangered the project of agricultural cooperation, Poe believed, because close social and economic bonds between black and white neighbors were dangerous and threatened the racial purity of their communities.[110]

Poe also encouraged farmers to take charge of their situation by refusing to spend money they did not have. (The idea was that they could start to purchase modern conveniences once they had gained control of their finances.) He encouraged them with statements such as the following:

You can get out of debt if you will. The way is hard, and steep, and thorny.
It is not a path for weaklings or cowards, or men who lack grit and

guts. . . . You will need all the courage and dogged persistence that kept our Confederate-soldier fathers fighting, fighting, fighting, with unfaltering determination, when their uniforms were ragged and their shoes were soleless and their food was parched corn or whatever they could get. . . . And much as you will gain in money and property by making this fight, you will gain even more in manhood and character and self-respect.[111]

Of course, farmers could not win this fight, no matter how full of grit they were, without reform also coming from government. Their determination could not help them buy the seeds they needed, nor could their courage help them acquire fertilizer. Thus Poe worked through state government to study the problem and propose a solution. He served on a committee appointed by Locke Craig, governor of North Carolina from 1913 to 1917, on the "Needs of North Carolina Farmers with Regard to Credits, Marketing, and Co-operation." The committee's report, which Poe helped write, criticized banks for refusing to lend money to small farmers, thus necessitating that farmers look to "the land loan shark," who charged between 6 and 20 percent interest and "subjected [the farmer] to extortion, usury and exploitation." Because farmers disliked bring "robbed," they preferred to let "about 14,000,000 acres of land . . . remain in a state of waste that is a menace to the health and happiness of the entire population of our state." The committee argued that farmers needed to do more "self-help" by working together to obtain credit, buy or share equipment, run gins and mills, and sell their products, but the state, too, would need to play a role in protecting farmers from "blood suckers" and helping them obtain credit.[112]

Poe promoted a 1917 bill backed by Craig's successor as governor, Thomas Walter Bickett, to cap prices on credit purchases at the cash price plus 10 percent interest. Governor Bickett was a man after Poe's heart: he too wished to improve rural life, and he understood that conditions would need to change for small farmers for this to happen. The bill said that at the time of purchase, merchants would be required to give the purchaser a memorandum with the cash price of the items purchased, and that anyone lending money to a farmer could charge "in lieu of interest, a commission of not more than ten per cent of the amount of money actually advanced." Though high, this 10 percent commission was still much less than what some farmers were paying.[113] It was not uncommon for customers buying goods on credit to pay 30 to 60 percent more than those who paid cash.[114]

Poe hoped that reforms to the crop lien law would make the credit system more conservative, with less credit advanced and fewer unnecessary purchases made. This, he believed, would help small farmers who had formerly accumulated debt with a fatalistic attitude begin to save money. "Instead of continuing in virtual serfdom," farmers freed of the shackles of credit could "begin work for wages as a farm laborer or rent with some resident white farmer" rather than "working for themselves on the merchant's land."[115]

Even stances that seemed sympathetic to black southerners were part of an agenda meant to benefit whites. Poe took on lynching because he considered lynching an embarrassment to the white South. Lynching went against the image of the South as modern and "civilized" that Poe tried to promote. Poe wished to see southerners show respect for the U.S. Constitution by following legal procedures regarding the punishment of crime. Lynching, Poe believed, was a first step toward "anarchy." First it was black men who were being lynched, but soon enough it would be white men, too. Even if whites were not lynched, they would suffer from "that greatest danger of all—the inevitable brutalizing of any people that is cruel to the weak, the curse of God that must fall upon our race if we are unjust to another."[116]

Poe hoped to end lynching through reforms to the judicial system and through changes to rural society that would discourage the rape of white women—"the crime which nourishes and sustains" lynching. Good roads, telephones, rural police protection, enforced vagrancy laws, and Prohibition would help protect white women in remote areas, as would addressing "ignorance, idleness, thriftlessness" among black southerners through improved education.[117] Poe did not acknowledge that not all lynched African Americans had been accused of rape—or that many lynchings were perpetrated against individuals innocent of crimes.[118]

Poe's reform agenda focused on the needs of small white farmers and the reputation of the white South. It showed little concern for improving the situation of African Americans in the region—though it would have had the secondary effect of doing this in some areas. It looked to both the farmers to improve their situation through self-help and to the state to enact legislation that would protect small farmers.

THE MIGRATION OF SMALL FARMERS TO CITIES

Poe dreamed of a countryside full of thriving white yeoman farmers, well-educated men who used the latest "scientific" technologies to work the land. He feared a countryside depleted of white land owners, where those white farmers who remained would not be able to fill churches and schools. In the first decade or two of Poe's editorship, he watched the mass exodus of farmers to southern cities and devoted himself to enhancing the appeal of the countryside to small white farmers. But Poe could not stop the transformation of the economy, which was taking place rapidly between around 1885 and 1910 as members of the planter class diversified their investments by pumping money into industry. In 1890, 3,667 factories employed 36,214 workers in North Carolina, 6.7 percent of the workforce in the state. Ten years later, 73,571 people worked in industry, making up about 12 percent of the state's workers. Textiles were the state's largest industry, employing more workers than either the lumber or tobacco industries.[119]

Winston and Salem (the two were separate until 1913) show some of the trends that developed as industrialization came to North Carolina. A number of textile mills operated in Salem, while Winston housed tobacco factories. Textile mills employed white families to run their machines as well as black men to sweep floors and unload cotton; industrialists believed that black people were not "suited" to working with machines. Meanwhile, tobacco factories—which were not mechanized—hired African Americans. Both the textile and tobacco factories hired mostly female workers because employing women and children allowed industrialists to pay lower wages. While the hours, pay, and conditions were not good in these factories, migrants coming from the countryside judged the pay at least to be better than what was offered on the farm. Thus the population of Winston rose from about 2,800 in 1880 to over 8,000 in 1890 and almost 14,000 in 1900.[120]

Salem began as a quiet Moravian town. The church, which governed the town, opened the Salem Manufacturing Company in 1837. The company's workers, who lived in company boardinghouses, produced textiles. Most of the company's employees were white women and girls working as spinners and weavers, though men also worked at the mills. These workers, who were not paid during company shutdowns, had varied levels of commitment to their jobs, and many left for periods of time to help out on their family farms. Francis L. Fries was the first individual to build a factory in town, which he did in 1840. Fries used the labor of enslaved people to operate his wool mill, viewing the enslaved as a more stable labor force than that of the Salem Manufacturing Company. Several years after its founding, the Fries factory was expanded and began to produce cotton textiles in addition to woolens (during the Civil War, it produced Confederate uniforms).[121]

Textile mills sprang up at a rate of six per year in North Carolina between 1880 and 1900, and by 1900 there were 177 in total (the vast majority of them in the Piedmont).[122] Labor in textile mills was challenging, as workers had to keep up with the fast pace of the machines. They "spent the whole day walking among the machinery, reaching, pushing, and pulling as they tended the looms and frames." They repaired broken threads and made sure that the process of weaving thread into cloth went smoothly. The machines frequently caused worker injuries.[123] The mill worker Alice P. Evitt described workers getting their aprons and even hair caught in the machines. One woman Evitt knew had to wear a wig because the machine "pulled her hair all out—every bit of it."[124]

Evitt, born in 1898, who started full-time work at age twelve in mills in Charlotte and other parts of North and South Carolina (her family moved often), described additional problems at the mills, including foremen yelling at workers for taking bathroom breaks, noisy machines that made "so much fuss and clatter," and heat emanating from the machines that made it so "you'd come out of there, your clothes was plumb wet."[125] Yet there was also much she enjoyed about mill life, including playing and singing in the mill as a child and working with people she liked. She described an attractive mill town wherein "every house on the mill hill had flowers. They had shrubbery in front of it—hedges; had colored people to keep it up and keep it clean. We didn't have to clean it. The company cut it and put the flowers around and all. It was beautiful here."[126]

Instead of employing a workforce made up of single women, as the textile mills in Lowell, Massachusetts, were famous for doing in the 1830s,

North Carolina's textile mills tended to hire families. They achieved this by underpaying adults and offering wages to children like Evitt. Children made for desirable workers because their labor was cheap and they could enter and leave the workforce according to the demands of the market. As textile mills tended to be located by the rivers that provided them with power, workers generally lived in company towns rather than in towns with preexisting housing. Through their ownership of worker housing and the stores in which they shopped—and the placement of superintendents in the villages—industrialists were able to exert a high level of control over workers' lives. Mill owners set the rules in the villages, and superintendents would try to regulate workers' bedtimes, church attendance, and habits of smoking and drinking.[127] Partly through their paternalism, mill owners were able to create a myth that the mills were "not a business, but a social enterprise" meant to save poor whites from degradation—that elite whites and poor whites were tied together by bonds of intimacy, rather than that elite whites were looking to exploit the labor of poor whites, who had few other options.[128]

Lack of autonomy and exploitation meant that transition to mill life could be a difficult change for migrants coming from the countryside. Accustomed to organizing their days around the seasonal demands of agriculture, these workers now had to match the speed of machines, spurred on by managers. As Jacquelyn Dowd Hall and her coauthors describe it in *Like a Family*, "Millhands rose early in the morning, still tired from the day before. For ten, eleven, or twelve hours they walked, stretched, leaned, and pulled at their machines. Noise, heat, and humidity engulfed them. The lint that settled on their hair and skin marked them as mill workers, and the cotton dust that silently entered their lungs could eventually cripple or kill them."[129] To many migrants coming from the countryside, taking mill work was an unfortunate and distressing step, as it meant that any independence they might have had on the farm was gone. Indeed, many things made mill work less than ideal, but farm families continued to flock to the mills, drawn by the reliable pay.[130]

At the same time that white people left the countryside for work in textile factories, African Americans did the same for employment in the tobacco industry. Winston, Durham, and a number of other North Carolina towns became cities because of the growing businesses of tobacco manufacturing and marketing—businesses with relatively low start-up costs because they were not mechanized. Winston began its rapid growth after a railroad line connected it to nearby Greensboro in 1873, thus allowing for tobacco and tobacco products to be transported in and out. It was this rail line— along with Winston's proximity to the tobacco-growing countryside— that attracted R. J. Reynolds to the town in 1874, at age twenty-four. Reynolds purchased a lot near the railroad tracks on Depot Street, the site of his first factory. His company, which specialized in plug (tobacco fla-vored and pressed into bricks) and twist (tobacco twisted in cords), flour-ished, and by the 1880s Reynolds "built additions or new factories or bought out competitors every two years." In 1889, Francis H. Fries built a new rail line connecting Winston to Roanoke, Virginia, providing even better access to markets.[131]

Reynolds hired former farm people. Many of them had been recruited to work from the South Carolina countryside or from eastern North Caro-lina. These laborers carried out difficult work. Men would use their own muscle to move heavy hogsheads (wooden barrels) of tobacco into the fac-tory (this position was called "mule"). They emptied the hogsheads, and women steamed the tobacco so that it could be worked with more easily. The tobacco was then picked through, with the nicest leaves kept as "wrap-pers" for the tobacco plugs and the remaining leaves sent to be made into chewing tobacco. Women graded tobacco and removed the stem from the leaf. Men fed coal into fires and stirred boiling pots of tobacco in sugar or licorice flavoring. After the tobacco had been dried, lumpers shaped it into twists or plugs. Rollers put the plugs in wrappers, then shapers pressed and oiled the plugs. Boys—tobacco factories had a number of roles for children, including stemming—then labeled and boxed the finished product.[132] While Reynolds was a paternalist—he funded his workers' churches and tried to hire his workers' family members, for example—the business model of tobacco factories was less paternalistic than that of the textile mills. Tobacco companies did not provide their workers with housing, as did the textile mills, and thus they were not able to supervise workers' lives outside of work to the extent possible in mill villages.[133]

For their hard work, tobacco workers earned barely enough to live on, and some augmented their pay by stealing chewing tobacco or cigarettes from the company. Robert Black, an R. J. Reynolds employee, explained:

> There were many people that was forced to steal from the company because most of the people during those years had large families. And during certain periods there, probably the husband was in Reynolds and the wife was doing domestic work or things like that. . . . But the stealing was done mostly among the husbands and the fathers, because there was the greatest pressure for survival. And I'll tell you now, I know of many people who followed this stealing over a period of years that were able to buy a little house and maybe help his family to live a little better.

Black described both African Americans and poor whites living in miserable conditions in Winston-Salem, using outdoor toilets, their houses overrun with rats.[134]

Winston's tobacco companies (thirty-five existed by 1890, most of them small operations) provided jobs to thousands of workers and kept in operation the stores and other businesses that provided services to tobacco workers. In a sample of eight hundred individuals in one census enumeration district who lived in East Winston in 1910—a sample that includes children and wives who did not work as well as male and female workers—213 (26.6 percent) worked in tobacco factories. These tobacco workers generally rented their homes, which was typical for both whites and for African Americans in this part of the city (almost 35 percent of whites and 8.6 percent of blacks owned their homes). The heads of the households of white families that did own their homes worked as bookkeepers and merchants in grocery stores, as a physician, a minister, a policeman, and a railroad engineer. Some worked as laborers (odd jobs), and a few were employed in tobacco factories as coffers, foremen, or machinists. Quite a few were tradesmen—a brick mason, a blacksmith, and three carpenters. White renters worked most frequently in the tobacco factories, for the railroads, and in retail, but they also worked as managers, carpenters, foremen in knitting mills, wagon manufacturers, real estate agents, blacksmiths, ministers,

TABLE 1.2 Numbers of individuals, households, owners, and tobacco workers in part of East Winston

Individuals	Black households	Black owners	White households	White owners	Tobacco workers
800	127	1	86	30	213

Source: Department of Commerce and Labor, Bureau of the Census, Thirteenth Census of the United States: Population, 1910, Forsyth County, Winston Township, City of Winston, First Ward, Enumeration District 69, sheets 1–8B, http://familysearch.org.

and in other professions. These were the middling whites who animate this study. Less and less, middling whites made their living as artisans; the day of the independent craftsman was coming to a close, in part because of the factory-made goods from the North that came south on trains.[135]

The African Americans in the census sample worked primarily in the tobacco factories—as rollers, machinists, stemmers, casers, firemen—but also as laborers, teachers, shoemakers, teamsters, coachmen, and in retail. Black women also worked as washerwomen, running operations out of their own homes, and as cooks in restaurants and private homes. African Americans who were able to pull themselves into homeownership did so as washerwomen, tobacco workers (stemmer, roller, laborer), and carpenters. In 1910, except where a neighborhood immediately switched from white to black, African Americans did not live among white people, with the exception of live-in servants. The streets in East Winston were all white or all black and mulatto, except for a very occasional white family living among African Americans.[136] This had not always been the case: Forsyth County, home to Winston-Salem, experienced a rapid spike in residential segregation—marked by whether African Americans lived next door to white people or to other African Americans—between 1880 and 1900. After 1900, segregation increased even more, until by 1940 it was one of the most segregated counties in the state.[137]

Middling white people were not in the position they wanted to be in. An unstable group, they moved from farm ownership to factory work and sometimes back to farm work (the fluidity between agricultural and industrial jobs should be noted, as well as the fact that factory jobs provided paychecks that helped relatives who remained on the farm to stay there).[138] Neither farming nor factory jobs provided workers the lives they wanted. Just as small farm owners were in a better situation than croppers, those whites who worked as foremen in factories or who ran the businesses that served factory workers were better off than factory laborers. But their position was still more precarious than it had been, and they would come to feel anxious as African American neighborhoods expanded into formerly white areas and as a few African Americans—their population in cities continuing to expand—moved into their neighborhoods after 1910. Middling white people's perception of black neighbors as threats was to a large extent shaped by political leaders, which is the subject of the next chapter.

2

Fusion, Democrats, and the Scarecrow of Race

Clarence Poe cherished his connection to Governor Charles Aycock. Poe forged a strong personal alliance with Aycock beginning as early as the spring of 1902, when the two men met to discuss "educational matters." As the years passed, the relationship deepened. Poe sent the governor reading material, including a copy of a resolution adopted by the North Carolina Farmers' Alliance and articles and books that Poe had published, including *Cotton* (1906) and *A Southerner in Europe* (1908). Aycock praised young Poe in the letters he sent him. "I wish to express to you my continued appreciation of the excellent work which you are doing for the State," he wrote in 1904. "It is not too much to say that no young man is doing so much." With his term coming to a close in the fall of 1904, Aycock wrote Poe, "I shall follow your future career when I return to private life with deep interest and much hopefulness." In 1910 and 1911, Poe encouraged Aycock to run for a seat in the U.S. Senate. In 1912, when Poe became engaged to marry Aycock's daughter, Alice, Aycock wrote Poe that "My regard for you has been of long standing and has grown with the years." Strong ties of affection connected Poe and Alice, and Alice and her father, but also Poe and Charles Aycock. "I make no doubt that the closer relation in which we have now come will more and more endear you to me," Aycock wrote Poe. "I shall hope for a real companionship unmarred by our difference in years." A month before his death, Aycock wrote Poe from the hospital, ending the letter warmly: "I am feeling fine to-day, really much better. Give my love to Daught, but keep a proper share for yourself." Charles Aycock's heart failed while he addressed the Alabama Educational Association on April 4, 1912. A little over a week after Aycock's death, Poe wrote to the governor's friends to solicit "any anecdote, incident, story, conversation, or fact of any kind ... revealing the Governor's character, power, or personality" to be collected in a book along with his speeches and letters, a hagiographical volume published in 1912 as *The Life and Speeches of Charles Brantley Aycock*.[1]

How did Poe, raised on Populist ideas, become an eager Democrat and an ardent admirer of a man who rose to power on a platform of white supremacy (rather than, say, economic reform)? As it happens, the shift from Populist to Democrat was not one that required a revised perspective on race; white leaders of all three major parties at the time—the Populist, Democratic, and even Republican parties—held and embraced racist views.[2] Populists and Democrats both wielded racism to influence the voting of the masses. The shift did, however, mean putting the so-called problem of race above economic problems as a priority. For the political agenda of the Democrats to appeal to Poe and others who saw the world as he did, there needed to be a change in the way that white southerners viewed their problems—a change wherein they viewed the most pressing problem they faced as created by African Americans. The Democrats, displeased by the increased effectiveness of their political opponents—who had put into office successful black politicians like George White and James H. Young—brought about this change in perspective by leading a campaign for white supremacy that made black people out to be dangerous not only in the political arena but also as neighbors.[3]

Populism, a political movement meant to help producers (that is, the class of farmers and other workers who made the goods that kept the American economy afloat), sought to force the government to make reforms that benefited working people rather than the wealthy and powerful. Both black and white farmers became Populists, and they fought a common enemy in "business interests." But the biracialism of the Populist moment had clear limits.[4] White Populists wished to see political power remain with whites, and they embraced some types of segregation. Even if they did not set aside their attachment to white supremacy, white Populists were pragmatic, however, and were mostly willing to work with Republicans and black Populists to push forward their joint economic interests, generally by lending political support to the same candidates.[5] They believed it was important to ignore what they called the "scarecrow" of race so that Americans could focus on the economic problems that mattered more.[6] (One person explained in a Populist newspaper how the cry of "negro domination" obscured economic issues: "whether there is any danger of 'negro domination' or not, this battle-cry so inflames the whites that no appeal to reason, or force of argument or strong presentation of real issues has any weight.")[7]

The pragmatism of the North Carolina Populists is visible not just in their notion that "negro domination" should be put aside as a focus of energy but also in their sense of what farmers might achieve. They saw that the industry of the day offered few potential rewards, and they sought to make real changes to the economic system—through what the North Carolina Populist leader Leonidas Lafayette Polk described as "the mightiest, social, industrial and economic revolution the world has ever witnessed"—that would make it possible for farmers to prosper.[8] They were not looking to go backward in time, to premarket days; instead, they had a modern vision of what agriculture could look like, and they envisioned reforms to make this possible.

The practical economic goals of the Populists were undermined, unfortunately for farmers, when the Democrats shifted the debate away from economic problems and back to the "scarecrow of race" in their successful statewide campaign for white supremacy in 1898. This campaign devastated the Populists and destroyed their fragile alliance with Republicans. While in some parts of the state they stayed focused on the economic picture, many Populists felt they had no choice other than to engage the Democratic Party in its tactic of race-baiting in order to keep voters. They did not know what to do when Democrats accused them of failing to protect white women from "black beasts" other than to puff up their own chests and present themselves as tougher on black lawbreakers than the Democrats. Their inconsistent message on their relationship with African Americans, as well as internal fighting, which had been going on for months over questions such as whether they should unite politically, or "fuse," with the Republicans or Democrats, weakened North Carolina's Populists. By 1898, Populism had faded as a political possibility, and the Democrats, with their full-fledged racial animus, had come to dominate politics in the state.

Populism offered North Carolina's white farmers a vision of politics in which they could not only play a role but also reshape their government to make it more democratic. It also provided self-respect, a sense of common purpose shared with other Populists, and the satisfaction of having a plan for how to improve their lot in life. It offered farmers something significant enough that they held onto many Populist ideas even after the party's demise. Indeed, after the Populist Party withered away and many (though not all) former Populists—including Poe—joined the Democratic Party, they brought to the Democratic Party ideas about the importance of producers to the U.S. economy and certain aspects of the Populist agenda.[9] But after those who were to join the Democratic Party did so and it became clear that economic reforms were not on the table, they turned to other methods of fighting for their interests—methods shaped by "Progressive" Democrats— such as residential segregation. Thus the story is more complex than that of a Democratic coup; the Populists played a role in the white-supremacy campaign by producing racist rhetoric about African Americans, joining the Democratic Party after their own party had met its end, and embracing so-called reforms meant to take rights away from African Americans.

THE POSSIBILITIES AND PITFALLS OF POPULISM

Populism grew out of earlier nonpolitical movements on the part of farmers. The Patrons of Husbandry established over five hundred local chapters, called granges, in North Carolina in the 1870s, which served primarily a social function. Finding themselves in need of more than social connections, however, farmers embraced the Farmers' Alliance when it spread from Texas to North Carolina in 1887. The Farmers' Alliance and Industrial Union was a national group rapidly gaining influence among farmers in the South and West. The North Carolina planter L. L. Polk, who rose through the granges to become the state's first commissioner of agriculture in 1877, became president of the alliance, and his *Progressive Farmer* became its organ.

Under Polk's leadership, local chapters of the alliance were formed in all of the state's counties except for one, and membership exceeded ninety thousand.[10]

Until his death in 1892, Polk was the state's leading Populist leader; the role then fell to Marion Butler, who served as chairman of the Populist National Committee, state senator, and U.S. senator. Like Polk, Butler came up through the Farmers' Alliance, serving as president of Sampson County's chapter. He also became in 1888 editor of the Clinton *Caucasian*, an alliance newspaper with the motto "Pure Democracy & White Supremacy" (a motto highlighting just how essential white supremacy was to the Populists). Both Polk and Butler came from families with significant land holdings, showing that Populists were united not by whether they owned land but by a perspective on how government should treat farmers.[11]

The alliance brought farmers together socially, but it also made political demands. The idea was that connecting socially would allow farmers to share their problems and ideas for solutions (much like the idea of consciousness-raising in the women's movement decades later). As Butler explained it, farmers suffered because of their lack of "cohesion," their "failure to pool our divergent opinions and agree upon a common line of action that would represent the combined wisdom of all." Once farmers decided on a course of action, they could then lobby for political change. This was the reason for organizing—to unite with others who shared a common interest, then promote this interest in the political sphere. It was essential to do this in order to compete with their opponents, the powerful business groups promoting their own interests through politics. The government protected business interests to the detriment of farmers, insisted the alliance: "[Business leaders] use their power to inaugurate and execute hostile legislation against other classes not organized, or poorly organized and weak," argued Butler. "The latter exercise of this power in defiance of right, but too often under the cover of unjust laws, is the snake in our body politic, and the curse of our civilization. This is the frightful game where the big fish eat the smaller fish, and then turn to eat each other."[12]

Polk explained that the alliance was not connected to either of the two major parties because it did not wish to "interfere or abridge in any manner the most perfect freedom of its members as to their political action." Instead, it advocated engaged citizenship.[13] It encouraged farmers to push their parties of choice to promote their agenda. This agenda included a reversal of the nation's monetary policy, which in 1873 limited the amount of greenbacks in circulation, made greenbacks convertible to gold, and excluded silver from the nation's money supply, even though bimetallism had been U.S. policy since the late eighteenth century. The new policy worked to keep the value of money high—a problem for farmers, who tended to be in debt and would have benefited from being able to repay their debts with money that was worth less. The solution offered by the alliance was for the federal government to issue greenbacks and allow for the free coinage of silver. Increasing the money in circulation would have caused crop prices to go up and debts to be lightened—both of which farmers believed would have given them much relief.[14] As Polk explained: "Scarcity of money means high priced money; a plentiful supply of money means cheap money. The high-priced dollar lessens the price of labor products, the cheap dollar raises the price of labor products." Polk offered an example of two farmers who had $1,000 in 1870. One farmer kept his money in cash, and by 1891 his money had increased in value by 50 percent. The other farmer bought 500 bushels of wheat as an investment. By 1891 his investment was worth $333, decreasing in value by 66 percent.[15]

The alliance also wanted the federal government to regulate railroads—upon which farmers relied to get their crops to market—or own and operate them. Its members saw this as essential because railroad barons restricted competition to keep rates high—and enjoyed undue political influence and, along with this, low taxes. They also demanded that tariff laws be reformed. As it was set up at the time, the tariff left American farmers vulnerable to the world market by not protecting their crops; it did protect American manufacturing, though, which as a result made manufactured goods more costly for the farmers who had to buy them. Members of the alliance also wanted, among other things, the direct election of senators by the people, government control of telegraph lines, and a system of graduated income tax. Perhaps the demand closest to the heart of farmers was a government-run subtreasury system that would offer farmers low-interest loans using their nonperishable crops, stored in government warehouses, as security. Members of the Farmers' Alliance in North Carolina made demands on state government, too. They wanted more resources put into public education and reform to the tax system, which placed much of the burden on land owners rather than on those people who earned the most money.[16]

The Farmer's Alliance attracted different types of farmers, including croppers, small owners, and large owners and landlords. While some of these farmers aspired to operate as yeomen, participating in the market but also growing crops for their own use, others were totally market oriented and wished to see government shift preferential treatment from railroad and other nonfarm business interests to farmers. Whatever their economic position, the farmers in the Farmers' Alliance were white. The alliance was restricted to white members, and it supported the segregation of textile mills and railroad cars and opposed the hiring of black postal workers. It also viewed white supremacy and segregation as essential for the "reconciliation" of northern and southern farmers to take place. African Americans who supported the cause joined the Colored Farmers' National Alliance and Cooperative Union, a separate group that took an active interest in the special needs of black farmers. It supported the ill-fated Lodge Election, or "Force," Bill of 1890, which would have provided for federal oversight of elections, thus protecting the voting rights of African Americans in the South, and it opposed the convict lease system, for example. Members of the Colored Farmers' Alliance and the white Farmers' Alliance worked separately toward their goals.[17]

Farmers in the alliance tried to push for political change through the two major political parties of the time. The Republican Party, the party associated with Lincoln and the Union, was less powerful in the South than the Democratic Party; it did have many supporters among North Carolina's white voters, though, especially in the mountainous west, and black voters were quite loyal to the party, as it supported political rights for all men. African Americans made up two-thirds of the Republicans in North Carolina. The Democratic Party—the party of the "Redeemers" who had "rescued" the South from Northern control during Reconstruction—was dominant. Support for the Democrats was strong among elites, but nonelite whites had reasons to be unhappy with the party. They viewed the party as too busy catering to the interests of corporations, banks, and merchants to care about small farmers and thought that it operated as a political machine that engaged in unfair tactics. The Democrats frequently engaged in race-baiting; they pointed out that African Americans were heavily represented in the Republican Party and claimed that "black domination" in the state had had a destructive effect on the political process.[18]

By 1892, Farmers' Alliance leaders had come to believe that the two major parties were not going to provide sufficient help for farmers, and the more radical wing of the group, led by Polk, formed the Populist Party. North Carolina Populists considered their party in opposition primarily to the Democrats, though voters left both the Democratic and Republican parties—often at considerable personal and professional sacrifice, as switching parties affected people's social and professional networks—to become Populists.[19] The Populist agenda echoed that of the alliance, and it included low tariffs, the free coinage of silver, and a subtreasury system. Shaping this reform agenda were ideas about the importance of agriculture to the nation and its people and the importance of those people who made the land produce. Butler described this class as "the bone and sinew, the wealth producers of the land." Polk described them as long-suffering: "No class of men work so hard, or so many hours per day, or live so hard and receive such little reward for their labor, as the average American farmer."[20]

Populists considered farmers to be important citizens who would correct a federal government that had fallen under the spell of big business. As protectors of their government and of the public good more generally, Populists viewed themselves as demonstrating character and strength of purpose and being driven by principle. This character was developed in fighting an enemy; the agrarianism of the Populists, like that of Jefferson, was shaped through opposition to dramatic economic changes of the day—industrialization, incorporation, monopolization—that hurt producers. Government ought to provide the most good to the most people, Populists believed. Farmers' interests should be represented in government. The political process should be clean. A flier directed to the voters of New Hanover County reveals how the Populists presented these ideas to the people. The flier attaches great significance to the election and the political process, arguing that by voting "you may save your political liberties for the future." Promising "a free and fair and peaceful election," the flier argues that it is through voting that the people can most fruitfully oppose "the Democratic Machine and its methods."[21]

Populists criticized their society for being set up to allow the rich to continue getting richer, while the poor were unable to pull themselves into prosperity. Witnesses of this society saw "centralized capital allied to corporate power, invading our temples of justice, subsidising the press, controlling conventions, corrupting the ballot box, dictating the platforms of parties, overriding individual rights, intimidating official authority and directing legislation, State and national."[22]

Populism was not a way for farmers to recreate the days of the past. It looked forward rather than backward. Charles Postel describes it as a "modernizing force" in the sense that members of the movement "understood that the transformations they sought required the uprooting of rural ignorance, inertia, and force of habit." The Populist critique grew out of a market-oriented context. Populists were not yeomen who lived apart from the market but farmers—including large-scale farmers—who depended on commerce and suffered because crop prices and the cost of transporting goods to market did not favor them. Thus, they supported using modern tactics. Indeed, a publicist for the Farmers' Alliance recommended organizing like the enemy: "Nothing could withstand their power . . . if the farmers of America would organize as intelligently and solidly as the Standard Oil Company has."[23]

One way for farmers to gain leverage was by joining together to operate as larger business units. Populist programs helped farmers purchase goods in bulk in order to secure lower rates, for example. As Butler explained this tactic:

> Competition is destructive—it is the devil's game. When we learn this lesson, when we overcome this fatal defect in our own organization, and unlearn the false education that has been taught us by selfish and designing monopoly, when we begin to practice co-operation, we will not only be able to protect ourselves, but to advance our mutual interests. Then we will not only be prosperous, but also well nigh invincible.[24]

Self-help could only go so far, though, the Populists believed. It was essential that government be reformed. Polk insisted that the problems of farmers were caused by the unjust, partial, discriminating and wicked financial system of our government; a system that has imposed upon agriculture an unjust and intolerable proportion of the burdens of taxation, and has made it the helpless victim of the rapacious greed and tyrannical power of gold; a system under which . . . our currency has contracted to a volume totally inadequate to the demands of the legitimate business of the country with the natural and inevitable result—high-priced money and low-priced products.

Populists like Polk insisted that government should offer farmers not special treatment but "an open field and an equal chance with every other great interest in the race of progress." It was essential that this be done in order to prevent America from becoming a nation of "paupers and millionaires"—indeed to "protect and preserve that great middle class which, in all ages, in all civilizations, in all countries, has always proved itself the surest and safest defender of civil liberty."[25]

African Americans who joined the Populist Party generally did so with their own set of goals and methods. As Omar H. Ali argues, "Black Populism neither mirrored nor derived from the parallel white-based movement, though it did share in common certain demands." Black Populists joined their white brethren for certain things, such as "patronizing white Alliance cooperative stores, lobbying for the subtreasury loan program, joining the boycott on jute bags, and fighting the Conger Lard Bill." They parted ways from white Populists in other areas, however, for example when they demanded civil rights for African Americans such as the right to serve on juries or when they backed the Lodge Bill. White Populists, in many cases, endorsed Jim Crow legislation. Historians write of "biracial cooperation" between black and white Populists; often, this meant no more than voting for the same candidates.[26]

FUSION

In the election of 1892, Populists in North Carolina won 17 percent of the total vote, electing fourteen of their own to the state legislature (three to the Senate and eleven to the House of Representatives). By the next election, it was clear that the party would have to decide whether it wished to continue as a third party that might never achieve real political power but that might weaken the Democratic Party enough to empower the Republicans in the state or instead "fuse" with one of the two major parties. They decided for fusion with the Republicans in 1894, and in that year's election the Fusion ticket did very well in North Carolina, gaining a majority of seats in the General Assembly and even the governorship. This success was thanks in part to the support of African Americans, who voted for the Fusion ticket overwhelmingly.[27] The votes of African Americans had a real impact in elections like this one; as Barbara J. Fields explains it, "If allowed the rights of citizenship, Afro-Americans potentially held in their own hands the balance of power between contending groups of white people."[28]

Daniel Lindsay Russell, elected on the Fusion ticket, was the only Republican to serve as governor of North Carolina in close to one hundred years, from the end of Reconstruction through the 1970s. Russell came from a family of wealthy Whig planters from the Wilmington area—one of the few North Carolina families that owned a huge estate. In spite of his background, Russell developed an affinity for the state's lower classes. A Radical Republican during Reconstruction, he supported equal rights for African Americans. As time passed, however, and Russell saw the Democrats defeat their opponents by accusing them of allowing "Negro rule," he came to represent white Republicans who were tired of the focus on race.[29]

The Fusion government, led by Governor Russell, initiated reforms to benefit the common man rather than business interests. It increased school funding, capped interest rates at 6 percent, required that corporations pay property taxes, began to regulate railroads, and shifted some control from state government to local government.[30]

As might be expected, Democrats criticized Fusion. They opposed it because it made possible the victories of the North Carolina Republicans and Populists, who enjoyed real political power until 1898. During campaigns, Democrats accused the Fusionists of plotting to allow "negro rule" once they won office. They claimed that Fusionists had pulled African Americans off the ballot to get the votes of whites but that they had also made a deal with black voters: "If the negro will be content to wait a few months, if the Fusionists can be elected, then a negro-loving Legislature will make new places for him and a negro Governor will appoint him to them," a Democratic circular argued. "The treasury will be looted, the white citizen taxed to keep the compact with clamorous negro politicians."[31]

But it was not just the Democrats who disliked Fusion. A number of Republicans and Populists did, too, and both parties weakened as a result of internal disagreement about whether the two parties should unite. Andrew D. Cowles, for example, a minor Republican leader in the state, wrote a letter to the Republican Party of Iredell County in 1894 that laid out his case against Fusion. The Populists and Republicans stood for different things, he argued. "There is not a plank in our platform on which the Populist party would stand, and not one in theirs on which a Republican *should* stand. Expediency is the only bond of union. I have tried to reconcile it with conscience and principle. I can't do it. . . . Temporary success means permanent loss."[32]

Populists, too, saw compromise as watering down their goals. L. L. Polk opposed fusion before his death in 1892, arguing that "the only true and manly course to take, is to strike out boldly on our own hook."[33] He saw fusion as dangerous to Populism: "I can see in it elements of great weakness and I think, defeat."[34] Indeed, "the *people* are ripe and ready and will not tolerate a dilly-dally policy. A straight manly fight will win."[35] He noted that Butler disagreed with him on the issue of fusion. Internal discord over issues such as fusion, James Beeby argues, "demoralized and disillusioned the rank and file of the People's Party at a time when unity was desperately needed" and indeed "precipitated the decline of the Populists *before* the 1898 white supremacy campaign."[36]

In North Carolina and several other southern states, Populists fused with Republicans; to Populists in other parts of the country, fusion with the Democrats made more sense because the Democrats had co-opted various Populist goals, such as free silver. In the presidential election of 1896, both the Democrats and the Populists backed William Jennings Bryan, who spoke for farmers among others when he vowed that those who supported the gold standard "shall not crucify mankind upon a cross of gold."[37]

Fusion with the Democrats disheartened some Populists, especially African Americans.[38] J. Z. Greene, the editor of *Our Home*, wrote Marion Butler in 1896 that "our people are disorganized and not in good fighting trim, which, of course, is due to the peculiar and unsettled state of things. Lots of our best men may not vote this year. They think they see in this movement a deep-laid plan by which they will again be placed under rule of Democratic Maclune politics." Greene believed that the "program of the Democrats is to absorb the Populist party of the West and destroy it in the South."[39] A Populist from Cherryville, North Carolina, wrote to Butler that he "will follow you anywhere in Populism, but follow you back into the Democratic party, I will not."[40]

A Populist circular written by N. A. Dunning noted that the Populist National Committee, led by Marion Butler, considered Bryan a "good enough Populist and . . . the Democratic platform represents good enough Populist doctrine." Dunning disagreed with the committee, insisting that "Mr. Bryan is not a Populist. . . . He does not fully endorse a single Populist principle. He is not in favor of government ownership of railroads; does not believe in a graduated income tax and does not endorse absolute full legal tender paper money. He endorses simply the free coinage of silver, but not for the same reason that we Populists do."[41] Dunning urged Populists not to vote or to vote for whoever they thought would be best in office, party notwithstanding. Thomas Watson, a vice presidential candidate during the 1896 election who grew disenchanted when the Democrats put the banker Arthur Sewell on their ticket instead of him, urged the same. Marion Butler scolded him, noting that his advice would put McKinley in office. "Can any personal or party injustice, however great, justify us in being responsible, either directly or indirectly, for placing in power the stock jobbers, monopolists, trusts, the British gold ring, and all of the combined robbers of the people and enemies of good government[?]" Butler asked Watson.[42] Watson replied that he could not support Sewall, who stood for everything the Populist Party opposed:

"Equal rights to all and special privileges to none," was the bedrock principle upon which the great Alliance movement and the Peoples [sic] Party were founded. If we vote for Sewall the representative & beneficiary of "special privilege" we give the lie to all we have been crying for the last eight years. . . . If we compel the Populists to vote against their reform principles, in supporting Sewall, we kill the spirit which vitalizes and inspires our movement.

Watson took a personal jab at Butler, who he felt had betrayed him by urging Populists to vote the Bryan-Sewall ticket: "A fusionist you have always been, and you bargain with the Republicans in one Campaign and with the Democrats in the next. In this Campaign you have bargained with both Republicans & Democrats. God only knows which bargain you intend to keep."[43] One Populist described the problem within the party clearly in 1898: "It is discouraging to think there are three factions in what ought to be one united Populist party. Something ought to be done by which we all could come together and form one solid phalanx against the common enemy."[44]

Populists made their decisions on fusion at the local level, showing the democratic processes that meant so much to them at work. The result was disorganization and, ultimately, losses at the polls. Weakened by internal disagreement, the Populists would lose their grip on political power, and the farmer-friendly reforms made by Fusion government would be overturned.

RACE AND THE POLITICAL LEADERSHIP
OF NORTH CAROLINA

Racism runs deep through the speeches and other writings of the white political leadership of the day. The white supremacist views of L. L. Polk are fairly typical of the white Populists. A former slaveholder and Confederate officer, Polk believed that slavery was an appropriate way of regulating and making productive "a race of strong animal passion, unchecked by any moral force." Polk, previously a Whig, joined the Democratic Party after the Civil War because he objected to the extension of voting and civil rights to African Americans—he described this as "the greatest crime of modern times." He believed that black people contributed to American society only under the control of white supervisors; if this model was not viable, a possible solution was emigration. A number of other Populists, including Lon Livingston and James R. Sovereign, embraced the idea of the removal of blacks.[45]

Marion Butler, too, was an ardent white supremacist. He studied at the University of North Carolina (where he absorbed New South ideas about reform) and trained to become a lawyer. He was not able to do so at that point, however; his father died, and he had to return to Sampson County, where he had grown up. Butler led the North Carolina Populists through the troubles the party faced with the Democratic resurgence. Butler's desire for both white supremacy and political reform is typical of the Populists; as he explained it, "we are in favor of white supremacy, but we are not in favor of cheating and fraud to get it." He wanted white people to retain political power in the state, but he also wanted government to pay attention to the needs of nonelite whites. The 1898 Populist Party *Hand-Book of Facts* presented this perspective to voters, complaining that Democrats used the question of what role African Americans should play in state government to draw attention away from more important issues: "In the campaign of 1898, this Democratic party no longer attempts a discussion of issues of political and economic significance, but flies back to its old cry of 'nigger' on which it managed to exist so long, with the insane and drivelling hope that such a

FIGURE 2.1 Marion Butler.
Source: Courtesy of the State Archives of North Carolina.

cry will resuscitate it, and give it a few more years of license to plunder the State."[46]

Populist leaders generally looked down upon African Americans and wanted to keep them subordinate to white people, but their primary concern was improving the situation of farmers, and they did not want a focus on race to distract from that. They sought to address the concerns of different classes of farmers.[47] Democratic leaders, meanwhile, also wished for African Americans to be subordinate to whites, and they deployed fear of racial difference, which they heightened through their rhetoric, to capture the attention of nonelite whites who were choosing between two parties that looked more similar after the Democrats adopted much of the economic platform of the Populists in 1896.

Charles Aycock—called the "idol of the East"—was a masterful speaker who drew enormous crowds to the Democrats' rallies, where he would exhort his listeners to help save the state from "Russellism, Fusionism, and Black Domination."[48] Josephus Daniels probably did not exaggerate when he claimed that "no man ever converted so many Republicans or Populists" as Aycock.[49]

Governor of the state from 1901 to 1905, Aycock was the youngest of ten children of Serena and Benjamin Aycock, a planter who owned over a thousand acres and thirteen enslaved people and who served as clerk of court of Wayne County, North Carolina, and then in the state senate from 1863 to 1866. Charles grew up sympathetic to the Confederate cause, a great admirer of Confederate heroes such as General Robert E. Lee and Zebulon Baird Vance (Vance led a North Carolina regiment and served as governor of the state during the Civil War). Aycock attended the University of North Carolina, after which he practiced law in Goldsboro, North Carolina, and taught school. He became superintendent of public instruction of the Wayne County school district, a presidential elector for Grover Cleveland (which meant speaking on behalf of the party throughout his district), and U.S. attorney for the Eastern District of North Carolina, a position he held between 1893 and 1897. According to his biographer, Aycock cherished agricultural society, considering it more valuable than industrial society. He also held dear the Democratic Party and the "Anglo-Saxon race." Aycock proved his loyalty to the "race" during the violence in Wilmington in 1898, when telegrams were sent from Wilmington to nearby towns asking for armed men to help the white-supremacist cause. Aycock, telling the story a decade later, said that "in less than half an hour, there were five hundred men at the depot [in Goldsboro] with guns on their shoulders waiting for the train and I was one of them." Before they boarded the train, however, a second telegram arrived that said they would not be needed after all.[50]

The Winston family from Bertie County, with its four prominent sons, provides another example of the Democratic Party's elite and racist leadership. Their father, Patrick Henry Winston, owned fisheries on the Roanoke River and slave-operated plantations. An esteemed lawyer, Patrick Henry represented his county at the North Carolina Constitutional Convention in 1865 and served in a number of other public positions. "Old Man Pat" was an aristocrat and a Whig who very reluctantly "put on the trappings of the mob" to join the Democratic Party after the war. His son Robert recalled that the Democratic Party was unpopular in North Carolina in those days—secessionists were viewed, along with "the fanatics of the North," as "guilty of the most wicked, and the most useless war ever waged."[51]

FIGURE 2.2 Charles Brantley Aycock.
Source: Courtesy of the State Archives of North Carolina.

Robert, born in 1860, practiced law and served in the state legislature and as a judge. He viewed enslaved people as "overgrown children" and slavery as a burden reluctantly borne by paternalistic masters. Innocuous as blacks might be on the plantation, however, they were dangerous as voters. Indeed, Republicans made a grave mistake when they "took the ballot from the master and entrusted it to the slave. They put the bottom rail on top, one of the darkest tragedies in all history." Men like Winston's father joined the Democratic Party in response to the Republicans' eagerness to extend political power to African Americans. Patrick Henry Winston became a Democrat because "the heel of the despot was on the brow of his state"—that is, he feared the "danger" of black control. Members of the white elite took umbrage at the sight of their formerly enslaved workers enjoying political power. "How fresh in my memory is the year 1868," Robert Winston recalled, "when negroes of all ages and all degrees of ignorance took possession of Bertie County, did the voting, filled the offices, and spread dismay." He was horrified to witness African Americans out to vote in 1868. As he described the spectacle, "a brass band gave forth wretched music as savage shouts tore the air. Unearthly guffawing and wild cheering for Gineral Grant and de 'Publican party were incessant."[52]

While the Winstons had no problem living among African Americans as masters, they were less happy in their proximity to black people after emancipation. Now they were surrounded by "worthless tenants" and "the sons of some of the old families [who] had lost their bearings and were living in concubinage with mulatto women." Patrick Henry Winston objected to this change in affairs and "had he been able to dispose of plantations and fisheries he would have moved up the country to a white section." His properties, however, were "unsaleable," and he had to "remain in a land remote from the centers of trade and blighted by an excess of negroes."[53]

The Winstons considered white supremacy essential. Under the direction of Furnifold Simmons, Robert's brother Francis founded White Government Union (WGU) clubs throughout the eastern part of North Carolina. Francis would encourage the white masses to support the Democratic Party and worked to suppress the black vote in 1898. The WGU worked to register white voters, send Democratic campaign literature to them, and convince them to vote Democratic when they came to the polls. Robert described Francis as also "in charge of the Red Shirt campaign to eliminate the ignorant Negro from politics." The Red Shirts would play a crucial role in the Democratic victory through their intimidation of voters.[54]

As a member of the state House of Representatives, Francis would also introduce a bill to disfranchise black voters. Francis considered "Negro suffrage" to be "the last rotten remnant of the Civil War. It still remains, a shameful memorial of sectional folly, hatred and passion. It was the climax of fanaticism, the weeds and nettles and brambles of humanitarianism."[55] After serving in the House of Representatives, Francis was appointed judge in the Second Judicial District by Governor Aycock, then served in a number of other political positions, including lieutenant governor from 1905 to 1909. The Democrats thought highly of Francis, according to his brother, and gave him a number of prominent roles in the party. Robert was also well regarded among Democrats. A member of the state Democratic Committee, he became Charles Aycock's law partner in Raleigh after Aycock's retirement from office.[56]

The political leadership of the state was not all white, however. African Americans rose up through the Republican and Populist parties in spite of the prevalence of racism in the parties. George Henry White, for example, an African American Republican, represented North Carolina's Second District in the U.S. House of Representatives from 1897 to 1901. A 1877 graduate of Howard University, White (b. 1852) moved to Republican-controlled New Bern, where he taught school and studied the law. After passing the bar exam, he practiced law in New Bern while continuing to work as a schoolteacher, then a principal. He also ran for various state-level offices, winning seats as a representative for Craven County in 1880 and as a senator in 1884, then winning election as a prosecutor in the "Black Second." In office, White fought against colleagues who sought to undercut the Fifteenth Amendment and other laws protecting black people's civil rights.[57]

White understood that an important part of the story of the rise of white supremacy was black success. In his famous 1901 farewell address to Congress—at which he acknowledged that he was the last African

FIGURE 2.3 George Henry White.
Source: Courtesy of the State Archives of
North Carolina.

American to serve in a now all-white body—he pointed out what black
people had been able to achieve.

> Since [thirty-two years ago] we have reduced the illiteracy of the race
> at least 45 per cent. We have written and published nearly 500 books.
> We have nearly 300 newspapers, 3 of which are dailies. We have now
> in practice over 2,000 lawyers, and a corresponding number of doc-
> tors. We have accumulated over $12,000,000 worth of school prop-
> erty and about $40,000,000 worth of church property. We have
> about 140,000 farms and homes, valued in the neighborhood of
> $750,000,000, and personal property valued about $170,000,000. We
> have raised about $11,000,000 for educational purposes, and the prop-
> erty per capita for every colored man, woman and child in the United
> States is estimated at $75. We are operating successfully several banks,
> commercial enterprises among our people in the South land, includ-
> ing one silk mill and one cotton factory. We have 32,000 teachers in
> the schools of the country; we have built, with the aid of our friends,
> about 20,000 churches, and support 7 colleges, 17 academies, 50 high
> schools, 5 law schools, 5 medical schools and 25 theological seminaries.

We have over 600,000 acres of land in the South alone. The cotton produced, mainly by black labor, has increased from 4,669,770 bales in 1860 to 11,235,000 in 1899. All this we have done under the most adverse circumstances.[58]

The African American Republican James H. Young, born in 1858, attended Shaw University, a Baptist institution for the education of African Americans in Raleigh. He left the university in 1877 to start work as a laborer in the Office of the Collector of Internal Revenue. Rising up the ranks at this office, he became chief clerk and cashier; after this, he held other appointments, including chief clerk in the Register of Deeds for Wake County and special inspector of customs. Editor of the black Republican publication *Raleigh Gazette* for five years starting in 1893, Young won election to the North Carolina General Assembly in 1894 on the Fusion ticket and in fact played an important role in bringing about Fusion. Young also helped with Daniel Russell's campaign for the governorship, and after Russell won, Young won appointment to the board of directors of the state's institution for the deaf and blind. He was also appointed colonel of the Third North Carolina Infantry, a black regiment that served in the Spanish-American War and was a source of great pride to the state's African American population.[59]

African Americans worked in major as well as minor political jobs in the state, and in doing so, they drew the ire of many white supremacists who could not stand to see African Americans enjoying roles that put them above some whites in status. There were not many African Americans in such roles, but they attracted a lot of attention and cries of "Negro domination." George White argued that "there never has been, nor ever will be, any negro domination in that State, and no one knows it any better than the Democratic party." As he pointed out, such claims served a political purpose: "It is a convenient howl, however, often resorted to in order to consummate a diabolical purpose by scaring the weak and gullible whites into support of measures and men suitable to the demagogue and the ambitious office seeker, whose crave for office overshadows and puts to flight all other considerations, fair or unfair."[60] The success of African American men in attaining and carrying out public office was an affront to white supremacy, and the backlash, when it arrived, was enormous.

FIGURE 2.4 Officers of the Third North Carolina United States Volunteer Infantry, Spanish-American War, commanded by Colonel James H. Young, 1899.
Source: Courtesy of the State Archives of North Carolina.

THE CAMPAIGN FOR WHITE SUPREMACY
IN THE *NEWS AND OBSERVER*

Central to the white-supremacy campaign was the depiction of black men as dangerous—especially to white women. Newspaper editor Josephus Daniels of the Raleigh *News and Observer* portrayed African Americans as angry, dangerous, disrespectful, and eager for sexual encounters with white women.[61] Other newspapers followed Daniels's lead. The way the press depicted black men encouraged white men to fear the possibility of black men intruding on the sanctity of their homes and marriages. Indeed, the American dream of these men was less attainable if their women were vulnerable to sexual advances. Their sense of ownership—of their farms and homes but also of their women—was threatened by the possibility that black men would "take" their women. As Michael Honey explains it, the Democrats needed something significant to "silence reform" coming out of "the highest level of anger on the part of agrarian and working-class people the state had seen since the Civil War." Stoking the racial fears of whites did the trick: "Much like the McCarthyite witch-hunts of the 1950s, the white supremacy campaign had its own kind of magic, which it worked through the media, campaign rallies, lynchings, and white race riots."[62]

James H. Young became the focus of Daniels's attention as his career flourished, and Daniel used the *News and Observer* to provoke fear about Young's position on the board of directors of the state institution for the blind and deaf in political cartoons and numerous articles. Daniels did not accuse Young of any actual impropriety but argued that Republicans endangered white girls through this appointment.[63]

In a political cartoon from August 1898, Young—belittled as "Jim Young"—stands in the bedroom of a white woman, conducting an inspection (a task his position made possible). The shocked and powerless occupant of the room stands in front of him, her bed suggestively placed behind her. Democrats knew better than to put a black man in such a position, argued the *News and Observer*, but the Republicans and Populists cared more about their own advancement than about the safety of the state's white women.

Jim Young, the Negro Politician, Inspecting Apartments in White Blind Institution at P

Jim Young controls the Board of Directors of the only Institution in the State at which the white blind children can be taught. Article 4 of the By-Laws require "the Committee of Inspection to visit each department of the Institution twice every month, and make a written report to the Board." It is the custom to appoint the members of the Board by turns on the Inspection Committee, who shall visit the rooms and apartments of the Institution, make an inspection, and report "as to their condition." This picture illustrates the power conferred upon a negro politician in an institution in which most of the teachers and pupils are white ladies.

FIGURE 2.5 Political cartoon from the Raleigh *News and Observer*: "Jim Young, the Negro Politician, Inspecting Apartments."
Source: *News and Observer* (Raleigh), August 19, 1898, 1.

Daniels was prone to exaggeration. One of his contemporaries described Daniels as someone who saw the world in black and white: "He never doubted, never hesitated. He did not pause to think, he acted.... He saw neither to the right hand nor to the left, only to the goal ahead, and to that he flashed like an arrow to the mark."[64] Poe, a friend of Daniels, years later acknowledged that Daniels had not "always been quite fair to one under-privileged class—our Negroes." He excused Daniels as a product of "the policies and passions" of his time and noted that he had "later fully supported Governor Aycock's universal education campaign and defended the Negroes against extremists who wished to limit the Negro school support to taxes paid by Negroes themselves."[65] Daniels, too, later described his headlines and stories as "sometimes too lurid" (although in line with the times), citing an example from the issue of June 16: "*Burned to Ashes, the Black Devil, Riddled with Bullets First, a Righteous Judgment, Ravished and then Killed a White*

Lady, Paid the Penalty for his Crime, an Outraged People Chased the Fiend for Two Days and When They Caught Him Made Short Work of Him.[66]

Decades later, Daniels described the time as one "when the race feeling was very tense and growing worse, day by day."[67] He did not cast blame upon himself for worsening "race feeling," though he did note that his stories had political repercussions because rural white female readers were afraid that their isolation would leave them vulnerable to attack. "All these cases of miscegenation, rape, and outrage, followed up by the reports of drinking and immorality in the State Prison, which were duly printed day by day," had consequences: the feeling of fear of the women in the country "was one of the factors which, in 1898, caused many farmers who had joined the Populists in 1894 to help drive the Fusionists out of power."[68] These stories about rapes also, happily for Daniels, increased circulation: "*The News and Observer*, at the end of 1898, had reached high water mark in circulation . . . [which] in two months, had grown from fifty-one hundred to sixty-two hundred."[69] Lurid and exaggerated it might be, but "the Old Reliable" was, according to Robert Winston, "our political Bible."[70]

Glenda Elizabeth Gilmore presents the negative portrayal of African American men as a conscious strategy employed by Democrats to undermine faith in Populists and Republicans by suggesting that only Democrats would protect white women. The number of rapes committed by black men against white women in 1897 and 1898 was no higher than usual, but Democrats effectively created a "black-on-white rape scare" using "propaganda" to plant "seeds of hysteria that ripened in the minds of an economically threatened people."[71] Even Josephus Daniels, who did more than perhaps anyone else to stir up fear of black men as rapists, afterward admitted that there were not actually many rapes.[72] Gilmore argues that men were primed to "commit mass murder" in Wilmington by the "hysteria that swelled from the belief that their wives and daughters lived in danger," a belief encouraged by the Democrats.[73] Democrats also linked rape to the new political positions African Americans were taking by arguing that blacks aspired to hold office with the goal of winning better access to white women and that black rapists were emboldened by black office holders, thinking that now they could get away with anything.[74] White supremacists argued that black men, no longer kept in check by slavery, were reverting to "barbarism."[75] Having depicted blacks as violent aggressors, Democrats argued that they would protect whites, especially white women, from the dangers posed by these "brutes." With Democrats having captured the attention of the people by creating hysteria, all Populists could do was claim that they—not Democrats—were the true champions of white women.

THE DEMOCRATIC PARTY'S "COUP"

Democrats ousted the coalition of Populists and Republicans in North Carolina in 1898. Their success can be attributed to Aycock's masterful campaigning, Francis Winston's violent Red Shirts, and Josephus Daniels's shaping of a message that created and stoked fear among white people through the *News and Observer*.[76] Heightened racism—fanned by the Democrats—played an important role in bringing about the party's triumph. Racism distracted small farmers, pulling their attention away from the potential benefits of the Populists' economic program and the potential mismatch with the Democratic agenda. Put another way, racism was used to mask the class implications of the Democratic victory. Barbara Fields, drawing upon C. Vann Woodward, makes the point that white people did not all benefit equally from white supremacy: "the question was not white supremacy but '*which whites* should be supreme.'"[77] Robert Korstad highlights the class dimensions of this story: "These Bourbon Democrats, so called by their Populist opponents because of their elitist base and goals, established a system of racial capitalism that they called 'white supremacy,' a term that helped to obscure the class presumptions of their undemocratic project."[78]

The Democrats argued that it was essential for the preservation of society that white Americans wield political power and enjoy a status superior to that of African Americans. Thus they made it their single driving purpose to "return" government to "able" voters and to separate black from white people in public accommodations. As Jack Kirby explained it, the disfranchisement and segregation of black southerners could be considered the "seminal 'progressive' reform of the era," a reform that "made possible nearly every other reform they [white southerners] might undertake—from building better schools to closing the saloons."[79] Putting power back into the hands of whites, the Democrats argued, would improve the South, enhancing the efficiency of government and business and improving the well-being of the public. In order to achieve this, Democrats instructed white voters, they would first need to remove the opposition: "We said to them: 'Help us overthrow the Republican bosses; help us eliminate the Negro ballot, which is the basis of their power; help us put away the Negro vote and the Negro issue, which hitherto have tended to veto all progressive measures— and we promise you that this State shall go forward as never before.'"[80] The Democrats' campaign for white supremacy was meant to improve government and to return "mastery"—lost after the Civil War—to white southerners. According to Stephen Kantrowitz, the term "white supremacy" describes several different things. It was "more than a slogan and less than a fact," an ideology that shaped the political agenda of the Democrats, a set of "practices, promises and threats, oratory and murder." As white supremacists stripped blacks of political and social rights as well as economic opportunity, white supremacy also became Democrats' crowning achievement.[81]

The Democratic seizure of political power in Wilmington in 1898 illuminates the link between "reform" and white supremacy. It also provides an example of the determination of Democrats throughout the state to regain political power and shows the violent and illegal measures they were willing to take to do so. White and black people throughout the state paid attention to what happened in Wilmington. It empowered white people to seek their own supremacy, and it imparted a lesson to African Americans: their political and economic rights could be forcibly taken from them.

A large and bustling port city with a majority-black population— Wilmington, North Carolina, had 8,731 white and 11,324 black residents— and one with a tradition of black militancy, Wilmington was a place where whites felt particularly threatened by African Americans. Black men held political offices in the city, and many black professionals owned property in majority-white sections of town. Wilmington was considered an example of what could go wrong with "Negro rule," and fabricated or embellished stories of black atrocities there abounded.[82] In the fall of 1898, an interracial "Fusion" coalition of Republicans and white Populists held together by their opposition to the Democratic Party led Wilmington. Business leaders and the planter class, who tended to be Democrats, felt threatened by the coalition. They listened, aghast, as the coalition demanded popular control of local elections and regulation of business; Democrats then began a campaign to destroy the coalition. Alfred Moore Waddell, a Wilmington Democrat, revealed the deep racism that motivated the campaign to end "these intolerable conditions" when he vowed that "we will never surrender to a ragged raffle of negroes, even if we have to choke the current of the Cape Fear with carcasses."[83]

What happened in Wilmington has traditionally been called a "riot," though historians consider this term inaccurate. Glenda Gilmore describes it as "upper-class whites [leading] a racial massacre against middle-class blacks."[84] Timothy Tyson and David Cecelski argue that the word "riot" does not reflect what happened, as it was not a spontaneous event but rather "an orchestrated campaign to end interracial cooperation, restore white supremacy, and in the process assure the rule of the state's planter and industrial leaders," led by a group of nine prominent white Wilmingtonians—the "Secret Nine."[85] White supremacists readied themselves to "take back" their city—they joined new white-supremacy clubs, together called the White Government Union, and a labor movement emerged along with the White Government Union that worked toward the goal of "the substitution of white for Negro labor." The opportunity to take control of Wilmington arose when Alexander Manly, the Hampton-educated African American editor of the *Daily Record*, published an editorial about lynching in August 1898.[86] Democrats would ride this editorial to victory over the Fusionists.

Manly's editorial responded to a speech given by Rebecca Felton before a meeting of the State Agricultural Society of Georgia, which was reprinted in the *Wilmington Messenger*. Felton, the wife of a Georgia congressman (she too would become a politician), called for white men to protect white women from black men, even if this required an orgy of lynching.[87] If it was necessary to lynch "to protect woman's dearest possession from the ravening beasts," Felton declared, "then I say lynch, a thousand times a week, if necessary." Lynching was just one measure that Felton, an ardent supporter of white women's rights, thought would improve the lot of rural women—she was also a member of the Women's Christian Temperance Union and a proponent of improved education for white women, including admission to the University of Georgia. She told a story about looking out her window while riding the train and seeing young white women hoeing cotton alongside black men; witnessing these "unwholesome conditions," she claimed, made her "heart sick." One reason for advocating better educational opportunities for white women, then, was to pull them out of the fields—and from this proximity to black men. Felton disapproved of sexual relations between white men and black women, too, but only because she thought it devalued the white wives and children of the white men who engaged in interracial intimacy.[88]

Felton assumed that all sexual relations between white women and black men were rapes, a belief Glenda Gilmore describes as increasingly common during this period—that all white women were pure and all black men rapists.[89] Alexander Manly disagreed with Felton, arguing in his editorial that many so-called rapes were actually instances of white women seeking out sexual relations with black men and that such relations "go on for some time until the woman's infatuation, or the man's boldness, bring attention to them, and the man is lynched for rape." He also pointed out that white men often sought out black women for the same purpose. "Tell your men that it is no worse for a black man to be intimate with a white woman than for the white man to be intimate with a colored woman," he instructed white readers. "You set yourselves down as a lot of carping hypocrites in fact you cry aloud for the virtue of your women while you seek to destroy the morality of ours. Don't ever think that your women will remain pure while you are debauching ours." Manly himself was believed to be descended from a white governor of North Carolina, Charles Manly (although he may actually have been descended from Charles Manly's nephew or grandson). White newspapers reprinted selections of Manly's editorial, calling it an "outrageous, mendacious attack on white women" that showed "the effects of Russellism and Butlerism."[90] (Governor Russell and Senator Butler had led the efforts to fuse the Republican and Populist parties in the state.)[91]

Manly's editorial, according to Josephus Daniels, "went like wildfire from house to house, particularly in the rural districts," where people "were righteously indignant."[92] White supremacists used the editorial to rally whites against African Americans. In October, the Democrats staged a huge political rally in Fayetteville, at which South Carolina's senator "Pitchfork" Ben Tillman stirred further animosity toward African Americans. "Why didn't you kill that damn nigger editor who wrote that?" Tillman asked the audience. "Send him to South Carolina and let him publish any such offensive stuff, and he will be killed."[93] Anger toward African Americans was harnessed by leaders like Furnifold Simmons, whom Daniels called "a genius in putting everybody to work—men who could write, men who could speak, and men who could ride—the last by no means the least important."[94] The men who rode around on horseback, terrorizing African Americans, were inspired by the "terrifying" Red Shirts who accompanied Tillman.[95] Josephus Daniels described the effect these riders had on witnesses.

> Wherever [Ben Tillman] spoke he was attended by a cavalcade of men who would meet him at the station and ride through the county with him, riding through the colored sections of the towns, all wearing red shirts, shouting white supremacy. Some of them carried shotguns and would shoot in the air. They created terror. I had read about Red Shirts but had never understood how three hundred men on horseback, wearing red shirts, with pants tucked in their boots, and carrying guns, could make such a terrifying spectacle.... As always happens in the South when there is a contest of this kind and the white people are greatly aroused, ready to wear red shirts and to carry pistols, many Negroes felt that the contest was unequal and stood aside.[96]

One can envision how empowering it would have felt for whites who had little real control over the forces that shaped their lives to join this cavalcade. They might have worked jobs just as menial as African Americans and felt burdened by debt and other troubles. But on horseback, dressed in their red shirts, they were given a psychological boost.

As part of the backlash against Manly's editorial, a committee of twenty-five white community leaders put together a list of resolutions that they named "The White Declaration of Independence." This declaration asserted the right of whites to govern themselves and retain economic opportunities for themselves and announced that Manly would have to leave Wilmington within twenty-four hours. The group of twenty-five then met with African American leaders to deliver their list of demands.[97] Wilmington's African Americans put up no protest, responding that "we ... beg most respectfully to say that we are in no wise responsible for nor in anyway endorse the obnoxious article that called forth your actions." They agreed to "most willingly use [our] influence to have your wishes carried out."[98]

In spite of the acquiescence of the city's African Americans, Wilmington's whites turned to violence. A mob destroyed Alexander Manly's printing press and offices—Manly was not harmed, as he had fled to New Jersey before this—then ran rampant, shooting African Americans willy-nilly in the streets and driving hundreds of black residents from their homes to nearby swamps. Estimates of the death toll resulting from this rout vary widely, ranging between seven and over three hundred.[99] One of Wilmington's black ministers, J. Allen Kirk, was among those forced to flee. He described the losses of the city's black population:

> We are exiled and scattered over the country from our pulpits and our people, without having time to get our property or our money or any other means of protection for our families, but left them in the woods and country places to flee for our lives, hoping that we might be able to gather them home at some future time and in a place of safety. . . . The shrieks and screams of children, of mothers, of wives were heard, such as caused the blood of the most inhuman person to creep. Thousands of women, children and men rushed to the swamps and there lay upon the earth in the cold to freeze and starve. The woods were filled with colored people. The streets were dotted with their dead bodies.[100]

The federal government did nothing to punish the murderers. The U.S. attorney for the Eastern District of North Carolina, claiming a lack of information from witnesses, told the U.S. attorney general that he could build a case only with substantial federal resources to help him gather information. It was decided not to move ahead.[101] Alfred Waddell, one of the riot's leaders, argued that federal inaction showed tacit approval: "The great majority of the people in all parts of the country justified the movement—if not by expressed approval at least by abstaining from any condemnation of it, and a very convincing evidence of the spirit in which it was regarded by the Federal authorities was given by their silence and inaction concerning it."[102]

FIGURE 2.6 "The Revolution at Wilmington NC" (*Collier's Weekly*, November 26, 1898). The man on the left is Alfred Waddell; on the right is Wilmington's chief of police, E. G. Parmele. Bottom center is the mob after destroying Manly's printing press.
Source: Courtesy of the North Carolina State Archives.

As they ran African Americans out of the city, Democrats, led by the chairman of the state Democratic Executive Committee, Furnifold Simmons, also stripped political power from the Fusionists. They had used fraud and fear tactics to vote out Fusionist candidates who were up for election on November 8, 1898; on November 10, they forced political opponents who had not been up for reelection out of office and ran black professionals out of the city. As a response to the political coup and the violence, 1,400 African Americans left Wilmington over the next month.[103]

The events in Wilmington were led by middle- and upper-class whites, though the leaders were able to attract poor white followers by focusing on the "threat" posed by black men to white women. The Democratic leadership also tried to convince poor whites that it was in their economic interest to support the party—that the party would attract outside investment to the state, thus creating jobs, and that it would make sure that jobs held by blacks would be handed over to whites. Party leaders also convinced poor whites that the elevated position of blacks in Wilmington was attributable to unfair racial preferences under Fusionist government.[104]

Republican and Populist leaders were outraged by the massacre—Marion Butler thought that Democrats had "won by the most contemptible and infamous methods."[105] Democratic leaders, meanwhile, cheered for what the rioters had accomplished. Speaking about the coup a few years later in his 1901 inaugural address, Governor Aycock described North Carolina under Fusion rule as lawless and dangerous and praised the white-supremacy campaign, including the events in Wilmington, for returning government to Democrats.

Under [Fusion] rule, lawlessness stalked the State like a pestilence—death stalked abroad at noonday—"sleep lay down armed"—the sound of the pistol was more frequent than the song of the mocking-bird—the screams of women fleeing from pursuing brutes closed the gates of our hearts with a shock. Our opponents unmindful of the sturdy determination of our people to have safe and good government at all hazards became indifferent to or incapable of enforcing law and preserving order. . . . The campaign of 1898 ended in a victory for good government. That was not a contest of passion, but of necessity. When we came to power we desired merely the security of life, liberty and property. We had seen all these menaced by 120,000 negro votes cast as the vote of one man. We had seen our chief city pass through blood and death in search of safety. We did not dislike the negro, but we did love good government. We knew that he was incapable of giving us that, and we resolved, not in anger, but for the safety of the State, to curtail his power.[106]

Aycock engaged in a tactic typical of white supremacists by fanning fears about the rape of white women—his language about "the screams of women fleeing from pursuing brutes" is hardly subtle—to spread fear and win support for himself. During his campaign for the governorship, he told listeners that "the safety of our women is dependent upon" his winning and the prevailing of white supremacy. Because the violence in Wilmington cleared out "dangerous" blacks, it was a reform. Accepting the Democratic nomination for governor, Aycock emphasized the improvements that would come with white supremacy. Among them were safety, peace, and an end to the fighting over the status and rights of African Americans: "We unfurl anew the old banner of Democracy. We inscribe thereon 'White Supremacy and Its Perpetuation.' Under that banner we shall win and when we shall have won we will have peace in the land. There will be rest from political bitterness and race antagonism."[107]

The violence in Wilmington brought "reform" to government, according to Aycock, and improved opportunities for whites. It also led to a decline in opportunities of all kinds for African Americans. Black leaders were targeted for expulsion; as Reverend Kirk described it, "the decent families of our race have been assailed and routed like beasts from their God given positions as leaders of their race."[108] Professional opportunities shrank; the black press, for example, was silenced after the destruction of Manly's office. Black firemen and policemen lost their jobs. After the fall of 1898, a higher percentage of the city's African Americans held low-wage, low-status jobs. The 1898 events also destroyed the political opportunities blacks had enjoyed since Reconstruction. White supremacists removed African Americans from local political offices. Segregation was strengthened throughout the city not right after the coup but by 1905; before this, there had been a number of integrated "transition" blocks between black and white neighborhoods. Black-owned businesses in white areas were put out of business or forced to relocate. Funding for black schools was cut after 1898—as it was throughout the state—and literacy rates among African Americans declined compared to whites.[109] The *Southern Workman* reported in 1908 that hundreds of African Americans fled North Carolina after the Wilmington massacre and that about twenty families from the state had settled in Whitesboro, New Jersey, an all-black community founded by former congressman George H. White as a refuge from the violence and restrictions of Jim Crow.[110]

RACE AND THE EVOLUTION OF THE POPULIST PARTY

Populist literature and the correspondence and speeches of Populist leaders reveal a sincere commitment to democratic principles.[111] But, believing there was no alternative, the Populists set aside their principles, especially after 1898, to engage in race-baiting. In much of the state, the Populists felt compelled to take on the "scarecrow of race" in response to the Democratic attack. The *News and Observer*, for example, provoked Populists by arguing that they were wishy-washy on "race." The newspaper reprinted a statement of Butler's from 1888 and argued that he had switched from an earlier white-supremacist perspective to one that favored blacks for political expediency, for example. "For White Supremacy Then" argued that Butler had walked away from his former position that "this is a Caucasian government, founded by the courage, framed by the wisdom and won by the partiotism [*sic*] of white men. . . . Therefore it is of right, ought to be, and must be, MANAGED BY WHITE MEN ONLY."[112]

Populists responded to attacks like these by lowering themselves to the level of the Democrats in presenting their party as the true representative of the white masses and their opponents as overly friendly with African Americans. "The People's Party is and has always been more distinctly than any other party in North Carolina a white man's party, and is more anxious than any other party to solve the race problem," claimed a party publication that argued against the proposed disfranchisement amendment of 1899.[113] Under Butler's editorship, the *Caucasian* was full of articles such as "'White Mans Party' Democracy Shown Up; It Elects Negroes to Office by Hundreds, Then Squalls 'Nigger Domination.'" This article argued that the Democratic Party "blows hot and cold alternately" on African Americans:

One day it will be squalling "nigger" worse than a man with delirium tremens. Then some Democratic candidate will go to the machine, or some parts of it and say: "Look here! if you keep this thing up we won't get a single negro vote." And on the very next day that same machine or parts of it will say: "We have nothing against the negro; we have always been his best friend." . . . But while the Democratic machine relapses into its delirium tremens howl of "nigger," it tries to *use* him by elevating him to office and otherwise playing with and equalizing him.[114]

Disorganized and scrambling for a message that would lift the party's prospects in the face of the Democrats' unethical campaign tactics, Populists argued that the Democrats were inconsistent in their approach to dealing with African Americans and that because of their desire for the votes of blacks they exposed the most vulnerable whites to danger. The *Caucasian* reported that the "Democratic Board of County Commissioners of Mitchell county farmed out two helpless little white orphans to a negro woman of the lowest intelligence" after their mother died, stating that the children died under her care.[115] It also argued that the Populists did more than the Democrats to protect white women from the threat of sexual relationships with black men. According to the *Caucasian*, Alamance County Democrats forced a nineteen-year-old white girl who had been convicted of "receiving stolen goods" to shovel dirt in a roadside ditch alongside black male convicts. "She was a white girl and deserved to be treated as a human being," scolded the newspaper.[116] Democrats hired a black notary public who met privately with white women as part of his job.[117] Meanwhile, the paper claimed that Populists fought this trend. For example, it praised Senator Butler for blocking the appointment of a handful of African Americans to federal offices such as that of postmaster.[118]

It was not just the leadership of the Democratic and Populist parties but also the white masses—many of whom were Populists—who worked to make the South a white man's country. One black Populist who grew up in North Carolina but became politically active in Texas, John Rayner, complained about the "agrarianism of white tenant farmers" as motivating whites to limit the rights of African Americans. African Americans viewed Populists as using blacks to their own political advantage. For example, Isaac

Sad and Disgraceful Scene in Alamance county, where "White Man's Party" Democrats work White Girls on Public Roads with Negroes.

FIGURE 2.7 Political cartoon from *The Caucasian*: "Sad and Disgraceful Scene in Alamance County."
Source: Supplement to *The Caucasian*, October 20, 1898, 2.

Smith, an African American who represented Craven County in the North Carolina House, complained that the way Populists treated blacks made him think of

> a horse that you get for nothing, and then you ride him and ride him and half-feed him, and finally turn him aloose, and say he's no good; anyhow. That's the way you Populists have done my race. We have elected them to good fat offices; we've made them Governor—the returns in the office of the Secretary of State show it—and now you turn and tell us we ought never to have been allowed to vote, anyhow.[119]

Gerald H. Gaither argues that North Carolina's African Americans generally stayed in the Republican Party. They viewed the Populist Party as hostile toward them and faced social pressure within their community to remain true to the Republican Party.[120]

A Democratic Legislature Electing 107 Negro Magistrates.

FIGURE 2.8 Political cartoon from *The Caucasian*: "A Democratic Legislature Electing 107 Negro Magistrates."
Source: Supplement to *The Caucasian*, October 20, 1898, 2.

As the Populist Party declined in power, Democrats took advantage of the opportunity to woo Populist voters into their own party. As Josephus Daniels pointed out, many Populists had been Democrats before they were Populists, and they were returning to the fold. Daniels tried to lure these people back to the Democratic Party through his newspaper. "*The News and Observer*," he recalled years later, "believing that the bulk of the Alliance men had joined the Populist party because of the distress and poverty on the farms and that the bulk of them had no sympathy with the Russell administration, wanted to make it easy for them to come back to the Democratic Party." Democratic leaders made this easier by shifting aspects of the Democratic agenda to parallel that of the Populists, embracing reforms like free silver.[121]

One of the tactics Daniels used to bring Populists back to the Democratic Party was suggesting that Fusion was somehow responsible for supposed atrocities committed by African Americans. As Daniels explained this,

The indignation over cases of assault and rape of white women by the Negroes, though these were few in number, was such that women in the country who at first had been strong for the Populists, now convinced that Fusion had some part in the increase of attacks, began to turn against the Fusionists. . . . This illustrates the feeling of fear of the women in the country. It was one of the factors which, in 1898, caused many farmers who had joined the Populists in 1894 to help drive the Fusionists out of power.[122]

Butler looked back on the bitter campaign of 1898—the campaign wherein Democrats used all the dirty tactics they could think of to take political power—as one in which Populists had made costly mistakes. He had wanted to "take such [action] as was necessary to shift the issue from the negro," but the state committee "decided against the proposition and allowed matters to drift." As a result,

The Democrats won by the most contemptible and infamous methods that a party ever resorted to, but they could not have done it if we had played the cards that were in our hands, and which we could have played, to execute a flank movement on them, shift the negro issue, and put them on the defensive. The result is due as much or more to our mistakes than to their shrewdness or their tremendous campaign barrel contributed by the railroads.[123]

It turned out that the Populist approach on the "negro question" was not as effective politically as that of the Democrats; nor could the Populists compete with Democrats' tactics. Trying to please both sides—by cooperating with African Americans at the same time that they denied them, by supporting certain rights for blacks at the same time that they engaged in race-baiting—pleased no one. Their ill-conceived political approach, which was a response to Democrats' race baiting, fraud, and violence, could not resuscitate their political fortunes.

THE DISFRANCHISEMENT AMENDMENT

African Americans in North Carolina were keenly aware that disfranchisement was on the horizon in 1898. It had come to South Carolina and Louisiana already. The *Gazette*, James Young's newspaper, pointed out that the 1898 election would "determine whether the Democratic party is to be allowed to disfranchise negro voters of this State under the forms of law as it has done in the other Southern States, or whether the voters belonging to that race are to continue to exercise the God given right of casting their ballots." The paper pledged to "uncover their wicked plans, schemes and methods in order that the people may be warned."[124] White Republicans also opposed disfranchisement; as the *Union Republican* explained it, responding to accusations that it favored "negro domination," "The only thing that The Republican or the Republican party in N.C. has advocated for the negro is that he be allowed the same privileges at the polls and the same rights of citizenship that any other citizen has, just as our constitution and the laws of the land provide."[125] Republicans white and black considered disfranchisement "the most impudent assault upon the Constitution of the United States and the most shocking act of party perfidy ever attempted by men who recognize the obligation of an oath or the sanctity of a public pledge."[126] But there was little that those who favored equal rights for African Americans could do to protect voting rights from the Democratic onslaught.

In 1899 Aycock joined other Democratic leaders in promoting an amendment to the state constitution that would disfranchise African Americans, a measure that Aycock argued would help prevent the occurrence of another Wilmington.[127] For Aycock, electoral reform necessitated removing African Americans from the franchise because they were "easily led to form combinations with a small minority of white men [thus bringing] to the State intolerable government." Aycock claimed that North Carolina's experiment with universal male suffrage had turned out to be a "failure" because of the "ignorance" of black voters.[128] The amendment—introduced by Furnifold Simmons, Francis Winston, and George Roundtree—was passed in August 1900, and Aycock was elected governor at the same time on a platform of educational reform, winning the governorship with a large majority.

The amendment put in place a literacy test that potential voters would have to pass before they could register, as well as a poll tax. White men who were able to vote on or before January 1867 or descendants of such voters were exempted from the literacy test through a "grandfather clause," in effect through December 1908. The reason that Aycock—remembered fondly by some North Carolinians as the "education governor"—proposed improving the public-education system was to prepare white voters to pass the literacy test after 1908. Simmons recalled years later that until they promised to prepare white voters through an "educational campaign," the Democrats "had a great deal of trouble" gaining support for the amendment in the western part of North Carolina, "where a large number of white adults were unable to read or write" and where white men feared being disfranchised. Populists, especially Marion Butler, pointed out to these whites that they were in danger of losing the vote. Afraid that Republicans would push to have the grandfather clause declared unconstitutional, Democrats decided that the amendment would go forward only if it included both the literacy test and the grandfather clause (to protect illiterate white voters). These measures were necessary to convince small white farmers and other whites who were likely to be illiterate that the Democrats were not out to disfranchise them, but African Americans.[129]

The amendment disfranchised the vast majority of black North Carolinians; 120,000 African Americans were registered to vote in the state in 1896 but only 6,100 in 1902. Some illiterate whites who also faced disfranchisement nevertheless supported the amendment because they believed Democratic leaders who promised that the amendment would protect their women. If African American men could not vote, these white men believed, they would not be able to put themselves in offices that gave them access to white women, and they would no longer enjoy an elevated position in society, a position it was believed made them feel entitled to white women.[130]

Aycock sought to assure nonelite white voters that they would be able to participate in their government by highlighting the educational reform that would "prepare" them for citizenship. During Aycock's administration, hundreds of schools were constructed, 877 rural schools gained libraries, and spending on public education was increased. This money came from increased tax revenue; in 1900, local school taxes were collected in thirty districts, but by 1904 they were collected in 229 districts. It should come as no surprise that Aycock's approach to improving the education system reflected his racial bias. While the enrollment of both white and black children rose by about 10 percent, the rate of spending on black schools did not match that of spending on white schools.[131] A paternalist, Aycock argued that his administration made every effort to advance the interests of African Americans who could no longer protect their own rights through the ballot. As an example of this, he pointed to the state's provision of "equal" education for its black residents. "The negroes pay but little of the taxes for the conduct of the public schools," Aycock claimed, "and yet our laws provide and carry into effect the public school system which secures equal facilities for the negroes with those provided for the white." Aycock's claim of equal education ignores the fact that African Americans were taxed "proportionally more than whites," while the state spent less money per capita on their education.[132]

The battle over the amendment reflects the differences between the Democrats and the Populists. Democratic leaders knew that they would gain political power as black voters and nonelite white voters were taken off the voter rolls, and most Populists understood that the disfranchisement of these voters would have the opposite effect on their party. In North Carolina, unlike other southern states, the Democrats had a relatively small numerical advantage over the Republicans (in gubernatorial elections after 1876, there were usually fewer than twenty thousand votes' difference between the two parties). Black voters were essential to the victory of Populist and Republican candidates in the state.[133] Senator Butler, aware that the Populists needed black voters, decried the amendment as illegal as well as dangerous. Butler argued that African American men had a constitutional right to vote and that the amendment violated the Fifteenth Amendment, which said that the right to vote could not be "denied or abridged . . . on account of race, color, or previous condition of servitude." The Fifteenth Amendment, Butler insisted, "whether its adoption was wise or unwise, is a part of the organic law of this Republic, and is as binding as any other section of the Federal Constitution; and while it so remains it should and must be respected and obeyed, not only by every State but by every citizen and voter." He went on to explain that the disfranchisement amendment violated the Fifteenth Amendment by targeting former slaves and their descendants. "Why was the arbitrary date of 1867 adopted? Why not 1875 or 1880 or 1899?" Butler demanded. The reason, as he explained it, was that the framers of the amendment were trying to eliminate a "class of citizens who were in servitude and who, therefore, could not vote in 1867."[134]

Not all Populists agreed with Butler. According to Josephus Daniels, the Populists in the state legislature were split on the amendment:

> Every Republican in the Legislature voted against its submission. The Populists divided, and the vote of the Populists on this question forecast their future political alignment. It was a clear-cut issue between those who wanted to remove the bulk of ignorant Negroes from the exercise of suffrage and those who wanted to continue them. Pritchard and Butler saw, in the elimination of the ignorant Negro vote, their undoing. They were ready to go to any length to defeat any plan that denied the ballot to every Negro, even the most ignorant.[135]

One thing the Populists did agree on: it was to the detriment of their cause if poor white men lost the vote. Butler argued that the amendment would take the vote away from illiterate whites, white men "who compose some of the very best and most substantial citizens of our State," men who had fought in the Civil War.[136] The *Caucasian* published a letter to the editor from "A Populist" who criticized the Democratic modus operandi as being "We can afford to cut off one white man who cannot read, in order to cut off two negroes."[137] One article in the *Caucasian* showed anxiety that African Americans were doing more to educate their youth than were poor whites and that because of this poor whites would be hurt more by the amendment than would blacks. "The negroes for various reasons send their children to school during the school months," an article claimed, because "they cannot find employment for them . . . and send it to school in many instances to get it out of the way." Not wishing to suggest that blacks were intellectually superior to poor whites, the article described black children as able to "learn to read and write quite readily, [though they] have difficulty in getting much further."[138] Another article accused the Democrats of aiming to disfranchise poor whites: "It was to strike down the political rights and liberties of these honest, sturdy and patriotic yeomanry that this amendment was brought forward."[139] Figure 2.9 shows a political cartoon in which a well-dressed young black man, whose coat states "I Can Read," is allowed past the election constable to cast his ballot, while an older white man, "Illiterate White Voter," is blocked. The cartoon declares that this is "what will happen at the next election if the amendment is adopted. . . . The negro dude will vote while the illiterate white man will be pushed aside by one of Simmons' election constables."[140]

White Populists were not so different from Democrats on the issue of race. That is to say: most were racist. Because they relied on the votes of black men—and, in certain cases, because they believed in the principle of it (Cyrus Thompson, for example, announced in a speech in 1900 that "the negro was the equal of the white man in hereditary fitness to govern")[141]— some Populists stood up for the voting rights of blacks. Some even risked their own lives to help African Americans register to vote after the disfranchisement amendment was passed.[142] They generally objected to African Americans holding political office that would put them into contact with whites, however, and depicted black men as "brutes" when it suited them to do so. As Charles Postel points out, Populists faced a "politically difficult and dangerous undertaking": finding a balance between "attract[ing] a section of the black vote without undermining [the Party's] support among white farmers."[143] By 1900, the Populist experiment had failed in North Carolina; Democrats had successfully used racism to push Fusionists out of office and take the vote away from those people who would have been most likely to support the Populist cause.

Clarence Poe, meanwhile, supported disfranchisement—so strongly, apparently, that he was willing to risk his job to garner support for it. At the time the amendment was under consideration, Poe worked as editor of the *Progressive Farmer* under the owner of the publication, John Denmark. Eager to collect letters from readers in support of the amendment, Poe worked behind Denmark's back to encourage a letter-writing campaign. As T. B. Parker, a correspondent of Poe, explained the situation,

> I have had a confidential request from the editor of the *Progressive Farmer*, for something in favor of the Amendment for his paper. He also gives me permission to get others to write for it. *He must not be*

FIGURE 2.9   Political cartoon from *The Caucasian*: "The Simmons Machine at Work."
Source: *The Caucasian*, June 14, 1900, 1.

known as soliciting these contributions, as he might loose [sic] *his job if it were known.* Get your friends in different sections to write along the same lines; but suggest to them to write on the merits of the Amendment and not in a partisan spirit as that might cause suspicion. You see and understand the situation.[144]

Poe also published an article on disfranchisement in another publication, *North American Review*, in 1902, arguing that disfranchisement was essential for getting corruption out of politics. Tracing the history of African American suffrage, Poe depicted the Fifteenth Amendment as a mistake causing different problems: not only the scheming of whites who took advantage of "the ignorance and recklessness of the newly-enfranchised blacks" to achieve their own ends but also the "undivided slave-like support" of African Americans to the Republican party, which meant that their votes shaped elections when whites split their votes among the Republican, Populist, and Democratic parties. Whites eager to end "negro rule" participated in "election frauds," which Poe considered a step toward "lawlessness." The movement to disfranchise black voters, Poe believed, would lead to freedom "from our nearly four decades of bondage to the race issue." It would allow white southerners to cast their votes focusing on issues other than race and for the fraud and corruption that characterized the southern political system to be cleaned out.[145]

Clarence Poe's political trajectory illustrates a trend common enough in North Carolina: like a number of other middling white people, he shifted from the Populist Party to the Democratic Party. Poe's family had embraced Populism, which offered small farmers the hope of significant economic reform. By the time Poe was a young man, however, the party was in disarray, and the Democratic Party was the only option for a man who wanted to make his name in the state. Poe made the intellectual connection between Populism and the Progressive wing of the Democratic Party; according to Poe, "William J. Bryan once told me that he regarded the Farmers' Alliance as the forerunner of the Progressive movement in politics, later represented by himself in the Democratic party and by Theodore Roosevelt in the Republican party."[146] Leaders in the Democratic Party (and in the press) gained the political support of poor and middling white folk, including former Populists, by stirring up fear of African Americans and promising to provide protection from the threat they posed. Even as Poe built close professional and personal ties to Democratic leaders, he held onto some of the best ideas from the Populist experiment, which shaped Poe's agrarian perspective and that of the *Progressive Farmer*. The problems of small farmers did not disappear after Populism faded as a political possibility, and Poe continued to look to ideas offered by the Populists for inspiration.[147]

Not all of Poe's ideas about cooperation were derived from Populism; he studied the cooperative movement in Ireland under Horace Plunkett, too, for example, and was inspired by European "romantic agrarianism" during his 1908 and 1912 trips to rural England, Ireland, and Denmark.[148] Daniel Rodgers presents Poe as one among many Progressive reformers operating on both sides of the Atlantic, inspired by one another's work, who promoted cooperative efforts among farmers.[149] As important as European influences were, however, Poe's sense of what southern farmers needed was very much based on the Populist ideas he had grown up with.

Years after Populism's demise, Poe looked back on Populism as "the surest way for farmers to help themselves at a time when the national government did nothing to help." Financial troubles had brought his family, like so many southern and western farmers of the time, to look to the Farmers' Alliance. The alliance movement swept through Chatham County, where Poe was born, its fires fanned by L. L. Polk. Poe's father and uncle listened to Populist orators and socialized with alliance men, and Clarence grew up embracing the reforms advocated in the Ocala Platform of 1890 such as the levying of income tax, the direct election of U.S. senators, and the public control of railroads. Poe claimed that he "share[d] nearly all the hardships and struggles of our Southern farm people" and argued that this was why he was "inspired to fight long years for their betterment."[150] Perhaps, too, southern farm families like Poe's liked the emphasis on social ties that came with the Populist vision. In order to cooperate, farmers had to work together. This mattered in an isolating way of life. Poe's brand of populism, which offered white farmers ways of trying to control their fate such as buying and selling together and wearing worn clothing in order to save money, felt empowering to people who wielded very little power in their lives. No doubt these people experienced the sense of worth bestowed by Populism on poor farmers that Lawrence Goodwyn describes as "individual self-respect and collective self-confidence, or what some would call 'class-consciousness.' "[151]

Clarence Poe identified with small white farmers, or claimed that he did. While he may have had humble beginnings, as his career advanced he worked with and befriended many of North Carolina's most illustrious men, including Democratic leaders.[152] One venue through which Poe met the Democratic Party's emerging leadership was the Watauga Club, founded by Walter Hines Page and other young leaders to encourage the New South idea of "progress"—particularly industrial progress—for the region. (The idea of a "New South"—no longer characterized by slave-run plantations but by modern factories—was publicized by another editor, Henry Grady of the *Atlanta Constitution*, in the late 1880s.) At the Watauga Club, which he joined in 1902, Poe met and socialized with Josephus Daniels and Francis D. Winston, among others. The Watauga Club, which argued that agricultural reform was essential for progress, focused on what could be achieved in the future, and because of this "nobody old enough to have been in the Civil War was admitted." While the Civil War generation was admired by the leaders of the New South, they were seen as relics of the past.[153]

Poe's most important connection in the state was Governor Aycock. Aycock shared with Poe a belief that whites would be safer and happier without black people as social equals and the notion that blacks would benefit from staying apart from whites. Aycock told African Americans at a 1901 Negro State Fair that whites like him had "for your race aught but the kindest feelings" and that they wished " to see you grow into the highest citizenship of which you are capable." In order for this to happen, though, black people would need to "remain distinct" from whites. "Inside of your own race you can grow as large and broad and high as God permits, with the aid, the sympathy, and the encouragement of your white neighbors," Aycock told them. "If you can equal the white race in achievement, in scholarship, in literature, in art, in industry, in commerce, you will find no generous-minded white man who will stand in your way; but all of them in the South will insist that you shall accomplish this high end without social intermingling. And this is well for you; it is well for us; it is necessary for the peace of our section."[154]

Years later, Clarence Poe would take Aycock's ideas about the benefits of "remain[ing] distinct" to the next logical step with his campaign for rural segregation. As was the case with the governor whom he so admired, Poe was in no way less of a southern Progressive because of his racist ideas for how to "improve" the South.[155] By 1912, even as he held onto some ideas put forward by the Populists, Poe had assimilated the rhetoric of the Democrats. He viewed solidifying the position of whites above African Americans as a "reform" worth fighting for, and he worried about the "threat" black neighbors posed to the social and economic opportunities of white farmers. He wrung his hands, too, about interracial sex and the resulting "mongrelization" of the southern countryside. Indeed, Poe is representative of something we might think of as a new and lasting fusion—one in which many former Populists joined the Democratic Party and embraced its racist goals (labeling them "Progressive"). Poe's Democratic friends did not help him come up with a plan for addressing the threat posed by African Americans who lived near white farmers—for that, he would have to look beyond the borders of the United States and across an ocean to South Africa.

3

Inspirations for Residential Segregation

In May 1912, thirty-one-year-old Clarence Poe married Alice Aycock in a quiet ceremony at the Aycock family home. The wedding had originally been planned as a grand affair to take place at the First Baptist Church in Raleigh, but coming a month after the death of Governor Aycock, it was held with only "the smallest number of relatives" present. After the wedding, Poe took his bride on a train to Wilson, North Carolina, then on to New York. In New York, they boarded the SS *Caledonia*, setting sail for Europe, where the couple would honeymoon; Poe would also study conditions among farmers in the European countryside.[1] It was on the *Caledonia* that Poe met Maurice Smethurst Evans of South Africa.

Evans, almost thirty years Poe's senior, author of *The Native Problem in Natal* (1906) and *Black and White in South East Africa: A Study in Sociology* (1911), had just completed a trip through the southern states on which he would base his 1915 book *Black and White in the Southern States: A Study of the Race Problem in the United States from a South African Point of View*. An influential politician who played an important role in bringing to fruition the pre-Apartheid system of segregation in South Africa, Evans introduced Poe to the notion that the countryside could be segregated. One can imagine the two men in earnest discussion of relations between black and white people in their respective countries, the new bride left to entertain herself.

Certainly the vision of residential segregation that emerged in North Carolina was a local product, shaped by the peculiarities of the state. Yet it did not come out of nowhere. As is illustrated by the chance encounter with Evans—which would provide an ideological framework for Poe's residential segregation campaign, begun a year after the voyage on the *Caledonia*—North Carolina's segregationists followed with interest the enactment of policies establishing residential segregation in other nations and other states, and these policies influenced their thinking.

THE SEGREGATION OF PUBLIC SPACE
IN NORTH CAROLINA

Southern states enacted the first Jim Crow laws during Reconstruction and the bulk of them just after the turn of the twentieth century. North Carolina kept pace with other southern states in its segregation laws. The state required segregation in public schools in 1875 and prohibited intermarriage between African Americans and whites in the same year. It required that trains and steamboats "provide separate but equal accommodations" for black and white passengers "at passenger stations or waiting rooms, and also on trains and steamboats carrying passengers" in 1899. Exemptions included "relief trains in cases of accident" and "Negro servants in attendance on their employers." Companies that did not comply could be fined $100 per day in violation.[2] The state segregated street cars in 1901. C. Vann Woodward noted that Jim Crow extended far in the South, reaching "entrances and exits . . . toilets and water fountains, waiting rooms and ticket windows"—even without laws requiring this. North Carolina was no exception.[3]

Gilbert Stephenson, a contemporary observer, saw a pattern in Jim Crow laws. The first set of laws (such as the Black Codes), passed shortly after the Civil War, sought to control the labor of black people by "regulating the relations of the master and his colored apprentice [and] of the employer and his colored laborer" and "restrict[ing] the movement of negroes." These laws "have been repealed or become inoperative." Stephenson considered these first laws different in nature from later laws, which worked to "prevent any sort of social association between the races." Stephenson envisioned laws separating black and white people socially staying on the books and considered them essential in creating "harmony." Stephenson pictured a society in which African Americans would be granted political rights and treated fairly but would exist separately from whites. This was not a temporary measure for Stephenson: "in matters social we may expect the races to drift further and further apart."[4]

Segregation of public space served a number of purposes. It worked to "solidify racial difference," to mark black and white people as different, and one as inferior to the other after the institution of slavery had ended.[5] According to Paul Escott, segregation had a larger purpose than this, however—it was connected to disfranchisement, which was the larger aim of Democrats by the late 1890s (by which time it had become clear that they could no longer control the voting of African Americans, even through violence and intimidation). Wishing to "put a stop" to the voters who had ushered in Fusion politics, the Democratic leadership envisioned segregation as a way of preventing lower-class whites from aligning themselves with black voters. "The purpose of an 1899 Jim Crow law covering trains and steamboats," Escott argues, "was in major degree to stigmatize the Negro race and thereby stigmatize all cooperation with Negroes. . . . An expanding system of segregation . . . placed blacks in an official pariah caste." It also boosted the self-esteem of poor whites, Escott points out, but this was more "by-product" than intention.[6]

Glenda Elizabeth Gilmore describes the segregation of public space as reining in upwardly mobile blacks and keeping them in "their place":

> As a living testament to capability, successful African Americans' lives provided a perpetual affront to whites. The black lawyer, doctor, preacher, or teacher represented someone out of his or her place. The danger lay not in their numbers, but in the aspirations they inspired in their fellow African Americans and the proof they gave to the white lie of inherent African inferiority.[7]

Upwardly mobile African Americans were a new "problem" in the late nineteenth century. Stephen Berrey points to the changes that came as a generation of African Americans that had never been enslaved entered adulthood, "occup[ying] new spaces" as well as "familiar spaces in new ways." Troubled by the new experience of "[finding] themselves in public spaces where African Americans insisted on playing the part of social equals," whites looked to segregation, which provided roles for each race to play in a type of "performance."[8] Grace Elizabeth Hale describes segregation as offering whites a solution to their fears about "racial disorder in a changing southern society" (that is, black people entering middle-class spaces) and helping them sort out who was black from who was white. It addressed a problem that came with modernity: now that black and white people were meeting in anonymous cities, freed of the personal relationships common in small towns, it was difficult to tell how some people should be racially categorized.[9]

White supremacists proposed residential segregation after the series of laws segregating public space. Quite a few segregationists considered the segregation of public space and private property to be similar, arguing that if they could do one, then they should also be able to do the other. As one put it, "Negro children are not allowed to attend school with whites; Negroes do not sit in the same cars, loaf in the same depots and feed at the same hotels as the white folks. Why, then, should landlords be allowed to impose them on white farmers and ruin entire sections of the country?"[10] Yet there was a difference between these two types of segregation, and one withstood legal scrutiny for decades longer than the other. Laws providing for the segregation of public accommodation proved more successful than residential segregation laws because they offered benefits to all—not just some—white southerners.

RESIDENTIAL SEGREGATION EFFORTS IN CALIFORNIA

Interested southerners paid attention to efforts to set up residential segregation on the West Coast in the last decades of the nineteenth century. In 1880, California passed a residential segregation law allowing the state's cities to exclude Chinese residents or limit where they could live. Ten years later, San Francisco enacted a residential segregation ordinance. Anti-Chinese sentiment was high in the city, most likely fueled by the fact that the Chinese were occupying prime real estate near the business district. White residents of San Francisco also feared the spread of the Chinese into "the old aristocratic quarters [such as] Nob Hill." The ordinance limited people of Chinese descent to live and work in an area that "had by previous legislation been set aside for slaughterhouses, tallow factories, hog factories and other businesses thought to be prejudicial to the public health or comfort." The Chinese government, angered by the ordinance, demanded that the federal government step in on behalf of the Chinese in San Francisco, pointing to the 1880 treaty between the United States and China, which promised protection to Chinese people treated unfairly in the United States. A federal court judge declared the city ordinance unconstitutional in 1890, the same year it was enacted. This judge, Lorenzo Sawyer, who after his decision in the case would be called "Mandarin Sawyer," pointed to the 1868 treaty with China as well as to the Fourteenth Amendment to the Constitution and Section 1977 of the Revised Statutes of the United States.[11]

While Poe did not reference the earlier ordinance, he did point to efforts to deny land to people of Japanese descent in California at the same time he began his residential segregation campaign through the *Progressive Farmer*. These efforts led in 1913 to the passage of the Alien Land Law, which prevented people who were not eligible for citizenship—namely, people from Asia—from buying land in California.[12]

Citing an article by P. F. Macfarland published in *Collier's Weekly*, Poe argued that white farmers in California faced the same problem as their counterparts in the South: "This writer points out the same identical evils resulting from Japanese buying farms in white California communities which we pointed out as resulting from Negroes buying farms in white Southern communities." Just as in the South, in California white farmers chose to leave when nonwhites entered their neighborhoods. "When the Japanese farmers move in numbers into a community," Poe claimed, citing Macfarland, "the white farmers, for social reasons, that is to say, in order to have an adequate white society of their own, are forced to move out." Eager to flee, they would "sell . . . at a sacrifice because so few white men are willing to move into a part-white community."[13] Poe quoted Macfarland at length:

"The white farmer's wife does not run in and sit down to gossip with the Japanese farmer's wife, and she does not want the Japanese farmer's wife running in to gossip with her. Their children cannot play together. Jenny Brown cannot go for a buggy-ride with Harry Hirada (Japanese). The whole idea of social intercourse between the races is absolutely unthinkable. . . . So, in the fruit-growing districts of California, when the Japanese get a foothold through ownership or a long-term lease, there is nothing for the American family to do but to move."

Substitute Negroes for Japanese and does not this describe the situation in the South today?[14]

Poe put his full support behind Californians who proposed legislation limiting land sales to Japanese Americans. He considered legislation essential for two reasons, "social and economic." One was the great fear that through social interaction would come "a mongrel civilization." The other was that competition with the Japanese would lower the prospects of white Californians—indeed, white Californians had to look to legislation because of what he described as "the lower standard of living of the Japanese, and the determination of white Californians that they will not be forced to compete with the Japanese in any line of California's industry."[15]

RESIDENTIAL SEGREGATION IN SOUTHERN CITIES

Southerners did not segregate their cities by race before the Civil War—indeed, enslaved people in cities lived with their masters—and it took until around 1890 for distinct black and white neighborhoods to emerge in some cities. "It was in the fast-rising cities of the New South, including Nashville and Atlanta, that the modern forms of competition and segregation between the races appeared earliest," according to Don H. Doyle. "Traditions of intimacy and paternalism" continued to influence older cities, which did not experience influxes of African Americans as large as in the newer cities, which had expanding job markets. As African Americans poured into newer cities in search of jobs and housing, competition with whites ensued. While many jobs were categorized as appropriate only for white or for black workers, black and white workers competed over a class of "middle levels of skilled and semi-skilled occupations."[16]

In Baltimore—the first southern city to pass a residential segregation ordinance—"there was no Negro quarter or ghetto," according to Garrett Power, and blacks resided in all twenty of the city's wards in the years after the Civil War. African Americans moved in large numbers to Baltimore between 1890 and 1900, with their population expanding by 47 percent in those years, from 54,000 to 79,000. Meanwhile, the white population in the city increased by 54 percent during the same period, as the same forces that pushed African Americans out of rural areas also pushed white migrants into cities and as immigrants from Russia (many of them Jews) and Poland moved to Baltimore. As impoverished African Americans moved to town, they "rented shanties and doubled up in small houses," according to Power, "resulting in Baltimore's first sizeable slums." Native white residents fled the slums, as did black residents who had the means to do so. Meanwhile, white immigrants sought out cheap places to live, competing with African Americans for housing in the slums.[17]

With an economic downturn starting in 1890, Baltimore's residents accepted low-paying jobs in terrible conditions and packed two or three families in each housing unit. They received few municipal services; they lacked a sewer system, for example. Poverty, crime, and disease were rife. Progressive reformers appeared into this milieu, eager to bring clean water and clean government to Baltimore and to the nation's other cities, which suffered from many of the same ills that plagued Baltimore. Many of the reforms put into place by these Progressives did little to improve conditions, as they ignored the causes of urban problems. They sought to ban spitting in public, for example, as part of an effort to curb tuberculosis. They also fought the slums and the slum dwellers rather than the conditions that caused slums.[18]

Historians have often pointed to segregation as a focus of Progressive reformers.[19] George Fredrickson viewed segregationist thinking as a sign that Progressive reformers considered African Americans unredeemable and segregation as their solution to the problem of blacks' degradation. As he put it:

If blacks were a degenerating race with no future, the problem ceased to be one of how to prepare them for citizenship or even how to make them more productive and useful members of the community. The new prognosis pointed rather to the need to segregate or quarantine a race liable to be a source of contamination and social danger to the white community, as it sank even deeper into the slough of disease, vice and criminality.[20]

Yet fear of contamination only went so far. As Progressives segregated many aspects of southern city life—such as streetcars and public parks—and even as African Americans moved to separate neighborhoods, black domestic workers continued to work in the homes of whites. In newer cities, these servants might commute in on streetcars, but in older cities, they often lived in the alleys behind the houses of whites.[21] Grace Elizabeth Hale describes the "white home [as] a central site for the production and reproduction of racial identity precisely because it remained a space of integration within an increasingly segregated world." In their homes, white children learned that it was appropriate to have black servants but not black friends, and they learned to consider themselves superior to these servants. Black "mammies" and other domestic workers "physically crossed the color line on a daily basis, traveling from 'Colored Town' to 'White Town'"; they were accepted in the most private spaces of whites and allowed—the only exception to the rule of "whites only"—in public spaces reserved for whites such as parks. Mammies did the essential work of raising white children—from breastfeeding them to teaching them manners. White children loved their mammies but were taught that as they became adults, their love for their mammies and the "integrated living" they had enjoyed had to be "packed up with the baby clothes."[22]

Even as the presence of black domestic workers "integrated" the homes of whites, white southerners considered it essential that African Americans did not live near them as peers. They would accept black servants living in their homes or in buildings in the alleys behind their homes but not African Americans who could afford to live on the main streets of their neighborhoods.

Americans have historically found much meaning in home ownership. Part of this meaning comes from the financial stake people have in their homes. Homes are generally the largest investment people make, and they fear anything that could be perceived as lowering their property values. They hope their homes will gain in value; if the opposite occurs, it can cause a family to fall to a lower class. But homes are important for more than their economic value. Homes house families—the center of American life—and offer, in the words of Kenneth Jackson, "a retreat from the compromises and unpleasantries of competitive life."[23]

The American system of home ownership was based on the British model, in which power resided in real estate. As Kenneth Jackson explains, European settlers in America single-mindedly focused on "organizing the landscape into private parcels and somehow procuring a share of the division." The American ideal became a single-family home with a yard. Attainment of such a home meant that a man had found success—he had provided for his family and achieved the American dream. A man's house showed his status.[24] LeeAnn Lands argues that whiteness became an essential quality of desirable neighborhoods in Atlanta starting around 1900— that white homeowners who had previously "been concerned only with what was contained within their property boundaries" came to "look past their property lines" at who lived nearby, coming to see "residents as part of the landscape, as part of the *view*."[25]

African Americans moving into a neighborhood jeopardized the achievement that a home represented, many white people believed. Homes represented an extension of the self, and for many whites, that self could not be interracial. Whites also feared that blacks would lower property values by running properties down, thus making a neighborhood less attractive, or that they would endanger white neighbors. As an editorial in *The Crisis*, the publication of the NAACP, pointed out, however, if the presence of black people lowered property values, it was mainly because "an exaggerated and persistently encouraged racial prejudice" encouraged whites with black neighbors to sell at any price. Lawyers arguing against Louisville's segregation ordinance would compare this fleeing of whites to suicide:

It is nothing in the conduct of the negro, but simply the prejudice that the white man feels against the race which he formerly enslaved and regards as inferior, which is the reason for the ordinance in question. It is not his moving into a street but the prejudice which leads white people to move out that depreciates property; the loss comes not from hostile attack but from suicidal action.[26]

Middle-class African Americans would buy property in lower-middle-class white neighborhoods, sometimes paying more than white buyers. Once they had established a foothold in a neighborhood, their white neighbors would flee (note that lower-class whites fled as middle-class blacks moved in, showing that their concern was race, not class), and as they did so, property values generally declined, though sometimes they rebounded if black buyers could continue to pay high prices.[27] In general, once middle-class African Americans had moved into a neighborhood, working-class black people would follow, doubling or tripling up in order to pay high rents.[28] In this way, cities became ordered by race rather than class; middle-class black homebuyers, moving into middle- or lower-middle-class white neighborhoods, saw those neighborhoods become—as whites fled—black ghettos.[29]

An example of such a neighborhood "turning black" was seen in the case of Winston's William Darnell, a man convicted of breaking the city's residential segregation ordinance. At the time Darnell purchased his property on Highland Avenue, his block was majority white. But shortly after he moved into his new home, white residents left and African Americans moved in. In Darnell's trial in the Forsyth County Superior Court, his defense attorney argued that Darnell should be allowed to occupy the home because his neighborhood had turned black by the time his case had made its way through court.[30]

Home ownership meant as much to African Americans as it did to white Americans—perhaps even more. Their homes provided one of the few places (another being the church) where African Americans could enjoy autonomy and where they could build a sanctuary from the indignities and humiliations that the outside world directed toward them.[31] Like white people, black home buyers wanted to provide safe homes for their families near good schools, and they wanted their investment in a home to appreciate. For these reasons, many looked to move to majority-white neighborhoods, which offered safe streets, and public amenities like streetlights.[32] They also wanted to get away from illicit activities like prostitution, gambling, and drug use. As an article in a black newspaper explained, "Negroes ... want to live in a community where the controlling people will see that decency and order are maintained. The charge is made that white communities neglect the sections in which the Negroes live, and allow all kinds of vice and crime to pile up about the Negro homes."[33]

George McMechen, for example, a graduate of Yale Law and a successful attorney, moved with his family in the summer of 1910 into a house they had purchased in Eutaw Place, a white neighborhood in Baltimore. The McMechens were "a cultured and educated family striving to live decently and to rear their children in as good environments as they could secure." As they moved into white neighborhoods, African Americans like the McMechens were greeted with vandalism and worse. In Baltimore, whites welcomed black newcomers to their neighborhoods by "breaking the window lights, putting tar on the white marble steps, and in other ways mutilating the property." "Ruffians" in the community sought to intimidate the McMechen family, for example, succeeding enough that their house received police protection.[34]

As black people began to move into their neighborhoods, white residents also turned to the law for "protection." The Baltimore City Council passed the first southern residential segregation ordinance in December 1910, in doing so lending its name to ordinances that followed the "Baltimore idea." It took this step after receiving many complaints about black people flooding white neighborhoods. After the McMechens moved to Eutaw Place, over ten thousand community members petitioned the City Council, looking for a stop to such so-called outrages. White attorney Milton Dashiell proposed a law that would prevent blacks from continuing their advance into white neighborhoods, and Councilman Samuel L. West introduced the bill to the City Council. Passed by the council in a partisan vote—all Democrats voted for it and all Republicans against it—the ordinance set up a system of residential segregation by block; black people and institutions could not move onto majority-white blocks, and white people and institutions could not move onto majority-black blocks. The Baltimore ordinance was challenged in court by African Americans and by white realtors and landlords, who complained that white owners of property on blocks primarily occupied by whites but with some black residents would not be able to rent their property to African Americans if they were unable to find white renters. The Baltimore City Council then passed a new ordinance in April 1911 that addressed the court's objection. In its new iteration, the law applied to all-black and all-white blocks but not mixed-race blocks. A third version of the law, enacted in May 1911, prohibited the establishment of black churches and institutions on all-white blocks and white churches and schools on all-black blocks. After *State v. Gurry* invalidated the third version of the law for taking "vested rights of use" from people who had purchased their property before the ordinance was enacted, city government passed a fourth iteration that was "prospective only" in its application, applying only to new people moving into a neighborhood.[35]

Other cities enacted a slew of copycat ordinances. In Virginia, Ashland and Richmond, for example, passed segregation ordinances similar to Baltimore's. In 1912, the state of Virginia passed a statute encouraging its other cities and towns to set up "segregation districts" and to prohibit black people from residing in majority-white districts. The Ashland and Richmond ordinances were tested and determined to be constitutional by the state Supreme Court in 1915 in *Hopkins v. City of Richmond*.[36] An editorial in *The Crisis*, pointing to the increase in black property owning in the state between 1891 and 1911, argued that the Virginia ordinances came into being as a response to black success in the state: "This astounding advance of over 100 per cent. in property holding in a decade is the real reason for the attack on Negro property rights in Virginia, where three cities have tried to erect Negro Ghettoes."[37]

Ordinances in different cities worked toward the same goal but through different methods. Gilbert Stephenson, the author of *Race Distinctions in American Law* (and city solicitor in Winston at the time that city's ordinance was enacted), described these methods in an article that examined different cities' segregation laws. While the Baltimore model applied only to all-white and all-black blocks, the model adopted by Roanoke, Virginia, created " 'segregation districts,' [which] designate which districts are to be for white people and which for negroes, and make it unlawful for white people to live in negro districts and for negroes to live in white districts." The Richmond, Virginia, model (adopted in Winston) "undertakes to legislate for the whole city, declaring that a block is white whereon a majority of the residents are white and colored whereon a majority of the people are colored." The model used in Norfolk, Virginia, "like the Richmond type . . . undertakes to apply to mixed as well as all-white and all-negro blocks, but unlike the Richmond type, it determines the color of the block by the ownership as well as by the occupancy of the property thereon."[38]

Who was behind residential segregation in cities? Generally, middling white residents were the ones who sought to resolve the "problem" of black neighbors through segregation ordinances. According to Gretchen Boger, the effort to enact residential segregation in Baltimore was not part of the Progressive reform, led by elites, that did shape other Jim Crow policies. A few elite Baltimoreans participated because they had, as Boger put it, "something personal to lose." Charles Grasty, the editor of the *Baltimore Sun*, for example, used his paper to promote the segregation campaign because he had real estate investments that would have benefited from the segregation ordinance.[39] But most of the leaders in the segregation campaign in Baltimore were middle class, and their hold on middle-class status was "tenuous." These white people sought higher status by moving into neighborhoods abandoned by elites, who had started their own shift to tony suburbs. They hoped that by moving into these neighborhoods as owners or renters they could "guarantee themselves stability and reputation." They resented African Americans who moved along with them into these neighborhoods. When it became clear their new neighborhoods were "abruptly chang[ing] character" on them, they tried "to inscribe order on the living space in the modern city according to their need to secure their own often precarious status."[40]

Milton Dashiell, the man with the dubious distinction of drafting the Baltimore segregation ordinance, fits this bill. An unimpressive lawyer— W. Ashbie Hawkins, the black lawyer who fought residential segregation in *State v. Gurry* and hoped to see his case go before the Supreme Court, dismissed Dashiell as "briefless" and using the ordinance to win for himself "glory and a possible clientage"—Dashiell rented in a white neighborhood one block away from an infamous slum inhabited by African

Americans with the highest tuberculosis rates in the city.[41] Perhaps Dashiell hoped to drum up business from other marginal whites who would have appreciated the ordinance. Hawkins described the people who supported Dashiell's measure as unaccomplished and insignificant, too: "A call was issued for a meeting of the greatly offended citizens, most of whom didn't own the property they occupied, nor any other, and with this start for weeks and months these hitherto obscure personages managed to keep themselves in the limelight by their appeals to race prejudice."[42]

While the claim that these people were propertyless may not have been generally true, their marginal status was. The *Baltimore Afro-American* described them thus: "Sentiment for the law was bolstered up by the wails of whites of moderate station in life, aided by Democratic politicians."[43] While these whites sometimes pointed to public health issues such as the spread of tuberculosis among African Americans, their primary interest was in maintaining their own position. As the *New York Sun* explained it, the ordinance's "frank purpose is to protect the property interests of the stronger race." To this end, segregationists did not have sweeping plans for reordering the city, and they did not force black people who already resided in primarily white neighborhoods to move. Instead, they aimed to stop additional African Americans from moving into their neighborhoods. They exempted black servants living in white neighborhoods, as they did not consider servants a threat, thus showing that, in the words of Homer Plessy's counsel, "the real evil lies not in the color of the skin but in the relation the colored person sustains to the white."[44]

White elites generally did not attend the hearings on the segregation ordinance in Baltimore. This did not necessarily mean that they opposed segregation. Rather, they did not need to worry about black people "invading" their neighborhoods, as doing so was out of the realm of possibility for almost all African Americans.[45] (Here it is important to distinguish between elite neighborhoods—high status, not in danger of declining in value—and mixed neighborhoods, which occasionally had some elite residents.) Residential segregation did not matter much to residents of elite neighborhoods, as it did not affect them. When African Americans moved into mixed neighborhoods with some elite residents, these residents did in fact support segregation ordinances.

In Louisville, Kentucky, middling whites were again the people most motivated to pursue separate neighborhoods. There, "a segregation movement" was "agitating what appears to be a small element of her population, and that element mostly unknown, poverty stricken whites, aside from the editor of the Times, a member of one of Kentucky's most distinguished families," one newspaper reported.[46] *The Crisis* argued that the ordinance failed to "represent the real feeling of the best white people of Louisville" and described disagreement among the city's white residents regarding the ordinance.[47] Speakers in favor of the Louisville ordinance at a 1914 hearing included a laborer who argued that much of his life savings had disappeared when his greatest investment—his house—lost value as African Americans moved into his neighborhood. Apparently the members of the council who listened to these speakers found the argument about the need to protect property values from depreciation persuasive. Louisville's residential segregation ordinance became law in May 1914.[48]

LeeAnn Lands argues that Atlanta's residential segregation programs were pushed forward by white elites in Jackson Hill. These elites first attempted to relocate Morris Brown College, an African American institution located in their neighborhood, which drew a number of black residents to the area and helped keep in business a number of local black-owned businesses and black churches. They offered the college a larger space in the western part of the city, near Atlanta University and Spelman College. Morris Brown's leaders refused to move the college, however, and Jackson Hill's white elites turned to a different approach. In October 1910, they set a boundary line designating a section within the neighborhood as reserved for the residences of whites. Lands quotes the *Atlanta Constitution*'s report that the neighborhood's "prominent citizens" led this effort.[49] While no doubt the individuals leading Atlanta's residential segregation efforts were indeed elites—bankers, real estate investors, and the like—it seems that their neighborhood was not as securely elite as these individuals would have liked. It was a mixed neighborhood—inhabited by African Americans and non-elite whites as well as elites—and some people feared that property values in the neighborhood were in danger of declining. The focus on property values was strongest and residential segregation most embraced in owner-occupied sections of the neighborhood, not tenant-occupied sections; it was owners who had the most at stake, as their property values would plummet if white residents began to flee the neighborhood.[50]

The boundary declaration proved ineffective, and in 1913, Atlanta passed a segregation ordinance after the model of Baltimore, though Atlanta's law was harsher. The Atlanta ordinance disallowed blacks from moving to mixed-race blocks if the previous occupant of the intended residence was white and required that black would-be residents get the permission of white neighbors if the residence they wished to move to adjoined a residence occupied by whites. The state Supreme Court declared Atlanta's ordinance invalid in *Carey v. City of Atlanta* (1915). By prohibiting an owner from occupying his own property (if he belonged to the "wrong" race), the ordinance in effect took his property from him without due process of law, the court determined. The court later reversed its ruling in *Harden v. City of Atlanta* (1917), deeming a new Atlanta residential segregation ordinance legal because it did not retroactively apply to owners who had purchased property before the ordinance was enacted.[51]

As segregation ordinances passed in city after city, African Americans and their allies reacted with alarm. The ordinances would not lead to "separate but equal" neighborhoods for black people, they believed—and the right of African Americans to own any property at all might be the next right to be lost. The NAACP's Mary White Ovington expressed this fear:

> In a democracy, of white voters only, the city would not be ruled with impartiality. Colored people would be forced to remain in such localities as the white people did not like. And if by chance the colored should succeed in beautifying their quarter, they would have no assurance that their white neighbors might not any day steal it from them. Why not, indeed? The white [*sic*] have the power to say where the colored shall live; it is they who segregate, and it is they who can give and take away. One can imagine this policy creeping from the city into the country, and one can see the ordinances changing as the white citizens change their minds regarding the most desirable land. If anyone doubts the probability of this thing's happening, let him read the story of the white man's treatment of the North American Indian.[52]

Blocked from the political system, black people in cities had no power to stop segregationists from chipping even further into their property rights. Residential segregation ordinances, if they stood, might be just the first step in a process that would take away such rights altogether. African Americans also feared that once they were limited to certain neighborhoods, the rents in those neighborhoods would increase—as, *The Crisis* reported, took place in Baltimore, where "real estate sharks" raised rents "at least 20% in the restricted Negro districts."[53] Once African Americans were put in a vulnerable position (that is, restricted to certain neighborhoods), they were open to even more exploitation at the hands of realtors and landlords.

RURAL SEGREGATION'S SOUTH AFRICAN INSPIRATION

Recent scholarship has explored the international dimension of the "assertion of whiteness" in the early twentieth century.[54] In various places around the world, white people anxiously watched the challenges nonwhites made to white hegemony, aware that something would have to be done to preserve their status, and they worked to shore up white supremacy through policies such as segregation. Carl Nightingale describes a " 'segregation mania' [spreading] across Asia, Africa, and the Atlantic world."[55] One of these places where white people worked to strengthen their own position, of course, was South Africa, and the example of South Africa proved quite instructive to segregationists in the United States, including Clarence Poe.

After meeting Maurice Evans in 1912 and hearing his perspective on territorial segregation, Poe publicized South Africa's efforts to maintain white supremacy. As Poe saw it, South Africa provided a model of rural segregation for southerners to observe and follow.

Nowhere else in the world are Negroes and whites in great numbers living together side by side as here in the South, except in South Africa. For years and years our brother English people there—white farmers who went from England there just as our ancestors came from England here—struggled with just such conditions as we now face in the South. On a trip abroad three years ago the writer discussed the subject with one of the most eminent white statesmen of South Africa

[Maurice Evans] and he declared that they saw but one remedy, race segregation in land ownership. Accordingly, on June 19, last year, the law went into effect—a law which prohibits any Negro in the Union of South Africa from buying or leasing land in the districts set apart for white ownership.[56]

Poe hoped that anyone troubled by the implications of a policy separating blacks from whites in the southern countryside—to American democracy or to the southern economy—would be reassured on hearing that a similar policy had been enacted in South Africa. South Africa, after all, he argued, was also a civilized nation shaped by the British system, a nation that like the United States valued individual rights. The British in South Africa were the brethren of white southerners, and whatever policies they adopted would likely be perceived as fair in the American South.

Similarities to South Africa notwithstanding, the South's situation was unique among societies that sought to separate their white and black populations. In South Africa and in many other countries, a large native population lived under colonial rule, generally retaining their own languages and cultures. Meanwhile, people of African descent whose ancestors had been forcibly brought to the region made up a minority of the population in the U.S. South, and African Americans were fluent in the language and customs of the white ruling class. As Evans observed, racial mixture meant that territorial segregation would have been a great logistical challenge. Yet Poe, after studying the ideas circulating in South Africa and the policies that came out of these ideas, came to believe that the "solutions" adopted there would help with the South's own "race problem."

Evans was not Poe's only international inspiration. His travels in Western Europe also influenced Poe's vision for what the countryside should look like, a vision shaped by what Andrew C. Baker describes as a "romantic agrarianism" born of the Country Life movement. In England, which he visited in 1908, Poe was enchanted by "neat homes, well-tended gardens, trimmed hedges, and picturesque cottages"—and racial homogeneity. Baker describes this visit as "a form of racial tourism—an accounting of . . . Anglo-Saxon cultural achievement." Poe came to believe that the countrysides of England, Ireland, and Denmark flourished partly because they lacked a black population.[57] Yet Poe's "racial tourism" in Western Europe—while it did reemphasize his commitment to white farm communities—did not help Poe come up with a policy to propose. It was South Africa and Evans that did that.

Evans delivered Poe the missing piece in a puzzle he had been working on for years: how to create what he called a "great rural civilization" for whites by untangling small white farmers from the African American neighbors who he believed undermined their prospects. South Africa gave him the example he needed to envision how rural segregation could be put into political action. It gave him a case study to refer to and a connection to a global movement of shared white identity—just what he needed to launch his segregation campaign. Through Evans, Poe became a part of an international conversation on how to improve the position of white men vis-à-vis nonwhite men, learning about a new possibility and gaining confidence from being part of a global trend.

Evans, born in Manchester, England, in 1854, immigrated to the British colony of Natal, South Africa, in 1875. He worked in agriculture there for a number of years and won election to the Natal parliament in 1897, a position he held for many years. He had various experiences that would come to shape his views on segregation. These included sitting on the Natal Native Commission of 1906–1907 after the Zulu rebellion of 1906 and attending the International Conference on the Negro at the Tuskegee Institute in April 1912, where he met with black leaders—newspaper editors, missionaries, and most importantly, Booker T. Washington—who offered him guidance on the needs of people of African descent who lived in nations governed by whites. At the conference, Evans learned more about the gospel of self-help (he noted that this was the only perspective available at the conference; to hear the African-American critique of discrimination and "injustice," he would have to look "elsewhere").[58]

Participants at the International Conference on the Negro discussed "the practical work that is being done to educate and uplift the Negro, either in Africa or America." The conference attracted people from near and far: "Eighteen foreign countries, or colonies of foreign countries, and twenty-five different missionary societies, representing twelve different religious denominations were represented in some way, officially or unofficially at the

Conference."[59] Speakers discussed questions such as whether missionaries should teach "natives" in European languages or in their own languages, how African American missionaries could "have their part in the redemption of the dark continent," and whether people of African descent were capable of adopting "the culture of the white man, and participat[ing] in the white man's civilization" (the conclusion was yes, with proper education).[60]

Evans delivered a paper explaining what he considered to be South Africa's predicament: as an observer explained his main point, "[South Africa] can't allow the natives to remain uneducated and uncivilized because they are so numerous that they would constantly menace the lives of the white people; on the other hand it seems inexpedient to civilize and train them to be skilled workmen because this would be resented by the white population."[61] Evans reported that he told his audience he embraced segregation as a solution and that he was surprised to learn from a number of African Americans in attendance at the conference that they considered "separation rather than further commingling . . . the right policy to pursue in the United States." Evans did not expect the support, as "I had been assured by those belonging to what I have termed the militant Radical School, that what the negro race wanted above all was equal treatment, equal justice, equal opportunity, to be treated as the immigrant, so that they might, like him, blend with the many races which go to make the American people."[62] Evans's African American supporters may have believed, as did Booker T. Washington, that there were certain advantages to living and working separately from white people but that laws forcing them to leave behind hard-won property to live in all-black communities were the wrong way to achieve this.[63]

Evans considered separate paths necessary for both white and black people to prosper in the new Union of South Africa, formed in 1910, eight years after the British won the Boer War and annexed Afrikaner colonies to their own holdings. He hoped to see the vast majority of black South Africans living on territories overseen by a fair commission. A benevolent paternalist—he had seen the exploitation of black South Africans and sought to protect them from it—Evans urged the new government, which represented the white minority (Parliament, for example, had 161 members, of whom 157 represented whites and four represented blacks), to be "sensitive to the rights of the unrepresented majority." He did not want black people to participate in governing South Africa—that had failed in the United States, he thought—but rather for government to protect blacks from the harm that came to them from living among whites, particularly in cities.[64] Evans made the case for the large-scale separation of white and black South Africans in his writings. One historian of South African segregation and apartheid described his work as "the first thorough-going and broadly disseminated theory of segregation," and it was often cited in political debate.[65]

The years Evans spent in Natal influenced his vision for what the status of blacks should be in the Union of South Africa. Diplomatic Agent to the Native Tribes and Secretary for Native Affairs Theophilus Shepstone, who believed that it was preferable for blacks to retain their traditional African culture rather than to assimilate to British ways—and that they could best do this on reserves apart from whites—shaped British policy in Natal in the late 1840s and 1850s. While the reserves did allow for retention of some aspects of native culture, heavy taxes obliged many black South Africans to leave the reserves to take low-paying temporary jobs.[66]

In 1906 Zulus, who had been moved to reserves in and just outside Natal, rebelled against the Natal government's attempt to collect a poll tax from each adult man in the colony. After the uprising, the Natal government set up the Native Affairs Commission to study what had motivated the Zulu to rebel. Africans who testified to the commission claimed that settlers exploited them, that the Natal government ignored them, and that their traditional way of life was crumbling. Their leaders were pawns of the colonial government, and they were being pushed off of their homesteads to take jobs as wage laborers. Probably Evans's desire for white government to treat native Africans fairly was related to hearing these testimonies as a member of the commission.[67]

Evans emerged from the context of Natal a benevolent paternalist. Many of the other South Africans who played a role in bringing about segregation between around 1905 and 1925 were also concerned with "helping" native Africans. They included Jan Smuts, prime minister of South Africa between 1919 and 1924 and again between 1939 and 1948, and the historian Edgar Brookes. These liberal segregationists favored segregation as the best way of preserving "an Africa for Africans." They believed that the various "races" were different from one another and that they would best cultivate their own talents separately. They feared that "the simpler, more fragile African way of life" would be destroyed by "the stronger, more complex economy of the Europeans" if blacks were not removed from the influence of the Europeans. South Africa's segregationists embraced Johann Gottfried von Herder's idea that different peoples had their own "genius" and extended this idea to the separation of black and white people, which they believed allowed for separate "race development" and the protection of each group's special qualities from "contamination" by other groups. (Some of South Africa's liberals—like Brookes, who later advocated for blacks as a senator and through the multiracial Liberal Party—ultimately decided that embracing segregation had been a mistake.)[68]

Evans, a liberal in this vein, sought to keep the white "race" free from the influence of blacks (that is, protect its "purity") and the African "race" free from exploitation at the hands of whites. The phrase he felt best presented the challenge of meeting these two goals was written by an African American, W. E. B. Du Bois, and he took it—without citation—for the beginning of *Black and White in the Southern States*: "The problem of the Twentieth Century is the problem of the colour line." Addressing this "problem," as Evans understood it, meant protecting the two "races" from interacting with each other, from "clashing" and "fusion." Addressing the problem also meant allowing each group to excel in its own areas of expertise.[69]

Evans believed that black South Africans were different from white South Africans and that it would not be to the advantage of whites to let them influence white society. Part of the problem was that black people were not able to mirror whites in their social complexity or keep up with modern technology, according to Evans. Yet their numbers continued to increase—they did not die out like some other groups whose homelands had been invaded and transformed by whites. They "persisted," and in early-twentieth-century Natal the ratio of native to white South Africans was ten to one. This "persistence" of blacks created a problem that appeared "wherever a strenuous European people, imbued with the desire to keep their race intact and pure, and intent on the utmost economic development, live alongside a conservative one at a lower stage of culture and yet withal virile and increasing in numbers": the problem was how to keep the "higher race" from being negatively influenced by the "lower race."[70]

Evans's thinking on how whites would be negatively impacted by blacks was influenced by a number of thinkers, most obviously by Thomas Jefferson. For example, Evans argued that taking on a role of domination destroyed the character of whites, especially the young. Poor whites were susceptible to complacency about their social position, which was artificially boosted by the presence of blacks. White supremacy created "a white oligarchy, every member of the race an aristocrat; [and] a black proletariat, every member of the race a server; the line of cleavage as clear and deep as the colours," according to Evans. Weaker whites were lifted up as by a rising tide in South Africa, allowed "an ease, a comfort, a recognition to which their personal worth would never entitle them in a homogenous white population." Reminiscent of Jefferson's warning in *Notes on the State of Virginia*, Evans argued that wielding power over others led to the affectation of "a domineering and masterful tone." When whites affected superiority, it did not necessarily harm blacks, Evans thought, but it did hurt whites.[71]

The presence of black workers also hurt white men by freeing them from physical labor, Evans claimed. In South Africa, black people did all the unskilled labor, which led to the physical weakening of white men and to dependency on black workers. "To plough, to dig, to hoe, to fetch and carry, to cook—all laborious and menial toil is the duty of the black man," Evans observed. Black laborers did all the grunt work for white jobs, and whites then became unwilling to do things for themselves. They were so set on not doing "black men's work" that they put up with sloppy work—if that was what their laborers and household servants gave them—rather than laboring themselves.[72]

This system had detrimental effects aside from shoddy work; it wasted black labor, as "big, strong, capable men" were kept from doing "useful and suitable labour" in order to run minor errands for white people; this also discouraged the development of labor-saving technologies. More detrimental to society, white men became lazy, with even recent immigrants who came to South Africa intending to work instead falling into the prevailing way of life. "Their hard hands become soft, their muscles flaccid, as compared with their peers in the lands they have left," Evans claimed. "It matters not whence they came, Norway, Germany, England, Scotland, Ireland, Australia, Canada, New Zealand: we have had them all and all fall under the spell."[73]

Evans considered the weakening of white men in South Africa a danger because the white working class was "the solid foundation" of a society; when this class was lacking or unmanned, he thought, it jeopardized society. As Evans understood it, "society tends to die out at its apex, and must be constantly renewed from its base." This idea would resonate with Poe, who was also concerned about the white men who made up society's "base." This was yet another idea reminiscent of Jefferson, who argued that a self-sufficient, hard-working yeomanry would keep the young United States safe from what he viewed as the corrupting influences of industrialism. Jefferson's focus was independence and citizenship more than virility, but his point is reinforced by Evans's argument that a society is threatened by a lack of physical labor.[74]

Like Jefferson, Evans worried about how the presence of black people would affect white society, trying to balance the need for low-cost workers with what he considered the negative influences of these workers on a young nation. Jefferson described the dilemma of needing black workers whose presence threatened the ideals of the nation—and might threaten the safety of its white citizens—as "holding a wolf by the ear." Indeed, Jefferson thought the best solution would be sending African Americans to Africa when their labor became less necessary, and he tried during his presidency to arrange for African Americans to relocate to Sierra Leone. Evans recast some of Jefferson's ideas for the age of Theodore Roosevelt, exploring how the presence of blacks affected white peoples' "race development" and arguing that white men needed to be strong and "virile" in order to carry out the white man's burden. The "heavy and onerous . . . responsibilit[y]" of "govern[ing] an overwhelmingly numerous, prolific, vigorous people," Evans argued, required physical as well as mental strength, and physical strength came from the kind of labor that white South Africans were no longer doing. Thus, reliance on the labor of black South Africans would lead to the physical and moral degeneration of white South Africans.[75]

Evans believed that separating black from white would solve the problems he saw in South Africa. Separation would mean that white men would have to perform their own labor, with an attendant increase in wages and the development and use of labor-saving technologies. White people would become strong and self-reliant. Meanwhile, black people would do well in separate rural areas, where they were protected from exploitation and the

corrupting influences of cities, to which he considered them highly susceptible. Without separation, competition would ensue, Evans argued, and hos-
tility between white and black would brew. White South Africans would
not set black people up for success if doing so meant competing with them,
and if they withdrew their "guidance and assistance and applie[d] the conditions of equal competition to all," blacks would suffer.[76]

Evans envisioned black people living on large territories as in Natal, not
on lands scattered among white properties. These territories would be
reserved for black residents, though some whites would be allowed on
them to work for the administration or as missionaries or teachers. Evans
considered his plan "a generous policy," one where black people would be
free of "the irritation and overlordship of individual whites." Off the reservations, however, the black man "has no such privileges. Should he go [into
white areas] for any purpose, he must conform and submit to laws and
regulations made by the white man for the benefit of the white man." Segregation would not be complete under this plan, because Evans understood
that there would still be a need for the labor of black workers on farms and
in industry. But the majority of black South Africans would not live among
whites.[77]

In 1912, Evans traveled around the American South, the region he considered most similar to his own nation.[78] He moved by train between New
York and New Orleans, making frequent stops to visit schools, churches,
farms, factories, and other places where southerners carried out their business. He spoke with black and white southerners and compared the peculiarities of the South with those of South Africa. Evans was not particularly
interested in helping fix the problems of the region; instead, he wished to
use the South's story to push his agenda in his own country. He painted the
American South's experience as "tragic," describing it as a region ruined by
its reliance on and exploitation of African Americans. Both the southern
environment and the character of its white inhabitants had been damaged
by slavery and its aftermath, and the black residents of the region were so
deeply embedded in the South that it would be impossible to uproot them,
he believed. Evans found a lesson for South Africa in the story of the South,
and he advised his countrymen to enact territorial segregation to avoid making the same mistakes.[79]

His studies and trip through the South convinced Evans that relations between black and white southerners were bad and that both black and lower-class white people suffered, but territorial segregation on the model of South Africa was not the solution for the American South. The South and South Africa were too different to follow the same model for addressing their common "problem." African Americans shared a culture with white Americans in the South, and the influx of "white blood" into their makeup meant that their "racial traits and characteristics ha[d] been modified, and are in [some ways] much more white than black." Thus, very little could be done to fix the problems of the South other than encouraging African Americans to save money and purchase land in their own communities.[80]

White South Africans who watched the unfolding of segregation in the American South convinced themselves that the problems of the South resulted from segregation's failure there. They saw competition between whites and black people, interracial sex, lynching—all of which benefited neither "race," in their opinion—and judged that segregation had not gone far enough. This persuaded them that segregation in their own country would have to go further than segregation in the United States in order to truly protect "race development." It was not enough to let black South Africans segregate themselves; large-scale territorial segregation was the only solution.[81]

The historian John W. Cell describes the United States as a "magic mirror" through which white South Africans observed what they feared could be their own future if they did not separate whites and blacks, a future of "frequent lynchings and race riots, political corruption, unspeakable crimes against white women."[82] This "magic mirror" helped them decide what their next steps should be. Act number 27 of 1913, the Natives Land Act (which stayed on the books until 1991), was part of a broader segregationist program in South Africa that included the Mines and Works Act (1911), the Native Labour Regulation Act (1911), the Native Affairs Act (1920), and the Natives (Urban Areas) Act (1923). One historian of the Natives Land Act describes its importance in being "the first major piece of legislation that would later comprise the legal structure of apartheid."[83] The act determined the boundaries of the reserves set aside for native Africans, which made up about 7 percent of the nation's lands. It also prohibited black South Africans from purchasing or leasing lands outside of these areas and white people from buying land within the reserves. Its purpose was not actually to separate black and white people, as it did allow black laborers to work in white areas on a temporary basis, as contract wage laborers on farms or as migrant workers in the industrial areas, as their labor was essential. The act had devastating effects on black South Africans. Many were evicted from the farms they worked. With an expanding population on the reserves, lands were overgrazed and soil became eroded, hurting native farmers. The reserves also became "the cornerstone of a key part of the apartheid system" after apartheid was instituted in 1948: the homelands.[84]

The Natives Land Act came out of an effort to make black labor both available and cheap in the mines and on white-owned farms and to establish white supremacy in the Union of South Africa. It made black labor available by preventing black people from settling in white areas as an independent peasant class and by providing them with too little land on the reserves to make do without supplementary wages. It made black labor cheap by keeping the families of workers on the reserves, where they could support themselves through subsistence farming.[85] Laws also regulated Indians ("coolies"), another source of essential and exploited labor. White men wished for laws to strengthen their position in the nation, which they perceived as precarious because they made up a minority of the population. There were about four million black people living in South Africa in 1910, making up about 70 percent of the population. They controlled little land (white people controlled 90 percent of South Africa's land in 1910) but were thought to pose a threat to whites nonetheless because of their numbers. The Natives Land Act was a response to this fear.[86]

Poe published an article in the *Progressive Farmer* in July 1912—shortly after he met Evans—recounting Evans's thoughts on the situations in South Africa and the American South. It took Poe almost a year to process Evans's ideas and develop a plan for how rural segregation might work in the South. He began writing of rural segregation for the South—sometimes citing the example of South Africa—in June 1913.[87]

In the July 1912 article, Poe relayed Evans's views on whether segregation would benefit the southern countryside. Evans did not recommend a sweeping policy like what would become the Natives Land Act for the South but rather a more gradual, voluntary separation in the region. As Poe told it, Evans argued

> that no far-reaching plan for the immediate separation of the races is practicable. Nevertheless, if the people of both races once realize and consciously accept the doctrine as wise and imperatively necessary to peace and safety, it can be worked out silently, gradually and steadily, the black sections becoming blacker and the white sections whiter through the voluntary migration and segregation of each class.[88]

As Poe recounted it, Evans acknowledged that segregation—forced or voluntary—would not be embraced by wealthy whites who profited from cheap, black labor. Evans considered these men misguided in thinking that they benefited from the exploitation of African Americans through the charging of high interest rates and other practices. In reality, he believed, these whites would prosper more from the presence of an "intelligent, progressive and thrifty working class," and the region itself would benefit from being a "white democracy of thrifty home-owning, small farmers" rather than a plantation-ridden oligarchy. Evans told Poe that he hoped to see African Americans owning small farms in their own communities and living under the leadership of Hampton and Tuskegee graduates.[89]

Once Poe began to articulate and promote his idea of rural segregation for the South, he ignored Evans's argument that South Africa–style segregation would not work in the South and embraced many of Evans's other ideas, especially regarding how the presence of African Americans caused the labor and property of white men to be devalued. When manual labor was designated "Negro work," he insisted, white men—no matter how poor—became unwilling to do this labor and therefore missed out on rewarding work. They also took a step toward the decline of their "race," for "no people who refuse to work and work hard can remain strong and dominant," Poe argued, in a point reminiscent of Jefferson and Evans. If African Americans were removed from neighborhoods, certain jobs would no longer be considered appropriate for black workers only, and—Poe hoped—"the job will be elevated by employing advanced and intelligent means of performing it." Also, because black labor was so cheap, white landowners tended to hire black workers rather than investing in new technologies that would in the long run make agriculture more efficient and productive. "No sooner is the Negro element eliminated from farm work than the landowner will immediately be forced to adopt methods and use implements that will offset the increased cost of white labor," claimed one *Progressive Farmer* reader who supported rural segregation, echoing Poe. Southerners were undermining their society and the white men upon whom success rested by seeking short-term profits.[90]

Like Evans, Poe insisted that his policy would help both black and white people and that he proposed it in the spirit of interracial harmony. "I know in my heart of hearts that I want to be just to the Negro," he opined, "and I believe the average Southern white man has the same feeling. It is bred in me to believe that whatever we sow we reap." These words most likely meant less for Poe than they did for Evans. While Poe claimed that rural segregation helped African Americans as well as whites, he devoted very little time to explaining what black farmers had to gain from the policy. He did not view African Americans as exploited by whites and thus did not argue that segregation would protect them.[91]

Evans seems genuinely to have wished to protect black South Africans (though the Natives Land Act did the opposite of this), and Evans-style paternalism was fairly common among South African segregationists. It was, however, less common among American segregationists. Poe, unlike Evans, did not believe that different "races" had their own significant contributions to make to the world; instead, he believed that African Americans "made no important contribution to civilization . . . no great achievement in science, government or religion . . . [and that they were the great beneficiaries of] contact with the white man's own opulent civilization." Thus it was all the more galling to him that their ability to live on less than whites would help black farmers "outdo the white man in getting possession of the land, the ultimate source of all wealth." The white man needed more protection than the black man, Poe believed.[92]

The story of Poe's engagement with Evans's ideas shows Poe's efforts to have been rooted in a context of international segregationist ideology. Poe viewed southerners as part of a worldwide effort to take up the "white man's burden"—a burden that they had already "borne for more than thirty years," he wrote in 1902. Poe's understanding of what this entailed was different from that of white supremacists overseas, some of whom felt a pressing responsibility to protect blacks; for Poe, the "white man's burden" meant that white farmers were burdened with black people in their midst and would need to find a way to improve their situation—and segregation was just the solution he sought. Poe may not have been true to all of Evans's ideas, but he did hold tight to one: that the countryside could be segregated.[93]

Ideas about segregation from other states and from South Africa were in circulation in North Carolina before the state's own residential segregation campaigns began. Segregationists in the state no doubt found these ideas exciting. In the city of Winston, for example, middling white people who felt threatened by a black "invasion" of their neighborhoods looked to the Baltimore plan with hope. Yet what took place in North Carolina was not as easy as borrowing ideas from other places and plugging them into the Tar Heel State. North Carolina had unique characteristics—from the prevalence of its small farmers to the power wielded by its tobacco manufacturers, who preferred black labor—and these characteristics, as we will see, influenced how the campaigns for residential segregation unfolded there.

4

Separating Residences
in the Camel City

On June 13, 1912, the board of aldermen of the city of Winston held a special meeting with the mayor and almost two hundred members of the white public—so many that it was "necessary to throw back the sliding doors between the council chamber and municipal court room in order to accommodate the crowd," which "had not been found necessary before in many months."[1] The aldermen had convened at the request of S. J. Bennett, an attorney who, according to the minutes from the meeting, "stated that he represented the citizens of East Winston and had asked the mayor to call the meeting of the Board of Aldermen that he might present an ordinance and ask its adoption, as the negroes who are buying property and moving to the Eastern part of the City are damaging the property of the [white] citizens of that part of the city." After a few people spoke in favor, the ordinance was unanimously adopted. This ordinance made it a misdemeanor for African Americans to own or live on property on a specified section of East Fourth Street between Depot Street and the city limits on the east and for white people to live in (but not own) property on sections of Third and Depot Streets. People convicted of breaking the ordinance would be subject to a hefty fine—twenty dollars for the first day and five dollars for each day they remained on the property—or imprisonment for thirty days.[2] The

Winston-Salem Journal reported that many people considered this ordinance "the most important and far reaching action taken by the board in a decade." The paper recognized that the ordinance might not be legal and noted that the North Carolina Supreme Court had never addressed the question of whether a city had the right to segregate the residences of its people. It expected that a "test case" would follow.[3]

The June meeting ended with one of the aldermen, G. E. Webb, arguing in favor of extending the ordinance to cover the entire city; this the aldermen did at their next regular meeting, on July 5, 1912, after coming to the conclusion that it was unconstitutional to segregate only certain parts of the city.[4] In its next iteration, the Winston segregation ordinance forbade white and black people to live in homes on blocks where the majority of occupants were not of their racial designation. It did not say anything about the ownership of these homes; it made illegal just the occupying of these homes. Allowing whites to own property in black-occupied areas and forbidding blacks to own in white-occupied areas would have set the ordinance up for legal challenges, as that was clearly not equal treatment. The ordinance was prospective and would even require that building permits declare whether buildings were "designed to be occupied by white or colored people." Those who already inhabited homes on blocks designated for the other race would not be forced to move. The ordinance was intended to halt the shifting of neighborhoods from one racial makeup to another and to help them become over time all white or all black. The penalty under this version of the ordinance increased to a fine of fifty dollars, with the possible addition of a thirty-day stay in prison for each day that the ordinance was disobeyed.[5]

White people in East Winston wanted a residential segregation ordinance because they were uncomfortable with what they viewed as an "invasion" of African Americans. The two hundred people who attended the June meeting of the aldermen claimed that, if the aldermen would not act, they would flee the neighborhood, abandoning a school that had recently been built for their children. As they saw it, "On every side the negroes are intruding, because some of them are willing to pay much more for real estate than the average white man can, and more than the property is actually worth, in order that they may establish their residences in the more favorable location." In the words of the newspaper coverage, it was not wealthy but "average" whites who called for an ordinance as African Americans flooded into neighborhoods in the eastern part of the city near the tobacco factories. These were people who could not outspend prosperous African Americans, people whose greatest investment—their homes—would be hurt if the value of their property declined as white neighborhoods became black ones. White residents of Winston had tried limiting where blacks could live through restrictive covenants starting around 1890, but to no avail. Thus they turned to the municipal government for a residential segregation law. "Never in the history of the city have the people of any section been more apparently aroused upon a question" than were these white residents, the *Winston-Salem Journal* reported. Bennett explained the position of these people to the aldermen:

> The white people had purchased property along East Fourth street, with the understanding that negroes would not be permitted to live alongside them, but that now they were threatened with invasion by the colored race, which would mean a great depreciation in the value of the real estate, besides the bringing about of unbearable conditions for the white people. "If you let this matter run on as it is running," declared Mr. Bennett, "we shall be obliged to sacrifice our homes. We do not bear any ill will towards the colored people, but we must protect ourselves."[6]

Bennett too was eager to enter the ranks of the elite. He was not born to privilege; he did farm work during his childhood in Surry County, North Carolina, then owned and operated a tailoring and clothing-cleaning business in Winston, which he and his partner sold in August 1911. At that time, though in his thirties, Bennett attended Wake Forest College, where he studied law and was elected class president. After completing his course of studies, he began working as an attorney in Winston early in 1912. Over the summer and fall of 1912, he ran for a seat in the state legislature as a progressive Democrat. In an endorsement of candidate Bennett published in a newspaper, a "Voter" (likely someone in Bennett's camp, if not actually Bennett) described Bennett as "a self-made man, [who] has come to the front more rapidly than any man I know in this county—a man that is settled in his habits and knows a business profession from its face."[7]

As he advanced professionally, Bennett changed his residence from one part of East Winston to another. In August 1912, Bennett moved from a home at 904 East Fifth Street to one at the corner of Highland Avenue and Seventh Street, which occupied a lot he had recently purchased for $3,075. Bennett's assets also included an expensive horse; a newspaper reported that his $200 horse had become sick and died while Bennett was out campaigning. He began his career as an attorney in private practice, but by 1917 Bennett was the attorney for Winston's Home Mutual Insurance Company. As Bennett rose, he gained status; for example, he became a trustee at the new Greenwood Avenue Baptist Church in East Winston in 1913.[8]

Bennett had political and financial aspirations that likely led to his promotion of the ordinance. Surely Bennett understood the mood of the white people of East Winston—the people he wished to represent—as they watched white neighborhoods turn over to African Americans. As a resident of East Winston, someone who had invested significant capital into a home in the area, and a striver who sought to continue advancing in status and wealth, Bennett also likely considered a residential segregation ordinance a prudent way of protecting his economic interests.

This chapter examines the effort to legislate residential segregation in Winston, an effort led largely in behalf of marginal white people, as well as the unenthusiastic response of elite whites to the question of urban residential segregation in North Carolina. While middling whites in Winston were able to persuade the Board of Aldermen to heed their desire for segregation, well-educated and paternalistic elite whites—including perhaps even the lawyer who argued the city's case to the state's supreme court—preferred an approach to race relations in which blacks were paid little but not denied economic opportunity, unwelcome in white schools and other institutions but encouraged to enjoy such institutions of their own, and unable to fraternize with whites as equals but not denied the right to live near them. Without the support of the state's leading white men—including R. J. Reynolds and Walter Clark—the residential segregation ordinance would falter.

African American leaders in the city did little to fight the ordinance. These leaders, such as the educator Simon G. Atkins, lived in a separate neighborhood—an attractive one that befitted their elevated position among their people—called Columbian Heights. For various reasons, including, perhaps, the fact that a residential segregation ordinance would increase demand in Columbian Heights, Atkins and others kept silent.

RESIDENTIAL SEGREGATION ORDINANCES FOR MOORESVILLE, WINSTON, AND GREENSBORO

One month before Winston put in place its residential segregation ordinance, the town of Mooresville, North Carolina, enacted an ordinance. *The Crisis* reported the story: "The movement to keep Negroes from buying property in desirable sections in cities is moving on apace. In Mooresville, N.C., Mr. A. Coble, who had been owning land on McLelland Avenue for four years, started to build a house. Immediately the town passed the following ordinance."[9]

Mooresville's ordinance, about which little information survives, prohibited African Americans from moving into homes within a set of "boundaries" marking an all-white neighborhood.[10] The *Washington Bee* described Coble as "a self-respecting colored carpenter" whose lot lay "in a decent section of the city."[11] Mooresville, a Piedmont town just north of Charlotte in Iredell County—home to the Mooresville Cotton Mills, Mooresville Furniture Company, and a few other industries—had a population of 3,400 in 1910. McLelland Avenue was accessible to the factories but not too close, and its houses sat on spacious lots.[12] Mooresville's ordinance, like so many of the other ones, was a response to black success. The ordinance failed in removing the Coble family: the U.S. Census lists Alexander Coble and his wife Georgia as living at 220 West McLelland Avenue in 1940. (By then, Coble worked as an ice wagon driver.) The ordinance, or the memory of it, may have played a role, however, in keeping the neighborhood from "turning" black; the Cobles were the only black family on the street.[13]

Winston (about whose residential segregation ordinance more information survives, thanks to local newspaper coverage and the legal challenge to the city's ordinance), which would merge with nearby Salem in 1913, was a city shaped by tobacco processing and, in particular, by the R. J. Reynolds Tobacco Company. Reynolds, born in Patrick County, Virginia, in 1850, grew up in the family business of tobacco. His was not a rags-to-riches story, as Reynolds's father was one of the largest slave owners and tobacco growers in the state. Reynolds moved to Winston around 1874 and there built a tobacco empire. Reynolds selected Winston for his plug-tobacco company (plug was a type of chewing tobacco mixed with a sticky sweetener) because the city was connected by rail to productive tobacco-growing areas. With Reynolds expanding his business from a factory run by twelve workers—a factory in which he initially slept both to save money and to protect the facility from fire—to a company with five hundred workers when it incorporated in 1890, Winston became North Carolina's wealthiest city. By 1897 it was also the nation's third-largest tobacco manufacturing city, behind St. Louis and Louisville. Over time, Reynolds expanded from plug tobacco to cigarettes, hitting the jackpot with the Camel brand, introduced in 1913. Winston-Salem's white residents enjoyed the prosperity brought by the growth of the tobacco industry, but they were of two minds about the African American workers whose numbers strained the city's resources—particularly its housing. (The black population of Winston rose from 4,686 in 1890 to 7,828 in 1910.) Generally loyal to employers like Reynolds, who paid their wages and doled out money to their churches and schools, these workers did not always accept the restrictions placed upon them by the city's other whites.[14]

Middling whites were rarely able to control black people as employers. While African Americans did work in the homes of elite and middling whites in Winston, most of the city's black folk labored in the tobacco factories. This meant that the vast majority of Winston's African American population generally did not rely on middling whites for jobs.[15] A sampling of the occupations of African Americans listed in the 1912 Winston-Salem city directory shows that the great majority of black men found work in the tobacco factories or as laborers. The next most common occupations—though far behind the first two—were drivers and proprietors of small businesses. Small numbers of black men also worked as porters, tailors, barbers, firemen, pastors, waiters, shoemakers, carpenters, plasterers, and as managers and other employees at small businesses. Women worked most frequently as tobacco workers, cooks, and laundresses. Women did not have as much freedom from working in the homes of white people as men, though

FIGURE 4.1 R. J. Reynolds.
Source: Courtesy of the Reynolda House Museum of American Art Archives.

they were more independent than black women had been in the past, as they typically lived in their own homes rather than in the homes of their employers.[16]

It was usually African Americans employed in the tobacco factories in East Winston who were moving into the part of Winston from which the residential segregation movement emerged. Fourth Street, the eastern part of which the first iteration of the Winston ordinance applied to, ran from the western part of the city, where well-to-do whites lived, through downtown Winston, to the industrial eastern part of the city. Whites who could not afford to live in the western part of Winston lived in East Winston, and they were separated from the affluent side of town by a black neighborhood that lay just east of the city center. This black neighborhood lacked amenities like street lights and paved roads. Prone to flooding, it was also noisy, as it lay near the rail lines that carried tobacco in and out of the city. As more and more African Americans moved to Winston to take jobs processing tobacco, this black neighborhood expanded northeast and southeast, cutting East Winston's white residents off from West Winston.[17]

While black neighborhoods expanded, Winston was not in any sense integrating. The city was made up of black and white neighborhoods, with very little intermixture. As the *Winston-Salem Journal* described it, "It is the exception, not the rule, to find negroes and whites living alongside each other in Winston-Salem. Now and then a member of one race will intrude upon a section occupied entirely by the members of the other, but the occurrence of such intrusions is seldom indeed. It is to prevent these intrusions that the segregation ordinance was passed."[18]

Census records and Sanborn Fire Insurance maps for a section of Fourth Street east of Depot Street, near the Reynolds Tobacco buildings, reveal hints of why residents demanded a segregation ordinance. This was the section that the original segregation ordinance applied to before it was broadened to include the entire city. In 1900 (figure 4.2), there were no houses on the 500 block, between Sycamore and Linden Streets, just east of some Reynolds Tobacco storage facilities (which lay east of the Reynolds factory buildings); by 1910 (figure 4.3), a number of African American renters—single men, many of them employed by tobacco factories—lived on this block. Continuing east on Fourth Street past Linden were blocks occupied by middling white families, in both 1900 and 1910. The heads of their households worked as salesmen and grocers, on railroads, and as foremen in tobacco factories. Some of them had one African American servant (unlike elite families, which generally had a number of black servants in various roles). In 1900, this area housed eleven white families that rented and seven that owned their homes; by 1910, ten owned and ten rented.

There was an extremely high turnover rate on this block from 1900 to 1910—even among home owners. It is quite possible that the turnover rate was related to the influx of African Americans on the 500 block of Fourth Street. The white families residing on these blocks—many of them tied to property in what was evidently a neighborhood in flux—feared that the African Americans moving onto the block just west of them would soon move into their own neighborhood or that the presence of African Americans nearby would make their own homes less valuable.[19]

Figure 4.5 is a map of the Reynolds factory and its immediate vicinity in 1912. Note the residences labeled "Negro tenements" between Vine and Depot Streets as well as the services provided to tobacco workers along East Fourth and Church Streets. These include restaurants, cobblers, barbers, the Rex Moving Picture and Vaudeville Theatre (Negro), drugstores, and laundry. Figure 4.6 shows one of the Reynolds factory buildings on Depot, a location full of factory buildings and tobacco-storage facilities that African Americans were increasingly moving into. Figure 4.7 shows some of the shacks that housed black workers in East Winston. Often these shacks were owned by tobacco or textile companies. Each shack typically had three rooms and would be rented out for $1 or $1.25 per week, and up to fifteen people might live in each one. Unpaved roads served these shacks, and residents used outdoor toilets, which were supposed to be sprinkled with lime and connected to drainage but often were not. Flies made themselves at home in these houses, which lacked screens. Diseases such as tuberculosis that thrived off of poor sanitation ran rampant. Residents made extra money through illegal means. Gilbert Stephenson, the city solicitor, addressing African Americans in the city, described "the condition of Winston as regards criminality [as] alarming," reporting hundreds of convictions in 1912 (the majority of them for African Americans) for crimes including assault, gambling, selling alcohol, and prostitution. While noting the possibility that African Americans "feel that they have no voice in making the laws and regard them much as in former days slaves regarded the orders of their masters," he stressed the importance of law for the protection of one's "person and property." It is not hard to imagine why African Americans who had saved up enough money to move out of these areas would wish to do so. Only 16 percent of Winston's black population had pulled itself into homeownership by 1910, but this population was slowly gaining wealth. In

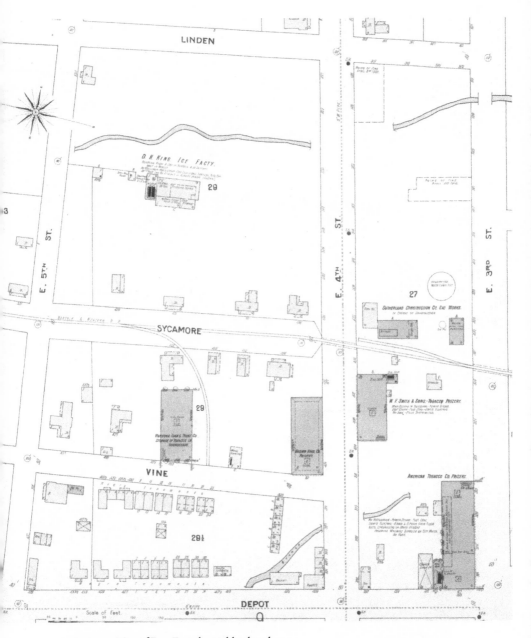

FIGURE 4.2 Map of East Fourth neighborhood, 1900.
Source: Insurance Maps of Winston-Salem, North Carolina, Sanborn-Perris Map Company. North Carolina Maps, https://web.lib.unc.edu/nc-maps/.

FIGURE 4.3 Map of East Fourth neighborhood, 1912.
Source: Insurance Maps of Winston-Salem, North Carolina, Sanborn Map Company. North Carolina Maps, https://web.lib.unc.edu/nc-maps/.

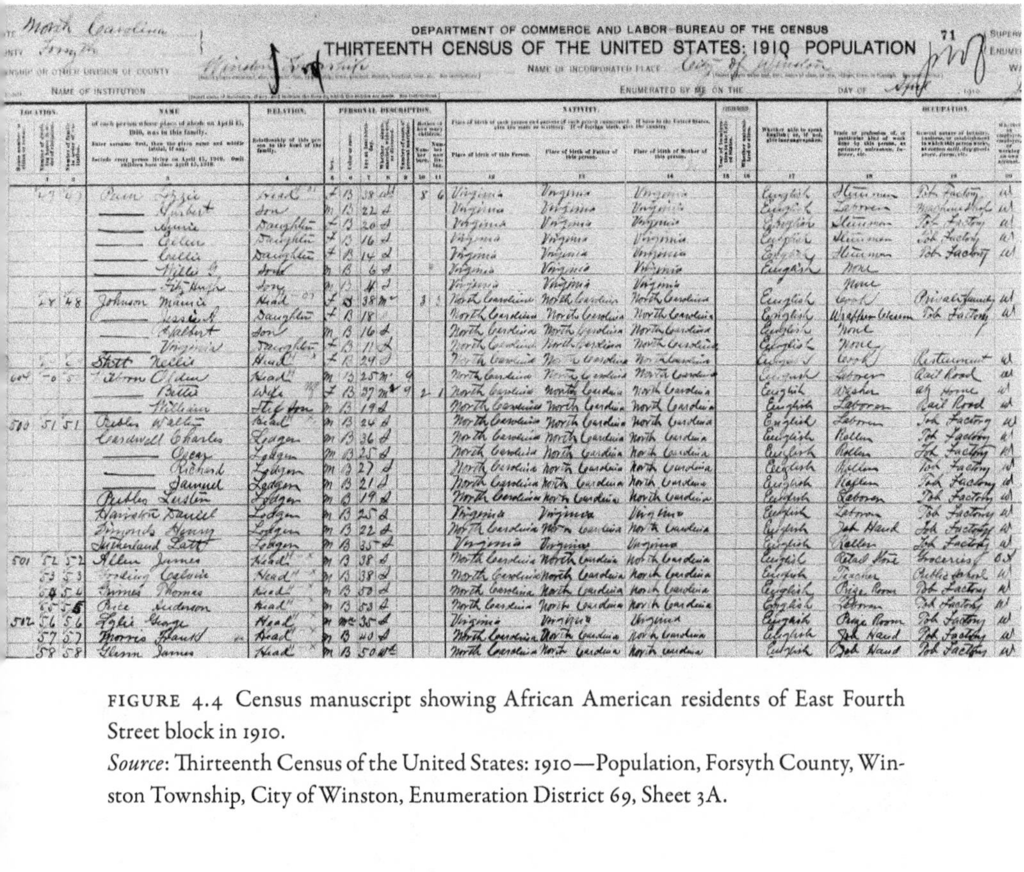
DEPARTMENT OF COMMERCE AND LABOR—BUREAU OF THE CENSUS

THIRTEENTH CENSUS OF THE UNITED STATES: 1910 POPULATION

State: North Carolina. County: Forsyth. Township or other division of county: Winston Township. Name of incorporated place: City of Winston. Enumerated by me on the ... day of April, 1910. Sheet 71.

Location	Name	Relation	Sex	Color or race	Age	Marital	Place of birth of this person	Place of birth of father	Place of birth of mother	English	Trade or profession	Industry	Class
47 49	Penn Lizzie	Head	F	B	38	Wd	Virginia	Virginia	Virginia	English	Stemmer	Tob Factory	W
	—— Herbert	Son	M	B	22	S	Virginia	Virginia	Virginia	English	Laborer	Machine Shop	W
	—— Annie	Daughter	F	B	20	S	Virginia	Virginia	Virginia	English	Stemmer	Tob Factory	W
	—— Eileen	Daughter	F	B	16	S	Virginia	Virginia	Virginia	English	Stemmer	Tob Factory	W
	—— Callie	Daughter	F	B	14	S	Virginia	Virginia	Virginia	English	Stemmer	Tob Factory	W
	—— Willie G.	Son	M	B	6	S	Virginia	Virginia	Virginia	English	None		
	—— Fitz Hugh	Son	M	B	4	S	Virginia	Virginia	Virginia		None		
48 48	Johnson Mamie	Head	F	B	38	M	North Carolina	North Carolina	North Carolina	English	Cook	Private family	W
	—— Jessie A.	Daughter	F	B	18		North Carolina	North Carolina	North Carolina	English	Wrapper Classer	Tob Factory	W
	—— Albert	Son	M	B	16	S	North Carolina	North Carolina	North Carolina	English	None		
	—— Virginia	Daughter	F	B	11	S	North Carolina	North Carolina	North Carolina	English	None		
	Stott Nellie	Head	F	B	24	S	North Carolina	North Carolina	North Carolina	English	Cook	Restaurant	W
604 50 50	Thorn Olden	Head	M	B	25	M	North Carolina	North Carolina	North Carolina	English	Laborer	Rail Road	W
	—— Bettie	Wife	F	B	37	M	North Carolina	North Carolina	North Carolina	English	Washer	at Home	W
	—— William	Step Son	M	B	19	S	North Carolina	North Carolina	North Carolina	English	Laborer	Rail Road	W
510 51 51	Peebles Walter	Head	M	B	24	S	North Carolina	North Carolina	North Carolina	English	Laborer	Tob Factory	W
	Cardwell Charles	Lodger	M	B	36	S	North Carolina	North Carolina	North Carolina	English	Roller	Tob Factory	W
	—— Oscar	Lodger	M	B	25	S	North Carolina	North Carolina	North Carolina	English	Roller	Tob Factory	W
	—— Richard	Lodger	M	B	27	S	North Carolina	North Carolina	North Carolina	English	Roller	Tob Factory	W
	—— Samuel	Lodger	M	B	21	S	North Carolina	North Carolina	North Carolina	English	Roller	Tob Factory	W
	Peebles Lester	Lodger	M	B	19	S	North Carolina	North Carolina	North Carolina	English	Laborer	Tob Factory	W
	Hairston Daniel	Lodger	M	B	25	S	Virginia	Virginia	Virginia	English	Laborer	Tob Factory	W
	Simmonds Henry	Lodger	M	B	22	S	North Carolina	North Carolina	North Carolina	English	Tob Hand	Tob Factory	W
	Sutherland Latt	Lodger	M	B	35	S	Virginia	Virginia	Virginia	English	Roller	Tob Factory	W
501 52 52	Allen James	Head	M	B	38	S	North Carolina	North Carolina	North Carolina	English	Retail Store	Groceries	OA
53 53	Fielding Calvin	Head	M	B	38	S	North Carolina	North Carolina	North Carolina	English	Teacher	Public School	W
54 54	Grimes Thomas	Head	M	B	50	S	North Carolina	North Carolina	North Carolina	English	Prize Room	Tob Factory	W
55 55	Price Anderson	Head	M	B	53	S	North Carolina	North Carolina	North Carolina	English	Laborer	Tob Factory	W
502 56 56	Ogle George	Head	M	Mu	35	S	Virginia	Virginia	Virginia	English	Prize Room	Tob Factory	W
57 57	Morris Frank	Head	M	B	40	S	North Carolina	North Carolina	North Carolina	English	Tob Hand	Tob Factory	W
58 58	Glenn James	Head	M	B	50	Wd	North Carolina	North Carolina	North Carolina	English	Tob Hand	Tob Factory	W

FIGURE 4.4 Census manuscript showing African American residents of East Fourth Street block in 1910.

Source: Thirteenth Census of the United States: 1910—Population, Forsyth County, Winston Township, City of Winston, Enumeration District 69, Sheet 3A.

1903, black property (including businesses) in the city totaled $126,022, but by 1920 it had increased to $4,060,868—rising from less than 2 percent to 3 percent of the value of all property in Winston-Salem. Real estate made up much of this property. White residents of Winston-Salem may have perceived a real trend, which was that black people were gaining real estate more quickly than whites. For example, they owned 804 town lots in 1910, up from 354 in 1904, buying at twice the rate of white lot buyers. Those African Americans who did purchase property could secure loans from the Twin-City Building and Loan Association, founded in 1903 to encourage African Americans to buy homes, and the Forsyth Bank, but not from the lenders who served white buyers.[20]

The gains in property made by Winston-Salem's African Americans are all the more noteworthy considering that many black residents of the city lacked education, wealth, and opportunity. Simon G. Atkins described the

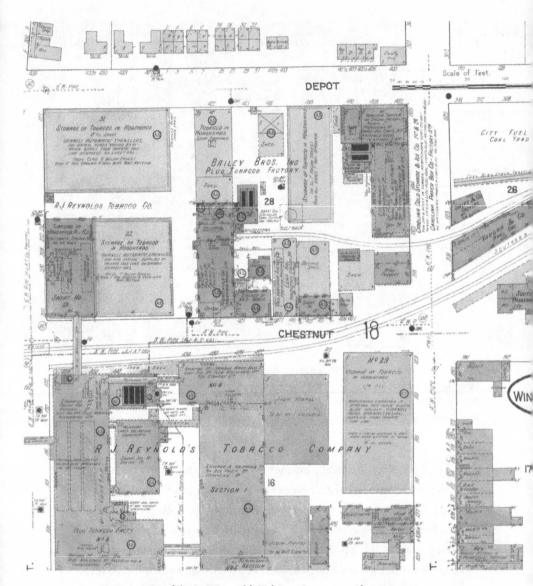

FIGURE 4.5 Map of the R. J. Reynolds Tobacco Company and vicinity, 1912.
Source: Insurance Maps of Winston-Salem, North Carolina, Sanborn Map Company. North Carolina Maps, https://web.lib.unc.edu/nc-maps/. Sections of two Sanborn maps were combined to make this map.

FIGURE 4.6 A Reynolds factory building on Depot Street.
Source: Courtesy of the Forsyth County Public Library Photograph Collection.

city's black population with condescension as "backward and raw, as well as ignorant":

> The interesting and serious thing about this population increase [from 1890 to the 1920s] is that these new people were largely the submerged element in sections where negroes had little or no opportunity and their object in coming to Winston-Salem has been chiefly a bread and butter one. They are people who have formerly had almost no advantage of schools, and among whom no type of uplifting social work had been done, so that they necessarily came to our city very backward and raw, as well as ignorant.[21]

White realtors used the increasing prosperity of African Americans to enrich themselves, convincing white homeowners in mixed parts of the city to sell to them (lest their homes lose value as more black people moved in), then selling their properties to African Americans at above-market prices that middling whites could not afford. They also sold property at high prices

FIGURE 4.7 Undated photograph of housing for black workers in east Winston. Areas like this were prone to flooding, which is why the houses were raised off the ground. *Source*: Courtesy of the Forsyth County Public Library Photograph Collection.

to whites moving out of mixed areas into new all-white neighborhoods, which they committed to keeping white. A newspaper also reported another way that realtors used the prejudices of whites to exploit them: "Certain real estate dealers are now robbing the white people by selling them land at exorbitant prices, all the time holding over their heads the threat that they will sell it to negroes, unless they pay the price demanded." Middling whites demanded that realtors lower prices so that they would not be boxed out of the market, but realtors would not comply. Here we can get an idea of the cost of "de facto" segregation to middling whites as well as to African Americans.[22]

East Winston's white residents argued that African Americans would not be injured by the segregation ordinance, as it applied to white as well as black people. Indeed, some believed, "many of the better class of colored people look with favor upon the ordinance."[23] Yet it was not long before African Americans began to challenge it. In May 1913, the *Winston-Salem Journal* reported on a case in which a black man, George W. Penn, requested that he be allowed to construct a house on property he owned in a white-designated area in Winston, arguing through his lawyer, John C. Buxton, that "more colored people live near that part of the lot on which Penn proposes to build than white people." White residents in this area signed a petition opposing Penn's request and presented it to the board of aldermen, who stood behind the ordinance.[24]

In June 1913, a black tobacco worker, William Darnell, moved into a house that he owned on Highland Avenue, on a block occupied primarily by whites. Darnell, who had moved to Winston in 1906 at age forty-seven, had saved enough money to relocate from a home near the railroad yards in southeastern Winston to a more attractive neighborhood in northeast Winston. He purchased his home from Emily Sledge, wife of F. M. Sledge, a realtor who apparently disliked the segregation ordinance. Sledge signed a petition, along with three other white property owners on the block (all the owners save one), in which he "agree[d] to sell our property, to colored people, owing to the fact that the City's School for colored people already occupies the East side of the Square," and then sold (or had his wife sell) the property to Darnell. And when Darnell was charged for violating the ordinance, Sledge paid Darnell's court bonds. Darnell was tried and found guilty in municipal court in July 1913 and, on appeal, in the Forsyth County Superior Court in January 1914; he appealed next to the North Carolina Supreme Court.[25]

As Darnell's case moved through the courts, agitation in support of residential segregation law came to the state legislature. On September 27, 1913, Senator George L. Peterson of Sampson County introduced a bill to allow cities and towns in North Carolina to create "segregation districts." The bill, purportedly meant to protect "public morals, public health and public order," was sent to the judiciary committee. A logistical nightmare, the proposed law would have laid the legal groundwork for de jure residential segregation in cities and towns (thus addressing the question of whether boards of aldermen had legal authorization to pass ordinances to segregate their communities). It allowed for the white people who governed cities and towns to decide to prepare "a map showing boundaries of the segregation districts and showing the number of white and colored people residing in each district." White people would not be permitted to move into black districts or black people into white districts, unless they resided with white employers. The senate tabled the bill on October 11.[26]

A few months later, in December 1913, Greensboro newspapers reported that an African American man named William B. Windsor—a ten-year veteran teacher in the public schools who would less than two years later be acting president of Bennett College, an institution for black women in Greensboro—had purchased a house on Gorrell Street at the corner of Martin Street, in eastern Greensboro, in a neighborhood occupied by white people (it was actually Windsor's sister who had purchased the house). Greensboro, twenty-five miles east of Winston-Salem, was known for its textile mills and its universities, supporting both working-class and middle-class jobs. The city's white population worked in poorly paid mill jobs—by 1910, the mills hired only white workers—or in middle-class jobs at insurance companies or universities. While most African Americans in Greensboro worked in service jobs, there were also good teaching jobs at Dudley High School, North Carolina A&T, and Bennett College. Newspaper accounts differ on whether Windsor planned to live in the house with his sister or without her and on whether Windsor or his sister owned the property. Windsor, "a tall, exceedingly light negro, with few of the facial characteristics of the race," was someone who "might easily pass among strangers for a white man" as well as "a man of considerable intelligence." His appearance, intelligence, and professional success did not mitigate the perceived threat—in fact, they probably made it worse—and white Greensboro panicked. "A number of white people live close by," one newspaper reported. "One family lives within twenty-five feet of the place."[27]

In response, white people living nearby demanded a segregation ordinance, which they hoped would force Windsor out. A segregation ordinance, passed on February 16 as "an emergency measure," went into effect "immediately, without the 20 days' notice required for an ordinary ordinance." Commissioners considered the case an emergency because "residents of that section of the city came down on the authorities with blood in their eyes, promising that if something were not done for their relief by means of the law that they would see to it that their own interests were defended." The ordinance passed by the commissioners was "a copy of the Winston ordinance, modified enough to apply to the present situation."[28]

A newspaper listed a "delegation of Gorrell street citizens . . . all of whom either live or own property in the neighborhood," who led their neighborhood in demanding that Windsor be removed: B. E. Smith, T. T. Brooks, Frank Brooks, C. V. Clark, and E. P. Wharton. These men seem to range from middle class to well-to-do; this was not an elite neighborhood but a mixed one. The presence of men who might be considered elite in the delegation shows that elites would back residential segregation law when black people moved into their neighborhoods and when it was in their financial interest to do so. B. E. Smith, a significant property owner in the city, showed up in the local papers from time to time for failure to pay taxes and paving assessments on various properties he owned in Greensboro. T. T. Brooks founded a lumber company in 1895 along with four others. Over time, T. T. Brooks and his son Frank were "sole owners," until T. T.'s death in 1926, at which time Frank Brooks became sole owner. C. V. Clark worked as an engineer on the Southern railroad between Greensboro and Goldsboro. E. P. Wharton, probably the most successful of the group, ran various businesses in the city, starting with a dairy, then the Wharton-Hunt Lumber Company, then a real estate firm named E. P. Wharton and Company, and the Southern Stock Mutual Fire Insurance Company. President of the Greensboro National Bank for ten years starting in 1912, he also volunteered as a health officer in Greensboro; his job included keeping track of whether stable owners were doing enough to combat flies and reporting those who were not cleaning their stables properly. Wharton was both a white supremacist and a progressive, considered "one of the leaders in the movement for education of the negroes in his community and state," and he served as a trustee of the North Carolina College for Negroes in Durham. Wharton owned numerous properties in Greensboro.[29]

The neighborhood that Windsor moved into was not elite, and it did not have a buffer separating it from nearby black neighborhoods. In 1910, African Americans lived just east of the house that Windsor's sister had purchased, to the north and the south, on the 500 block of Martin Street, the 500 and 600 blocks of Macon Street, the 500–700 blocks of Gorrell, and the 600 block of East Lee. The white families that they lived near (whites lived on the 300 and 400 blocks of Gorrell and on Pearson Street) generally owned their homes, and they worked as railroad dispatchers and clerks, shoe salesmen, bookkeepers, and merchants. No doubt the men who led the charge for a segregation ordinance feared that with Windsor, the black neighborhood was moving west onto their own blocks.[30]

During the uproar over Windsor's purchase, the *Greensboro Record* made threats of violence, noting that while "violence [against black homeowners] is a rare thing" in the city, "yet the habitation of this colored woman may be made very uncomfortable to say the least" (at the time this article was written, local whites had come to believe the house would be inhabited by Windsor's sister).[31] A group of residents of the neighborhood also demanded of the mayor and board of commissioners that they strip Windsor of his job, arguing in a petition with five hundred signatures that while they had "no prejudice against the negro race," they believed that "the close intermingling of our houses and the association of our children would be extremely detrimental to both races: and would probably result either in familiarity or constant friction, each of which might lead to dangerous results." They also claimed to fear "great damage to the value of our property as many of the white people would wish to move out, and would find it impossible to sell their property for any reasonable price." This group did not consider Windsor's reasons for wanting to move onto a nice property—they considered "his conduct [in purchasing the property] . . . reprehensible and . . . dangerous." Such a person should not be working in the public schools, the group argued, and asked that "you remove him at once, and select in his place some one of his race who will realize the responsibility of his position and his obligation to both races." It is hard to say what percentage of Greensboro's white residents considered the petition fair and what percentage agreed with H. L. Hines, who wrote a letter to the *Greensboro Record* complaining that such a demand went against the rules of "fair play" and would "kindle animosity instead of promoting peace."[32]

After it became clear that the ordinance would not affect Windsor, as he had purchased the property before the passage of the ordinance, the *Record* noted ominously: "It is possible . . . that he will see what is likely to result if he remains in the locality and will dispose of the property. He is a man of sufficient intelligence to know what will happen if he persists in remaining."[33] Violence turned out not to be necessary, however, as threats proved enough to force Windsor to sell his property. Initially unwilling to sell, Windsor was persuaded by City Attorney Wayland Cooke to, as a reporter put it, "sink his personal stake and consider the good of his own people, as well as the whites."[34] A "committee representing the protesting citizens from South Greensboro" paid Windsor $2,700 for his property, which it promptly resold for $2,500. Windsor or his sister had paid $1,800 for the property and had made improvements (including installing plumbing and electric lights) costing $1,202. Factoring in interest on the property, the *Record* calculated that Windsor had lost $428 on the property.[35] The *Record* applauded what it considered the happy outcome: "A great deal of feeling had developed and it was getting worse. Windsor himself is to be congratulated upon having the good sense to sell out and move from a white section where he was not wanted." After selling his home, Windsor moved elsewhere in Greensboro.[36]

The fate of the Greensboro and Mooresville ordinances would hang on the *Darnell* case. As the *Greensboro Record* pointed out right after the *Darnell* decision came out, "this knocks Greensboro's segregation ordinance out of the box." It did the same for other cities in the state that were considering enacting such an ordinance; Charlotte's board of aldermen, for example, were reported to be "mak[ing] further investigation into the success of the plan as adopted elsewhere" in the fall of 1913, planning to move ahead with their own ordinance after investigation.[37]

THE *DARNELL* CASE

When the *Darnell* case came before the North Carolina Supreme Court, it was not an abstract legal question but an economic and moral question to Winston's middling whites.[38] Yet Walter McKenzie Clark, the court's chief justice and author of the *Darnell* opinion, did not prioritize the desire of these people to order their neighborhoods by race. On April 8, 1914, ruling in favor of Darnell, Clark demonstrated that he cared more about issues of property rights (such as the right of property owners to dispose of their property as they wished) and the concerns of elites (such as industrialists like Reynolds who relied on black workers).

Darnell's case, like Penn's, was argued by John C. Buxton, a former mayor of Winston and state senator. Buxton, as the Raleigh *News and Observer* reported, "held that [the ordinance] is unconstitutional because it takes away from the occupant of the residence the right of residence without due process of law. 'Even the Legislature cannot do this,' Mr. Buxton said, 'and it cannot give the right to violate that portion of the constitution that insures life, liberty and the pursuit of happiness.'" Buxton claimed a number of other problems with the ordinance, including the fact that the Board of Aldermen had not published notice of the ordinance before its passage and that it had not been signed properly.[39] Also on Darnell's legal team was Cyrus B. Watson, a former state legislator and the Democratic nominee for governor in 1896 (he was defeated by Republican Daniel Russell). Buxton and Watson were among Winston's most prominent citizens; we see here elites defending an African American man against a law meant to benefit middling whites.[40] As the historian Clayton McClure Brooks argues in her book on interracial activism in Virginia, we should not view this generation of elite white Progressives who worked to help African Americans as undermining white supremacy. Rather, these people can be understood through "lingering paternalism," and their work "helped build and reinforce . . . segregation." "Concerned with a pretense of civility," according to Brooks, they believed that paternalism offered a better and more orderly alternative than violence to control African Americans.[41] While segregation laws might have appealed to their commitment to order, these elites believed that unfair laws limiting where African Americans could live would provoke unrest among black workers and make it harder to keep them at hand.

Chief Justice Clark, a Progressive and a Confederate veteran who—like Reynolds—grew up on a slave-operated plantation, supported reforms such as extending suffrage to white women. He had a paternalistic approach to dealing with African Americans, preferring to keep them nearby as subordinates than to ban them to all-black parts of town. He thought white southerners should consider themselves "our brother's keeper" and look out for the African Americans whose lives intersected with their own.[42] Looking out for African Americans meant educating them and helping them become property owners, in Clark's view:

It is to the interest of the entire people of the State that the colored people should be educated and aspire to obtain a higher standard of living and well being and to become owners of property, and especially of real estate. Educated men owning a stake in the country, living in their own homes, whether in country or town and on good terms with their neighbors, can never be a dangerous element to the stability of government, but will be a strong support to the maintenance of law and order.[43]

Clark believed that African Americans who did well helped white people do well, too—rather than that blacks who did well did so at the expense of whites. This view was fairly typical of the group Clark referred to as the "best white people in the South" (that is, elite paternalists). Thus, when "a northern man not long since told me that the greatest drawback at the South was what he called the 'Negro Problem,'" Clark claimed, "I told him that frankly there was no 'Negro Problem.'" As Clark saw it, white and black southerners got along better than did different groups of Europeans in Europe—after all, southerners spoke the same language and were not divided by religious differences. Of course, they also got along because black

FIGURE 4.8 Chief Justice Walter Clark.
Source: Courtesy of the State Archives of North Carolina.

southerners accepted a subordinate role. "The colored people do not wish social equality," Clark insisted, "and the white people would not tolerate it, and there the matter ends. It is not a matter of debate, but is settled and not a cause of strife like the divergence in language, in religion, in national aspirations which exists in nearly every other country."[44]

In the opinion of the court for *State v. Darnell*, Clark argued that the Winston city charter did not give the aldermen the authority to enact such a law—and he argued so without explicitly standing up for the rights of African Americans. As Clark saw it, African Americans did not have much in the way of rights. Disfranchisement was legally valid, as suffrage was "not an inherent right." Laws that limited the "social rights" of African Americans, such as prohibiting intermarriage and requiring Jim Crow cars, were not only valid but also proper.[45]

According to Clark, the city did not have the authority to pass such an ordinance, because to do so "would give to the words 'general welfare' an extended and wholly unrestricted scope." Such broad powers, he pointed out, could be used to separate Republicans and Democrats, Protestants and Catholics, or any other groups based on "the arbitrary judgment . . . of a majority of the aldermen." The ordinance, in the words of the legal historian John Wertheimer, was "unauthorized, not unconstitutional." Thus, the *Darnell* decision was based not on the Fourteenth Amendment but on the Winston city charter, which specified what the board of aldermen could do.[46]

Clark ruled against the residential segregation ordinance because it had been "adopted without authority of law," but he had other criticisms, too. The biggest flaw in the law was that it inhibited "the right of disposing of property, the *jus disponendi*," which Clark viewed as "one of the inalienable rights incident to the ownership of property, which no statute will be construed as having power to take away." This would be the U.S. Supreme Court's reason for invalidating Louisville's residential segregation law a couple of years later.[47]

Though *State v. Darnell* concerned urban residential segregation, Justice Clark used the opportunity of his opinion for the case to aim a blow, too, at rural segregation—clearly, he viewed the two as connected. Curtailment of the right to dispose of property would be a problem not just in cities but also in the countryside if "similar regulations are prescribed for the country districts." Property rights would be trampled if "one who should buy or inherit property in a section where the opposite race is in the majority could not reside on his own property, and he could not sell it or rent it out except to persons of such different race, since none other could reside there." And, preposterous in the plantation South, "neither a white manager nor any white tenants could reside on a farm where a majority of the tenants or hands are colored." The chief justice made it clear that any law that restricted such an important and "ancient" right as the right to dispose of one's property would have to be made through the General Assembly. While he declined to say whether such a law would be constitutional, he made it clear that such a law would certainly be ill-conceived, and its effects would be disastrous as it would lead to "a large exodus . . . of the most enterprising and thrifty element of the colored race, leaving the unthrifty and less desirable element."[48]

Clark did not base his opinion on legal reasoning alone. Because he favored the interests of elite businessmen like Reynolds who relied on black labor, Clark was also motivated by the need to retain black workers in the state at a time when many were leaving. He viewed the residential segregation ordinance as having the potential to drive African Americans out of the state in search of less restriction—something against the state's interest in "retaining the colored laborers in this State."[49] In Michele Gillespie's view, Clark's decision was influenced by Reynolds's need for labor. Reynolds could not publicly oppose the ordinance because he did not want to risk angering the poorer whites who purchased his products, but his influence helped put an end to the ordinance—perhaps through the hiring of Darnell's lawyers, who Gillespie notes had ties to Reynolds.[50] It is possible, too, though he did not mention this in his opinion, that Clark paid attention to North Carolina's reputation nationally, particularly in regard to attracting companies to locate in the state, and worried that it was not in the state's interest to be seen undermining property rights or driving off workers.[51]

Clark considered the needs of corporations like the Reynolds Tobacco Company to attract low-paid workers to Winston-Salem. No doubt he was also aware that in order to keep them in the city, Reynolds would have to pay them more, if the only housing available to them was overpriced (as a result of its being limited by the ordinance). In Clark's view, the needs of the Reynolds Tobacco Company—which brought revenue and prestige to North Carolina—took priority over the desires of middling white people to stop African Americans from moving into their neighborhoods. Clark did not directly address the corporation's rights, as other jurists were doing around this time, using the Fourteenth Amendment to claim legal protections for corporations. (People fought for corporate rights for "straightforward" reasons, according to Adam Winkler: "to fight laws and regulations that restrict business autonomy and interfere with the pursuit of profit.")[52] But he did put the corporation's needs first.

Ruling for the corporation was also ruling for elites, many of whom were corporate owners, investors, or employees. Elites would not have found their own social standing affected if African Americans were allowed to move into the white areas near the tobacco factories. Darnell's lawyers, Watson and Buxton, were elites who surely had additional financial reasons to fight against the city's ordinance: they both owned a huge number of properties in the city—including in East Winston—and perhaps feared that buildings would sit vacant if they could not rent units or sell property on mixed blocks to African Americans. Buxton, for example, purchased 1,187 properties between 1876 and 1912; he sold 292 of these properties during this time period (some to other elites, including R. J. Reynolds, C. B. Watson, and members of the Fries and Hanes families) and presumably rented out the others.[53] But there were other reasons too that elites fought against residential segregation. Indeed, Simon Atkins described Buxton as "readily" taking Darnell's case as he considered it "a principle of justice."[54] The position of elite North Carolinians in squashing urban residential segregation played a similar role in the countryside—in both cases, elites had not only moral scruples but also business interests that would have been undermined by residential segregation.

Clark may have had personal reasons for opposing residential segregation, too—particularly in the countryside. After an unsuccessful attempt to win the Democratic nomination for a seat in the U.S. Senate in 1912—Clark had run as a Progressive and had hoped to oust the machine politician Furnifold M. Simmons—Clark blamed Clarence Poe and the Raleigh *News and Observer*'s editor Josephus Daniels for his loss. "I am not complaining that any man did not support me," Clark wrote to Poe, "that is a matter for each man to decide for himself." But for Poe to embrace Progressive causes but not back a Progressive candidate meant that "Reactionary" candidates would prevail. Indeed, "I know that the heaviest drawback I had was that you two [Poe and Daniels] did not give me your support tho you had been publicly advocating the very measures that I stood for. . . . The Progressive leaders did not 'vote as they shot.' " Poe had supported Charles Aycock, the father of his bride-to-be, in the race. It may be that Clark harbored a grudge against Poe that made him inclined to undermine Poe's pet programs.[55]

C. B. Watson supported Clark in his run; in an editorial, he argued that Clark was the candidate who would best represent the people against monopoly, and he pointed to Clark's many contributions to the state, including his service in the Confederate army and his role in editing a number of books on North Carolina's war effort, "thus preserving that glorious history in permanent form." In an unusual argument, Watson pointed out what was at stake financially for Clark in the election, arguing that Clark deserved to earn a senator's wages:

> No one has done more for the Democratic party in North Carolina than Walter Clark, and yet in spite of the immense work . . . he has only held an office that pays a bare living and has required enormous labor at his hands. His two competitors [that is, Aycock and Simmons] have held the best paying offices the better part of their lives, and have each drawn in the neighborhood of a hundred thousand dollars in salary.

At the end of his glowing endorsement, Watson added that of course he wrote "these things freely with out reward or hope of reward."[56] Whether or not Watson sought benefits for himself, surely whoever hired Watson as a lawyer for Darnell was aware that Watson's friendship and political support for Clark would ensure that Clark—who publicly called Watson the "uncrowned king . . . of the Bar of North Carolina"—would give his arguments against the segregation ordinance careful consideration.[57]

Meanwhile, another member of the North Carolina elite argued the city's case for the segregation ordinance: Gilbert T. Stephenson, born in 1884, almost four years younger than Clarence Poe and a generation younger than many of the other figures involved in the residential segregation debate. Stephenson came from a family of plantation owners in northeastern North Carolina. After earning degrees at Wake Forest College and Harvard University, he settled in Winston in 1910 to work as an attorney. The board of aldermen elected him city solicitor in 1913. In this role, Stephenson prosecuted defendants in municipal court and defended the city's segregation ordinance.[58]

Stephenson was a paternalist, one who took a great interest in the situation of black southerners. He spoke publicly about issues related to black southerners from time to time, and he published a book and a number of articles on these issues, too.[59] Stephenson's interest in African Americans was shaped very much by his own position in society as an upper-class white person who tended to perceive southern society as fair; as such, he was often oblivious to the actual situation of blacks. For example, he noted that criminality, as marked by arrests, had risen dramatically among black people. Cut from different cloth than someone like Benjamin Tillman, Stephenson did not condemn black "criminals," and he viewed their criminality as shaped by environment rather than being their nature. He thought about

FIGURE 4.9 Gilbert T. Stephenson in 1928.
Source: Courtesy of the State Archives of North Carolina.

things like "a. ventilation b. privacy [and] c. comfort," as well as about the "attractiveness" of the home and amenities like sewers, and he argued that criminality would decline if "white landlords [would] furnish better houses" and if blacks did more to "beautify" their homes. Stephenson did not consider, however, that the increase in arrests might be linked more to white southerners' need for labor than to actual criminal behavior. Through the convict lease system, employers were able to take possession of African Americans' labor at low cost to themselves.[60]

Stephenson did not record his private views on the matter of urban residential segregation in his journal. It may be that he privately opposed the ordinance, though it was his job as city solicitor to defend it. If this were the case, it would make some sense because otherwise Stephenson's views on residential segregation seem inconsistent, as he spoke in public in favor of urban residential segregation but against rural residential segregation. If Stephenson did oppose the Winston ordinance, we get an impression of a class of people, including Darnell's lawyers (Buxton and Watson), Clark, Stephenson, and Reynolds, who were mostly well-educated, from wealthy families, and connected by social or professional ties, that favored a social hierarchy that kept African Americans at the bottom but viewed a residential segregation ordinance as going too far. It should be noted too (and can be seen in figure 4.9) that all of these people—except for Clark, who lived in Raleigh—resided in the western part of the city, the section that was not suffering from the "invasion by the colored race."[61]

The *Darnell* case was significant for Stephenson. It brought him to argue in the state supreme court in Raleigh—at the Winston-Salem municipal court, the cases were about minor crimes such as gambling, vagrancy, and stealing cabbages—and thus he spent a good amount of time preparing his brief.[62] Stephenson argued before the North Carolina Supreme Court that the segregation ordinance was legal, as "there is no fundamental difference between the segregation of the races as to residence" and segregation of "schools, public conveyances, and other public places." Residential segregation in Winston-Salem was also "fair," as "it affects only one property right—occupancy" (not ownership) and "applies equally to both races."[63] To support his case, Stephenson called two witnesses. The first, V. E. Barnes, testified that at the time William Darnell purchased his property, only whites resided on the block; the second, J. D. Welch, who had sold the property to the person who within about a month then sold it to Darnell, confirmed the block's racial makeup.[64]

Stephenson contended in court that Winston's ordinance was a positive good for society, as it was meant to "help" African Americans: "Wherever there is indiscriminate residence," Stephenson argued, "there is irritation, constant irritation, and it always works a hardship upon the negro. He gets the worst of every clash. It [the ordinance] will be a protection to him. It will help the weaker race."[65] Residential segregation in cities was not an example of discrimination, Stephenson claimed. In his 1910 book *Race Distinctions in American Law*, Stephenson argued that "race *discriminations*" ("A discrimination necessarily implies partiality and favoritism") were unacceptable, whereas "race distinctions" ("A race distinction connotes a difference and nothing more") were valid. Though the law might treat blacks and whites differently, "there is no discrimination so long as there is equality of opportunity," he argued.[66]

Stephenson explained in his book how distinctions protected those who needed help:

> The races should be separated wherever race friction might result from their enforced association. The white race cannot attain its highest development when continually venting its spite upon the less fortunate race. Nor, indeed, can the Negro race reach its highest development when continually subjected to the oppressions of the more fortunate race.[67]

As the African Americans who protested against residential segregation pointed out, what Stephenson described as "friction" was almost always white residents lashing out against black neighbors. Opponents of residential segregation argued that it was therefore unfair to in effect punish blacks for the inability of their white neighbors to control their anger.[68]

Stephenson probably understood this. Moreover, rural segregation such as that proposed by Clarence Poe *was* discrimination, according to Stephenson. In an April 1914 article that came out around the same time that the *Darnell* case was decided, Stephenson argued that the "moral aspect" of rural segregation was questionable. White southerners had an "obligation" to help blacks, an idea for which he drew support from the speeches of Charles Aycock. Stephenson used the work of the southern liberal Edgar Gardner Murphy to support his idea that "a policy of repression" toward African Americans would thwart their good qualities— "sympathy, the spirit of co-operation, fidelity, loyalty"—and encourage instead "envy, selfishness, [and] treachery." And rural segregation was such a policy because it would stir up "race prejudice." Blacks would suffer from a lack of opportunity and from the loss of "the example and advice of the white man." The region would look bad, as outsiders would believe that white southerners had "disfranchised the negro in order to perpetrate discriminations against him," and "desirable" white immigrants would be dissuaded from moving to areas where certain groups were not allowed to purchase land. Indeed, anticipating Justice Clark's argument about the effects of residential segregation policy on the retention of labor, Stephenson argued that if black workers were pushed out of white areas and immigrants decided not to move in because of residential segregation, "industrial conditions"—from the perspective of management, if not from that of labor, whose scarcity would allow them to win higher pay—would be quite difficult. Thus "the advantages to the white people" (or to *certain* white people—here, middling whites) brought by the policy did not "equal or overbalance the disadvantages to the colored people," and rural segregation was "short-sighted."[69]

A correspondence with Booker T. Washington, whom he wrote in late September 1913 to ask his thoughts on Poe's rural segregation campaign, helped bring Stephenson to the conclusion that rural segregation would heighten animosity between whites and blacks. Washington pointed out that urban residential segregation stirred up animosity, too, and connected rural to urban residential segregation:

If there is an attempt to carry [Poe's] proposition into effect, racial hatred, in my opinion, will be stirred up in a way that it has not been stirred up in the South since reconstruction days. . . . I think we should learn a lesson along this line from what is taking place in Baltimore and in other cities where segregation has been attempted. So far as I have been able to ascertain, in every instance there has been a stirring up of racial hatred and, in some instances, rioting.[70]

To Washington, both types of residential segregation limited African Americans' opportunities. Stephenson most likely understood this effect of segregation, too, but in order not to undermine the city's case, he used convoluted logic to claim that urban residential segregation protected black people, rather than hurting them by limiting their choices.

Another person who played a role in the *Darnell* case—either directly, through his influence, or indirectly, through his need for laborers—was R. J. Reynolds, in many ways the most powerful man in Winston. Articles written during Reynolds's lifetime attributed his business success not to good fortune but to his personal qualities, such as his "tireless enterprise." Reynolds was someone who "watches with the closest scrutiny and directs with extreme foresight every phase of his immense business."[71] It is quite plausible that someone like Reynolds who left very little to chance would use his influence to block residential segregation.

Reynolds gave money to the institutions that improved his workers' lives. According to Michele Gillespie, "R.J.R. worked at being a benefactor to the local black community, not necessarily because it was the ethical thing to do or because he felt some moral imperative to do so, but because the more money he put into black churches, schools, and orphanages, the more he was creating a desirable and more stable world for Winston blacks to make their homes in." This stability allowed him to keep black workers—who might otherwise have looked elsewhere for better-paying jobs—and made the influx of black workers more palatable to local whites, as these workers seemed capable of caring for themselves.[72] Whether Reynolds's philanthropy came out of genuine goodwill or was meant to keep his workers content enough to continue working for low wages in his factories, Reynolds gave the impression of concern about the well-being of his employees. After Reynolds's death, an editorial in a black newspaper, the *Twin City Advertiser*, described how at least some of Winston-Salem's African Americans viewed Reynolds.

The Advertiser a few days since styled him as our "Big Dad". This was not an expression of the familiar kind. We meant nothing shallow. We meant from the depths of our hearts that he never allowed the Negro of Winston-Salem to suffer. He was with us first and last. And when we had to, we did it; that is to go to him and tell him all our troubles. This is what all good children do to their parents. This raises the question, did he so feel to us as our "Big Dad". In his will this question is fully answered with a $120,000.00 gift for a hospital. . . . Every church, orphanage and all of these splendid homes we live in are the immediate products of "Big Dad". He helped in them all. Then to make the matter more definite, there is Reynolds Temple, the most complete church for colored people in the city. It came to us as a direct gift, costing more than $10,000.00.[73]

Reynolds bequeathed $120,000 for the construction of a hospital for African Americans in Winston. He bequeathed the same amount for a hospital for whites, showing that to him, the needs of Winston's black residents were as important as those of its white ones. Reynolds operated within the segregated framework of the day, as his plans for separate hospitals demonstrate. He did, however, seek to make life better for black Winston residents.[74] It makes sense that someone who aimed to keep his workers happy would oppose an ordinance that would reduce their access to housing and make them feel unwanted in the city.

Another piece of evidence shows that Reynolds did not oppose the movement of African Americans into housing in East Winston. In May 1909, Reynolds and his wife, Katharine, sold a parcel of land just west of the Reynolds tobacco factory on the corner of Church and East Fourth Streets to three African American men, Charles H. Jones, Humphrey H. Hall, and J. S. Hill.[75] Jones, born in 1875 and a former farm worker, would become a successful real estate broker. According to *The Crisis*, "the beginning of his financial prosperity" came in 1912 with the sale of "a small lot, 25 X 100 feet, to R. J. Reynolds Tobacco Company in Winston-Salem, [which] made $10,000 profit."[76] Jones, who started purchasing property in Winston in 1900, bought twenty-four properties through 1912, selling many of them and renting others; although a substantial property holder, he owned considerably less than white elites like Buxton.[77] Jones rented apartments to African Americans, and among other ventures, he also owned the Royal Palace Hotel and Yellow Truck Line (which operated several small buses), both in

East Winston. He was treasurer of the Twin City Building and Loan Corporation, of which Simon G. Atkins was president. Jones, who acknowledged that he "had to be very subservient to the whites" in his business dealings, made over $250,000 in various entrepreneurial activities in Winston-Salem. Jones and Hill were directors of the Forsyth Savings & Trust Company, a bank owned by African Americans. A graduate of Shaw University's Leonard Medical School, Hall opened a medical practice in 1889 in Winston.[78]

Whether Reynolds actively worked to undo the residential segregation ordinance (which we have no record of) or his looming presence in the city merely served as a reminder of the city's need for laborers, he represented an important type in the story of residential segregation: a wealthy white paternalist who benefited from the presence of African Americans and who stood to lose from an ordinance like Winston's. Clark, in writing in the *Darnell* opinion about the effect of the ordinance on the retention of laborers, would have been thinking of Reynolds and other such industrialists.

After the *Darnell* decision, an editorial in the *Winston-Salem Journal* expressed disappointment with the court's decision along with hope that the state legislature would again consider a law allowing cities to pass segregation ordinances. "The question now arises, If the General Assembly at its next session passes a law that will permit Winston-Salem, Greensboro and other cities of the State so desiring to segregate the races, will such State law be constitutional? The court did not go into this question at all." If it turned out not to be constitutional, the editorial expressed interest in "changing the constitution, whether that constitution be Federal or State or both."[79]

THE RESPONSE OF WINSTON-SALEM'S BLACK LEADERSHIP TO THE SEGREGATION ORDINANCE

Booker T. Washington, the principal of the Tuskegee Institute in Tuskegee, Alabama, earned himself a reputation as an accommodationist. Because his school depended on the largesse of white supporters, both southern leaders and northern philanthropists, Washington was reluctant to offend, and he tended to keep quiet on explosive issues even while he sometimes participated behind the scenes.

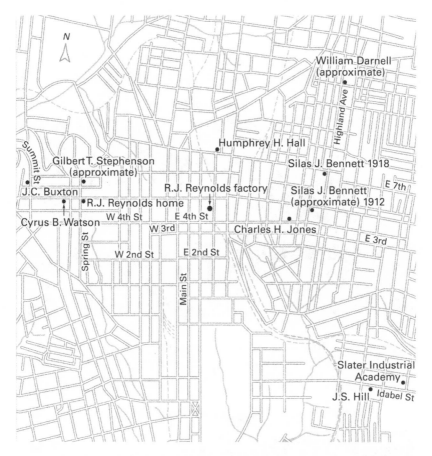

FIGURE 4.10 This map shows where Jones, Hall, Hill, William Darnell, and S. J. Bennett resided in east Winston and where Reynolds, Stephenson, Buxton, and Watson lived in the western part of the city. The stretch of Fifth Street upon which Reynolds lived (until he moved further out onto an estate in the suburbs in 1917) was called "Millionaire's Row." Not only wealthy industrialists but also the bankers who financed industry, lawyers, factory superintendents, and others lived in this area. These families had black live-in servants—often more than one, including cooks, nurses, housekeepers, and drivers—and they generally owned their homes. After the 1890s, many of these elites moved to the West End, just beyond the grid of west Winston, where the streets become curved.

Source: Ernest H. Miller, *The Winston-Salem, N.C., City Directory*, vol. 13 (Asheville, N.C., 1912) and vol. 14 (Asheville, N.C., 1918); David Foard Hood, "Winston-Salem's Suburbs: West End to Reynolda Park," in *Early Twentieth-Century Suburbs in North Carolina: Essays on History, Architecture, and Planning*, ed. Catherine W. Bishir and Lawrence S. Earley (Raleigh: Archaeology and Historic Preservation Section, Division of Archives and History, North Carolina Department of Cultural Resources, 1985), 61; Frank Tursi, *Winston-Salem: A History* (Winston-Salem: John F. Blair, Publisher, 1994), 146–47; for examples of families on Fifth Street who owned their own homes and employed live-in black servants, see Thirteenth Census of the United States: Population, 1910, Forsyth County, North Carolina, Winston Township, Winston City, Ward 2, Enumeration District 72, Sheets 9A, 10B, http://familysearch.org.

FIGURE 4.11 R. J. Reynolds's home on "Millionaire's Row."
Source: Courtesy of the Forsyth County Public Library Photograph Collection.

FIGURE 4.12 Reynolds's children in a pony cart in the 1910s. Note the black groom hold-ing Reynolds's baby; elites like Reynolds rarely took issue with proximity to African Americans, who posed no threat to their status.
Source: Courtesy of the Forsyth County Public Library Photograph Collection.

FIGURE 4.13 J. C. Buxton's home.
Source: Courtesy of the Forsyth County Public Library Photograph Collection.

Washington took an interest in segregation ordinances from the time they first appeared in the South, and he offered help in combating them. He encouraged Benjamin J. Davis of the black newspaper the *Atlanta Independent* to oppose Atlanta's ordinance, for example, writing in a private letter, "What are you all going to do about it? I advise that you hire the best lawyer you can get and fight the matter from now on. Let me know if you need any outside help and what your plans are."[80] Setting aside his usual resistance to publicly critiquing policies affecting blacks, in 1915 Washington published an article making a case against residential segregation laws in cities. (He published this article roughly a year after *The Crisis* reprinted an outpouring of criticism of Washington from the black press for advising the Negro Business League to ignore segregation ordinances.)[81]

Washington, a shrewd man who understood the politics of fundraising from whites, believed that the white donors on whom he depended for money and support did not back residential segregation. He said as much in a letter to Gilbert Stephenson: "there is no sentiment among the substantial white landowners in this section of the South in favor of such a

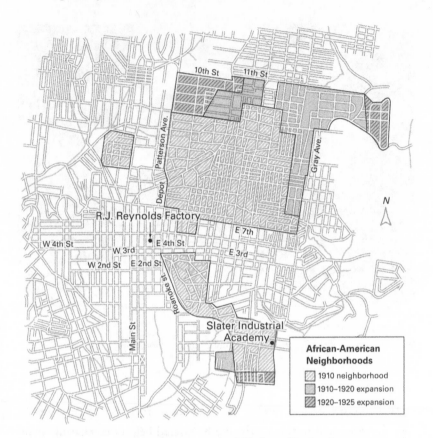

FIGURE 4.14   The expansion of Winston-Salem's black neighborhoods.
Source: Based on T. J. Woofter, *Negro Problems in Cities* (New York: Doubleday, Doran & Co., 1928), 66.

proposition." Indeed, white people, he noted, "like[d] to have just as many black people in 'calling distance' as possible."[82] This allowed Washington to make a strong argument against residential segregation, which he did in his 1915 article: whites who lived near black people were not harmed in the least; as proof, Washington pointed to the president of the United States and members of his cabinet who were "born and reared in the South in close contact with black people," some of them nursed by "black 'mammies.'"[83] Residential segregation was "unnecessary," continued Washington, as "both colored and whites are likely to select a section of the city where they will be surrounded by congenial neighbors."[84]

The reason that African Americans protested segregation ordinances was not that they wished to "mix with the white man socially" but because they viewed such ordinances as a sign that they would "receive inferior accommodations," according to Washington:

> If the negro is segregated, it will probably mean that the sewerage in his part of the city will be inferior; that the streets and sidewalks will be neglected, that the street lighting will be poor; that his section of the city will not be kept in order by the police and other authorities, and that the "undesirables" of other races will be placed near him, thereby making it difficult for him to rear his family in decency.[85]

Washington added to the latter point, pointing to examples of "house[s] of ill-repute" frequented by white men sited near black schools and churches. It was to get away from such situations that black people sought to move to "reputable" areas where "vice is not paraded."[86] Supporting Washington's claim, the Baltimore *Afro-American* reported that landlords kept the houses rented to African Americans—which were rented for much more than white people would have paid for them—in poor repair: "Bad bathrooms, broken bells, ceilings falling down and other evidences of need of repairs are to be seen."[87] James B. Dudley, the president of A&M College at Greensboro, argued that ordinances that limited black people to certain sections were morally suspect if those sections lacked sanitary measures such as water and sewer systems.[88]

Washington wished that rather than seeking to segregate African Americans in their own areas, whites would act as examples for their black neighbors; this would both teach black people proper behavior and cause white neighbors to conduct themselves well, knowing that their "hours, dress, manners, are all to be patterns for someone less fortunate."[89] Staying put would have also allowed whites to maintain the value of their property and middle-class blacks to enjoy a middle-class lifestyle.

Winston-Salem's Simon G. Atkins followed Booker T. Washington's lead on most things, but not on publicly criticizing residential segregation ordinances (until well over a decade had passed). President of the Slater Industrial Academy (later Slater Normal and Industrial School and now Winston-Salem State University), which followed the Hampton-Tuskegee model, and founder of Columbian Heights, a Winston suburb for middle-class African Americans, Atkins led a fiefdom created by self-segregation.[90]

Atkins, born into humble circumstances in 1863 in Chatham County, North Carolina, worked to ensure that Slater, established in 1893, would, as one newspaper described it, bring about "a better home life for the colored people, better teachers for the colored public schools and greater industrial efficiency, as well as a higher order of morals and the elevation of the colored race." The school sought to improve these aspects of black life by teaching trades that the white South had already approved for African Americans: "The boys are taught agriculture, blacksmithing, shoe making and dairying, while the girls are taught cooking, laundry work and general house hold economy."[91]

While Atkins enjoyed a prominent position in the segregated black community in Winston-Salem, this position was made possible by white largesse, and Atkins may have been wary of jeopardizing that. (Atkins has been described in a complimentary article as "a Christian statesman and patriot, who sees a new Southland in the molding and training of our youth, a lover of his race, and his State to that extent that he would not utter or say one word to irritate white or colored, hence a safe leader.")[92] It is also possible that Atkins supported the ordinance, which did not negatively affect him, as it did not push African Americans out of Columbian Heights. In fact, Columbian Heights stood to rise in desirability and value if the ordinance kept upwardly mobile African Americans out of white neighborhoods in the city. As president of the Twin City Building and Loan Association and Twin City Realty Company, Atkins would have benefited financially as demand to live in Columbian Heights grew.[93] One can only surmise what Atkins thought of the ordinance at the time it was enacted. The historian Elizabeth Lundeen came to the conclusion that he likely "found the policy tolerable albeit undesirable."[94]

In Atkins's world, African Americans chose to live apart from white people and sought to build up their own community. Black doctors, lawyers, educators, funeral directors, and ministers who served their own community benefited from the product of segregation: a self-contained

FIGURE 4.15 Atkins and the 1915 Slater student body. Atkins is seated in the front row.
Source: Courtesy of the Forsyth County Public Library Photograph Collection.

black community ready to purchase goods and services from African Americans.[95] While this world had some features in common with black nationalism, it was not economically independent, as Slater's reliance on white funding demonstrates. Nor was it a world in which the separate place of black people freed them from the oversight of whites. Atkins's black community found ways to live with discrimination, rather than actively fighting it or seeking to escape discrimination by moving out of the region.

Atkins's approach is evident in a letter he wrote, published in the *Charlotte Observer* (and described and quoted on the front page of the *New York Times* two days later) shortly after the passage of the disfranchisement amendment in August 1900. Described as "a direct appeal to the negro population to accept the inevitable and go to work to educate themselves and make themselves worthy citizens," the letter accepted at face value the "sincerity" of the state's leaders who claimed that they had no intention of using the amendment to take away government protection from African Americans. Atkins also offered African Americans some advice in his letter.[96] Through taking "pride in making ourselves useful members of the communities in which we live," black people might eventually gain rights. "Although our civil status may seem to be threatened, we owe it to our communities to contribute in every way we can to their prosperity, and thus shall we surely, if slowly, establish ourselves as helpful factors in our communities, and finally come into all the protection and privileges as such." Atkins made no criticism of the amendment and indeed offered his allegiance to a state that "will, I think, repeat her own history in the fair treatment of the negro as he rises up to . . . manhood and citizenship." Atkins, aware that few opportunities were open to African Americans outside of the South, decided not to criticize and thus anger white people but to strengthen ties with them. "The breasts of colored men all through the State," he wrote just after disenfranchisement, "heave with pride and gratitude whenever they remember the history and traditions of the Old North State."[97]

Atkins had moved to Columbian Heights in 1892, after asking that the city set aside the neighborhood in southeast Winston for African Americans. Before the development of this area, middle-class African Americans (doctors, lawyers, clergymen, teachers) had lived among working-class tobacco workers near the factories. Atkins aspired to move this middle class to a separate area that would reflect their status and serve as an example inspiring his students to achieve middle-class lifestyles (including homeownership) themselves. While this was the goal, the neighborhood did not exclude working-class black people, and in fact Atkins's neighbors included "a furniture finisher, a driver, a railroad porter, a carpenter, a grocery clerk, farmers, factory laborers, and tobacco rollers." While mostly made up of homeowners, the neighborhood included some boarders, too, showing that Columbian Heights was not as prosperous as Atkins intended. The neighborhood included about forty homes in 1906, and families living there planted vegetable gardens and raised hogs. Being able to eat off of the land rather than purchasing food was part of their strategy for gaining wealth and property.[98]

A letter to the editor of the *Union Republican* in 1896 that served as an advertisement for Columbian Heights described the neighborhood as idyllic:

> This beautiful and progressive little village is situated on the South-eastern surburb [*sic*] of Winston Salem, and within close proximity to the business centre of the Twin-City. Its high and rolling elevation places it within easy reach of the mountain breezes as they sweep from the towering peaks of the Blue Ridge—thus affording a climate pure and wholesome.
>
> The neat and attractive little cottages, scattered here and there "the Heights," [*sic*] surrounded with broad tracts of cultivated land, and the bright and cheerful aspect of every household, are speaking indications of the energy, thrift and refinement which characterize this community and contrast it so widely with the crowded and ill-appointed homes of the city.[99]

While close enough for residents to work in the city center, Columbian Heights looked and even smelled better than black neighborhoods in downtown Winston. Properties were "scattered here and there," in contrast to the overcrowding of the city that took place as workers poured into the city in search of tobacco-manufacturing jobs. The neighborhood's inhabitants demonstrated "energy," not laziness; their "thrift and refinement" revealed their desire to place themselves in the middle class.

For Atkins, the funding that his school gained from white benefactors was a priority—a larger priority than the property rights of African Americans in a different part of the city. As he viewed it, African Americans would advance not through protest but through gaining education at schools like Slater, which trained teachers who would teach the next generation of black North Carolinians. It was through relationships with whites—including local whites, state politicians, and white philanthropists from the North—that schools like Slater won funding; without these relationships, they would not have been able to operate, as black students could not afford to pay enough in tuition to cover operations.

FIGURE 4.16 Simon Atkins's home in Columbian Heights in 1903.
Source: "Slater Normal School Has Just Observed Its Tenth Annual Commencement Closing a Successful Year," *Winston-Salem Journal*, May 15, 1903, 1.

In 1895, the school received $460 from the Peabody Fund and $1,000 from the state legislature, for example; Simon Atkins's "personal appeal" to an agent of the Peabody Fund was crucial.[100] In 1917–1918, a committee chaired by the mayor of Winston-Salem and the treasurer of the R. J. Reynolds Tobacco Company raised over $10,000 from local whites, including $1,000 from R. J. Reynolds, for Slater.[101] The strong relationships with local whites built by Atkins and those who worked with him quite literally paid off. A letter written by the president of Slater's Board of Trustees to North Carolina's governor Thomas Bickett in 1918 emphasized these relationships in order to encourage Governor Bickett to convince the North Carolina General Assembly to provide the school with $10,000 (which it had promised to do if Slater succeeded in raising the same amount on its own). "The facts really are that while we asked our community for $5,000.00 they have in reality subscribed for $10,000.00, in order to emphasize the cordial realationship [*sic*] which is existing here between Professor Atkins and the colored people, and the white people of our community," the letter states.[102] Through currying favor, Slater won more money from local whites than from the state of North Carolina and northern philanthropists combined.[103]

THE BLACK RESPONSE TO RESIDENTIAL
SEGREGATION IN LOUISVILLE

Winston-Salem's leading African Americans followed the approach associated with Booker T. Washington (though, ironically, Washington did in fact criticize residential segregation ordinances after some prodding by the black press). It is worth comparing the response in Winston-Salem to that of African Americans in Louisville, Kentucky, to their city's segregation ordinance and considering why the response in Winston-Salem was more muted.

Louisville was a "gateway to the South"—a place where North and South met. Some people considered race relations in Louisville better than in other parts of the South; for example, Louisville's black citizens were not disenfranchised, and they continued to vote into the twentieth century (they voted Republican).[104] Voting rights notwithstanding, Louisville's African Americans were subject to discrimination on par with that faced by African Americans deeper in the South, as the city enacted a residential segregation ordinance and fought to keep it when black residents of the city and the NAACP objected.

Black and white people lived near each other in Louisville until the 1890s, at which point a few factors led to separation. For one, public transportation allowed many white people to move away from town and commute to jobs downtown. Rising sentiment in favor of segregation also led whites after 1890 to push for separate neighborhoods. Many African Americans resided in Downtown, a black residential area near the business district that had once been home to wealthy whites. Even as the area housed some of the city's most significant black businesses, churches, and other institutions, housing in Downtown was rundown, and all sorts of illicit activity, from prostitution to gambling, took place in the neighborhood. Uptown, another black residential area, was also considered a slum, as were other black neighborhoods such as The Bottoms and Little Africa. After around 1908, many African Americans who could afford to move out did so.[105]

As black people moved into areas occupied by whites, particularly the West End (a working- and middle-class neighborhood), a man named W. D. Binford led white residents in demanding a residential segregation law for the city. Binford, the superintendent of the mechanical department of the *Louisville Courier-Journal and Times*, proposed a residential segregation ordinance at a luncheon meeting of the Louisville Real Estate Exchange in November 1913. Binford made his case to the group: "There is no problem so grave, nor one fraught with so much danger to property values as the gradual influx of the negro into blocks or squares where none but whites reside." After this, white people who lived near black neighborhoods began to advocate for an ordinance, and one was introduced at Louisville's City Council in January 1914. Black residents in Louisville, including a number of ministers, quickly formed a branch of the NAACP (which was formally recognized by the national organization in August 1914) to fight against the ordinance, hoping to prevent it from being enacted. In spite of the pleas of these black leaders, the City Council unanimously approved the ordinance, as did the Board of Aldermen. Mayor John Bushemeyer signed off on the ordinance in May 1914.[106]

William Warley, who would become the leading voice in the fight against segregation in the city, was born in Louisville in 1884. He belonged to a "new generation of black leaders in Louisville" that, according to Patricia Hagler Minter, "had seen the hardening of racial separation both by statute and by custom" and "believed that to enact social changes African Americans would have to take the initiative themselves, instead of relying on the 'better element' of whites as their New South predecessors had." Warley had a respectable job working for the Postal Service (a job he would lose as a consequence of his activism). Chafing under the strictures of Jim Crow, in 1912 he started publishing the *Louisville News*, a weekly paper that promoted justice for African Americans in the city. In 1914, he used the paper in his boycott against the Louisville National Theater, whose policy on segregated seating he opposed. By leading this boycott, which won black patrons a somewhat improved situation at the theater, Warley became one of the city's antisegregation leaders. Active in the Louisville branch of the NAACP, he even served as branch president.[107]

Warley criticized Booker T. Washington's response to segregation ordinances in 1914. Washington had told the Negro Business League that African Americans should "spend less time in talking about the part of the city that we cannot live in, and more time in making the part of the city that we can live in beautiful and attractive." Warley responded with an article excoriating Washington that was reprinted in *The Crisis*: "It is doubtful if he has ever said anything that will so lower him in the respect and estimation of the whole race as this advice on segregation.... We do not merely express our private opinion when we say that the younger men and women, on whom the mantle of affairs must soon fall, speak of Dr. Washington's leadership with contempt."[108]

Warley was just the type of black leader that Winston-Salem lacked. Younger than Atkins (who was born into slavery) and more willing to resist segregation openly than Atkins, Warley had a sense of self tied to resistance to Jim Crow rather than to an institution like Slater that relied on the favor of white people. Working with the NAACP, he orchestrated a legal case that would test the constitutionality of legally mandated residential segregation.

BUCHANAN: THE SUPREME COURT RULES AGAINST RESIDENTIAL SEGREGATION LAW

Unlike North Carolina, which invalidated residential segregation ordinances on its own, other southern states argued that residential segregation laws were legal until the Supreme Court declared them unconstitutional on November 5, 1917, in *Buchanan v. Warley.*

Buchanan came out of a national campaign waged by the NAACP against residential segregation. The group viewed the Louisville, Kentucky, ordinance as critical in their fight; J. Chapin Brinsmade, one of the NAACP's lawyers, argued that the test case in Louisville would decide the issue. "The results in Louisville will be of the utmost importance in determining whether or not the Negro is to be segregated," Brinsmade argued. "It will not be easy to void the ordinance in the courts ... [as] Louisville has drawn its ordinance very carefully and the men who did the work had before them all the other similar ordinances and were able to profit by the defects. They believe that they have avoided all technical defects, and so all other cases will hinge on Louisville."[109]

The NAACP thus carefully set up its case, in which William Warley signed a contract to purchase a lot on a majority-white block from a white realtor named Charles H. Buchanan. A clause in the contract stated that Warley was purchasing the property with the purpose of living there and that "it is a distinct part of this agreement that I shall not be required to accept a deed to the above property or to pay for said property unless I have the right under the laws of the State of Kentucky and the city of Louisville to occupy said property as a residence." Warley reneged on the agreement because the ordinance would have prevented him from living on the property; Buchanan then sued Warley for breach of contract. The NAACP did not just set up the case; it also arranged for its president, Moorfield Storey, to join the Louisville counsel in arguing Buchanan's side once the case had moved past the appellate level.[110]

Buchanan examined a white man's right to sell his property as he wished. Charles Buchanan either sympathized with the desire of black citizens for equal rights or wished to protect his own right to sell property to people of either race—or both.[111] Buchanan's lawyers, Clayton B. Blakey and Moorfield Storey, argued that the residential segregation ordinance was invalid because it violated the Fourteenth Amendment. By prohibiting African Americans from living on the property because the block was majority white, the ordinance prevented Buchanan from selling the property and thus deprived him of his property. Buchanan was unlikely to sell the property to white buyers because it was located near properties occupied by black residents, which made the property undesirable to whites.[112]

In the Brief for the Plaintiff in Error, Buchanan's lawyers sketched out how the ordinance worked. Prohibited from selling his property to African Americans while the block was majority white, Buchanan would have to wait for six of the block's white residents to leave their homes vacant—which of course might never happen—after which time his lot could be sold to African Americans. Such a situation was obviously not ideal for a property owner. Even if his neighbors did eventually move out and leave their homes vacant, Buchanan would lose money as his own property sat empty "for an indefinite time." The ordinance allowed a property owner to live in a house on his property if one had been constructed before the passage of the ordi-nance, even if he was the "wrong race" for the block. But if no house had been constructed, that owner could not build until "the majority of occu-pants in the block are of his color." Such an owner would thus be "deprive[d] . . . of the right to live on his own land." This provision would have applied to Warley had he owned the property; he could not have built a residence on it until the block had turned majority black. Provisions such as these would have the effect of "stir[ring] up conflict and ill-feeling" between white and black residents of the city, according to the Brief for the Plaintiff in Error, and between neighbors. And all for the purpose—not the stated purpose but the purpose nonetheless—of "prevent[ing] the negro citizens of Louisville, however industrious, thrifty and well-educated they might be, from approaching that condition vaguely described as 'social equality.' "[113]

The *Buchanan* case was not cast as about discrimination against African Americans—and for this reason, it did not look to the Equal Protection Clause of the Fourteenth Amendment. Rather, the problem was the viola-tion of the right to property—a right enjoyed by both white and black citi-zens. (Hence the white plaintiff who claimed that he had been prevented from exercising the right to dispose of his property as he wished.) Indeed, the court pointed out the case was about not "the *social* rights of men" but "those fundamental rights in *property* which it was intended to secure upon the same terms to citizens of every race and color."[114]

Warley, of course, hoped to lose his case; the City of Louisville, which took over his defense before the Kentucky Court of Appeals and the U.S. Supreme Court, wished to win. The court's decision in *Buchanan* was a vic-tory for African Americans, whether the Supreme Court meant to stand up for the rights of African Americans or not, and it had the effect of improv-ing the lot of blacks. James Ely, a historian of property rights, argues that the case "had both practical and symbolic significance" as through it the court "made clear that there was a limit to legislation imposing racial segre-gation." The case also "spurred renewed civil rights activism" among Afri-can Americans. The legal scholars A. Leon Higginbotham Jr., F. Michael Higginbotham, and S. Sandile Ngcobo demonstrate the importance of the *Buchanan* decision by comparing residential segregation in the United States to that in South Africa. While state and city governments in the South "interpreted the Constitution in a racist manner," allowing the biases of judges to put prejudice above the requirements of the law, the Supreme Court made a stand for "equalitarian" principles and in doing so "allowed thousands and probably millions of black Americans" to enjoy "broader housing options." African Americans moving out of impoverished and segregated areas, the authors note, tended to be prosperous; *Buchanan* did not do much to help the poorest African Americans. If it were not for this case, however, "the plight of black Americans today concerning urban and suburban housing conditions could be almost akin to that of black South Africans" under apartheid, the authors argue.[115]

S. S. Field, the city solicitor of Baltimore, who filed an amicus curiae brief in *Buchanan*, criticized the decision for, in effect, standing with African Americans over white property owners who valued segregation. The case, he claimed, put blacks' property rights above whites' "personal rights." The Fourteenth Amendment, he argued, had been used "almost entirely to protect rights of property" rather than "rights of life or liberty." The right to dispose of property, he complained, "must be upheld, even though it is not certain that any damage would result to the individual from the enforcement of the ordinance, and it is certain that great damage would result to the neighborhood from the nullification of the ordinance." The city solicitor criticized white men like Buchanan who put their own right to sell property to black buyers for "$50 or $100 or $500 more from the negro than his property is worth" above the "right" of other whites to "protect" their investments. A person like Buchanan selling his property to African Americans "immediately limits the possible purchasers of the other houses in the block and depreciates the value of every other house in the block."[116]

The Baltimore city solicitor also viewed *Buchanan* as a threat to segregation in general. The court, he pointed out, failed to distinguish between laws providing segregation in public education and residential segregation. This presented a problem because if it did not consider segregation in public accommodation or in public education different from residential segregation, it might, down the road, prohibit these types of segregation, too. Meanwhile, residential segregation was necessary for the same reason that these other types of segregation were necessary:

If considerations of peace and good order justify the separation of the races in coaches; if there is sufficient danger of clashes between the races from meeting occasionally and for a short time in railway coaches, is there not far greater danger of clashes between the races from families, white and black, living side by side, with their front doors within a few feet of each other every day? [117]

Republicans in Congress envisioned the Fourteenth Amendment, added to the Constitution after the Civil War, as protecting the rights of African Americans, just emerging from slavery without economic power or legal protection. They wished to save these people from falling back under the exploitation of their former masters. Thus it declared them citizens, and it prohibited states from infringing upon their rights—including their right to property—without "due process of law."[118] There have been numerous attempts to subvert the Fourteenth Amendment over the years, to wipe it clean of its original purpose. Field tried to use the Fourteenth Amendment to protect the rights of middling whites to exclude African Americans, which, as he framed it, was their best chance at protecting the value of their own property. While the court discarded this argument, it did not stand up for the original purpose of the amendment by holding up the right of African Americans to buy and sell property. Rather, it protected the right of Charles Buchanan, a white man, to do this, and the court did not point out that in protecting Buchanan's right to property, it also protected that of African Americans.

Residential segregation ordinances were not the only way to keep property in the hands of whites, though they were the easiest to enforce. Restrictive covenants, for example, could be breached.[119] After *Buchanan*, whites had to look beyond ordinances to other measures. Thomas W. Hanchett describes efforts to put blacks in certain neighborhoods in Charlotte as part carrot and part stick:

White property owners offered blacks opportunities for improved housing in specific sections of the city, erecting clusters of shotgun dwellings for renters and even opening a streetcar suburb for African

American homebuyers. At the same time, opportunities vanished elsewhere. Downtown interests shunned black storekeepers, neighbors
pressured landlords to evict black tenants, and in the suburbs devel-
opers inserted restrictive covenants into every lot deed forbidding
ownership or residence by anyone of the "colored race."[120]

In Baltimore, white landlords who were willing to rent property in white
neighborhoods to African Americans were pressured not to; one such landlord agreed to stop renting to blacks after the inspector of buildings for
Baltimore threatened to cite him for code violations. Neighbors and the
Baltimore Real Estate Board also asserted pressure on white landlords who
considered renting to blacks in white neighborhoods.[121]

Without legal sanction for residential segregation ordinances, however,
residential segregation did not become as extensive as it might have. Consider the fact that the *Darnell* case not only blocked the ordinance in
Winston-Salem but also in Mooresville and Greensboro and that it notified cities like Charlotte that their time would be wasted if they moved ahead
with their own plans for ordinances. The decision also reassured African
Americans that while their situation was bad, there was a line past which
Jim Crow would not go. In 1929, Simon Atkins looked back on the response
of Winston-Salem's black community to *Darnell*: as he understood it, the
case "so reassured the negroes as to the spirit of our city in regard to their
rights under the law, that it prepared them the more readily to accept and
become content with the better policy of voluntary segregation."[122] While
the decision may have worked as an "opiate to the masses," so to speak, it
also allowed African Americans to hold onto property that they had worked
hard to purchase. This was the function of *Buchanan*, too.

5

Jim Crow for the Countryside

On a single page of the December 6, 1913, issue of the *Progressive Farmer*, a number of headlines made the argument that small white southern farmers needed rural segregation if they were to succeed: "Segregation Necessary to Develop Good Farming and White Farmers," "Present Situation Forces White Boys off the Farm," "The White Farmer's Hard Competition," "Many Large Landowners Blind to Their Own Interests."[1] These headlines, attached to letters to the editor sent in from all over the South, made the point repeatedly and forcefully that small white farmers in the region were suffering because of the presence of African American farmers in their neighborhoods. (These headlines appeared just a couple of weeks before Greensboro newspapers began publishing stories about the "threat" posed by William B. Windsor to the Gorham Street community.) The "scarecrow of race" had won; a number of North Carolina's small white farmers and their leaders were singularly focused on African Americans as the "problem" that kept them from success. They had internalized the message given to them through the Democratic Party about African Americans.

By 1913, a segregationist impulse had developed among many small white farmers in the South—an impulse deeply rooted in a tradition of agrarianism. Small farm owners, people who aspired to be small farm owners, and reformers like Clarence Poe who sought to help small farmers believed, at least in North Carolina, that white farmers would be able to expand their access to opportunity on the farm only if they lived and worked apart from African Americans. These agrarians viewed black farmers as competitors who prevented small white farmers from meeting their aspirations; in their view, "the really handicapped and disadvantaged man in the fierce industrial struggle in the South today is not the Negro but the white farmer and laborer who must compete with a race with lower living standards."[2]

"Conditions," Poe complained, "are simply not fair to the rural white man—he hasn't an equal opportunity with the Negro." Poe ignored the higher prices paid by African Americans for farmland, arguing that black farmers, because they were often willing to work for less money and live in worse conditions, hurt the prospects of poor white farmers, who had to accept lower standards of living to compete with African Americans. Property values, too, were a central concern: "Everybody knows that if white people are crowded thick around a Negro farm, the Negro's land values are not hurt. On the contrary, they are increased. But it is equally well known that if Negroes are crowded thick around a white farm its value is diminished—and diminished almost in direct ratio to the increasing number of Negroes."[3] Poe also argued that white women faced danger living among black men and that the presence of black farmers limited the opportunities for white farmers to socialize and work cooperatively with one another. He believed this situation was an important reason so many white farmers were moving to cities.[4]

The rural segregationist impulse was more than just a negative reaction to the presence of African Americans, however. Indeed, the driving force behind rural segregation was an agrarian worldview—a broad and energizing way in which small white farmers understood their land, their heritage, and their purpose on earth. These agrarians envisioned a rural countryside populated by thriving white yeomen. Even while this vision was premised on racism and exclusion, it had egalitarian elements, as it sought to reduce inequality among white farmers. Poe viewed segregation as the key "reform" that would enable small white farmers to build "a great rural civilization" in the South. This "great rural civilization," as Poe envisioned it, would be populated by thriving yeoman farmers, all of them white, and they would work together to buy and sell goods through agricultural cooperatives and enjoy a rich social life, unencumbered by black neighbors. Poe's vision of what rural life could become—a vision he "profoundly believ[ed] in . . . as the only way now in sight out of a perilous situation"—required segregation. Segregation was, as Poe saw it, a constructive way of building up a rich home and community life, of making property something that brought rewards beyond mere financial ones.[5]

The racism of agrarians was very much connected to their frustration regarding the inability of farmers to meet their aspirations. In other words, this racism was shaped by the economic context within which small white farmers struggled to make do. Small white farmers aspired to own land, gain independence, and work as stewards of the land. There was only so much good land, however, and black farmers were acquiring some of it. Anxious about their position, white farmers turned to blaming their problems on a group of people they considered different from themselves, and they tried to exclude this group from the land, hoping that doing so would allow them better access to the resources they wanted. They channeled their feelings of competition into racism.[6]

The desire of white agrarians to exclude African Americans was similar to that of white property owners in cities like Winston-Salem. Agrarians focused on farm ownership more than they did on property values, but the goal was the same: economic opportunity. Economic opportunity on the farm looked different from economic opportunity in cities. It was about more than how much value had accrued in the property; essential to economic opportunity on the farm was winning freedom from the credit system, which, if achieved, would allow farmers to keep the profits from the crops they grew. Farm ownership was necessary to achieve this.

POE'S RURAL SEGREGATION CAMPAIGN

Mark Schultz, one of the few historians to address the question of a segregated southern countryside, argues in *The Rural Face of White Supremacy* that segregation was designed to operate in cities, not the countryside. While they did forge personal relations in private spaces (spaces, like the home, where hierarchy was clear), urban black and white people also encountered one another as strangers in public spaces—modern spaces—such as street cars, train stations, and theaters. Progressive reformers responded to the so-called dangers associated with these anonymous encounters by designing "segregation codes [that] operated impersonally and uniformly to maintain African Americans in a conspicuous second-class status." The "premodern" countryside of Hancock County, Georgia, the focus of Schultz's study, was marked by "a culture of personalism and localism," meanwhile, and segregating public spaces there was both impractical and unproductive. In this county and many other parts of the rural South, black and white people had the most intimate of relations—with African Americans working in the homes and fields of their wealthy white neighbors, who often felt a paternalistic desire to look out for "their" blacks, and working alongside and socializing with poor white sharecroppers. These relations took place, of course, within the context of a rigid social hierarchy, and this shaped how white and black people interacted with one another when they met in public places.[7]

The dynamic described by Schultz does not apply to the entire rural South. Hancock County, most of it populated by large white landholders and white and black sharecroppers, was not a part of the South where small white landholders—the group most likely to support segregation—shaped the culture of interactions with African Americans.[8] The segregation of neighborhoods in the rural South may have been a logistical challenge, a legal nightmare, and an annoying obstacle for those who wished to see blacks working for whites, but it made sense to middling white people—the type of people who did not wield much influence in Hancock County.

Poe was not the only person working toward a segregated countryside in North Carolina. Hugh MacRae (1865–1951), an agitator for white supremacy in Wilmington in 1898 and a wealthy MIT-trained mining engineer, real estate developer, and industrialist, for example, believed planned rural communities would vastly improve the South, and he spent much of his own fortune constructing such communities in North Carolina. In 1905, Mac-Rae began to turn hundreds of thousands of acres into several farm colonies, each of them divided into ten-acre plots. He thought Europeans would bring desirable qualities to the South, and by 1908 had settled in his colonies eight hundred people, hailing from Italy, Greece, Holland, Poland, and

Germany. MacRae believed that European immigrants, once taught scientific agriculture, would improve "our vast areas of unused land" and make "desirable citizen[s]." He lured in settlers with promises of prosperity. In a pamphlet full of boosterism, he claimed that "from an agricultural standpoint, the South is a region of vast wealth; even single States may be classed as empires." MacRae did not envision African Americans living in his colonies, and he put a provision into the property deeds to ensure that the plots of land stayed in the hands of whites.[9]

The Outlook, a magazine edited by Lyman Abbott that reflected Progressive ideas, approvingly described the exclusionary policies of MacRae's farm communities. The article favorably compared the selection of types of people to live in farm communities to agriculture itself. Rather than letting nature decide which plants will grow, the farmer selects which plants he will cultivate. "He chooses for planting only those seeds which have demonstrated their possession of the desired qualities in the highest degree. Year after year he selects and plants until his crop has attained a superior level of excellence."[10] After selecting "superior" groups to live in his farm communities, MacRae even encouraged them to reproduce, rewarding parents with ten dollars for each child born in St. Helena.[11]

Poe and MacRae had different ideas for how to achieve their visions—MacRae, unlike Poe, did not seek a law to bolster segregation of the countryside—but their visions overlap in important ways. For both men, segregation was not an end in of itself; it was the first step toward creating a certain kind of rural community. Their idealized rural communities featured racial homogeneity, cooperation among farmers, and cultural cohesiveness. They worked not for a return to the plantation South—which would have benefited none but elites—but for something else: a world that protected middling whites from competition with nonwhites and helped them form strong social bonds.

In June 1913 (around the same time that William Darnell moved into his house in Winston-Salem), Poe began his campaign to segregate North Carolina's countryside—a campaign he hoped to see spread through the rural South and that he led through the *Progressive Farmer* and with the support of the North Carolina Farmers' Educational and Cooperative Union. Poe and his allies organized a political convention to meet in Raleigh in

April 1914 (the same month that the North Carolina Supreme Court decided *State v. Darnell*) with the purpose of putting forward a Progressive platform and backing politicians who supported it. Secretary of State William Jennings Bryan agreed to give the keynote address at the convention. Poe hoped that the platform adopted at the convention would include rural segregation as well as tax, school, and other reforms. In a blow to Poe and the Farmers' Union, which backed the idea, however, rural segregation was removed from the platform.[12]

According to one source—denied by Josephus Daniels, who had issued the invitation to Bryan[13]—Bryan "notified those in charge of the movement that unless that part of the proposed platform which referred to the 'segregation of the races' was stricken out he would not under any consideration consent to make a speech before the progressive meeting." It turned out that in spite of the fact that "the Farmers' union was committed to the segregation idea," conference planners cared more to "have the Nebraskan appear on the scene than to insist upon the segregation plank, and, therefore, that part of the proposed platform has been eliminated."[14] As it happened, Bryan canceled anyway, claiming to have a cold.[15]

The *Charlotte Daily Observer*, which opposed the rural segregation plank, offers some insight into why Bryan might have disapproved of rural segregation and why the idea was dropped from the platform. Rural segregation, along with child labor reform, split the state's Democratic Party. Those who wanted the Progressives to fall into line with the rest of the Democratic Party dismissed rural segregation as undesirable. In an editorial, the *Daily Observer* implied who within the party disliked rural segregation: "The segregation of farm labor is a question that perhaps should not be agitated seriously until an automatic farm hand is invented to take the place of the nigger." Clearly, the editor was thinking of landlords' desire for black labor. The editorial went on, "On all other items the Democrats of the State are practically united, and to that extent the Raleigh meeting will be in the nature of a ratification convention."[16]

The failure of rural segregation at the convention did not dissuade Poe. He claimed that rural segregation had been dropped simply because there was not enough time to include it on the schedule and that its omission did not reflect a lack of interest in the measure.[17] Poe continued his campaign by working in behalf of an amendment to the North Carolina Constitution that would allow the white residents of a community to prevent the sale of land within their community to African Americans. Poe understood that rural segregation might not be constitutional—he even admitted that some would consider his amendment "in conflict with the Fourteenth Amendment" of the U.S. Constitution. This, however, need not pose a problem. "If our people make up their minds that segregation is a good and necessary thing," he argued, "they will find a way to put it into effect—just as they did in the case of Negro disfranchisement despite an iron-bound Amendment specifically designed to prevent it."[18] (Poe had supported disfranchisement, believing that the Reconstruction amendments had made a mistake in allowing "a race only a few generations removed from African barbarism to take the reins of government into its own hands, [humiliating] the men and women who had built up the splendid civilization of the Old South.")[19]

Poe proposed that the North Carolina state constitution be amended to allow the majority of the population of a community to declare that no more land in the community could be sold to people of a particular race. He assumed that whites would more likely exclude blacks than vice versa, since blacks were less likely to make up the majority of a community's landholders. The amendment would not allow for the removal of black people who were already in the community; Poe recognized that inhibiting the ownership of land would violate the U.S. Constitution. He hoped that once a community had decided to restrict land sales, however, that community would over time become more and more "white" as properties owned by both white and black people were sold to white farmers. As Poe expressed it:

These communities would attract white settlers to them in increasing numbers. Wouldn't people from other sections begin to say, "I want to get into a permanently white community, with its better white social life, better white schools and churches, and better chances for a cooperation"—and wouldn't white people soon be willing to offer so fair a price for [an] absentee landlord's land that he could better afford to sell it rather than to continue renting it to shiftless, soil-destroying [black] tenants?

White farmers would pay a "premium" to buy land in such a community, a community shaped by their agrarian ideal.[20]

Communities that wanted to go "all white" would submit a petition saying the following: "We hereby petition to have this district set apart in future for the exclusive ownership, use and occupancy of the white race except that rights of persons who have already bought or leased shall not be destroyed, nor any man prevented from having laborers, croppers or tenants of a different race."[21] Poe did not intend for the proposed amendment to stop white landowners from renting their land to black farmers or from hiring black workers. The goal, as Poe articulated it, was "to prevent Negroes from coming into white communities and buying land as permanent and immovable residents." Poe understood that wealthy white landowners would oppose restrictions on their right to hire black workers—workers who were desirable because, having even less power than white workers, they were generally easier to exploit. Poe thought that if a community voted to go "all white," it would not be too difficult to get rid of black tenants, however.[22]

Poe proposed a system meant to look democratic. Poe's inclusion of a community vote would likely not have led to real democracy, however, as African Americans—disenfranchised at the time—would probably not have been allowed to vote on land restriction.

MIDDLING WHITE FARMERS AND RURAL SEGREGATION

An editorial in the *Winston-Salem Journal* published in September 1913, a few months after Poe had begun his campaign, applauded Poe's plan, claiming that Poe was "winning the approval of the best people of the South." The editorial—published a few weeks before the North Carolina Senate considered a bill authorizing the segregation of residences in North Carolina cities and towns—justified its support of the measure:

> It is inconceivable that a white man and a negro can live in harmony, with each the next door neighbor of the other. God never intended that such a condition should exist. That's why he put the negroes in Africa and the whites in Europe. He evidently intended that they

should not dwell on the same continent together. But we put them on the same plantation.

The paper probably also supported Poe's plan because its editor recognized the similarity to Winston's own segregation ordinance—the *Darnell* case was making its way through the courts—and thought that to support one was to support the other. The editorial also claimed that the *Charlotte Observer* "commend[ed]" the plan, arguing that it was a way of encouraging a "tendency"—segregation—that was occurring "naturally."[23]

Most support for the rural segregation plan came from small white farmers. Unlike large landholders and merchants, these farmers did not derive profits from black farmers, and they resented black farmers as competitors. They believed that successful black farmers hurt the prospects of their white neighbors by holding onto land that white farmers might want and that unsuccessful black farmers hurt them by driving farm wages down. The farmers who supported rural segregation did not do much to demonstrate their support, however. A petition drive organized by the North Carolina Farmers' Educational and Cooperative Union, which had a peak membership of 33,000, resulted in 234 petitions, signed by 5,867 farmers, being sent to the General Assembly in support of the amendment. As Jeffrey J. Crow reports, some petitioners wished they had had more time to collect signatures; a Nash County farmer commented that "I'm satisfied if I had the time I could get ever body in this communities, to sign it for ever body I saw sign[ed] it." Sixty out of one hundred counties in the state submitted petitions, with most of these petitioning counties in cotton- and tobacco-growing areas where tenancy was a great concern and fewer opportunities for small white farmers to own land existed. The old plantation belt was thus heavily represented in the petitions.[24]

An article by H. Q. Alexander, president of the North Carolina Farmers Union, appeared in the *Greensboro Daily News*. In it he argued that the efforts made by the Farmers Union did not reflect the strong interest of North Carolina farmers in rural segregation—thus implying a split within the union's leaders over rural segregation. "Because the officials of the North Carolina Farmers union have not been aggressive in urging the question of land segregation between the races . . . as was unanimously endorsed by our last State convention," Alexander claimed, "I find that some people in the towns have supposed that the farmers are not in earnest about the matter." In fact, the farmers supported the measure, according to Alexander, making "thousands of patriotic countrymen who will advocate and press this question until it shall be settled to the having of white communities and the protection of our homes and our women and children." Alexander compared the needs of white people in the countryside to those of urban dwellers. "If there is a demand for segregation in the cities, where the terrors of darkness flee before the electric light and armed police try to protect both day and night," he wrote, "how much greater the need for it to be the isolated country home, without the protection of lights or police, or the proximity of neighbors?"[25]

Rural segregation was just one way that southern small white farmers attempted to keep land in their own hands. Whitecapping, a form of terrorism used to intimidate black farmers and push them off their land, served the same purpose. Black landowners and sharecroppers were targeted as victims by, in the words of W. Fitzhugh Brundage, "those whites who bitterly resented their shrinking opportunities to move up the agricultural ladder from tenantry to landowning." These poor and middling white farmers aimed for violence (they sometimes employed lethal violence) to drive off black farmers, ensuring their own access to land and jobs. According to Brundage, they were not just "scapegoating" African Americans; "hardpressed [white] farmers had an acute sense of the tangible threat that black laborers posed to their access to land."[26]

Mark Schultz, writing about Georgia, argues that "small white landowners seem to have been the least secure in the superior status that white supremacy bestowed on them and the most willing to resort to organized violence in its defense"; they also made up a majority of the Klan's membership. Schultz does not have examples of these whites resorting to violence against black landowners in Hancock County, however, and notes that it may be that the same factors that allowed certain African Americans to purchase land (that is, personal relationships with influential white "patrons") protected them from lynch mobs.[27]

In other places, such as Georgia's Early and Miller Counties in 1899, whitecappers sought to use violence to create "entirely white counties." A local newspaper reported on one example: "the gang has issued an order that no negro shall live in the section in which the whitecappers are at work and the white people have been notified that negroes shall not remain on their places under penalty of violence." Brundage points out that members of the planter class used violence to control black farmers and punish individuals whose behavior they wished to correct, but they did not use it with the goal of creating white communities. Indeed, the actions of small white farmers who terrorized black farm laborers angered the planter class and often led to the prosecution of the offenders.[28]

Violence like whitecapping, as historians have pointed out, offers a glimpse into the history of the "inarticulate" (as perpetrators of such violence tended to be people who did not leave written records) and that of poor whites. A study of whitecapping in Georgia shows that over 50 percent of whitecappers were landless; an additional 20 percent owned less than $200 worth of property. Through whitecapping, less privileged whites were able to offer "challenges to the prevailing structure of power, whether these challenges came from groups contending for power, groups fearing loss of power, or groups affected by a shift of power from one level to another." Thus, violence such as whitecapping is not "an irrational phenomenon that defies explanation" but rather a logical expression of frustration about their social or economic position.[29]

Whitecapping did occur in North Carolina, and some of it may have even been inspired by Poe's campaign. In 1915, *The Crisis* reported, "in North Carolina the campaign of Poe, the latest Negro-baiter, is bearing its natural fruit. In two counties peaceful Negro farmers have been murdered for the new crime of land-owning."[30] It went on to quote the *Charlotte Observer*, a white newspaper, on the causes of this violence:

The *Observer* is in agreement with Mr. Garren in his theory as to the inciting cause. When, a few nights ago, the home of a Negro in Vance County was set on fire and the man and members of his family killed, this paper drew the inference that behind that crime was a feeling born of the segregation idea. The Catawba County case, following so closely, tended to strengthen that impression. . . . If it is true that these occurrences are the outgrowth of the segregation propaganda, that fact should be only the more reason why the hand of the law should be felt in its utmost severity at this time. . . . The *Observer* has always held that segregation of the races is a thing of ultimate achievement, not by statute process, but through the operation of moral and natural laws.[31]

Ideas like rural segregation had tangible effects even when they did not become policy. Racist ideas incited white people to commit acts of violence against African Americans.

In addition to whitecapping, small white farmers used intimidation to discourage black farmers from owning property. An African American from Mississippi argued in the *Progressive Farmer* that "If we own a good farm or horse or cow, or bird dog or yoke of oxen, we are harassed until we are bound to sell, give way, or run away before we can have any peace in our lives." Poe dismissed this man's claims as "wild," probably because he did not want to admit that the group he championed engaged in illegal and unethical behavior. Certainly, though, small white farmers who bitterly resented blacks who owned property found a number of ways of relieving them of this property.[32]

It may be that whitecapping and harassment were less likely to take place in parts of the South where small white farmers had other ways of pushing forward their agenda (such as through segregation laws), though the claims of *The Crisis* and the *Charlotte Observer* suggest that Poe's rural segregation campaign did not forestall—and in fact may have encouraged—violence. A rural segregation law makes sense as a Progressive reform as it would have achieved the same ends as whitecapping but would have done so legally.

Small white farmers also understood that a rural segregation law would be difficult to achieve because it pitted the financial interest of a relatively powerless group against the powerful elite. A small white farmer from Jackson, Tennessee, who signed his letter to the editor of the *Progressive Farmer* "O" voiced the belief that rural segregation would help his class while acknowledging that it was unlikely to happen as the interests of small white farmers were not aligned with those of wealthier whites: "There is not a respectable poor white man in the South but favors [Poe's] proposed law, not knowing any better plan to save the land for his children and his race; but the large landowners are on the other side." Economic interest, this farmer believed, motivated white elites: "Could they but love their people better than they love a dollar we would soon have at least an equal chance in life with a Negro." O praised Poe as a hero for standing with poor whites on a topic that he believed would be "strongly opposed" by wealthy whites. He noted that poor white farmers suffered in competition with African Americans, with white elites preferring the labor of black workers. Referring to how slave labor undercut free labor before the Civil War, O complained that the situation "is the same in effect as before 1865."[33]

Another letter argued that white landlords preferred black labor for nefarious reasons. A man from Bartlett, North Carolina, complained about "a certain class of white land-owners" who made their money taking advantage of black workers. This group of "land-owners don't want intelligent white tenants." Instead, they sought tenants that "they can use to their advantage." The writer offered an example of a black tenant who paid $150 for a mule that was worth $90 and then spent fifteen years unsuccessfully trying to pay for the mule before the mule died. During these fifteen years, the unscrupulous white man who had sold him the mule pocketed the black tenant's payments, which were large because of the high interest rate he charged. In complaining that landlords looked not for "intelligent" workers but for the most exploitable, this writer also showed that small white farmers were not the only group enduring a bad situation.[34]

Nonelite white farmers considered African Americans a threat to their economic prospects and to the racial purity of their families. The fear of a "mongrel breed" appeared again and again in the *Progressive Farmer*. Poe published an article and a series of letters under the ominous title "The Menace of the Mulatto Problem" in February 1914. Here, people who viewed segregation as Poe did expressed hope that segregation would end what they saw as the horror of interracial sex. The reverend A. H. Shannon combed through census data to come to the conclusion that "full-blood Negroes increased 17.6 per cent [between 1890 and 1910]; mulattoes increased 80.2 per cent!"[35] A reader from Cleveland County, North Carolina, who wrote a letter to the editor praising Poe as a visionary on the topic of African

Americans in the region revealed his fears of intermarriage and interracial sex: "Who knows but that God as he looks down on his different breeds of the human race . . . as they become more and more of the mongrel breed, has raised up a man to warn and lead the people?"[36]

Poe and his audience grappled with whom to blame for this situation. One Skippers, Virginia, tenant writing a letter to the editor "blame[d] the white man for the whole of it" (that is, interracial sex), aghast that "if you were to travel through my neighborhood at this time of the year, you would not know, on acount [*sic*] of amalgamation, whether to take off your hat to the lady in the carriage or not."[37] Poe printed an article by Senator Ben Tillman ("who is a subscriber to and reader of The Progressive Farmer") that Tillman had sent him, along with a note from Tillman saying that Poe's "headline, 'Women of the South Must Create Sentiment and Compel Laws to Save Us,' is the keynote to the agitation which should begin promptly and never cease." Tillman blamed white men who, "oblivious to their duty to their race and caste, are voluntary criminals in this regard . . . brazenly living openly with colored women." But African Americans, too, were not innocent, according to Tillman, as "amalgamation is the hope and ultimate purpose of the Negroes, the obliteration of the color line." Tillman's solution (he did not mention rural segregation): forcing white men to "observe the obligations of caste."

> I ask in all solemnity whether or not it is possible to prevent ultimate amalgamation if white men are not compelled by public opinion and by law to observe the obligations of caste. Can our Anglo-Saxon civilization withstand the undermining process of a constant increase in the number of mulattoes and quadroons? Our white women will guard the purity of the race in the bravest and most sacred manner. Shall white men be allowed to destroy what our mothers, wives, sisters and daughters are so bravely defending?[38]

A farmer from South Carolina linked the economic situation to interracial sex, complaining that "town landowners [that is, absentee landlords] and supply merchants . . . would willingly condemn their country to the mongrel civilization, for the sake of a little temporary profit."[39] The numerous letters and articles on this topic published in the *Progressive Farmer* served to rile up poor white farmers and strengthen their resolve to live near white farmers only.

OPPOSITION TO RURAL SEGREGATION

The rural segregation campaign laid bare the different interest groups in the countryside. Many small white farmers believed that a rural segregation amendment would benefit them. Elites, even if they shared the view that black men posed a threat to rural white women, generally refused to take the step that small whites asked of them. Many of those who opposed the amendment did so because they feared losing black workers; they did not believe Poe that their access to black workers would be protected if rural segregation was put into law. (And, indeed, their fears were reasonable, given the points made by many supporters of the idea, who assumed that segregation would lead to a removal of black labor.) They also envisioned a countryside that looked different from Poe's ideal, with its small farms operated by white farmers. They envisioned something akin to the Old South, in which an elite surrounded itself with African Americans, a symbol of their wealth and status and a reminder of a past they looked back on with nostalgia.

Landlords from states where such a policy was not even under consideration sent Poe their objections. W. H. Gould, of Livingston, Alabama, wrote a letter to the editor of the *Progressive Farmer* arguing that he stood against "your segregation movement" because he needed his black workers. "If it is raining so that no field work can be done, I tell the Negroes to fix the fence where it needs repair. I never have any argument about it but the fence is promptly repaired," he wrote. "What would a white man say if I rang my bell on a rainy morning and when he came I told him to get the necessary tools and fix the fence or get in the crib and shuck corn?" Without his black workers, Gould claimed, the value of his crops—and even of his land—would decrease by at least a half.[40] Another white landowner, W. M. Webster of Winona, Mississippi, complained that he had been unsuccessful with white farmworkers and that he would relocate to follow black workers if he had to.

The white man does not take to the hoe and plow like the colored man and is more expensive as a general thing. He wants his coffee three times daily and everything else in proportion. You can tell the colored man what to do and what you want done. My experience with the white man is if you so speak to him, he becomes highly indignant and winds up with a few cusswords. We cannot get along without the blacks. The day that comes when they are segregated, I want to go with the Negro. . . . Suppose in a neighborhood where all are white, who will cook your three meals a day? Not the white woman. Who will do your family's washing? Not the white woman. . . . You want to put in cultivation a new piece of land; who chops down, rolls the logs, burns and puts the ground in fix to plow? Not the white man. Who picks the cotton, gins and hauls the same to market, etc.? I could go on ad infinitum, but this will do. I want them around me as long as one is to be had.[41]

Webster's lack of respect for small white farmers is telling. In Webster's eyes, white farmworkers lacked an affinity for the work (they did "not take to the hoe and plow like the colored man"). In spite of this lack of affinity, they demanded higher pay than African Americans. They were difficult, unruly, rude, and resentful. They turned up their noses at certain kinds of work, including difficult tasks like laundry and clearing land. For these reasons, white sharecroppers and tenants were undesirable. No doubt poor whites were aware of how elites viewed them; the push for rural segregation must have been in part about setting up a situation in which small white farmers would be esteemed rather than dismissed and in which they could not be compared unfavorably with black farmers, as there would be no black farmers around to compare them with. Part of their agrarian dream was having the respect of others—being valued members of a community rather than scorned workers who were esteemed even less than black farmers.

In a printed response to Webster's letter, Poe twisted Webster's argument to support his position. If it was true that white workers were refusing to do physical labor in the South, it was all the more necessary to enact segregation so that they would be forced to learn the value of manual labor. Indeed, "no people who refuse to work and work hard can remain strong and dominant," Poe argued, in a point drawn from Thomas Jefferson and Maurice Evans. As Poe explained it, southerners paid black laborers little to do shoddy work, while white people in other parts of the country—such as the West—paid white workers well to do this same labor, and the excellent work done by these white workers paid off for their employers in better crops.[42] But Gould and Webster were less interested in improving white labor and more interested in protecting their supply of cheap black labor. For the reasons they articulated, many wealthy and powerful white southerners and the political leaders who represented them turned their backs on rural segregation.

Because black workers were essential to the economic position of wealthy whites, many wealthy landholders and merchants opposed Poe's plan. Landlords and merchants held the reins of power in Poe's society, and because Poe's rural segregation plan was unpopular with them, it would not become law. Southern elites were hardly less racist than Poe and his supporters, but they had no economic incentive to remove African Americans from their communities.

In March 1915, rural segregation went up for a vote in the North Carolina Senate. According to the *News and Observer*, the amendment had "received a favorable committee report on the part of the Senate and was placed as a matter of special order for a night session of the Senate."[43] The measure was debated for an hour, with the senators showing no desire "to discuss any measure at length, nor to enter into a spirited fight," according to the *News and Observer*. "With a lengthy session of the morning, followed by a solid two hours of routine in the afternoon, and with the same prospect before that body today, the members felt inclined to go easy." Senator Majette introduced the proposed amendment by pointing out that black farmers were increasing in number and in farm ownership faster than white farmers and by claiming that the amendment would benefit white farmers without harming black farmers. Majette made the case for the amendment in language influenced by Poe: "There is no white man, no matter how much intelligence he may have, no matter how poor he may be, who can live pleasantly or in an atmosphere of growth and progress with a [black] neighbor on one side of him and perhaps another one on the other side." One supporter of the amendment, Senator Snow, told the group that his constituents supported the measure and that he thought the people should be able to vote on it.[44]

Majette's argument was not enough to convince a majority of the senators present to vote for rural segregation. Using a roll-call vote, seventeen state senators voted against the amendment and fifteen voted in favor. A number of senators were not present for the vote, suggesting, perhaps, that they viewed the measure as controversial and did not want to anger middling white supporters of the amendment or elite opponents of it. However, for about half of the senators present to approve the amendment shows that Poe's plan received real consideration. Jack Temple Kirby claimed that "politicians with well-earned reputations as white supremacists thought [Poe's plan] bizarre," yet many state senators found the idea reasonable enough to vote for it.[45] As Poe pointed out, the amendment "received a clear majority of all the Democratic Senators voting" (some of those who voted against it were not Democrats) and that "from all that half of the state east of Greensboro where the people really know conditions, only four votes were cast against it."[46]

The amendment's opponents did not block rural segregation for economic self-interest alone. The biographies of the state senators who voted against the rural segregation amendment reveal a few different motivations for opposing rural segregation. State Senator Joseph Bivens Efird was a textile executive who ran the Efird Manufacturing Company in Albemarle, in central North Carolina, as well as other mills, and was director of two banks. A member of the state's elite, he would have had little interest in a policy that might have angered his peers. Charles Andrew Jonas, a Republican from Lincoln County in the western part of the state, was a founder and editor of the *Lincoln Times* and postmaster of Lincolnton; he served in the state's senate and house of representatives for a number of years and later represented North Carolina in Congress for one term. Jonas's constituents would not have been interested in rural segregation; Republicans sought to protect the rights of African Americans, and few enough African Americans lived in the western part of the state that they were not seen as the source of white men's problems there.[47] Jonas condemned the amendment in the senate debate: "I cannot sit here silent when such legislation is proposed. The great state of North Carolina and the people of North Carolina cannot afford to deprive a lower race of its rights. This is a blow at an already downtrodden people and a measure of even doubtful benefit to the white race."[48]

State Senator Frank Nash, a lawyer and writer who lived in Hillsborough, depicted the amendment as antithetical to the U.S. Constitution during the senate debate:

> I do not recall since the Legislature of 1868, perhaps, that there has ever been a measure proposed on the floor of this body so antagonistic to democracy, property rights, and the constitution. There is always an obligation resting upon the superior race to the inferior race, and if we do claim to be the superior race, that very claim imposes upon us certain duties, the very first and most fundamental of which is absolute justice.

Nash pointed out that the segregation of the countryside could never be "voluntary," since African Americans could not vote.[49] The *Winston-Salem Journal* mentioned another senator who presented the matter similarly when it was considered as a project for a rural-life commission (which the state senate blocked) in 1913: "Senator Ward raised the issue that there could be no segregation of the races in this country, so far as land owning is concerned, under the Federal constitution."[50]

The *Greensboro Daily News*, too, even while it printed an argument in favor of segregation for the countryside by H. Q. Alexander, printed next to this article the doubts of its editor. While claiming to be "as yet neither for segregation nor against it" and that particular elements of the idea "appeal to us," the editor pointed to the Fourteenth Amendment as posing a real challenge to the idea. This amendment did not cripple residential segregation ordinances in cities, as these are "a police regulation, designed to protect the persons of the citizens of the community," but residential segregation for the countryside would use a different type of law. "You can deprive a man more easily of his liberty [as in the ordinances] than his property," the editor observed, claiming that the ordinances generally affected where people could live—not whether they could own property.[51]

African Americans—who had no elected representatives in the state senate, as the vast majority of them had been disfranchised—opposed the amendment because they believed they had little to gain from it and everything to lose, including land they had worked hard to purchase. The NAACP kept African Americans all around the country apprised of the progress of the amendment. *The Crisis* reported on what it called "land segregation," informing readers of Poe's ideas and the response to these ideas in the South—reprinting, for example, the North Carolina Farmers' Union's endorsement of the idea.[52]

A public conference that was part of the NAACP's annual meeting took as its topic Poe's rural segregation campaign. An article about the conference described a speech given by W. E. B. Du Bois that painted rural segregation as part of the decades-long project of stripping African Americans of their rights. First they had lost political rights, then were trained for "'work, particularly farm work'" rather than the professions. As blacks "submitted" to these losses, they became subject to "complete social discrimination," and their schools were "neglected." When against all odds some African Americans did well and purchased farms, whites viewed their success as a problem rather than "as the working out of the solution suggested a quarter of a century ago."[53] (That "solution" was the deal brokered in 1895 by Booker T. Washington, who had urged white southerners to offer work opportunity to "these people who have, without strikes and labour wars, tilled your fields, cleared your forests, builded your railroads and cities, and brought forth treasures from the bowels of the earth" and had promised in return to set aside the demand for political and social rights.)[54] According to the article, Du Bois linked accommodation to Jim Crow, black economic success, and the rise of the rural segregation idea: "So long as the Negro accepted education as training to work for the white man there was no trouble, [Du Bois] said, but when he began to work for himself, objections at once suggested themselves. The result is the proposition of Clarence Poe." Du Bois drew a parallel between the plight of African Americans and that of Native Americans, who had been segregated from whites with resulting "degradation and failure"; for Du Bois, nothing beneficial could come from such a plan.[55]

Du Bois published his perspective on Poe's plan in the NAACP's *Fourth Annual Report*.

Has this [the success of black farmers] caused any rejoicing in North Carolina? I regret to say it has not. On the contrary, it has led to widespread proposal for the most vital attack on the economic rights of the Negro ever put forward in the United States. Let no one misconceive the significance of this. The Negro was asked to give up his political rights for the sake of advance. He finds that with the giving up of his political rights his educational rights are curtailed, the right to work is increased but inadequately, his right to hold property in cities is being questioned, and now, finally, there is a movement in the South to curtail his right to own agricultural land. This movement has not started with an ignorant agitator of the Blease and Vardaman and Tillman type. Its sponsor is Clarence Poe, editor of the Progressive Farmer, and a man representing in many ways the best traditions of the South.[56]

Du Bois focused not on the denial of social rights but on "economic rights"—the right to property. He considered this economic challenge deeply dangerous—indeed, "the most vital attack on the economic rights of the Negro ever put forward in the United States." He rooted this challenge in the white middle class, where it was led not by a demagogue but by "a man representing in many ways the best traditions of the South."

Booker T. Washington also opposed rural segregation, criticizing it privately to Gilbert Stephenson and helping Stephenson shape his argument against rural segregation in his 1914 article "The Segregation of the White and Negro Races in Rural Communities of North Carolina." While Washington disliked the policy, he did not think it would be enacted and said nothing publicly about it. Washington came under attack by NAACP leaders for not taking a stand against rural segregation. Oswald Garrison Villard, one of the founders of the NAACP, wrote in a letter sent to Washington's friend Robert R. Moton (who was then commandant of military discipline at the Hampton Institute but would become Tuskegee's second president after Washington's death in 1915) and Roger Baldwin (the nephew of one of Washington's advisers) that

One right after another is being taken away from the colored people, one injustice after another being perpetrated, and Booker Washington is silent. There has developed in North Carolina the greatest menace yet, a movement under the leadership of Clarence Poe, which will undoubtedly result in legislation, segregating the Negro on the farm lands, thus giving the lie to Washington's advice to his people that if they will only be good and buy land they will be let alone and will flourish.

Villard described Washington's silence as "pitiful beyond words" and noted that "His name is getting to be anathema among the educated colored people in the country, and he is drifting further and further in the rear as a real leader."[57] Washington responded by writing to Robert Moton dismissively of Poe:

> During the last four or five months I have been through practically every Southern state, and I have yet to find any persons, white or black, who take Mr. Clarence Poe's suggestion to segregate the race on the farm seriously. It is generally understood by people who have given the matter any attention at all that Mr. Poe is simply emphasizing this idea for the purpose of advertising his paper. The whole idea is so utterly impracticable and preposterous that I cannot see how people can grow excited over it.[58]

Washington argued that Poe offered "a generous sum to people who would write letters on the subject of segregation" to be published in the *Progressive Farmer* and that "he could find very few people who would even write on the subject" (a claim belied by the pages of letters that Poe printed). "Until I can be convinced that there is a serious intention or effort in the direction of farm segregation, I must refuse to take the matter seriously," Washington concluded.[59] He made similar comments about Poe a month earlier to James Edward McCulloch, a sociologist and general secretary of the Southern Sociological Congress, and asked that the Southern Sociological Congress ignore Poe at its meeting: "I very much fear the more attention the Congress gives to that subject the more it will be dignified and thus please those who are advocating what, in my opinion is a silly policy."[60] (Poe would attend the Congress and deliver a speech on rural segregation there.)[61] Two months after this letter, however, aware of the criticism directed at him, Washington had begun to take Poe more seriously, writing again to

McCulloch: "The main point . . . in writing you is to call your attention to a signed editorial by Mr. Clarence Poe in the Progressive Farmer under date of May 30. It seems to me this editorial indicates very clearly that the time has come when we cannot attempt to please all parties; we have got to take a position and stand by that position."[62]

A few months later, *The Crisis* reprinted a number of damning articles from the *Columbian Herald* (Louisville), the *Cleveland Gazette*, and the *Louisville News* about Washington's silence on residential segregation, inspired by the address to the Negro Business League in which Washington advised African Americans to, as the *Herald* explained it, "cease fighting segregation laws and to devote themselves to acquiring wealth and intelligence." The *Herald* condemned Washington's advice to the Negro Business League, arguing: "It is this obsequious doctrine that has resulted in growing up a generation of moral cowards among the Negroes of this country."[63]

The *Cleveland Gazette* presented Washington as a toady:

The prejudiced South and its northern sympathizers will "pat Dr. Washington on the back," continue to make his trips for his school, throughout the country, profitable, and to try to make our people accept him as our national leader, just as long as he continues to preach his infamous "doctrine of surrender" and endeavor to make us "ground arms" in the effort to enforce our rights, under the law.

The *Gazette* expressed frustration that a man as powerful as Washington would do so little for African Americans, when black people with fewer resources were doing more: "It is little less than an outrage for him to give that advice to the League, and make such a talk as that at Philadelphia, with our people in Louisville, KY., and several other points in the South, and the North, too, fighting desperately against segregation and kindred evils."[64]

The *Louisville News*, William Warley's publication, also condemned Washington.

Segregation has many champions even among our race, but almost without exception they are to be found among the element where there

is the least intelligence and where there is an inherent fear of opposing anything the white man chooses to do. But here [in Washington's
comments to the Negro Business League] we are smitten from an
unexpected quarter; a recognized leader of his race, an educator, tells
us to forget our manhood; to forget the sacred and inalienable rights
of political and personal liberty and to passively submit to the humil-
iation of being pushed aside as though we are a race of lepers, because
we would seek cleaner and healthier neighborhoods in which to live.[65]

The black supporters of segregation referenced by the *Louisville News*
were likely supporters of self-segregation rather than government-mandated
segregation. To Washington (who is famous for offering white southerners
a deal in which "in all things that are purely social we can be as separate as
the fingers")[66] and his African American critics, African American self-
segregation differed from segregation as required by law, and many black
people who supported self-segregation opposed segregation by law.[67] Republican George Henry White, for example, who fought against Jim Crow
during his time in Congress, after leaving the public sector became one of
the principal investors in Whitesboro, a two-thousand-acre colony in southern New Jersey purchased in 1901 and named after him in 1902. White and
the other investors envisioned Whitesboro—inspired at least in part by
Booker T. Washington's philosophy—providing African Americans a place
where they could prosper free of the interference of white people; it sold
black buyers lots of about one-sixth of an acre for a minimum of $50, which
they could pay off after a $5 down payment over a ten-year period. At the
same time that he was developing Whitesboro, White was also doing legal
work on a set of cases meant to test the constitutionality of disfranchisement in Alabama and Louisiana.[68]

Mary Rolinson's study of African American support for Marcus Garvey's
Universal Negro Improvement Association (UNIA) shows broad and deep
support for black nationalism and separatism across the South in the 1920s.
In North Carolina (unlike in other states, where much UNIA support was
rural), support for the UNIA was highest in tobacco-processing cities
like Winston-Salem, where a UNIA chapter was founded in 1921. Here and
elsewhere in the South, the UNIA appealed most to propertyless African

Americans living in mostly black communities—often tenant farmers and factory workers. Rolinson roots African American support for separatism in the desire of black men to protect their women from sexual exploitation at the hands of white men, which black women who worked in white men's fields or homes were particularly susceptible to.[69] (Robert Black, a worker at the R. J. Reynolds Company, described such exploitation at the company, where white foremen would "pat on [good-looking women]. . . . And I've seen those foremen do this: would take one of those good-looking Negro women out to his desk and maybe hold her out there for an hour.")[70]

Rolinson argues that Booker T. Washington's ideas about black economic self-sufficiency and social separation, which Garvey greatly admired, laid the groundwork for Garveyism (the black nationalist program associated with Garvey) to become popular in the rural South. And, of course, Washington was not the only African American proponent of separatism whose ideas black southerners would have heard. During slavery, many black southerners followed the colonization movement, and from the moment they gained their freedom, many viewed the situation as did Garrison Frazier, a former slave and minister from North Carolina, who told Secretary of War Edwin Stanton and Major-General William Tecumseh Sherman, "I would prefer to live by ourselves, for there is a prejudice against us in the South that will take years to get over."[71] Garveyism was even compatible with some of the ideas of white supremacists regarding the separation of black and white people; Garvey met with men like Atlanta's Edward Young Clarke, an imperial wizard of the Knights of the Ku Klux Klan, to discuss common ground (separatism and opposition to interracial sex) and possibly a donation to Garvey's shipping corporation, the Black Star Line, which was supposed to enable trade between nations with African-descended populations and ultimately bring African Americans to live in Africa. Even as Garvey expressed shared interests with white supremacists like Clarke, many black southerners continued to embrace his philosophy.[72]

Garvey would not speak in the South until 1917, however, and he did not reach the height of his popularity until the early 1920s. Black southerners in the years before Garveyism's arrival liked the idea of separate communities where black folk could govern themselves and where they would be free from the exploitation of whites. Even if the idea of self-segregation did appeal to them, a number of black leaders publicly criticized Poe's campaign, which they perceived as having the potential to cripple the gains African Americans had made in acquiring property. Those who spoke out against the campaign may not have cared about creating an integrated countryside, but they also did not want a decline in opportunity for black southerners.

An article in the *Washington Bee*, an African American newspaper, presented rural segregation as limiting economic opportunity for black farmers and described Poe's plan as an "evil consequenc[e]" of "Senator Tillman's reply to Colonel Roosevelt's 'open door of hope and opportunity' in which he cautioned the Colonel to remember that every such door open to a colored man was a door closed to a white one."[73] Here we see a perception of rural segregation as stifling opportunity for African Americans because white people viewed opportunity as a zero-sum game.

Charles Hillman Brough, a white professor of economics and sociology at the University of Arkansas, chairman of the University Commission on the Southern Race Questions, and governor of Arkansas from 1917 to 1921, agreed that rural segregation would mean less opportunity for African Americans in a report covered in the *New York Times* and the *Daily Arkansas Gazette*. Rural segregation was worse than other forms of segregation because it limited the economic opportunity of blacks in a way that other forms of segregation did not, according to Brough:

> Segregation in the departments of public service, railway and street cars, and even in cities, may be exceedingly just, but the idea of farm segregation, as proposed by Clarence Poe, editor of The Progressive Farmer, in my humble opinion, proposed as a means of giving the white man a better chance in agricultural and industrial competition with the negro, seems a travesty upon Anglo-Saxon superiority and an injustice to the negro.

Brough believed that rather than improving the situation of poor whites, rural segregation made things worse for them by crippling the region's African Americans, whose economic and moral degradation would rub off on white people.[74] Brough also believed the intimacy that he perceived as common between black and white people in the past had been replaced with the "social isolation of the negro," and he considered this dangerous. Far better would be for white people to influence their black neighbors, offering them a moral and intellectual example.[75]

Critics also viewed Poe's campaign as hateful. T. S. Inborden, an African American, complained in a letter to the editor of the *Progressive Farmer* of the "resentment" he felt because of this. Inborden had been a faithful reader of the *Progressive Farmer* who appreciated the journal's "sanity on agricultural and home matters." But, as he saw it, recently the journal had been "stirring up of race prejudice and animosity." Poe responded in an editorial note that his goal was to "lessen, not increase" animosity between white and black people. The idea was that separating whites and blacks would remove any potential for conflict.[76]

Regardless of how he wished to present his plan, however, Poe was perceived as promoting a policy that hurt black farmers by limiting their options. His stance against black landholders put Poe at odds with Booker T. Washington, who worked to create economic opportunity for African Americans (even as he was criticized for failing to stand up to segregation). Poe's vision clashed with that of Washington because—in spite of his words to the contrary—he did not see a way of building a "great rural civilization" for whites that respected the rights and prospects of African Americans. His supporters—middling whites—had little invested in the idea of paternalism, and they would not have appreciated efforts that actually might have helped black farmers.[77]

Local black leaders were able to criticize the rural segregation amendment because they did not depend on money from white benefactors, as Simon Atkins did, or because the white benefactors upon whom they depended did not support the amendment. James B. Dudley, president of the Agricultural and Mechanical College for the Colored Race in Greensboro (now North Carolina A&T State University), for example, published an article arguing that rural segregation was unfair. Because African Americans were disenfranchised and had "no representative at the seat of power," such legislation would result in inferior options for black people and in "flagrant, open breaches of justice," with no one heeding blacks' "faint plea for fair play." This, along with other Jim Crow legislation—"the disfranchisement of the race, the separate car laws, now . . . a law to hamper the

Negro in the purchase of property"—would "disturb industrious Negroes all over the State" and inspire them to leave, much to the detriment of the state. Dudley pointed out, too—critiquing one of the arguments white people made for rural segregation—that it offered no protection to white women.[78] "This legislation strikes not at the Negro criminal, but at the industrious Negro farmer who is just as ready and willing now to protect the white women of his neighborhood as his fathers did in the days of the civil war, when the masters left their wives and daughters in the charge of these slaves, who . . . were never known to violate their trust."[79]

Charles Henry Moore, one of the first African American graduates of Amherst College and an educator who helped found the Agricultural and Mechanical College, expressed his objections to Poe's plan in a letter to the Raleigh *News and Observer* in 1913. He pointed out that white people generally advised African Americans to focus on working hard and pursuing opportunities, such as purchasing land. He viewed the "agitating [on] the question of race segregation in the rural districts and in the towns and cities of North Carolina" as a turn toward limiting the opportunities available to African Americans. He hoped that "our real white friends in this State will always be vigilant that, the door of Hope and Opportunity shall always be kept open to the intelligent and thrifty colored citizen, not only for his own encouragement, but for the best economic interest of the commonwealth" (economic interests that benefited elites, not small white farmers). Poe took on Moore in his own letter, published on the first page of the *News and Observer*, arguing that Moore misrepresented his plan by suggesting that black landowners would be forced to move. Present land rights would be respected, but in the future, if communities voted for it, land would be sold only to members of one race. Poe ignored Moore's suggestion that his plan would diminish the opportunities available to blacks, even while implying that his plan would empower poor whites rather than blacks or wealthy whites: "if this matter can be constitutionally settled, by law by leaving [the law's] application to voters (which means in white hands) it will be better than if left to private agreement."[80]

Poe faced a lot of criticism of his idea of segregating the countryside, certainly more than proponents of residential segregation ordinances faced. Some critics viewed rural segregation as more unfair than residential segregation ordinances in cities—perhaps because land ownership was the only route to success in the countryside, as it was the only way to break free of the credit system. Urban dwellers could find economic success through their jobs as well as through the appreciation of their property. Or perhaps critics felt freer to speak against rural segregation because it was not tied to one particular place where residents had come together to demand residential segregation.

Rural segregation, a carefully thought-out and Progressive "reform," had roots in international efforts to protect the ascendancy of white men. Poe meant for this program to provide economic opportunity for small white farmers, a group he perceived as essential to the nation's future. As Poe conceived of rural segregation, it offered not just any economic opportunity to these farmers but the opportunity to meet their agrarian goals: to own and operate their own small farms, surrounded by others who were like them, others with whom they might work cooperatively without risk to their women. Rural segregation appealed to these farmers as a reform that seemed to be in their control. It seemed like something that could be achieved, as it was in keeping with objectives Democratic leaders purported to work toward (especially the protection of white women in rural areas). But, as much as the prices their crops brought in or the accumulation of debt as they spent season after season in pursuit of a payout from cash crops, attaining rural segregation was not in the control of small white farmers. Their lack of political power meant that rural segregation lay beyond their reach. An article from the *Independent* (a white newspaper published in Elizabeth City, in northeastern North Carolina), reprinted in the *Washington Bee*, explained why. The problem was that elites—not middling whites—held the reins of power.

> If the Negro's standard of living is low, so much lower than that of the white man, then who made it low?
>
> If the standard of living of the white tenant class in the South is higher than it should be, then who made it so high?
>
> When the foregoing questions have been answered we can discuss Dr. Poe's segregation scheme somewhat intelligently. . . . The answer

to both questions is found in the land-owning aristocracy of the South. This land-owning aristocracy has forced the lowest standard of living upon the Negro and attempted to keep him in subjection by starvation wages. On the other hand it has ever encouraged the white tenant class in the South to live beyond its means that it might hold this white tenant class in subjection by keeping it overloaded with debt. This landowning class is as much the enemy of the poor white as it is the enemy of the black. . . . The Negro has lived upon scraps and saved his money while the white tenant has gone to his landlord's store and run himself into debt and bad health by paying exorbitant prices for adulterated food-stuffs.[81]

According to the article, white elites, not African Americans, were the greatest threat to small white farmers. Elites consciously tried to keep wages low by "forc[ing] the lowest standard of living upon the Negro" at the same time that they sought to control small whites through debt. This article shows the perspective of at least some of the *Independent*'s readers and, likely, other middling whites in the state: they understood that nonelite and elite whites did not have shared interests and that elites in fact actively worked against the interests of nonelite whites. It is hard to say how widespread this viewpoint was. In any case, even while some small white farmers viewed elite whites as their greatest adversary, African Americans were the group upon which their class focused its ire, as middling whites stood a chance of winning when they fought the people furthest down.

Conclusion

Planning for Residential Segregation After *Buchanan*

Clarence Poe did not drop his interest in separate residential areas for black and white people after the failure of his segregation amendment or even after *Buchanan*. He may not have been able to bring segregation to the North Carolina countryside, but he did work to create a more segregated Raleigh in two ways. In the 1920s he served on the Raleigh school board, which chose to construct the city's new white high school in the well-to-do northwest, a neighborhood that excluded African Americans, and placed the black high school in downtown Raleigh rather than near emerging black suburbs. In doing so, the board fortified residential segregation, as black and white residents of the city looked to live near the schools that their children would attend.[1] Starting in 1938, Poe also developed much of his property in east Raleigh into Longview Gardens, a subdivision that excluded African Americans for years through restrictive covenants.

Undeterred by the lack of a legal scaffold, segregationists tried other means of separating the residences of black and white people in North Carolina, including a 1930 zoning ordinance in Winston-Salem and, starting in the 1950s, urban renewal projects that razed residences in East Winston, replacing them with highways and city government buildings. They faced setbacks along the way. The state supreme court ruled the Winston-Salem zoning ordinance unconstitutional, for example, and the restrictive covenants in Poe's Longview Gardens expired in 1965—though this expiration was meaningless: the Supreme Court had declared in 1948 in *Shelley v. Kraemer* that government would not enforce these private covenants.[2]

Even as local segregationists had trouble enacting segregationist programs, the federal government strengthened segregation through the Home Owners Loan Corporation (HOLC). A program designed to protect property values in elite neighborhoods, HOLC hurt the prospects of poor and middling whites and of African Americans of all classes who wished to buy homes—demonstrating yet again that the privileges of whiteness were not distributed evenly among white people.

SEGREGATING WINSTON-SALEM AFTER *DARNELL*

During World War I, Winston-Salem's black population continued to increase dramatically (growing 128 percent between 1910 and 1920, compared to 103 percent for the white population), straining the city's housing. This strain, along with the return of African American men from war, "rash and full of fire," expecting to be treated as equals, increased tension between the city's white and black residents.[3] This tension played no small role in bringing about a race riot in November 1918, which, along with a perception of black residents of the city contributing vice and immorality, fostered interest among many whites in segregated neighborhoods.

The spark for the riot came just a few days after World War I ended, when a white husband and wife, Jim and Cora Childress, claimed that a black man had shot Jim and sexually assaulted Cora along the road between their home in the mill village of Inverness and a nearby store. After word got out that a man being held in the Winston-Salem city jail might be the perpetrator (he was actually not, as he had been charged with something else), a mob of over two thousand formed to take this man from the jail, shouting, "We are the Inverness Mill crowd, and we've come after that nigger." Ordered to disperse and set upon with fire hoses, the mob began to shoot, killing Robert Young, a fireman who was directing a hose on them, and Rachel Levi, a white girl peering out a window, in addition to, according to one estimate, two other white and twenty black residents of the city.[4] One scholar viewed the mob as perhaps still angry about "the earlier housing segregation controversy," rioting to assert themselves.[5] Blacks mobilized to block the white mob's access to the jail and shoot back at the white gangs that roamed the city once the mob had been broken up. (It is not clear if they killed anyone.) Military support from nearby cities arrived to help bring an end to the riot, and soldiers remained in the city for about a week to check African Americans for guns and enforce a night-time curfew.[6]

White leaders in Winston-Salem wished to depict the riot as minor in order to dampen tension between the city's black and white residents and to maintain the city's reputation as a good place to do business. Black leaders felt the same way, and they also wanted to ensure that funding of their institutions from white sources would continue unabated.[7] The public response of African Americans to the riot shows how little had changed since Simon Atkins kept quiet about the segregation ordinance. A group of black leaders in the city that included Charles H. Jones and J. S. Hill published an article in one of the local white newspapers, the *Winston-Salem Journal*, arguing that they wished "to correct the impression that seems to have gone abroad that there is bad feeling between the races in Winston-Salem, and out of which feeling there was developed a race riot." In fact, the leaders claimed, "Winston-Salem has had no race riot." Complimenting the "best white people of Winston-Salem" for their "manly stand. . . . taken for the establishment and maintenance of law and order," they claimed that "nowhere in North Carolina is there a better race feeling than we have in Winston-Salem." Indeed, the city's white leadership were committed to "see that justice is meted out to all [the city's] people regardless of race or condition," and for this the city's "best colored people" wished to show their "profound gratitude and appreciation."[8]

Meanwhile, nervous white residents of the city kept an eye on East Winston, which they viewed as vice-ridden. Both white and black residents of this area sold cocaine and alcohol and engaged in gambling, particularly on Vine Street, which was often referred to in the press as "Cocaine Alley." A newspaper report in early 1919 described a "gambling event" that took place at the "cottage" of Amelia Smith at 408 Vine Street: "According to the testimony of chastened and repentant eye-witnesses, more than two thousand dollars adorned the table during the evening's operations." Among the evening's players were a man named Hunter Larkins, who claimed to have lost $300, and Arthur Gray, who gambled away $117. Police who arrived at the scene saw "a mad scramble for stakes, cash vanishing so swiftly that not even a bronze image of Honest Abe was left as evidence."[9]

A number of articles also reported cocaine hidden in people's homes. For example, police found seven ounces of cocaine hidden in a doorstop at the home of "Paul and Georgie Jolly, negro man and wife who reside in the notorious black section on Vine street, known as Cocaine Alley," according to one article. Police found the stash when "Policeman Thompson, wishing to go through a door leading from one room to another, reached down to remove a block of wood about two feet long which was obstructing his passage. Upon removing the block from the floor, a peculiar rattling sound was heard, and this, combined with the lightness of the block, aroused the suspicions of the officers." The police were pleased to find the stash, as they hoped it would lead them to information about the source of the "large quantity of the dope for sale in the negro sections of the city."[10] Apparently the Jollys were not the only people in the neighborhood hiding their illegal stores. "Lula Wright, fat and colored," had "whiskey in small quantities in almost every nook and corner of [her] home. There was whiskey between the mattresses, whiskey in the side board, whiskey in the dog house, etc., and so on. When it was all totaled up, there was about one gallon and one pint of the stuff."[11]

Perhaps the most notorious law breaker in East Winston, covered with great interest by the press, was Cora Smart, a divorced African American woman who quite frequently showed up in the local newspapers between around 1916 and 1925 for selling whiskey and cocaine out of a "dive operated on Vine street by 'the Wattie Greer gang'" and for vagrancy.[12] A colorful character, girlfriend of Wattie Greer, she enjoyed racing Greer's car through the neighborhood. Witnesses described her behind the wheel as "burn[ing] the wind. . . . whizzing by . . . at a rate of speed [varying] from forty to fifty miles per hour."[13] Tired of seeing Cora back in court day after day, in December 1921, a judge ordered her to leave the state. She reappears in the records in 1924 for her usual crimes.[14] By 1926, she was living in Greensboro, where she was again arrested for selling narcotics. A Greensboro reporter noted that she "had no trouble in making bond and was wearing a fur coat and seemed to be prosperous." He thought her to be about twenty-four years of age, which means that she would have begun her criminal activities in Winston-Salem as a teenager.[15] Cora's boyfriend, Wattie, meanwhile, appeared in the papers for assault with a deadly weapon, gambling, and selling cocaine and alcohol.[16]

Some of the vice in Winston-Salem grew out of what Gilbert Stephenson described as the city's "bad housing conditions": "let four or five grown men and women, little or no kin to one another, live together in a two-room cottage, and you are going to have impurity." What Stephenson described as "cottages" we would describe today as shacks. Few of these shacks had running water or toilets, even in the 1940s; according to one source, "one block of tenements with 32 families had one cold-water spigot and three toilets, two of which were stopped up." Figures 6.1 and 6.2 show East Winston slums in the 1950s.[17]

Many of the people who saw the slums and read about the activities going on in them feared a spreading moral contagion brought about by what they viewed as a lack of morality among African Americans. They blamed black people for their living conditions and extralegal sources of revenue—rather than blaming the companies that underpaid black workers. Fearful of riots and anxious about black criminality, appalled by living conditions in East Winston-Salem, white leaders began to work once more on an ordinance that would if not keep the city's white and black populations separate at least stop the expansion of black neighborhoods.

On December 12, 1930, Winston-Salem's Board of Aldermen adopted an ordinance dividing the city into different residential and industrial zones. The ordinance regulated everything from the uses and heights of buildings and the size of yards to where black and white people could live in the city. Using language similar to what had been used in 1912, city leaders claimed the need to "preserve and promote proper relationships between the two races . . . in order to promote public morals and the public welfare." The ordinance also purported to "protect and preserve valuable property rights in the area known as East Winston," including the City Memorial Hospital ("built at a cost of approximately $500,000"), which served white patients, the Union Railroad Station ("erected at a cost of approximately $883,000"), and a number of other institutions—including churches and

FIGURE 6.1 An east Winston slum in 1956.
Source: Courtesy of the Forsyth County Public Library Photograph Collection.

schools—designated for white people. The value of all of the white-serving institutions in this part of the city zoned for white people was $4,147,000, according to the city; the value of residences owned by white people in this area was $2,000,000.[18] City leaders feared that as black neighborhoods expanded, there would not be a large enough white population to make use of the hospital, railroad station, and other institutions in this part of the city.

Section 10 of the ordinance said that "In 'A-1', 'B-1' and 'C-1' Residence Districts, no building or part thereof shall be occupied or used by a person or persons of the negro race" (though it did provide an exception for "a negro

FIGURE 6.2   An east Winston slum in 1956.
Source: Courtesy of the Forsyth County Public Library Photograph Collection.

servant, chauffeur or other employee"). White people were prohibited from residing in Residence Districts A-2, B-2, and C-2. The ordinance, which brought new complexity to people's living arrangements, would soon be challenged in court.

A number of African Americans lived in a section that the ordinance reserved for white people on Greenwood Avenue in East Winston-Salem, and they continued to do so after the ordinance was adopted, with no action taken against them by the city. Mr. and Mrs. J. V. Little and Mrs. I. T. Stack owned houses on this section of Greenwood Avenue but chose not to live there, as they did not wish to live near African Americans. The Littles sold their home to Mr. W. A. Kelly Jr., a black man, and Mrs. Stack rented hers to black people and lived in a different part of the city, paying for her rent with the income from her Greenwood Avenue property. When "the Zoning Commission and Board of Aldermen attempted to amend the said Zoning Ordinance by moving the occupancy dividing line," owners on Greenwood Avenue sued, arguing that the ordinance, if enforced, "will amount to confiscation of their property . . . without due process of law."[19]

A number of white owners in this area had tried to rent their property to white people, the plaintiffs argued, "but were unable to rent, or were forced to rent for such a small amount of rental that it practically amounted to a confiscation of their property," so ended up renting to African Americans "who pay their rent promptly and give to the said persons a fair and adequate return on their investment." If the ordinance were enforced, these owners argued, they would lose income. Stack, who relied on that income to cover her rent in an area "where her neighbors are persons with whom she can associate," might be forced by these circumstances to move back into her property on Greenwood Avenue. Meanwhile, the Littles, who were still owed "a considerable balance" on the home they had sold to Kelly, feared that "they will be forced to take the property for the debt, and unable to rent the same," and Kelly was concerned that "the said ordinance, if enforced as threatened, will prevent his occupying property which he has purchased, and deprive him of his property without compensation, and without due process of law."[20]

Stack, the Littles, Kelly, and several other neighbors argued that the ordinance was unconstitutional. They won a temporary restraining order to halt enforcement while the court considered their case. Judge Felix E. Alley of the Superior Court of Forsyth County admitted that it would be difficult to rent the properties to "desirable white tenants," as "having been once occupied by negroes, it is very doubtful if they could be rented to white persons even though renovated." Yet he considered the ordinance "reasonable" and "valid."[21] The plaintiffs then appealed to the North Carolina Supreme Court.

In the appellants' brief, lawyers for the city admitted that the ordinance would be unconstitutional if its only purpose were segregating the residences of white and black people in the city. But a zoning ordinance was different from a segregation ordinance, they argued. Indeed, "Municipal zoning [was] a valid exercise of the police power," and "the use and occupancy of property for residence purposes [was just] one feature of a general plan for a city's growth and development."[22] The plaintiffs disagreed, pointing to the rulings in *Darnell* and *Buchanan v. Warley*. They noted, too, that Kelly was "in the incidental position of the plaintiff in error" in *Buchanan*— unable to occupy property that he owned—and that the U.S. Supreme Court had ruled in his favor.[23] The North Carolina Supreme Court agreed with the plaintiffs, arguing that

> the question for decision is whether reciprocal inhibitions of occu-pancy of residential districts by members of the white and Negro races, fairly apportioned, but admittedly invalid if they stood alone, may be inserted in a general zoning ordinance. . . . We think not. The law will not permit the indirect accomplishment of that which it directly forbids.[24]

The *Clinard* case offers glimpses into the shadows of some of the costs of segregation—glimpses into the cost of not just residential segregation but also the segregation of public institutions. It offers glimpses of money (some of it coming from middle-class taxpayers) spent building and maintaining separate hospitals, churches, and schools in Winston-Salem. It raises the question of how much value would have been lost to these segregated insti-tutions if the population they served lived in a different part of the city and no longer used these institutions. It also raises the question of how much rental income and property value would be lost to white and black families with markets for their properties limited to one group—especially when members of that group were unwilling to pay much for property they con-sidered too close to the other group.

Clinard also demonstrates the importance of the earlier cases. *State v. Darnell* and *Buchanan v. Warley* set precedents that segregationists could not easily slip past. They could not use the excuse of zoning to keep black people limited to certain areas. A New Deal program did provide them another method, though: declaring certain neighborhoods too risky for mortgages would strengthen segregation in the city.

The Home Owners Loan Corporation (HOLC), enacted during Frank-lin Roosevelt's first hundred days, provided loans for homeowners during the Great Depression. HOLC employed hundreds of workers to appraise neighborhoods; it then gave out loans based on its assessment of credit risk.

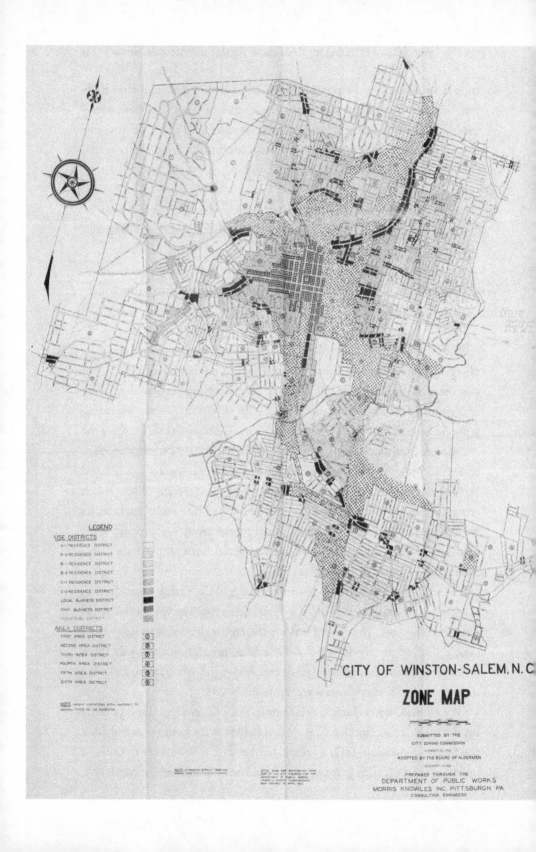

LEGEND

USE DISTRICTS
A-1 RESIDENCE DISTRICT
A-2 RESIDENCE DISTRICT
B-1 RESIDENCE DISTRICT
B-2 RESIDENCE DISTRICT
C-1 RESIDENCE DISTRICT
C-2 RESIDENCE DISTRICT
LOCAL BUSINESS DISTRICT
MAIN BUSINESS DISTRICT
INDUSTRIAL DISTRICT

AREA DISTRICTS
FIRST AREA DISTRICT
SECOND AREA DISTRICT
THIRD AREA DISTRICT
FOURTH AREA DISTRICT
FIFTH AREA DISTRICT
SIXTH AREA DISTRICT

NOTE HEIGHT LIMITATIONS APPLY UNIFORMLY TO
VARIOUS TYPES OR USE DISTRICTS.

CITY OF WINSTON-SALEM, N.C.

ZONE MAP

SUBMITTED BY THE
CITY ZONING COMMISSION

ADOPTED BY THE BOARD OF ALDERMEN

PREPARED THROUGH THE
DEPARTMENT OF PUBLIC WORKS
MORRIS KNOWLES INC. PITTSBURGH PA
CONSULTING ENGINEERS

While the agency helped many white homeowners by providing refinancing and brought millions of dollars into the coffers of the U.S. Treasury, HOLC also did something pernicious: it assessed neighborhoods occupied by African Americans as "declining" and "hazardous" (whatever the economic circumstances of the African American inhabitants), making it much harder for people in these neighborhoods to qualify for loans.[25]

HOLC maps of Winston-Salem show which neighborhoods were "redlined"—that is, which neighborhoods were given the least desirable designations. Most of the "Definitely Declining" (C) and "Hazardous" (D) neighborhoods lay on the east side of the city. The only "Best" (A) neighborhood and most of the "Still Desirable" (B) neighborhoods lay to the west. The "Area Description" of the A neighborhood notes that this neighborhood enjoys "all city conveniences—Uniform construction—Highly restricted." Its inhabitants, who lived in "large & Medium Singles [single homes]," were "capitalists" with family incomes above $4,000. (That was a lot; "In this area are located the residences of most of the wealthiest citizens of the city.") No one considered a "Negro" lived in the area.[26] The area to the immediate east of this neighborhood, labeled B-2, the formerly tony West End, suffered in the 1930s from "detrimental influences": "Home owners moving further west turning properties into double houses and rental properties." The inhabitants of this neighborhood were "Professional & Medium salaried class—some wealthier citizens," with salaries above $2,500, some with considerably higher salaries than that. No African Americans lived in this area.[27]

Moving east to C-5 lay a neighborhood that, while it "contains some very fine old homes in W. Fifth St.," suffered from "Smoke from factories. Old properties." Its inhabitants were "Laborers—mechanics, executives" earning $500 to $10,000 per year. African Americans made up 3 percent of this neighborhood.[28] Neighborhood C-4, meanwhile, occupied by "Mechanics—white & skilled colored laborers" who earned $500 to $2,000 per year, was

FIGURE 6.3 The Winston-Salem zoning map of 1930.
Source: North Carolina Supreme Court, Original Cases File, Fall 1939, *D. Elwood Clinard et als. v. City of Winston-Salem et als.* Courtesy of the State Archives of North Carolina.

seeing "Infiltration of Negro—slowly." The "Trend of desirability next 10–15 years" predicted "upward for colored property—downward for white." African Americans made up 50 percent of this area.[29]

All the D neighborhoods were majority black, full of frame houses, some with brick veneer. D-1 was 80 percent African American (seeing "Infiltration of Negro—rapid"). Inhabited by "Skilled and unskilled negro laborers, factory workers," the neighborhood still contained some people who were doing well economically, as family incomes ranged from $300 to $2,000 per year. While the neighborhood contained "cheap negro properties" and "old dilapidated houses," it also held "some fairly good negro properties along Cherry St." The owners of these nicer homes would have trouble accessing loans, even though some of them were earning as much money as residents of C areas.[30] D-2 and D-3, both 100 percent African American, had schools and parks for African American use. But they also lost value with "many narrow unpaved streets" and "Cheap negro properties."[31] D-5, also 100 percent African American, also lost value because of the factories in the area and the "creek running through center," which probably flooded periodically.[32]

Maps like the one in figure 6.4 were sent to lenders. These maps ensured that African Americans and poor and middling whites found it much more difficult to access home loans and thus to gain wealth through real estate, as some lenders made loans for residences only in A and B areas. The HOLC assessments also encouraged white homeowners to block the integration of all-white neighborhoods, as areas with African American inhabitants were all rated C or D. According to Thomas Hanchett, the HOLC map "influenced investment practices for decades" in Charlotte, where the boundaries between areas "became a self-fulfilling prophecy over the years." The map "encouraged disinvestment in existing low-income, mixed-use and black areas" along with investment in areas "as far as possible from 'lower grade populations.'" It likely had similar effects in Winston-Salem.[33]

Through HOLC, the government moved ahead with something that middling whites like S. J. Bennett had hoped the 1912 ordinance would achieve: protecting the value of property owned by white people and keeping this property for white people. HOLC's policy, however, protected elites at the expense of middling or poor white people, whose properties were

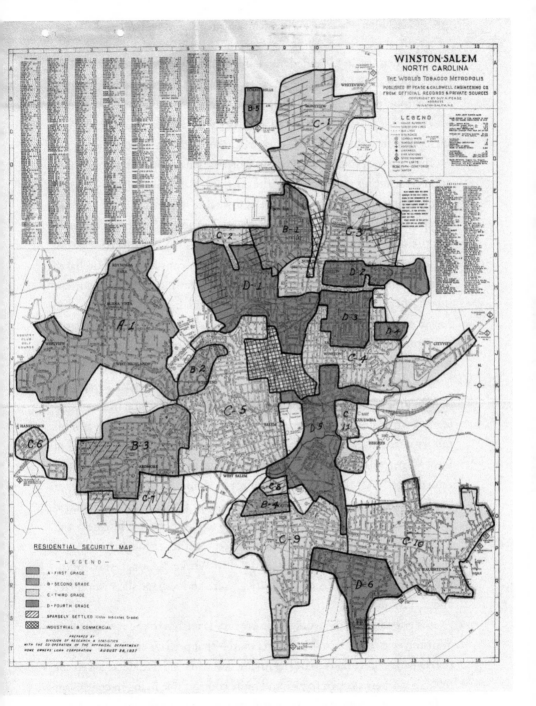

FIGURE 6.4 Residential Security Map of Winston-Salem, Home Owners Loan Corporation, 1937.
Source: From *Mapping Inequality*: *Redlining in New Deal America*, http://dsl.richmond.edu/mappinginequality.html.

more likely to sit in C-graded areas. The skilled white laborers and executives who lived in C areas lost access to loans, and their property lost value; as this took place, the possibility of economic mobility for these people lessened. They had been lumped together with African Americans, and their property values suffered—just what they had wanted to avoid.

Through the Home Owners Loan Corporation and numerous other programs (including the Veterans Administration and the Federal Housing Administration, which granted loans for white home buyers), the federal government created de jure segregation not just in the South but throughout the nation. The effects have been disastrous for African Americans. Because of these programs, many African Americans have not purchased homes. Those who have bought homes have spent more of their own savings (rather than borrowing money), which has left them with less cash to spend on other investments, like education. They have also purchased property in neighborhoods less likely to see real growth in value, which has led to their amassing less wealth than they would have otherwise.[34]

In May 1941, an African American man named Jasper Carpenter bought property in a white neighborhood near City Hospital in East Winston. A white mob threw stones at Carpenter's home, forcing him and his family out. This seemed a catalyst of sorts, and the white population of East Winston rapidly left, abandoning the neighborhood to African Americans.[35] Also in the 1940s, about ten thousand tobacco workers at the R. J. Reynolds Company, most of them African Americans, demanded changes from their employer. Objecting to low pay, abusive foremen, and high production quotas, the workers joined together through Local 22 of the Food, Tobacco, Agricultural, and Allied Workers–Congress of Industrial Organizations to develop a political voice and reshape their workplace and community.[36]

It is possible that the workers' insurgency is related to the razing of East Winston that took place shortly afterward—that perhaps city leaders found the demands of workers to be the final straw. Municipal leaders viewed the tobacco workers as open to vice and quite comfortable living in conditions unfit for human habitation, but—even worse—as beginning to assert themselves. Surely highway construction and urban renewal were partly about clearing out the places where workers organized themselves, where they made plans to stand up to authority.

By the end of World War II, Winston-Salem's leaders also believed that the traffic downtown, along with so-called festering slums, needed to be done away with to make the city appealing to people from other parts of the state and country, whom companies like Western Electric (later AT&T, which began operation in an old mill factory in 1946 and would soon employ thousands of people in the city) wished to attract. In 1948, the new City County Planning Board created a plan for redevelopment of the downtown. It worked to revamp neighborhoods abandoned by white residents, who now lived in new suburbs, and to sweep out black neighborhoods that lacked sanitation and other city services. Part of redevelopment was redoing the roads. In 1952, the city committed to building the East-West Expressway, which would bring traffic more efficiently into the downtown. Several years later, the expressway became part of Interstate 40 (deemed unsuccessful, however, the interstate was rerouted south of Winston-Salem in 1992). The residences of black workers in East Winston were razed to make room for this highway and for others, including U.S. 52 and University Parkway.[37]

In the 1960s, urban renewal projects destroyed many of the black neighborhoods—both slums and middle-class neighborhoods—that had not already been replaced with highways. Six hundred acres of houses were cleared out early in the 1960s, with four thousand families moved out of these houses. Thousands of additional houses, and over 1,600 additional acres, were cleared by the early 1970s. As neighborhoods went under the wrecking ball and bulldozer, new buildings went up—factories for the Reynolds Tobacco Company, for example, or new buildings for Winston-Salem State University (the former Slater Academy) campus, which meant the demolition of Simon Atkins's Columbian Heights. One of the only houses left standing from Columbian Heights today is Atkins's own house, which has been relocated and is now a university building. In December 1991 and January 1992, for example, Winston-Salem State razed seventy-five buildings to clear space for a $9 million dormitory for women. The destruction of black neighborhoods—the loss of houses and churches

FIGURE 6.5 View of North Church Street and East Fourth Street, 1963. This block in east Winston was razed.
Source: Courtesy of the Forsyth County Public Library Photographs Collection.

and doctors' offices, Y's, barber shops, cafes, funeral homes—caused the loss of a "sense of place and belonging" for many of the city's black residents. It also meant a loss of history: essentially all nineteenth- and early-twentieth-century black housing and historical landmarks were demolished.[38]

At the same time that the city was redeveloped, people from out of state flooded into Winston-Salem for industrial jobs. Traditionally over 90 percent of the city's population, by the 1950s native North Carolinians made up around 80 percent. Workers labored not only in tobacco companies (with R. J. Reynolds being the largest, employing 20 percent of the city's work-force by 1960) and textile factories (Hanes Hosiery and the P. H. Hanes Knitting Company produced hose and underwear and united as the Hanes Corp. in 1965) but also in factories making "electronic equipment, furniture, batteries, air conditioners, industrial machinery, mattresses, wagons, paint, swimming suits, toys, and chemicals." Winston-Salem, an industrial

FIGURE 6.6 Construction of Interstate 40 in a black neighborhood in Winston-Salem, 1957.
Source: Courtesy of the Forsyth County Public Library Photographs Collection.

powerhouse, manufactured "seven times more than any other city in the Carolinas."[39]

ROBERT WINSTON'S EMIGRATION PROPOSAL

Segregationist ideas continued to circulate in North Carolina beyond Winston-Salem, some of them coming from elites. Robert Watson Winston, from the elite North Carolina Winston family, believing that African Americans were "useful in inverse proportion to density and, therefore, should scatter," ran a sustained campaign to convince the public that the federal government should help African Americans emigrate starting in the 1920s. As Winston pointed out, this was not a new idea. Lincoln had supported such a plan, and Congress planned to fund emigration before Emancipation. "Washington, Jefferson, Madison, Clay, Webster, Lincoln, Grant and Lee" all wished to "give the negro a home."[40] Winston compared his idea to Indian removal, though he argued that black Americans should "be dispersed, not forcibly, as in the case of the Indians, but peaceably."[41] He described the force pushing black people out as "intelligent and sympathetic direction"—directed emigration, rather than the "haphazard" emigration that had been taking place.[42]

> I . . . pointed to Brazil, the Philippines and other islands, and likewise Liberia, French Guinea and British Sierra Leone, three countries contiguous to each other, almost uninhabited, easy to acquire and extensive enough to care for all American negroes for a hundred years. I . . . [argued] that a simple resolution by Congress, outlining a policy, would stop agitation and settle the issue. The resolution might read as follows, "The United States would welcome a fatherland for the Negro." The President would then appoint a commission to co-operate with leading negroes and set on foot a great independent, ideal, Negro Republic, with a Negro president, a Negro congress, Negro judges, Negro sheriffs. And all this in one of the most favored spots on the globe, with unsurpassed natural advantages: climate, water power, great, tall mountains, mineral products, ocean front.[43]

Winston did not explain the logistics of how the South's black population would be moved to a "fatherland" except to point out that during the World War the United States transported "millions of soldiers, in a few months, [across] the ocean dodging submarines, hostile ships, and aircraft."[44]

As with Poe, Winston's primary concern was helping white people, not black ones.[45] Yet Winston did believe that African Americans would want to go, that emigration would be "voluntary." Winston tried to sell his idea to black people with the argument that they could have "manhood rights" such as the right to vote and hold political office if they lived elsewhere. He also tried to make the idea appealing by linking it to pan-Africanism and voluntary emigration programs like Marcus Garvey's. "Were I a negro, facing the future, concerned about children and children's children," he opined, "I would cease to fight against white prejudice, but raising the banner of 'Pan-Africa,' I would herald that 'Unity of the Colored Races, sensed by far-seeing negroes,' as Dr. Burghardt Du Bois phrases it, until my latest breath."[46]

Winston claimed support from African Americans (while admitting that Moorfield Story, the first president of the NAACP, was "indignant" when he heard of Winston's plan to remove the nation's black population and accused him of "violating" the Constitution).[47] It is possible that Winston had some support from African Americans, in the same way that Marcus Garvey, toward the end of his life, found common ground with white supremacists. (In addition to meeting with the KKK leader Edward Young Clarke, Garvey supported legislation sponsored in Congress by Senator Theodore Bilbo of Mississippi that would have funded the emigration of African Americans to Africa.)[48]

That Winston, who certainly qualifies as elite, considered an emigration policy to be worthwhile and important shows that people have other interests that sometimes compete with their economic interests. Winston, in any case, was a former lawyer and judge who took up the life of the mind after retiring from the law, which he did by studying at the University of North Carolina and writing books about white supremacist leaders. He was not tied to the production of cash crops and had no direct interest in keeping black workers at hand. The unpopularity of Winston's emigration idea with other elites suggests that most others kept their eye on the economic interests of their class. Neither would they support Bilbo's emigration plan in 1939 (Bilbo represented lower-class whites). Winston explained why other elites rejected his idea.

> Now these thoughts of mine met with scant approval. Southern politicians and editors called them idle dreams. Chief Justice Clark . . . took sharp issue with me—he would hold conditions just as they were. But I fear both he and the Governor had missed the point and were what Williams called group-minded. They followed the crowd. The Governor, referring to an article of mine in *Current History*, declared I was wholly wrong. Southern conditions were ideal. There was no better laborer than the Negro, who was made for the South as the South was made for him. By this statement the Governor meant, of course, that George should continue to do the work, and the white

man continue to do the bossing! And, strange to relate, these good men—the Governor and the Chief Justice—seemed to imagine that the anomalous situation could permanently endure![49]

His critics, as Winston relayed it, valued the cheap labor provided by African Americans and wished to maintain the status quo. Winston believed that the status quo could not be maintained forever—that eventually, black people would demand more (leading to "conflicts and riots") or that, even worse in his view, there would be "amalgamation."[50] Winston viewed the South as overly tied to the past and believed that it was time to discard the region's fixation on the outcome of the Civil War—he recommended getting rid of its Civil War monuments, for example—and its reliance on black labor.[51]

Black emigration would help the South move toward a new day, argued Winston, and it would also save the region money through "the great burden of a double overhead" for "separate accommodations." Most importantly, it would help whites build the kind of society they would want to stay in. Like Clarence Poe (and Evans), Winston believed that black workers lowered the value of labor. With black people gone, "the Southern whites may overcome the notion that manual labor is for Negroes only." The "Solid South" would also wither away as blacks emigrated, leaving white individuals with room to think freely and disagree with one another. If African Americans moved out of the South, white people would stay. Winston shared Poe's fear that enterprising white people were leaving the South to get away from their black neighbors. The emigration of African Americans would leave a white South that offered more labor options to its inhabitants, Winston argued, thus retaining intelligent and capable white residents.[52]

Unpopular with elites and difficult to carry out, Robert Winston's plan never went beyond the initial stages of brainstorming and pleading a case. The plan's significance lies in showing the extent to which segregationist thinking percolated through the minds of white North Carolinians. Even an elite man had come to believe that white residents of the state would prosper only if they could be separated from African Americans. It also demonstrates that elites would oppose anyone—even their own—who proposed getting rid of the region's black workers.

CLARENCE POE'S LONGVIEW GARDENS

Starting in 1916, Clarence Poe purchased a number of properties to the east of Raleigh and by 1938 had amassed an eight-hundred-acre estate, which he and his wife named "Longview" in honor of their Progressive political perspective and the property's expansive views. Poe had grown up doing farm work but left the farm as a teenager—something he urged his readers' children not to do. He viewed his estate as a way of retaining a connection to farm life. Poe told the public that "this farm I have personally conducted as a means of keeping in daily touch with farm problems,"[53] but the "farm problems" he experienced were those of the absentee planter, not the small farmer. Poe hired men to manage the farm for him, and in spite of his criticism of absentee landlords for relying on black workers in the *Progressive Farmer*, he urged the white managers at Longview to hire African Americans to pick his cotton.[54]

The Poes lived on the estate in a large house constructed in 1925 of stone quarried from the property. One visitor to the estate described it thus: "no spot in Raleigh was lovelier than the high hill, approached through a long grove of crepe myrtle and providing a breathless view of blue-green rolling hills to the north."[55] Poe put his agricultural principles to work on the Longview farm, which produced wheat, tobacco, vegetables, and dairy. Even before the Great Depression pushed Poe and the *Progressive Farmer* to the brink of bankruptcy, he had planned to develop part of his estate; he hired Warren H. Manning, a Boston-based landscape architect trained by Frederick Law Olmsted, to design a subdivision in 1924. When the project began construction over a decade later, slowed down by the Depression, it was under the direction of Charles Gillette, who had at one time worked in Manning's office. Poe meant to create "Raleigh's Most Beautiful Subdivision." Longview Gardens, an attractive subdivision with curving roads, was built in three phases between 1938 and 1965, with each phase marked by a distinct architectural style (colonial and Tudor revival, ranch, and split level).[56]

In a 1939 article in the Raleigh *News and Observer*, Poe explained whom he intended to reside in Longview Gardens: middle-class white people. "While Longview Gardens has a rigid code of restrictions for the

FIGURE 6.7   Longview, Poe's home in eastern Raleigh, in 1938.
Source: Courtesy of the State Archives of North Carolina.

protection of home builders," he argued, "neither the price of the homesites nor the building restrictions are such to prevent any family of normal income from enjoying the exceptional environment."[57] The restrictions referenced by Poe—which were legal—included a minimum house cost ($6,000 for a house on a smaller and $7,000 on a larger lot), a ban on certain types of animals, and environmental-protection requirements, as well as a requirement that non-Caucasians could not own or occupy property in the neighborhood.[58] A typical deed for a property in Longview Gardens included the following restrictions:

> With the utmost respect and good will for all groups of people, but realizing that a high degree of homogeneity is necessary for that actively congenial community life desired for Longview Gardens, no land in Longview Gardens shall ever be sold, transferred, conveyed, mortgaged, or leased to, or occupied (servants excepted) by

any person who is not wholly Caucasian; and in those Blocks in Longview Gardens designated by letters of the alphabet on the recorded maps no land shall be sold, transferred, conveyed, mortgaged, devised, leased to, or occupied by any person who is not predominantly a descendant of those native North European national and racial stocks who comprise the bulk of North Carolina's white population (English, Scotch, Welsh, Irish, French, German, Dutch, Swiss, Belgian, Scandinavian).[59]

The writing in this covenant sounds very much like Poe, with its emphasis on encouraging social ties between whites and its interest in certain "racial stocks."[60] Even while Longview Gardens required that its residents be "wholly" white, however, the development suffered from its lack of proximity to a high school for white children. As Karen Benjamin has argued, "the location of new schools [in Raleigh] facilitated the shift of the city's white population to the north and west." White parents in east Raleigh, and Poe himself while he was on the school board, pushed for a more central location for the white high school, but the new high school, Broughton (opened in 1929), went up in northwest Raleigh.[61]

Longview did have appealing elements: an elementary school, a country club with an eighteen-hole golf course, and a shopping center, for example. It was able to attract a number of successful white residents. Poe's own adult children lived there (his son William Poe was vice president and treasurer of Longview Gardens, Inc.). By 1955, however, sales were slow.[62]

Meanwhile, African Americans, who made up a third of Raleigh's population after World War II, tended to live in east and southeast Raleigh, near Shaw University and St. Augustine's College, both historically black institutions founded in the 1860s. In the 1910s and 1920s, black residents in these areas had petitioned for a school, but Clarence Poe used his position on the school board to block the request. Black students from the St. Augustine's neighborhood had to commute to Washington High School in southwest Raleigh, a great inconvenience; African Americans notified the school board in 1948 that out of the high school's 650 students, only 110 lived within a reasonable commuting distance.[63] Most likely Poe objected to a black high school in east Raleigh because he would not have considered it desirable to encourage black residency so close to his landholdings. However, African Americans remained in the area, and they expanded into formerly white neighborhoods. White residents moved away. A construction boom was taking place, making available to whites freshly built subdivisions closer to the new white high school. Meanwhile, middle-class African Americans moved into vacated neighborhoods in the eastern part of the city near St. Augustine's. This is what happened with Longview Gardens. Blacks already resided in the area around Longview Gardens and, after the neighborhood's restrictive covenants expired in 1965, began to "trickle" into Longview Gardens proper.[64]

Poe died in 1964, so he never saw his Longview Gardens integrated. Meant to be a white island in a majority-black area, it is now occupied by white and black families. North Raleigh Boulevard, a busy four-lane road meant to separate the development from the black neighborhood around St. Augustine College, no longer serves as a racial barrier, though it does separate Longview from an economically depressed neighborhood. Longview Gardens is solidly middle class, with home values generally higher than $200,000 in 2017 (average home values in the neighborhood across North Raleigh Boulevard are at least $100,000 lower than in Longview Gardens). It is not the aristocratic oasis that Poe envisioned when he chose names like King Charles, Lord Ashley, and Lord Berkley for the development's streets. The development's shopping center is downmarket, and its most prominent store is a Family Dollar. The homes in Longview are small by today's standards (though the lots are quite large), and they are not all well maintained. The nicest house in the neighborhood is probably Poe's own, which sits at the top of a gentle hill at the end of Poe Drive and is now owned by Wake Medical Center. The neighborhood high school, William G. Enloe Magnet High School (Raleigh's first integrated high school, opened in 1962), is excellent and attracts a diverse student body from all over the county (39 percent are African American, 17 percent Asian, and 28 percent white), including local neighborhoods. Yet the school is not enough to attract Raleigh's affluent citizens, who generally choose to live in fancier neighborhoods.[65]

Longview Gardens demonstrates some of the costs of residential segregation, stunted in its development as a preeminent white neighborhood by

FIGURE 6.8   A typical house in Longview Gardens today.
Source: Courtesy of M. Ruth Little, Longleaf Historic Resources and the North Carolina State Historic Preservation Office.

its lack of proximity to a white high school, the investment of its original white inhabitants kept from appreciating dramatically. Clarence Poe worked for segregated neighborhoods, using the location of high schools to achieve this, but his own segregated neighborhood did not meet his vision for it because he did not prevail in his effort to put the new white high school in eastern Raleigh.

THE COST OF RESIDENTIAL SEGREGATION

Believing themselves threatened by the economic advances made by African Americans, middling white North Carolinians tried to limit African Americans' access to property in certain neighborhoods. Clinging to the belief that doing so would boost and protect their home values, they worked ardently for segregation ordinances and for a constitutional amendment allowing for segregated communities. Some elites in the state contested these efforts to put residential segregation into law.

We can see lurking in the shadows pieces of evidence that residential segregation laws, if successful, would have been a pyrrhic victory. They might
have kept home values stable in the short term but not the long term. White
neighborhoods depopulated by the flight to suburbs—inspired partly by
desires unrelated to race, including larger yards and curvilinear streets—
would have seen their home values plummet, as black buyers would not
have been able to purchase in these neighborhoods. Middling whites considered the failure of de jure residential segregation a setback, though, and
their commitment to residential segregation laws continued well after
Buchanan v. Warley.

Even without the state and local laws that middling whites wanted, residential segregation moved forward. It came about as school committees
decided to locate schools for black and white students in separate areas, as
white communities chose to exclude black buyers with restrictive covenants
and through other methods. Until the federal government imposed this type
of segregation through HOLC, though (doing so in a way that did not
undermine the property interests of white elites), residential segregation was
local and haphazard, despite the fact that it was inspired by global ideas and
trends.

Residential segregation—even when it was not required by law—imposed
immense costs on African Americans. Some of these costs were direct; black
people paid more money for substandard housing in black neighborhoods
than they would have spent to live in white neighborhoods, and they were
denied services like street lights that their tax dollars funded. Other costs
were more abstract but possibly even more damaging: African Americans
were kept out of networks where they might have developed what Pierre
Bourdieu called the "cultural capital" and "social capital" that would have
helped them advance into higher-paying jobs.[66] These costs were the tax
forced upon black people to keep them in their "place" and the penalty they
were to pay for success.

Residential segregation imposed real costs on middling white people, too,
including the cost of double overhead for segregated public institutions such
as schools and libraries, for example. The greatest cost borne by middling
whites was an opportunity cost: they missed the opportunity to address the
circumstances that actually held them back. Spurred on by the campaigns

for white supremacy, middling whites focused on competition from African Americans over property and white women as their most pressing "problem." They worked to achieve the things they yearned for—increased status and economic opportunity—by building firm lines of separation between themselves and African Americans, by fighting against the expansion of resources to African Americans. They devoted far less attention to addressing the power imbalances with white elites that prevented them from advancing in the ways they wanted to, and they failed to unite with African Americans, which would have given them the leverage they needed to win change. It is a tragic story: middling white people fixated on the "scarecrow of race" at the expense of their own betterment. Our nation and all its people would benefit if we learned from this story.

Notes

INTRODUCTION

1. W. E. Burghardt Du Bois, "The Upbuilding of Black Durham: The Success of the Negroes and Their Value to a Tolerant and Helpful Southern City," *World's Work* 23 (January 1912): 336. Du Bois thought that white people in Durham were pleased to see African Americans succeed because of the salutary influence of Trinity College (now Duke University), which benefited from "a president and professors who have dared to speak out for justice toward black men" (338).
2. In studying how white supremacy benefited white elites more than middling white southerners, I demonstrate that whiteness is not as tidy a concept as it is presented in whiteness studies, as is argued in the roundtable "Scholarly Controversy: Whiteness and the Historians' Imagination," *International Labor and Working Class History* 60 (October 2001).
3. Douglas A. Massey and Nancy A. Denton, *American Apartheid: Segregation and the Making of the Underclass* (Cambridge, MA: Harvard University Press, 1993), 41–42; Gilbert T. Stephenson, "The Segregation of the White and Negro Races in Cities," *South Atlantic Quarterly* 13 (January 1914): 1–18; "Segregation Ordinance: Spartanburg City Council Draws Color Line Regarding Residence," *Charlotte Observer*, February 3, 1915, 2.
4. See, for example, the Louisville ordinance, reprinted in *Buchanan v. Warley*, 245 U.S. 60–82 (1917), 70. See also Stephenson, "The Segregation of the White and Negro Races in Cities," 3.
5. *Buchanan v. Warley*, 245 U.S. 60 (1917); Mark V. Tushnet, *Making Civil Rights Law: Thurgood Marshall and the Supreme Court, 1936–1961* (New York: Oxford University Press, 1994), 83.

6. Massey and Denton, *American Apartheid*, 36, 42, 188; Tushnet, *Making Civil Rights Law*, 82; Colin Gordon, *Mapping Decline: St. Louis and the Fate of the American City* (Philadelphia: University of Pennsylvania Press, 2008), 71–79. On *Shelley v. Kraemer*, see Jeffrey Gonda, *Unjust Deeds: The Restrictive Covenant Cases and the Making of the Civil Rights Movement* (Chapel Hill: University of North Carolina Press, 2015); and Jeffrey Gonda, "Litigating Racial Justice at the Grassroots: The Shelley Family, Black Realtors, and *Shelley v. Kraemer* (1948)," *Journal of Supreme Court History* 39 (November 2014): 329–46.

7. No biography of Poe has been published, though his story has been told in Joseph A. Coté, "Clarence Hamilton Poe: Crusading Editor, 1881–1964," Ph.D. diss., University of Georgia, 1976; Joseph A. Coté, "Clarence Hamilton Poe: The Farmer's Voice, 1899–1964," *Agricultural History* 53, no. 1 (January 1979): 30–41; Jeffrey J. Crow, "An Apartheid for the South: Clarence Poe's Crusade for Rural Segregation," in *Race, Class, and Politics in Southern History: Essays in Honor of Robert F. Durden*, ed. Jeffrey J. Crow et al. (Baton Rouge: Louisiana State University Press, 1989), 216–59; Elizabeth A. Herbin-Triant, "Race and Class Friction in North Carolina Neighborhoods: How Campaigns for Residential Segregation Law Divided Middling and Elite Whites in Winston-Salem and North Carolina's Countryside, 1912–1915," *Journal of Southern History* 83, no. 3 (August 2017): 531–72; Elizabeth A. Herbin-Triant, "Southern Segregation, South Africa–Style: Maurice Evans, Clarence Poe, and the Ideology of Rural Segregation," *Agricultural History* 87, no. 2 (Spring 2013): 170–93; Jack Temple Kirby, "Clarence Poe's Vision of a Segregated 'Great Rural Civilization,'" *South Atlantic Quarterly* 68 (1969): 27–38; Jack Temple Kirby, *Darkness at the Dawning: Race and Reform in the Progressive South* (Philadelphia: Lippincott, 1972), 108–30; and Jack Temple Kirby, *Rural Worlds Lost: The American South, 1920–1960* (Baton Rouge: Louisiana State University Press, 1987), 232–71. Poe has made an appearance in transnational works, including Daniel Rodgers, *Atlantic Crossings: Social Politics in a Progressive Age* (Cambridge, MA: Harvard University Press, 1998), 322–23; and George M. Fredrickson, *White Supremacy: A Comparative Study in American and South African History* (Oxford: Oxford University Press, 1981), 253.

8. W. E. B. Du Bois, "The Last Word in Caste," in *NAACP Fourth Annual Report, 1913* (New York: NAACP, 1914), Moorfield Storey Papers, 1876–1929, Library of Congress, box 9, folder "Printed Matter, 1913," 73.

9. Joseph F. Steelman, "The Progressive Democratic Convention of 1914 in North Carolina," *North Carolina Historical Review* 46, no. 2 (April 1969): 95–97; Crow, "Apartheid for the South," 256.

10. Exceptions are Crow, "Apartheid for the South," 244–46, which surmises that the *Darnell* decision must have discouraged Poe in his efforts to enact a segregation program in the countryside, and Herbin-Triant, "Race and Class Friction in North Carolina Neighborhoods," 531–72. Crow's excellent article "Apartheid for the South" uses many of the same sources as my work, and we quote a number of the same sources. I have not indicated in my notes when quotations that I selected were also in Crow's article, because I came to these sources through my own review of the *Progressive Farmer* and the Poe Papers. Crow's interpretations of what motivated Poe and why various groups embraced or opposed his plan—along with those of Jack Temple Kirby—have been quite helpful for my research.

11. Joel Williamson has argued that segregation laws were important primarily "as symbols"—that a group of people he calls Radicals worked to put disfranchisement and

segregation, which were already widely in place, into law in order to reveal "explicitly and blatantly the power of whites." Joel Williamson, *The Crucible of Race: Black-White Relations in the American South Since Emancipation* (New York: Oxford University Press, 1984), 247, 225.

12. That segregation was necessary to help whites categorize people by race in confusing modern spaces is Grace Elizabeth Hale's argument, though her focus is on social more than economic gains. Grace Elizabeth Hale, *Making Whiteness: The Culture of Segregation in the South, 1890–1940* (New York: Vintage, 1998), 128–38.

13. There is a tendency among some historians to demonize elites, who, after all, exploited African Americans and other whites and excluded them from the halls of power, and to romanticize middling whites. Escott, for example, writes of "the depth of self-respect and democratic aspirations among ordinary North Carolinians," qualities that drove them to participate in "movements for greater justice in society." Paul D. Escott, *Many Excellent People: Power and Privilege in North Carolina, 1850–1900* (Chapel Hill: University of North Carolina Press, 1985), xviii.

14. Paul D. Escott, for example, sees "continuity" in class relations between 1850 and 1900 as the class animosity present during the Civil War extended through the decades that followed as elites continued to exclude lower-class white men from political power. Escott, *Many Excellent People*, xvii–xviii. See, on the different experiences and perspectives of poor whites (as compared to middling and elite white southerners), Keri Leigh Merritt, *Masterless Men: Poor Whites and Slavery in the Antebellum South* (New York: Cambridge University Press, 2017). Stephen A. Berrey discusses the historiography that shows "a diversity of responses and attitudes among white Southerners" in *The Jim Crow Routine: Everyday Performances of Race, Civil Rights, and Segregation in Mississippi* (Chapel Hill: University of North Carolina Press, 2015), 6. This historiography includes Berrey's work as well as Kevin M. Kruse, *White Flight: Atlanta and the Making of Modern Conservatism* (Princeton, NJ: Princeton University Press, 2007); Matthew D. Lassiter, *The Silent Majority: Suburban Politics in the Sunbelt South* (Princeton, NJ: Princeton University Press, 2007); Joseph Crespino, *In Search of Another Country: Mississippi and the Conservative Counterrevolution* (Princeton, NJ: Princeton University Press, 2007); Jason Morgan Ward, *Defending White Democracy: The Making of a Segregationist Movement and the Remaking of Racial Politics, 1936–1965* (Chapel Hill: University of North Carolina, 2011); and Keith M. Finley, *Delaying the Dream: Southern Senators and the Fight Against Civil Rights, 1938–1965* (Baton Rouge: Louisiana State University, 2008). Jason Sokol explores the varied responses of white southerners to the changes to their society that came with the Civil Rights Movement in *There Goes My Everything: White Southerners in the Age of Civil Rights, 1945–1975* (New York: Knopf, 2006).

15. See, on this theme, C. Vann Woodward, *Tom Watson: Agrarian Rebel* (New York: Oxford University Press, 1938).

16. William Cohen, *At Freedom's Edge: Black Mobility and the Southern White Quest for Racial Control, 1861–1915* (Baton Rouge: Louisiana State University Press, 1991), 5; Williamson, *Crucible of Race*, 5–7, 247–48.

17. David M. P. Freund's *Colored Property* makes for an interesting comparison. Freund argues that in suburban Detroit after World War II, the interests of working-class and middle-class whites coalesced around residential segregation and that their commitment to exclusion "helped unify a suburban population that was remarkably diverse" (41, 288). Freund does not, however, discuss where elites stood on the issue. David M. P.

Freund, *Colored Property: State Policy and White Racial Politics in Suburban America* (Chicago: University of Chicago Press, 2007).

18. T. J. Woofter, *Negro Problems in Cities* (New York: Doubleday, Doran & Co., 1928), 20.

19. Residential segregation was considered at a time when the effort to put segregation into law was losing its impetus throughout the South. Joel Williamson describes the "third wave" of segregation (1913–1915) as "feeble"; even though segregation continued to be passed into law after this period, these laws generally extended existing segregationist practices to "new technology or institutions" rather than orchestrating segregation into new arenas. Williamson, *Crucible of Race*, 255.

20. Barbara Jeanne Fields, "Slavery, Race, and Ideology in the United States of America," in *Racecraft: The Soul of Inequality in American Life*, ed. Karen E. Fields and Barbara J. Fields (New York: Verso, 2012): 111–48, esp. 128–31; see also Walter Johnson, *River of Dark Dreams: Slavery and Empire in the Cotton Kingdom* (Cambridge, MA: Harvard University Press, 2013); and Edward E. Baptist, *The Half Has Never Been Told: Slavery and the Making of American Capitalism* (New York: Basic Books, 2014). Fields explains changing ideology as follows: "Ideology is not a set of attitudes that people can 'have,' as they have a cold, and throw off the same way. Human beings live in human societies by negotiating a certain social terrain, whose map they keep alive in their minds by the collective, ritual repetition of the activities they must carry out in order to negotiate the terrain. If the terrain changes, so must their activities, and therefore so must the map." Fields, "Slavery, Race, and Ideology," 139–40.

21. As Barbara Fields puts it, "The racial ideology of the yeomanry therefore could not possibly replicate that of the planters." Fields, "Slavery, Race and Ideology," 134. Thomas C. Holt asks a series of important questions on this subject: "What enables racism to reproduce itself even after the historical conditions that initially gave it life have disappeared? And if we are to sustain an argument about its essential mutability, its historically contingent nature, how do we explain the seemingly endless repetitions of certain stereotypes?" Thomas C. Holt, *The Problem of Race in the Twenty-First Century* (Cambridge, MA: Harvard University Press, 2002), 20. The literature on racism and property has embraced the idea of racism as changing over time; see, for example, Freund, *Colored Property*, 7–13.

22. Edgar Gardner Murphy was a southern liberal who wrote about increasing racial tensions after 1900. See, for example, "Backward or Forward?" *South Atlantic Quarterly* 13, no. 1 (January 1909): 19–38.

23. On how the undoing of Populism and the problems that came with modernity (particularly urbanization) boosted racism and white people's commitment to white supremacy, see C. Vann Woodward, *The Strange Career of Jim Crow*, 3rd rev. ed. (New York: Oxford University Press, 1974), 67–109; John W. Cell, *The Highest Stage of White Supremacy: The Origins of Segregation in South Africa and the American South* (New York: Cambridge University Press, 1982), 82–90; and Hale, *Making Whiteness*, 128–138. These issues will be discussed later in this book.

24. David R. Roediger, *The Wages of Whiteness: Race and the Making of the American Working Class* (London: Verso, 2007), 10, 12, 13. The full quotation from Du Bois's *Black Reconstruction in America: Toward a History of the Part Which Black Folk Played in the Attempt to Reconstruct Democracy in America, 1860–1880* (1935; New York: Routledge, 2017), 626: "It must be remembered that the white group of laborers, while they

received a low wage, were compensated in part by a sort of public and psychological wage. They were given public deference and titles of courtesy because they were white. They were admitted freely with all classes of white people to public functions, public parks, and the best schools. The police were drawn from their ranks."

25. See, on the advantages that white people enjoyed, Eric Arnesen, "Whiteness and the Historians' Imagination," *International Labor and Working Class History* 60 (October 2001): 3–32, esp. 10–13.

26. See Woodward, *Strange Career*; and Cell, *Highest Stage*, 87–89. Joel Williamson points out that "segregation laws within each state were passed over a long period of time, related to different areas, varied widely from state to state, and varied even more widely within each state as towns, cities, villages, and other local communities made their own laws." Williamson, *Crucible of Race*, 255.

27. Jane Dailey, Glenda Elizabeth Gilmore, and Bryant Simon, *Jumpin' Jim Crow: Southern Politics from Civil War to Civil Rights* (Princeton, NJ: Princeton University Press, 2000), 4.

28. Berrey, *Jim Crow Routine*; Ward, *Defending White Democracy*.

29. Mark Schultz, *The Rural Face of White Supremacy: Beyond Jim Crow* (Urbana: University of Illinois Press, 2005), 5–9, 66–96.

30. Joel Williamson, Howard Rabinowitz, and others depart from C. Vann Woodward's focus on Jim Crow laws, arguing that African Americans were kept separate from whites in the South directly after the Civil War and that Jim Crow laws showed continuity with an earlier pattern of informal segregation or even exclusion. More recently, scholars including Matthew Lassiter have argued that both de jure and de facto segregation were brought about by state action and that they had the same effects. See, on this debate, John David Smith, introduction to *When Did Southern Segregation Begin?*, ed. John David Smith (Boston: Bedford/St. Martin's, 2002), 31–34; Joel Williamson, *After Slavery: The Negro in South Carolina During Reconstruction, 1861–1877* (Chapel Hill: University of North Carolina Press, 1965); Howard Rabinowitz, *Race Relations in the Urban South, 1865–1890* (New York: Oxford University Press, 1978); Matthew D. Lassiter, "De Jure/De Facto Segregation: The Long Shadow of a National Myth," in *Myth of Southern Exceptionalism*, ed. Matthew D. Lassiter and Joseph Crespino (New York: Oxford University Press, 2009), 25–48; and Carl H. Nightingale, *Segregation: A Global History of Divided Cities* (Chicago: University of Chicago Press, 2012), 7.

31. Mary White Ovington, "Segregation," *Crisis*, January 1915, 142.

32. Looking beyond North Carolina, three important books are Loren Schweninger, *Black Property Owners in the South, 1790–1915* (Urbana: University of Illinois Press, 1990); Andrew Wiese, *Places of Their Own: African American Suburbanization in the Twentieth Century* (Chicago: University of Chicago Press, 2004); and Todd M. Michney, *Surrogate Suburbs: Black Upward Mobility and Neighborhood Change in Cleveland, 1900–1980* (Chapel Hill: University of North Carolina Press, 2017). Schweninger surveys the property gains of African Americans throughout the southern states, which peaked in 1910. In *Places of Their Own*, Wiese examines where and why African Americans moved into suburbs and what was distinct about their suburbanization patterns. Michney looks into the movement of middling black families out of downtown Cleveland to what he calls "outer-city spaces" (4) in *Surrogate Suburbs*, a movement that took place as African Americans who could afford to do so sought out better living conditions.

33. Sharon Ann Holt, *Making Freedom Pay: North Carolina Freedpeople Working for Themselves, 1865–1900* (Athens: University of Georgia Press, 2000), xviii; Evan P. Bennett, "Of the Quest of the Golden Leaf: Black Farmers and Bright Tobacco in the Piedmont South," in *Beyond Forty Acres and a Mule: African American Landowning Families Since Reconstruction*, ed. Debra A. Reid and Evan P. Bennett (Gainesville: University Press of Florida, 2012), 179–204, esp. 187–89; and Evan P. Bennett, *When Tobacco Was King: Families, Farm Labor, and Federal Policy in the Piedmont* (Gainesville: University Press of Florida, 2014). See also Adrienne Petty, who examines small farmers, black and white, as a class, arguing that both groups were disadvantaged by racism along with "other, equally invidious tools of exploitation and inequality" and showing the commitment of this class to the agrarian ideal along with its struggle to purchase and keep farm land. Adrienne Monteith Petty, *Standing Their Ground: Small Farmers in North Carolina Since the Civil War* (New York: Oxford University Press, 2013), 6. Robert Kenzer examines how black North Carolinians came to acquire property in cities, as well as farmland, in *Enterprising Southerners: Black Economic Success in North Carolina, 1865–1915* (Charlottesville: University Press of Virginia, 1997).

34. LeeAnn Lands, *The Culture of Property: Race, Class, and Housing Landscapes in Atlanta, 1880–1950* (Athens: University of Georgia Press, 2009), 2.

35. Freund, *Colored Property*, 284–85, 304–5.

36. N. D. B. Connolly, *A World More Concrete: Real Estate and the Remaking of Jim Crow South Florida* (Chicago: University of Chicago Press, 2014), 7.

37. An article by Gretchen Boger, "The Meaning of Neighborhood in the Modern City: Baltimore's Residential Segregation Ordinances, 1910–1913," *Journal of Urban History* 35 (January 2009): 236–58, has had a strong influence on this book. Boger, examining the role of middling whites in excluding blacks in Baltimore, argues that these people were "a tier of whites with a tenuous hold on middle-class reputation" who sought ordinances in an "attempt to . . . secure their own often precarious status" (237–38). Boger notes that a few elite Baltimoreans participated in the campaign for residential segregation there because they had "something personal to lose" (237). Other articles that investigate different southern cities that passed residential segregation ordinances in response to African Americans moving into white neighborhoods are Garrett Power, "Apartheid Baltimore Style: The Residential Segregation Ordinances of 1910–1913," *Maryland Law Review* 42, no. 2 (1983): 289–328; Roger L. Rice, "Residential Segregation by Law, 1910–1917," *Journal of Southern History* 34 (May 1968): 179–99; John Wertheimer, *Law and Society in the South: A History of North Carolina Court Cases* (Lexington: University Press of Kentucky, 2009), chap. 3; and Russell Wigginton, " 'But He Did What He Could': William Warley Leads Louisville's Fight for Justice, 1902–1946," *Filson History Quarterly* 76, no. 4 (2002): 427–58.

38. Natalie J. Ring, "The 'New Race Question': The Problem of Poor Whites and the Color Line," in *The Folly of Jim Crow: Rethinking the Segregated South*, ed. Stephanie Cole and Natalie J. Ring (Arlington: University of Texas at Arlington Press, 2012), 97; Neil Foley, *The White Scourge: Mexicans, Blacks, and Poor Whites in Texas Cotton Culture* (Berkeley: University of California Press, 1997), 5–7.

39. Cheryl I. Harris makes the argument that whiteness is a form of property in "Whiteness as Property," *Harvard Law Review* 106, no. 8 (June 1993): 1709–91. Harris argues that the "core characteristic" of whiteness as property is "the legal legitimation of expectations of power and control that enshrine the status quo as a neutral baseline, while masking the maintenance of white privilege and domination" (1715). Also see C. B.

MacPherson, introduction to *Property: Mainstream and Critical Positions*, ed. C. B. MacPherson (Toronto: University of Toronto Press, 1978), 1–2.

40. W. E. B. Du Bois, *Darkwater: Voices from Within the Veil* (New York: Harcourt, Brace and Howe, 1920), 30.

41. In another example, which Andrew W. Kahrl calls "coastal capitalism," the southern coast was developed as a space for the leisure of whites—a process that involved gaining property from African American owners and reserving this property exclusively for the use of white people. Andrew W. Kahrl, *The Land Was Ours: How Black Beaches Became White Wealth in the Coastal South* (Chapel Hill: University of North Carolina Press, 2012). Something similar took place in greater Miami, where, according to N. D. B. Connolly, " 'whites only' beaches, hotels, apartments, and suburbs churned out millions of dollars on one side of the color line, while landlords and property managers in the region's hulking, cramped slums harvested millions in rent money on the other." Connolly, *A World More Concrete*, 6. Ta-Nehisi Coates describes segregation, along with slavery and other racist systems, as responsible for the "plunder" of African Americans. See Coates's keynote address at the Radcliffe conference "Universities and Slavery: Bound by History," March 3, 2017. See also Ta-Nehisi Coates, "The Case for Reparations," *Atlantic*, June 2014, https://www.theatlantic.com/magazine/archive /2014/06/the-case-for-reparations/361631/. Section 5, "The Quiet Plunder," highlights the United States' theft from African Americans starting in slavery and continuing into the twentieth century: "The federal government is premised on equal fealty from all its citizens, who in return are to receive equal treatment. But as late as the mid-20th century, this bargain was not granted to black people, who repeatedly paid a higher price for citizenship and received less in return. Plunder had been the essential feature of slavery, of the society described by Calhoun. But practically a full century after the end of the Civil War and the abolition of slavery, the plunder—quiet, systemic, submerged— continued even amidst the aims and achievements of New Deal liberals."

42. Manning Marable, *How Capitalism Underdeveloped Black America: Problems in Race, Political Economy, and Society* (Chicago: Haymarket, 2015), 2; my italics. Nancy Leong defines racial capitalism as "the process of deriving economic and social value from the racial identity of another person." Leong argues that while "nonwhiteness" has not historically been considered valuable, recently the "preoccupation with diversity" has led to nonwhiteness being "commodified" by people and institutions that reap economic gains by adopting the appearance of diversity (in this situation, nonwhiteness is valuable not so much to nonwhite individuals but to white people or institutions). Nancy Leong, "Racial Capitalism," *Harvard Law Review* 126, no. 8 (June 2013), 2153–56; See also W. E. B. Du Bois, "Of the Black Belt," in *The Souls of Black Folk: Essays and Sketches* (Chicago: A. C. McClurg and Co., 1903); and Cedric Robinson, *Black Marxism: The Making of the Black Radical Tradition* (London: Zed, 1983).

43. See David Brown, *Southern Outcast: Hinton Rowan Helper and* The Impending Crisis of the South (Baton Rouge: Louisiana State University, 2006), 2.

44. An example suggesting similar outlooks among middling whites elsewhere in the South: middling whites in Hancock County, Georgia, while not prominent in Schultz's study (as there were relatively few of them in the county), were more concerned than poor white sharecroppers and elites with "maintaining codes of interracial etiquette and seemed coldest and most distant in their relationships with blacks." Schultz, *Rural Face*, 95.

45. On corporate rights, see Adam Winkler, *We the Corporations: How American Businesses Won Their Civil Rights* (New York: Liveright, 2018).

1. MIDDLING WHITES IN POSTBELLUM NORTH CAROLINA

1. Clarence Poe, *My First Eighty Years* (Chapel Hill: University of North Carolina Press, 1963), 3.
2. Clarence Poe, "Some Traditions of the Poes and Hackneys of Chatham, 1675–1865: Being Mainly About the Family of Jesse Poe, Sr. (1768–1859)," *South Atlantic Quarterly* (January 1936): 3, 16, Poe Papers, North Carolina State Archives.
3. Clarence Poe, "William Baxter Poe: An Imperfect Tribute" and "Mrs. Susan Dismukes Poe," North Carolina Collection, Wilson Library, University of North Carolina at Chapel Hill.
4. Poe, "Some Traditions," 8; Poe, *My First Eighty Years*, 13.
5. Poe, *My First Eighty Years*, 29.
6. Clarence Poe, "William Baxter Poe: An Imperfect Tribute"; Poe, *My First Eighty Years*, 18–19.
7. Poe, *My First Eighty Years*, 27.
8. William Baxter Poe, "Negro Life in Two Generations: The Observations of a Southern Farmer," *Outlook* 75 (October 1903): 495.
9. Poe, "Negro Life in Two Generations," 497.
10. Poe, "Negro Life in Two Generations," 497.
11. Wm. Bullock Clark, "The Physiography of the Coastal Plain of North Carolina," in *Reports of the North Carolina Geological and Economic Survey*, vol. 3: *The Coastal Plain of North Carolina*, by Wm. Bullock Clark et al. (Raleigh: E. M. Uzzell and Co., State Printers and Binders, 1912), 23–24; North Carolina Board of Agriculture, *North Carolina and Its Resources Illustrated* (Winston: M. I. & J. C. Stewart, Public Printers and Binders, 1896), 16–17, http://docsouth.unc.edu/nc/state/state.html.
12. North Carolina Board of Agriculture, *North Carolina and Its Resources*, 27–29.
13. S. Huntington Hobbs Jr., *North Carolina: An Economic and Social Profile* (Chapel Hill: University of North Carolina Press, 1958), 63; William S. Powell, *North Carolina Through Four Centuries* (Chapel Hill: University of North Carolina Press), 4–5; North Carolina Board of Agriculture, *North Carolina and Its Resources*, 25; Federal Writers' Project, *North Carolina: A Guide to the Old North State* (Columbia: University of South Carolina Press, 1939), 9.
14. North Carolina Board of Agriculture, *North Carolina and Its Resources*, 21.
15. North Carolina Board of Agriculture, *North Carolina and Its Resources*, 156–63.
16. Jonathan Daniels, "Tar Heels All," in Federal Writers' Project, *North Carolina*, 4–5. See also North Carolina Board of Agriculture, *North Carolina and Its Resources*, 14; Powell, *North Carolina Through Four Centuries*, 328; James M. Beeby, *Revolt of the Tar Heels: The North Carolina Populist Movement, 1890–1901* (Jackson: University Press of Mississippi, 2008), 12–13.
17. Jonathan Daniels, "Tar Heels All," 7.
18. An example is the homestead provision in the North Carolina state constitution, added during Reconstruction, which protected debtors' homesteads from sale to pay off debts. This kept farms in the hands of small white farmers, preventing them from being sold to African Americans. See James W. Ely Jr., "Homestead Exemption and Southern Legal Culture," in *Signposts: New Directions in Southern Legal History*, ed. Sally E. Hadden and Patricia Hagler Minter (Athens: University of Georgia Press, 2013), esp. 294.

19. I am using the term "cropper," even though the term "tenant" continued to be used, as Woodman explains: "Southerners . . . did use the term *cropper* [rather than sharecropper] both in ordinary language and in the official language of legislation and judicial proceedings." Harold D. Woodman, *New South—New Law: The Legal Foundations of Credit and Labor Relations in the Postbellum Agricultural South* (Baton Rouge: Louisiana State University Press, 1995), 68.

20. Clarence Poe, "An Open Letter to the White Renters of the South," *Progressive Farmer*, September 11, 1915, 837; Harold D. Woodman, "Class, Race, Politics, and the Modernization of the Postbellum South," *Journal of Southern History* 63, no. 1 (February 1997): 7–8; Carl C. Taylor and C. C. Zimmerman, *Economic and Social Conditions of North Carolina Farmers: Based on a Survey of One Thousand North Carolina Farmers in Three Typical Counties of the State* (Raleigh: North Carolina Department of Agriculture, Tenancy Commission, 1923), 34–39.

21. Adrienne Monteith Petty, *Standing Their Ground: Small Farmers in North Carolina Since the Civil War* (New York: Oxford University Press, 2013), 8–10, 31–33. See also Allan Kulikoff, *The Agrarian Origins of American Capitalism* (Charlottesville: University Press of Virginia, 1992), 34–35.

22. Paul D. Escott, *Many Excellent People: Power and Privilege in North Carolina, 1850–1900* (Chapel Hill: University of North Carolina Press, 1985), 15, 28.

23. Powell, *North Carolina Through Four Centuries*, 328; Escott, *Many Excellent People*, 4–7. See also Dwight B. Billings, *Planters and the Making of a "New South": Class, Politics, and Development in North Carolina, 1865–1900* (Chapel Hill: University of North Carolina Press, 1979).

24. Eric Anderson, *Race and Politics in North Carolina, 1872–1901: The Black Second* (Baton Rouge: Louisiana State University Press, 1981), 4–5; Escott, *Many Excellent People*, 181.

25. Escott, *Many Excellent People*, 263.

26. Hinton Rowan Helper, *The Impending Crisis of the South: How to Meet It* (New York: Burdick Brothers, 1857), 45, 28, 43, 44.

27. Hinton Rowan Helper to Senator John Sherman, October 19, 1896, Marion Butler Papers #114, Southern Historical Collection, Wilson Library, University of North Carolina at Chapel Hill, box 3, folder 36.

28. Hinton Rowan Helper, *Compendium of the Impending Crisis of the South* (New York: A. B. Burdick, 1860), 104.

29. Daniels, "Tar Heels All," 5, 45; Powell, *North Carolina Through Four Centuries*, 368–70.

30. Powell, *North Carolina Through Four Centuries*, 356–81; Petty, *Standing Their Ground*, 37–39.

31. Michael L. Lanza, *Agrarianism and Reconstruction Politics: The Southern Homestead Act* (Baton Rouge: Louisiana State University Press, 1990), 1–4; Keri Leigh Merritt, *Masterless Men: Poor Whites and Slavery in the Antebellum South* (New York: Cambridge University Press, 2017), 326–31.

32. Woodman, *New South—New Law*, 75–76; Eric Foner, *Reconstruction: America's Unfinished Revolution, 1863–1877* (New York: Harper & Row, 1988), 403–6.

33. "The law that stipulated that the cropper was a wage laborer paid in kind meant that employers of croppers could exercise complete managerial control, determining what would be grown, the seed, fertilizer, tools, and work animals to be used, the hours and pace of work, and even the time and price of the sale of the croppers' shares. In short,

the law made it possible to make the croppers part of a rural proletariat on the pattern of the industrial proletariat in the North. Croppers, like northern workers, had a legal right to their wages but no legal right to the goods they produced and from which their wages would come; in both sections, employers owned the means of production, and they, not the employees, made all management decisions." Woodman, *New South— New Law*, 104–5.

34. C. Vann Woodward, *Origins of the New South, 1877–1913* (Baton Rouge: Louisiana State University Press, 1951, 1971), 183.

35. Woodman, *New South—New Law*, 11–13; Woodman, "Post–Civil War Southern Agriculture and the Law," *Agricultural History* 53, no. 1 (January 1979): 323–27.

36. Adam Jacob Wolkoff, "Possession and Power: The Legal Culture of Tenancy in the United States, 1800–1920," Ph.D. diss., Rutgers University, 2015, 124–25.

37. *Harrison v. Ricks*, 71 N.C. 7, 22 (N.C. 1874), 10–11.

38. *Haskins v. Royster*, 70 N.C. 600, 486 (N.C. 1874), 611.

39. Wolkoff, "Possession and Power," 102, 136–39, 141; Marjorie Mendenhall Applewhite, "Sharecropper and Tenant in the Courts of North Carolina," *North Carolina Historical Review* 31, no. 2 (April 1954): 135–38.

40. Escott, *Many Excellent People*, 174–79; Woodman, "Class, Race, Politics," 4.

41. Wolkoff, "Possession and Power," 15, 17.

42. Wolkoff, "Possession and Power," 154, 155, 158; *Curtis v. Cash*, 84 N.C. 41 (1881); *State v. Copeland*, 86 N.C. 691 (1882).

43. Woodman, "Class, Race, Politics," 18.

44. White tenants and croppers produced comparable numbers of eggs per family and had comparable percentages of families producing eggs to farm owners, however. The same was true of garden products. A higher percentage of renting than landowning whites produced molasses. Taylor and Zimmerman, *Economic and Social Conditions*, 22–26.

45. U.S. Census, 1910, http://socialexplorer.com.

46. Taylor and Zimmerman, *Economic and Social Conditions*, 5–7, 15–26.

47. Taylor and Zimmerman, *Economic and Social Conditions*, 6.

48. Steven Hahn, *The Roots of Southern Populism: Yeoman Farmers and the Transformation of the Georgia Upcountry, 1850–1890* (New York: Oxford University Press, 1983), 27–40, 52, 91; Eugene D. Genovese, "Yeomen Farmers in a Slaveholders' Democracy," *Agricultural History* 49, no. 2 (Spring 1975): 334–35; Escott, *Many Excellent People*, 8–9; Claire Strom, *Making Catfish Bait out of Government Boys: The Fight Against Cattle Ticks and the Transformation of the Yeoman South* (Athens: University of Georgia Press, 2009), 43–46.

49. North Carolina Board of Agriculture, *North Carolina and Its Resources*, 24–25.

50. University of Virginia Libraries, U.S. Historical Census Browser, http://mapserver.lib .virginia.edu/php/state.php.

51. Jeffrey J. Crow, "An Apartheid for the South: Clarence Poe's Crusade for Rural Segregation," in *Race, Class, and Politics in Southern History: Essays in Honor of Robert F. Durden*, ed. Jeffrey J. Crow et al. (Baton Rouge: Louisiana State University Press, 1989), 235–36; U.S. Census 1890 and 1910, http://socialexplorer.com.

52. Clarence Poe, "Education, Co-Operation, Legislation," *Progressive Farmer*, June 7, 1913, 681.

53. Loren Schweninger, *Black Property Owners in the South, 1790–1915* (Urbana: University of Illinois Press, 1990), 175; Crow, "An Apartheid for the South," 235.

54. Robert Kenzer, *Enterprising Southerners: Black Economic Success in North Carolina, 1865–1915* (Charlottesville: University Press of Virginia, 1997), 27.

55. Twelfth Census of the United States, Schedule no. 1—Population, 1900, Chatham County, North Carolina, Oakland Township, Enumeration District 13, sheets 3B, 4A, http://familysearch.org. The Goldstons are listed near Poe's farm, which shows proximity, as census enumerators went door-to-door from one household to the next. On this, see Trevon D. Logan and John M. Parman, "The National Rise in Residential Segregation," *Journal of Economic History* 77, no. 1 (March 2017): esp. 135–36. I noted the trend of white farmers living near black farm owners in other townships in the county, too.

56. See, for example, Thirteenth Census of the United States: 1910—Population, Chatham County, North Carolina, Oakland Township, Enumeration District 17; and Gulf Township, Enumeration District 10, http://familysearch.org.

57. Clarence Poe, "Racial Segregation Necessary to Education and Co-Operation," *Progressive Farmer*, August 9, 1913, 11.

58. Poe, "Racial Segregation Necessary to Education and Co-Operation," 11.

59. Neil Canaday, "The Accumulation of Property by Southern Blacks and Whites: Individual-Level Evidence from a South Carolina Cotton County," *Explorations in Economic History* 45, no. 1 (2008): 51–75; Robert Higgs, "Accumulation of Property by Southern Blacks Before World War I," *American Economic Review* 72, no. 4 (1982): 725–37; Robert A. Margo, "Accumulation of Property by Southern Blacks Before World War I: Comment and Further Evidence," *American Economic Review* 74, no. 4 (1984): 768–76; Neil Canaday and Charles Reback, "Race, Literacy, and Real Estate Transactions in the Postbellum South," *Journal of Economic History* 70, no. 2 (June 2010): 428–45 (examines blacks paying more for worse property on 438–42); Mark R. Schultz, "Interracial Kinship Ties and the Emergence of a Rural Black Middle Class: Hancock County, Georgia, 1865–1920," in *Georgia in Black and White: Explorations in the Race Relations of a Southern State, 1865–1950*, ed. John C. Inscoe (Athens: University of Georgia Press, 1994), 151.

60. Evan P. Bennett, "Of the Quest of the Golden Leaf: Black Farmers and Bright Tobacco in the Piedmont South," in *Beyond Forty Acres and a Mule: African American Landowning Families Since Reconstruction*, ed. Debra A. Reid and Evan P. Bennett (Gainesville: University Press of Florida, 2012), esp. 182, 185.

61. Petty, *Standing Their Ground*, 8.

62. Petty, *Standing Their Ground*, 44.

63. *The Portable Thomas Jefferson*, ed. Merrill D. Peterson (New York: Penguin, 1975), 217; Drew R. McCoy, *The Elusive Republic: Political Economy in Jeffersonian America* (Chapel Hill: University of North Carolina Press, 1980), 14–15, 38.

64. *Portable Thomas Jefferson*, 217.

65. Richard Hofstadter, *The Age of Reform: From Bryan to FDR* (New York: Knopf, 1965), 7, 24–5, 28.

66. Petty, *Standing Their Ground*, 10; "More Small White Farmers the Hope of the South," *Progressive Farmer*, March 15, 1913, 375.

67. Charles Aycock Poe, "The Education of Clarence Poe," address delivered to the Watauga Club, January 10, 1978, 1, North Carolina Collection, Wilson Library, University of North Carolina at Chapel Hill.

68. Poe, *My First Eighty Years*, 4.

69. While Poe's success did not bring immediate financial rewards, he did build an enterprise that would become quite profitable. In 1953, the *Progressive Farmer* made $5 million in advertising, and in 1954, its circulation was 1,235,000. Time Inc. purchased the Southern Progress Corporation, which included the *Progressive Farmer* and its sister publications, including *Southern Living*, for $480 million in 1985, roughly twenty years after Poe's death. In 1984, the *Progressive Farmer* had a circulation of 573,000. Chester Davis, "Clarence Poe: His Zeal for a Better Commonwealth Never Flagged in Fifty Years," *State* 21, no. 44 (April 3, 1954): 1, North Carolina Collection, Wilson Library, University of North Carolina at Chapel Hill; Cooley, "Dr. Clarence Hamilton Poe," A915; North Carolina State Historical Marker, http://www.stoppingpoints.com/north -carolina/sights.cgi?marker=Clarence+Poe+1881–1964&cnty=Wake; Alex S. Jones, "Time Inc. Will Buy Magazines: $480 Million for Group in South," *New York Times*, February 22, 1985.

70. W. O. Saunders, "The 'Dixie Plowboy': Remarkable Story of Clarence Poe—Friend of Roosevelt: His Rise to Fame," *Success: The Human Magazine*, May 1924, 56, 116, North Carolina Collection, Wilson Library, University of North Carolina at Chapel Hill. See also Davis, "Clarence Poe: His Zeal for a Better Commonwealth," 1–2.

71. Poe, "The Education of Clarence Poe," 4; see also 6, 8–9.

72. Anne Jackson Williams to her "homefolks," November 12, 1920, 2, Anne Jackson Williams Papers, #3308, folder 2, Southern Historical Collection, Wilson Library, University of North Carolina at Chapel Hill.

73. The *Progressive Farmer* was read primarily by white southerners, though it influenced black farmers as well. For example, the Extension Service bought copies of the journal for its black agents in Alabama, who then taught the journal's lessons to the farmers with whom they worked: "I have your recent letter telling me that the Extension Service South has raised a question requiring an explanation in justification of the expenditure of $10.00, December 2, 1919, for subscription to the *Progressive Farmer* sent to local (negro) farm demonstration Agents," an Extension official wrote. "In reply I would say that the training and equipment of negroes is so inadequate for the varied character of work they should attempt and they are so almost completely without any agricultural books, that on careful deliberation it was concluded that the most economical way to add to their information along lines of seasonal work from week to week was by furnishing them weekly with copies of the agricultural paper published in this state and dealing with local questions of the same character that the agent faces every week. The expense was many times less than would have been required to get even one-tenth of the same information to the agents by means of circular letters. You will note that no such expenditure was made for white agents because of their better training, possession of college text books, or other books on agriculture, etc." Letter from J. F. Duggar, director of Experiment Station of Alabama Polytechnic Inst. to S. J. T. Price, Auburn, Alabama, December 18, 1920, Correspondence of Alfred C. True (Director, States Relations Service, March 1914–June 1923), entry 6, box 1, Extension Service Records, National Archives II. "The *Progressive Farmer*: 1886–1926: Something About Its History and Its Ideals," *Progressive Farmer*, February 13, 1926, 193; Joseph A. Coté, "Clarence Hamilton Poe: The Farmer's Voice, 1899–1964," *Agricultural History* 53, no. 1 (January 1979): 2; Crow, "An Apartheid for the South," 218–19; "*Progressive Farmer* Is Now Largest in the World," *News and Observer* (Raleigh), May 18, 1930, Clarence Poe Papers, North Carolina State Archives.

74. Connie Lester argues that farmers in Tennessee held onto aspects of Populism such as cooperativism through the Progressive Era. Connie Lester, *Up from the Mudsills of Hell: The Farmers' Alliance, Populism, and Progressive Agriculture in Tennessee, 1870–1915* (Athens: University of Georgia Press, 2006), 4–5.

75. Harold D. Cooley, "Dr. Clarence Hamilton Poe: Extension of Remarks of Hon. Harold D. Cooley of North Carolina in the House of Representatives," Congressional Record—Appendix (February 4, 1954), A915, North Carolina Collection, Wilson Library, University of North Carolina at Chapel Hill.

76. Later in life, Poe published additional books: *True Tales of the South at War* (1961) and *My First Eighty Years* (1963).

77. Charles Aycock Poe, "The Education of Clarence Poe," 7.

78. Davis, "Clarence Poe: His Zeal for a Better Commonwealth," 2.

79. Cooley, "Dr. Clarence Hamilton Poe," A915.

80. Anne Jackson Williams to her family, November 20, 1920, 3, AJW Papers, folder 2.

81. "Clarence Poe's Life of Service to the South Is Recognized," collection of reprints from various newspapers in the Poe Papers, box 29.

82. Josephus Daniels to FDR (August 5, 1940), FDR to Josephus Daniels (August 21, 1940), "Subject: Proposed Appointment of Dr. Clarence Poe, President and Editor 'The *Progressive Farmer* and Southern Ruralist,' to Fill out Unexpired Term of Secretary Henry A. Wallace," Poe Papers, NCSA.

83. W. D. S., "Interlude at Longview Gardens," *Daily News* (Greensboro), October 18, 1964, 57.

84. For evidence that African Americans read the *Progressive Farmer*: there are occasional letters to the editor that mention the race of the writer. See, for example, T. S. Inborden, "A Negro Reader Protests," *Progressive Farmer*, September 20, 1913, 995 (discussed in chapter 5). Aside from the span of years when Poe promoted rural segregation, the journal did not have a hateful tone toward African Americans, and some may have found its advice on farming appealing.

85. Cooley, "Dr. Clarence Hamilton Poe," A915.

86. Davis, "Clarence Poe: His Zeal for a Better Commonwealth," 2.

87. Charles Aycock Poe, "The Education of Clarence Poe," 7.

88. Charles Aycock Poe, "The Education of Clarence Poe," 13.

89. Charles Aycock Poe, "The Education of Clarence Poe," 14.

90. Clarence Poe, "Can the Little Farmer Survive? Or Are We Headed for Corporation Farming with Hireling Cultivators?" *Progressive Farmer*, August 15–31, 1931, 532–33.

91. "The True Test of Success—Love for One's Work," *Progressive Farmer*, April 2, 1910, 293.

92. "Love Your Work," *Progressive Farmer*, May 28, 1910, 454.

93. A. L. French, "The New Appreciation of Farming," *Progressive Farmer*, April 16, 1910, 356.

94. Poe, "'We Are Tenants of the Almighty': What Then Is Our Duty to the Soil He Entrusts to Our Care?" *Progressive Farmer*, May 5, 1923, 487. See also Poe, *My First Eighty Years*, 142; D. N. Barrow, "Ministers Meet to Discuss Country Life Problems," *Progressive Farmer*, February 25, 1911, 205.

95. "The Country Boy's Creed" (written by Edwin Osgood Grover for the Boys' Corn Clubs of Virginia), *Progressive Farmer*, May 20, 1911, 478.

96. "The Land of Opportunity—Who Shall Possess It?" *Progressive Farmer*, April 23, 1910, 365.

97. Clarence H. Poe, *The Case for Prohibition in North Carolina* (Raleigh: Mutual Pub. Co., n.d.), 4, North Carolina Collection, Wilson Library, University of North Carolina, Chapel Hill; Crow, "Apartheid for the South," 216–25; Jack Temple Kirby, "Clarence Poe's Vision of a Segregated 'Great Rural Civilization,'" *South Atlantic Quarterly* 68 (1969): 28–29.

98. "'Scientific Farming' and Better Marketing Both Essential," *Progressive Farmer*, October 14, 1911, 13.

99. Daniel Rodgers, *Atlantic Crossings: Social Politics in a Progressive Age* (Cambridge, MA: Harvard University Press, 1998), 320–321.

100. Poe, "What I Saw in the Middle West—III," *Progressive Farmer*, June 4, 1910, 477.

101. Poe, "Round the World Travel Letters: XX—Asia's Most Important Lesson for the South," *Progressive Farmer*, March 18, 1911, 295; *Progressive Farmer*, March 25, 1911, 321.

102. Tait Butler, "A Boy's Most Important Problem," *Progressive Farmer*, June 25, 1910, 522.

103. Minnie C. Middleton, "College Training for the Country Girl," *Progressive Farmer*, June 25, 1910, 525.

104. "The College-Trained Farmer's Opportunity for Leadership," *Progressive Farmer*, February 25, 1911, 201.

105. "Legislation the Farmers of North and South Carolina Need," *Progressive Farmer*, January 25, 1913, 105.

106. "The School the Hope of the South," *Progressive Farmer*, June 25, 1910, 517; Tait Butler, "$500 More a Year Farming: How to Get It By the Improvement of the Rural Schools," *Progressive Farmer*, June 25, 1910, 519.

107. Stephen Kantrowitz, *Ben Tillman and the Reconstruction of White Supremacy* (Chapel Hill: University of North Carolina Press, 2000), 87–88.

108. Poe, "Two Big Measures White Farmers Should Support," reprinted article from the January 2, 1915, issue of the *Progressive Farmer*, n.p., Poe Papers, box 29; Woodward, *Origins of the New South*, 184.

109. Poe, "Two Big Measures White Farmers Should Support," n.p.

110. Poe, "Racial Segregation Necessary to Education and Co-operation," *Progressive Farmer*, August 9, 1913, 865.

111. Poe, "Start on the Great Adventure: The Man in Debt Should Begin His Fight for Freedom Now," *Progressive Farmer*, October 25, 1924, 1121. Poe's italics.

112. Committee on Agricultural Credit, Marketing, and Co-operation, "Report of Committee Appointed by the Governor of North Carolina on Needs of North Carolina Farmers with Regard to Credits, Marketing, and Co-operation, Addressed to Hon. Locke Craig, Governor of North Carolina for Transmission to American Commission on Finance, Production, Distribution, and Rural Life," Raleigh, North Carolina, n.d., 3–4, 12–13, North Carolina Collection, Wilson Library, University of North Carolina, Chapel Hill.

113. "A Bill to Be Entitled 'An Act to Relieve the Crop Lien Evil,'" passed by the North Carolina State Senate 33 to 11, 1917, reproduced in an untitled pamphlet; Poe, "The Crop Lien Bill—An Explanation," in the same pamphlet (previously published in the *News and Observer* (Raleigh), February 18, 1917; clipping from the *Sumter Watchman and Southron*, no title, n.d., n.p. All of these materials in the Poe Papers, box 5.

114. Gilbert C. Fite, *Cotton Fields No More: Southern Agriculture, 1865–1980* (Lexington: University Press of Kentucky, 1984), 23.

115. Poe, "Two Big Measures White Farmers Should Support." See also Poe, "The Crop Lien Bill—An Explanation."

116. "The Foulest Blot on Southern Civilization," *Progressive Farmer*, January 4, 1913, 15.

117. Clarence H. Poe, "Lynching: A Southern View," *Atlantic Monthly* 93 (February 1904): 156, 161.

118. Ida B. Wells put the percentage of lynched African Americans accused of rape at one-third in *Southern Horrors: Lynch Law in All Its Phases* (New York: New York Age Print, 1892), "The New Cry," https://www.gutenberg.org/files/14975/14975-h/14975-h.htm. The historian W. Fitzhugh Brundage gives different numbers: "There is a measure of truth in Clarence Poe's claim that the stimulus for lynching initially had been alleged sexual crimes. During the 1880s and 1890s, alleged 'outrages' did prompt the majority of lynchings by all mobs. As the practice of mob justice persisted into the twentieth century, however, the number of lynchings for alleged outrages declined steadily.... Between 1880 and 1889, alleged sexual infractions in Georgia led to more than 60 percent of all lynchings in the state. During the next two decades the percentage of lynchings for sexual transgressions declined to 27 percent. After 1910, 'outrages' accounted for roughly one in six lynchings." W. Fitzhugh Brundage, *Lynching in the New South: Georgia and Virginia, 1880–1930* (Urbana: University of Illinois Press, 1993), 68.

119. Escott, *Many Excellent People*, 197–201. On the movement of rural southerners to cities, see Louis M. Kyriakoudes, *Social Origins of the Urban South: Race, Gender, and Migration in Nashville and Middle Tennessee, 1890–1930* (Chapel Hill: University of North Carolina Press, 2003).

120. Roger Biles, "Tobacco Towns: Urban Growth and Economic Development in Eastern North Carolina," in *North Carolina Tobacco: A History*, ed. Billy Yeargin (Charleston: History Press, 2008), 109–10; Robert Rodgers Korstad, *Civil Rights Unionism* (Chapel Hill: University of North Carolina Press, 2003), 43–44; Jacquelyn Dowd Hall et al., *Like a Family: The Making of a Southern Cotton Mill World* (New York: Norton, 1987), 67; Frank V. Tursi, *Winston-Salem: A History* (John F. Blair, 1994), 116.

121. Tursi, *Winston-Salem*, 69–80.

122. Hall et al., *Like a Family*, 26.

123. Michael Shirley, *From Congregation Town to Industrial City: Culture and Social Change in a Southern Community* (New York: NYU Press, 1994), 190–91.

124. Transcription of interview with Alice P. Evitt by Jim Leloudis, July 18, 1979 (H-162), 36, Southern Oral History Program Collection #4007, Southern Historical Collection, Wilson Library, University of North Carolina at Chapel Hill, https://dc.lib.unc.edu/cdm/compoundobject/collection/sohp/id/11756/rec/10.

125. Evitt interview, 1–5, 37, 39.

126. Evitt interview, 7–8, 39, 43–44, 48.

127. Hall et al., *Like a Family*, 52, 114–24.

128. Gerald W. Johnson, quoted in Escott, *Many Excellent People*, 204.

129. Hall et al., *Like a Family*, 53.

130. Escott, *Many Excellent People*, 222.

131. Korstad, *Civil Rights Unionism*, 42; Tursi, *Winston-Salem*, 107–10, 146.

132. Tursi, *Winston-Salem*, 118–19; Shirley, *From Congregation Town*, 193–94.

133. Michele Gillespie, *Katharine and R. J. Reynolds: Partners of Fortune in the Making of the New South* (Athens: University of Georgia Press, 2012), 86, 98; Korstad, *Civil Rights Unionism*, 43–44.

134. Transcript of interview with Robert "Chick" Black by Robert Korstad, June 1, 1976 (E-0093), n.p., Southern Oral History Program Collection #4007, Southern Historical Collection, Wilson Library, University of North Carolina at Chapel Hill, https://dc.lib.unc.edu//utils/getfile/collection/sohp/id/17177/filename/17219.pdf.

135. Tursi, *Winston-Salem*, 116; Department of Commerce and Labor, Bureau of the Census, Thirteenth Census of the United States: Population, 1910, Forsyth County, Winston Township, City of Winston, First Ward, Enumeration District 69, sheets 1–8B, http://familysearch.org; Korstad, *Civil Rights Unionism*, 43–44.

136. Department of Commerce and Labor, Bureau of the Census, Thirteenth Census of the United States: Population, 1910, Forsyth County, Winston Township, City of Winston, First Ward, Enumeration District 69, sheets 1–8B, http://familysearch.org. Cell describes segregation as more common in cities like Winston-Salem than in older southern cities: "The Old South cities had long histories of interracial economic and social relations, of master-servant ties between white and black families that sometimes went back several generations. Many of these bonds, of course, had already dissolved. But the housing patterns that had been based on them remained. By contrast, the new towns of the Piedmont, where the people of both races were recent arrivals, could be model cities from the first." John W. Cell, *The Highest Stage of White Supremacy: The Origins of Segregation in South Africa and the American South* (New York: Cambridge University Press, 1982), 135.

137. Based on the research of Trevon D. Logan and John M. Parman, who shared with me data collected for their article "The National Rise in Residential Segregation," *Journal of Economic History* 77, no. 1 (March 2017): esp. 129–30. The article explains the methods used to create a neighbor-based segregation index (138–41). The closer to 0 this number is, the less segregated a county; the closer to 1, the more segregated. Forsyth County increased from 0.12 in 1880 to 0.62 in 1900, to 0.74 in 1910, to 0.85 in 1920, to 0.89 in 1930, and to 0.92 in 1940.

138. Korstad, *Civil Rights Unionism*, 44, 73.

2. FUSION, DEMOCRATS, AND THE SCARECROW OF RACE

1.   Charles Aycock to Clarence Poe, May 17, 1902; Aycock to Poe, August 14, 1903; Aycock to Poe, January 27, 1904; Aycock to Poe, November 15, 1909; Aycock to Poe, January 27, 1910; Aycock to Poe, May 29, 1911; Aycock to Poe, January 5, 1912; "Miss Aycock to Wed May 29th," newspaper clipping (probably the *News and Observer* [Raleigh]), February 15, 1912; all in Charles B. Aycock Papers, North Carolina State Archives, box 4. Poe and R. D. W. Connor, "A Personal Appeal to Friends of Charles B. Aycock," April 11, 1912, Aycock Papers, box 3.

2.   James Beeby, ed., *Populism in the South Revisited: New Interpretations and New Departures* (Jackson: University Press of Mississippi, 2012), xv. For an example of the similarity of views of whites in these parties (and of their movement from one party to another), consider William A. Guthrie, a silverite Republican who became a Populist and was the Populists' candidate for governor in 1896 (running against Cyrus Watson, a Democrat, and Daniel Russell, a Republican). By 1900, Guthrie was "advocating the

[disfranchisement] amendment and doing all [he could] for white supremacy." "White Men's Rally!" *Chatham Record* (Pittsboro, NC), July 19, 1900, 3.

3.   See, on the Democrats' efforts to stoke racism in order to take votes from Populists, C. Vann Woodward, *The Strange Career of Jim Crow*, 3rd rev. ed. (New York: Oxford University Press, 1974), 78–79.

4.   For examples of historians pointing to the biracialism of Populists, see C. Vann Woodward, *Tom Watson: Agrarian Rebel* (New York: Oxford University Press, 1938), 220–22, 239–40 ("Never before or since have the two races in the South come so close together as they did during the Populist struggles," 222); C. Vann Woodward, *Origins of the New South, 1877–1913* (Baton Rouge: Louisiana State University Press, 1951, 1971), 254–58; Lawrence Goodwyn, *Democratic Promise: The Populist Moment in America* (New York: Oxford University Press, 1976), 276–306. On the limits of biracialism, see Steven Hahn, *A Nation Under Our Feet: Black Political Struggles in the Rural South from Slavery to the Great Migration* (Cambridge, MA: Harvard University Press, 2003), 432–41.

5.   The literature on Populism in North Carolina includes Helen G. Edmonds, *The Negro and Fusion Politics in North Carolina, 1894–1901* (Chapel Hill: University of North Carolina Press, 1951); Paul D. Escott, *Many Excellent People: Power and Privilege in North Carolina, 1850–1900* (Chapel Hill: University of North Carolina Press, 1985); Goodwyn, *Democratic Promise*; Lawrence Goodwyn, *The Populist Moment: A Short History of the Agrarian Revolt in America* (New York: Oxford University Press, 1978); Bruce Palmer, *"Man Over Money": The Southern Populist Critique of American Capitalism* (Chapel Hill: University of North Carolina Press, 1980); Eric Anderson, *Race and Politics in North Carolina, 1872–1901: The Black Second* (Baton Rouge: Louisiana State University Press, 1981); James L. Hunt, *Marion Butler and American Populism* (Chapel Hill: University of North Carolina Press, 2003); and James M. Beeby, *Revolt of the Tar Heels: The North Carolina Populist Movement, 1890–1901* (Jackson: University Press of Mississippi, 2008).

6.   Populist Party (NC) State Executive Committee, *People's Party Hand-Book of Facts. Campaign of 1898* (Raleigh, NC: Capital Printing Company, Printers and Binders, 1898), 95, North Carolina Collection, Wilson Library, University of North Carolina at Chapel Hill, Documenting the American South, http://docsouth.unc.edu/nc/peoples /peoples.html. Beeby uses this term, too, in *Revolt of the Tar Heels*.

7.   James B. Lloyd, "A Plan to Solve Race Issue in Politics: Prohibit Negro from Holding Office," *Caucasian*, April 12, 1900, 3.

8.   L.L. Polk, "The Protest of the Farmer: Address of President L. L. Polk to Citizens Alliance No. 4 of Washington, D.C. at Concordia Hall," April 14, 1891, 2, Rare Book/ Special Collections Reading Room, Library of Congress.

9.   On the continuing influence of deeply held Populist values, such as producerism, see Jarod Roll, "Agrarian Producerism After Populism: Socialism and Garveyism in the Rural South," in *Populism in the South Revisited: New Interpretations and New Departures*, ed. James M. Beeby (Jackson: University Press of Mississippi, 2012).

10.   Robert F. Durden, "North Carolina in the New South," in *The North Carolina Experience: An Interpretive and Documentary History*, ed. Lindley S. Butler and Alan D. Watson (Chapel Hill: University of North Carolina Press, 1984), 315–16; Federal Writers' Project, *North Carolina: A Guide to the Old North State* (Columbia: University of South Carolina Press, 1939), 60; Edmonds, *Negro and Fusion Politics*, 23. Sources on

the Farmers' Alliance in North Carolina include John D. Hicks, "The Farmers' Alliance in North Carolina," *North Carolina Historical Review* 2 (April 1925): 162–87; Lala Carr Steelman, *The North Carolina Farmers' Alliance: A Political History, 1887–1893* (Greenville, NC: East Carolina University Publications, 1985); and Lala Carr Steelman, "The Role of Elias Carr in the North Carolina Farmers' Alliance," *North Carolina Historical Review* 57, no. 2 (April 1980): 133–58.

11. Charles Postel, *The Populist Vision* (Oxford: Oxford University Press, 2007), 197; "The Address of President Marion Butler, to the North Carolina Farmers' State Alliance at Greensboro, N.C.," in *Addresses of Marion Butler, President, and Cyrus Thompson, Lecturer, to the North Carolina Farmer's State Alliance, at Greensboro, N.C., Aug. 8, 9, and 10, 1893, at Its Seventh Annual Session* (Raleigh: Barnes Bros., 1893), 5, North Carolina Collection, Wilson Library, University of North Carolina at Chapel Hill, Documenting the American South, http://docsouth.unc.edu/nc/butler93/butler93.html; Goodwyn, *Populist Moment*, xvi.

12. "Address of President Marion Butler, to the North Carolina Farmers' State Alliance at Greensboro, N.C.," 1–2.

13. Polk, "Protest of the Farmer," 15.

14. Durden, "North Carolina in the New South," 316–17.

15. Polk, "Protest of the Farmer," 7–8.

16. Durden, "North Carolina in the New South," 316–18; Polk, "Protest of the Farmer," 20–21; Edmonds, *Negro and Fusion Politics*, 24.

17. Steven Hahn, *The Roots of Southern Populism: Yeoman Farmers and the Transformation of the Georgia Upcountry, 1850–1890* (New York: Oxford University Press, 1983), 273–74; Adrienne Monteith Petty, *Standing Their Ground: Small Farmers in North Carolina Since the Civil War* (New York: Oxford University Press, 2013), 49–50; Postel, *Populist Vision*, 177–82. On African Americans in the Colored Farmers' Alliance and Populist Party, see Omar H. Ali, *In the Lion's Mouth: Black Populism in the New South* (Jackson: University Press of Mississippi, 2010).

18. Deborah Beckel, *Radical Reform: Interracial Politics in Post-Emancipation North Carolina* (Charlottesville: University of Virginia Press, 2011), 3–10; Beeby, *Revolt of the Tar Heels*, 1–4; Edmonds, *Negro and Fusion Politics*, 25.

19. Woodward, *Origins of the New South*, 244.

20. "Address of President Marion Butler, to the North Carolina Farmers' State Alliance at Greensboro, N.C.," 3; Polk, "Protest of the Farmer," 9.

21. "Vote!" (1898), Broadsides and Ephemera Collection, Duke University Library, http://library.duke.edu/digitalcollections/broadsides_bdsnc061806/#info.

22. Polk, "Protest of the Farmer," 9.

23. Postel, *Populist Vision*, 9, 16.

24. "Address of President Marion Butler, to the North Carolina Farmers' State Alliance at Greensboro, N.C.," 3; Beeby, *Revolt of the Tar Heels*, 15.

25. Polk, "Protest of the Farmer," 9–10, 13.

26. Ali, *In the Lion's Mouth*, 8, 75–76. On black Populists, see Gerald H. Gaither, *Blacks and the Populist Revolt: Ballots and Bigotry in the "New South"* (Tuscaloosa: University of Alabama Press, 1977). Woodward describes the alliance of white and black Populists as follows: "The Populist experiment in interracial harmony, precarious at best and handicapped from the start by suspicion and prejudice, was another casualty of the political crisis of the 'nineties. While the movement was at the peak of zeal the two

races had surprised each other and astonished their opponents by the harmony they achieved and the good will with which they co-operated. When it became apparent that their opponents would stop at nothing to divide them, however, and would steal the Negro's votes anyway, the bi-racial partnership of Populism began to dissolve in frustration and bitterness. Many of the Negroes became apathetic and ceased political activity altogether. Some of the white Populists understood that the Negro was merely one of the hapless victims rather than the author of the party's downfall. But for the majority it came much easier to blame the Negro for their defeat, to make him the scapegoat, and to vent upon him the pent up accumulation of bitterness against the legitimate offenders who had escaped their wrath." Woodward, *Strange Career*, 80–81.

27. Edmonds, *Negro and Fusion Politics*, 27, 37; Beeby, *Revolt of the Tar Heels*, 51. According to Omar Ali, Populist or Fusion candidates won 15.95 percent of the vote in North Carolina in 1892 and 53.78 percent in 1894. Ali, *In the Lion's Mouth*, 119, 136–37. See also Joe Creech, *Righteous Indignation: Religion and the Populist Revolution* (Urbana: University of Illinois Press, 2016), 134.

28. Barbara J. Fields, "*Origins of the New South* and the Negro Question," *Journal of Southern History* 67, no. 4 (November 2001): 813.

29. Jeffrey J. Crow, "Cracking the Solid South: Populism and the Fusionist Interlude," in *The North Carolina Experience: An Interpretive and Documentary History*, ed. Lindley S. Butler and Alan D. Watson (Chapel Hill: University of North Carolina Press, 1984), 337. See also Jeffrey J. Crow and Robert F. Durden, *Maverick Republican in the Old North State: A Political Biography of Daniel L. Russell* (Baton Rouge: Louisiana State University Press, 1977).

30. Edmonds, *Negro and Fusion Politics*, 13; Bruce E. Baker, *This Mob Will Surely Take My Life: Lynchings in the Carolinas, 1871–1947* (London: Continuum, 2008), 98–99.

31. "A Brazen Steal! Some Lessons of the Wake Republican Convention," Duke University Libraries, Broadsides and Ephemera Collection, folder NC11, http://library.duke.edu/digitalcollections/broadsides_bdsnc112242/.

32. Andrew D. Cowles, "A card to the Republican party of Iredell County," October 29, 1894, Duke University Libraries, Broadsides and Ephemera Collection, folder NC6, http://library.duke.edu/digitalcollections/broadsides_bdsnc061827/.

33. L. L. Polk to James W. Denmark, March 12, 1892, L.L. Polk Papers, #3708, Southern Historical Collection, Wilson Library, University of North Carolina at Chapel Hill, box 16, folder 226.

34. Polk to Denmark, March 15, 1892, Polk Papers, box 16, folder 226.

35. Polk to Denmark, March 16, 1892, Polk Papers, box 16, folder 226.

36. Beeby, *Revolt of the Tar Heels*, 7–8.

37. William Jennings Bryan, "Cross of Gold" speech, in *Official Proceedings of the Democratic National Convention Held in Chicago, Ill., July 7th, 8th, 9th, 10th and 11th, 1896* (Logansport, Indiana: Wilson, Humphreys & Co., 1896), 234.

38. On African Americans objecting to fusion with the Democrats, see Ali, *In the Lion's Mouth*, 114–15.

39. J. Z. Greene to Marion Butler, October 19, 1896, 1, 3–4, Marion Butler Papers #114, Southern Historical Collection, Wilson Library, University of North Carolina at Chapel Hill, box 3, folder 35.

40. P. L. Gardner to Marion Butler, October 20, 1896, Butler Papers, box 3, folder 37.

41. N. A. Dunning, "An Appeal to Populists and a Defense of Mr. Thos. E. Watson," October 20, 1896, Butler Papers, box 3, folder 38.

42. Marion Butler to Thomas E. Watson, October 26, 1896, 2, Butler Papers, box 3, folder 38.

43. Thomas E. Watson to Marion Butler, October 28, 1896, 4, 7, 12, Butler Papers, box 3, folder 38.

44. W. B. Felton to Marion Butler, July 7, 1898, 3, Butler Papers, box 9, folder 104.

45. Postel, *Populist Vision*, 183–88.

46. Postel, *Populist Vision*, 199; State Executive Committee, *People's Party Hand-Book of Facts*, 5.

47. Woodward, *Origins of the New South*, 193–94; Goodwyn, *The Populist Moment*, xvi.

48. H. Leon Prather Sr., "We Have Taken a City: A Centennial Essay," in *Democracy Betrayed*, ed. David S. Cecelski and Timothy B. Tyson (Chapel Hill: University of North Carolina Press, 1998), 22.

49. Josephus Daniels, *Editor in Politics* (Chapel Hill: University of North Carolina Press, 1941), 298.

50. Oliver H. Orr Jr., *Charles Brantley Aycock* (Chapel Hill: University of North Carolina Press, 1961), 5–19, 135–36.

51. William S. Powell, ed., *Dictionary of North Carolina Biography*, 6 vols. (Chapel Hill, NC, 1979–1996), 6:249; Robert Watson Winston, *It's a Far Cry* (New York: Henry Holt, 1937), 8, 26–28.

52. Winston, *It's a Far Cry*, 11, 31–32, 28.

53. Winston, *It's a Far Cry*, 54–55.

54. Winston, *It's a Far Cry*, 237.

55. Francis Winston, letter concerning African American suffrage, 3–4, Francis Donnell Winston Papers, #2810, Southern Historical Collection, Wilson Library, University of North Carolina at Chapel Hill, series 2, folder 74.

56. LeRae Umfleet, "1898 Wilmington Race Riot Report," in Wilmington Race Riot Commission and the North Carolina Office of Cultural Resources (May 31, 2006), chap. 3A, 66–68, http://www.ah.dcr.state.nc.us/1898-wrrc/report/report.htm; Winston, *It's a Far Cry*, 237–38, 250–54, 259.

57. Benjamin R. Justesen, *In His Own Words: The Writings, Speeches, and Letters of George Henry White* (Lincoln, NE: iUniverse, 2004), xiii–xv. See also Benjamin R. Justesen, *George Henry White: An Even Chance in the Race of Life* (Baton Rouge: Louisiana State University Press, 2001).

58. *Congressional Record: Containing the Proceedings and Debates of the Fifty-Sixth Congress*, 2nd sess. (Washington, DC: Government Printing Office, 1901), 34:1636.

59. Collins & Goodwin, *Biographical Sketches of the Members of the General Assembly of North Carolina, 1895* (Raleigh: Edwards & Broughton, 1895), 52–53; *National Cyclopedia of the Colored Race*, ed. Clement Richardson (Montgomery, AL: National Publishing Company, 1919), 1:350–51; Willard B. Gatewood, "Young, James Hunter," NCpedia, https://www.ncpedia.org/biography/young-james-hunter.

60. *Congressional Record*, 2nd sess., 34:1635.

61. In addition to the *News and Observer* (Raleigh), the *Charlotte Observer*, *Messenger* (Wilmington), and *Morning Star* (Wilmington) played key roles in stirring up resentment toward African Americans. Umfleet, "1898 Wilmington Race Riot Report," chap. 3A, 56.

62. Michael Honey, "Class, Race, and Power: Racial Violence and the Delusions of White Supremacy" in *Democracy Betrayed*, ed. David S. Cecelski and Timothy B. Tyson (Chapel Hill: University of North Carolina Press, 1998), 170.

63. See, for example, "Jim Young Did Inspect—His Report," *News and Observer* (Raleigh), August 28, 1898, 4; "No Amount of Squirming or Lying Will Avail," *News and Observer* (Raleigh), September 15, 1898, 4. There are many other similar articles about Young's position at the institution.

64. Winston, *It's a Far Cry*, 173.

65. Clarence Poe, *My First Eighty Years* (Chapel Hill: University of North Carolina Press, 1963), 116.

66. Daniels, *Editor in Politics*, 253.

67. Daniels, *Editor in Politics*, 255.

68. Daniels, *Editor in Politics*, 253–55.

69. Daniels, *Editor in Politics*, 335.

70. Winston, *It's a Far Cry*, 259.

71. Glenda Elizabeth Gilmore, *Gender and Jim Crow: Women and the Politics of White Supremacy in North Carolina, 1896–1920* (Chapel Hill: University of North Carolina Press, 1996), 83. Writing about the 1898 white-supremacy campaign in North Carolina, Gregory P. Downs concludes that fear about outrages committed against white women was perhaps less important to the campaign than the notion that blacks were competing with whites for "government access." Cartoons published in the Raleigh *News and Observer* were less often about black men threatening the virtue of white women and more focused on "suggest[ing] that whites were friendless and abandoned, while African Americans profited from their relationship with, and access to, white Republican politicians." Access to government, whites believed, "meant access to jobs," and "this access was a zero-sum competition between white and black men." Gregory P. Downs, *Declarations of Dependence: The Long Reconstruction of Popular Politics in the South, 1861–1908* (Chapel Hill: University of North Carolina Press, 2011), 195, 199.

72. Daniels, *Editor in Politics*, 253–54.

73. Glenda E. Gilmore, "Murder, Memory, and the Flight of the Incubus," in *Democracy Betrayed*, ed. David S. Cecelski and Timothy B. Tyson (Chapel Hill: University of North Carolina Press, 1998), 77.

74. Prather, "We Have Taken a City," 21; Gilmore, *Gender and Jim Crow*, 77.

75. Honey, "Class, Race, and Power," 165.

76. There is much more to the story of how the Democrats took political power from the Fusionists than I am able to explain in a single chapter. For information about the Democrats' changing economic policies, other factors that weakened the Populists in North Carolina before 1898, and how Democrats changed election laws to influence the 1900 election, see James Beeby, *Revolt of the Tar Heels*.

77. Fields, "Origins of the New South and the Negro Question," 815.

78. Robert Rodgers Korstad, *Civil Rights Unionism* (Chapel Hill: University of North Carolina Press, 2003), 5.

79. Jack Temple Kirby, *Darkness at the Dawning: Race and Reform in the Progressive South* (Philadelphia: J. B. Lippincott, 1972), 4.

80. Furnifold Simmons, *Memoirs*, in *F. M. Simmons: Statesman of the New South: Memoirs and Addresses*, ed. J. Fred Rippy (Durham, NC: Duke University Press, 1936), 32.

81. Stephen Kantrowitz, *Ben Tillman and the Reconstruction of White Supremacy* (Chapel Hill: University of North Carolina Press, 2000), 2.

82. Prather, "We Have Taken a City," 16; Gilmore, "Murder, Memory, and the Flight of the Incubus," 75; Honey, "Class, Race, and Power," 170–71.

83. Tyson and Cecelski, introduction to *Democracy Betrayed*, 4.

84. Gilmore, "Murder, Memory, and the Flight of the Incubus," 88.

85. Tyson and Cecelski, introduction to *Democracy Betrayed*, 6.

86. "11 Negroes Dead, War in Wilmington," *Union Republican* (Winston), November 17, 1898, 1.

87. In 1922, Felton would become the first female U.S. senator, when she was appointed at age eighty-seven by Georgia's governor Thomas Hardwick—who wished to curry favor with female voters—to fill the seat of Tom Watson, who had died suddenly, until Walter George was sworn in. Felton served for a mere day after taking the oath of office. "First Woman Senator," http://www.senate.gov/artandhistory/history/minute/First_Woman_Senator_Appointed.htm.

88. LeeAnn Whites, "Love, Hate, Rape, Lynching: Rebecca Latimer Felton and the Gender Politics of Racial Violence," in *Democracy Betrayed*, ed. David S. Cecelski and Timothy B. Tyson (Chapel Hill: University of North Carolina Press, 1998), 149, 152–53; Joel Williamson, *The Crucible of Race: Black-White Relations in the American South Since Emancipation* (New York: Oxford University Press, 1984), 124–30. On Felton's work against the convict leasing system (which she believed corrupted the morality of black women and made them more likely to entice white men), see Sarah Haley, *No Mercy Here: Gender, Punishment, and the Making of Jim Crow Modernity* (Chapel Hill: University of North Carolina Press, 2016), 141–55. Crystal N. Feimster also examines Felton in *Southern Horrors: Women and the Politics of Rape and Lynching* (Cambridge, MA: Harvard University Press, 2009).

89. Gilmore, *Gender and Jim Crow*, 83, 87.

90. Gilmore, "Murder, Memory, and the Flight of the Incubus," 78; Prather, "We Have Taken a City," 23–24; *Wilmington Record*, August 18, 1898, quoted in Robert H. Wooley, "Race and Politics: The Evolution of the White Supremacy Campaign of 1898 in North Carolina," Ph.D. diss., University of North Carolina at Chapel Hill, 1977; Umfleet, "1898 Wilmington Race Riot Report," 270–71; *News and Observer* (Raleigh), August 24, 1898, 3.

91. Beeby, *Revolt of the Tar Heels*, 156.

92. Daniels, *Editor in Politics*, 287.

93. Quoted in Prather, "We Have Taken a City," 25.

94. Daniels, *Editor in Politics*, 284.

95. Simmons, *Memoirs*, 24.

96. Daniels, *Editor in Politics*, 292–93.

97. "The White Declaration of Independence," Alfred M. Waddell Papers, #743, folder 2b, Southern Historical Collection, Wilson Library, University of North Carolina at Chapel Hill; Umfleet, "1898 Wilmington Race Riot Report," 114–17.

98. Letter from the Committee of Colored Citizens to A. M. Waddell, Chairman of the Citizens Committee, n.d., Alfred M. Waddell Papers, folder 2b, Southern Historical Collection, Wilson Library, University of North Carolina at Chapel Hill.

99. Tyson and Cecelski, introduction to *Democracy Betrayed*, 4–5.

100. J. Allen Kirk, "A Statement of Facts Concerning the Bloody Riot in Wilmington, N.C. Of Interest to Every Citizen of the United States" (1898?), 8, 10, http://docsouth.unc .edu/nc/kirk/kirk.html.
101. Gilmore, "Murder, Memory, and the Flight of the Incubus," 86–87.
102. Alfred Moore Waddell, *Some Memories of My Life* (Raleigh: Edwards & Broughton Printing Company, 1908), 243; Tyson and Cecelski, introduction to *Democracy Betrayed*, 4–5.
103. Tyson and Cecelski, introduction to *Democracy Betrayed*, 4–5; Hayumi Higuchi, "White Supremacy on the Cape Fear: The Wilmington Affair of 1898," MA thesis, University of North Carolina at Chapel Hill, 1980, 119–20.
104. Honey, "Class, Race, and Power," 173–77.
105. Beeby, *Revolt of the Tar Heels*, 187.
106. Charles Aycock, "The Ideals of a New Era" (inaugural address, January 15, 1901), in *The Life and Speeches of Charles Brantley Aycock*, ed. R. D. W. Connor and Clarence Poe (Garden City, NJ: Doubleday, Page & Co., 1912), 229–30.
107. Charles Aycock, "The Keynote of the Amendment Campaign (Address Accepting the Democratic Nomination for Governor, April 11, 1901)," in *Life and Speeches*, 224.
108. Kirk, "Statement of Facts," 16.
109. Prather, "We Have Taken a City," 37–38; Umfleet, "1898 Wilmington Race Riot Report," chap. 6, 190–93; chap. 8, 224–48.
110. Richard R. Wright Jr., "The Economic Condition of Negroes in the North III: Negro Communities in New Jersey," *Southern Workman* 37, no. 7 (July 1908): 385–93. Whitesboro is discussed on 393.
111. According to James Beeby, so does examination of contested election testimony, which he examined in his essay " '[T]he Angels from Heaven Had Come Down and Wiped Their Names off the Registration Books': The Demise of Grassroots Populism in North Carolina," in *Populism in the South Revisited: New Interpretations and New Departures*, ed. James Beeby (Jackson: University Press of Mississippi, 2012).
112. "For White Supremacy Then," *News and Observer* (Raleigh), October 4, 1892, col. D.
113. "The Proposed Suffrage Amendment. The Platform and Resolutions of the People's Party," 9, North Carolina Collection, Wilson Library, University of North Carolina at Chapel Hill, Documenting the American South, http://docsouth.unc.edu/nc/ populist/populist.html. See also Postel, *Populist Vision*, 173–76.
114. " 'White Mans Party' Democracy Shown Up; It Elects Negroes to Office by Hundreds, Then Squalls 'Nigger Domination,' " Supplement to *Caucasian*, October 20, 1898, 1.
115. "Helpless Orphans Hired Out to Die," Supplement to *Caucasian*, October 20, 1898, 2.
116. "The Democratic Board of County Commissioners of Alamance County Work a Young White Girl on the Public Roads with Negro Men," Supplement to *Caucasian*, October 20, 1898, 2.
117. "Negro Notaries Public Are Necessary for 'White Man's Party' Democrats," Supplement to *Caucasian*, October 20, 1898, 3.
118. "Held Up by Butler: The Senator Was Opposed to Negro Postmasters, Secured the Rejection of One," *Caucasian*, December 8, 1898, 3.

119. Postel, *Populist Vision*, 18–19; "The Negro Smith Scores Populist Johnson" (Raleigh?, 1900?), 1, North Carolina Collection, Wilson Library, University of North Carolina at Chapel Hill, Documenting the American South, http://docsouth.unc.edu/nc/negrosmith /negrosmith.html.

120. Gaither, *Blacks and the Populist Revolt*, 87.

121. Daniels, *Editor in Politics*, 243–44.

122. Daniels, *Editor in Politics*, 253–54.

123. Marion Butler to J. S. Mitchell, November 15, 1898, Butler Papers, box 10, folder 119.

124. "A Happy New Year to You," *Gazette* (Raleigh), January 1, 1898, 2.

125. "A Clear Cut Policy," *Union Republican*, November 17, 1898, 2.

126. "Republican State Platform Adopted by the Republican Party at the State Convention Held in Raleigh N.C.," *Union Republican*, July 12, 1900, 4.

127. Prather, "We Have Taken a City," 39. On disfranchisement in the South, see J. Morgan Kousser, *The Shaping of Southern Politics: Suffrage Restriction and the Establishment of the One-Party South, 1880–1910* (New Haven, CT: Yale University Press, 1974); and Michael Perman, *Struggle for Mastery: Disfranchisement in the South, 1888–1908* (Chapel Hill: University of North Carolina Press, 2001).

128. Charles B. Aycock, "The Disfranchisement of the Negro," *World To-Day* 5, no. 4 (October 1903): 1305.

129. Simmons, *Memoirs*, 27–28.

130. Beeby, *Revolt of the Tar Heels*, 193–95; John Haley, "Race, Rhetoric, and Revolution," in *Democracy Betrayed*, ed. David S. Cecelski and Timothy B. Tyson (Chapel Hill: University of North Carolina Press, 1998), 220.

131. Overview to Governors' Papers: Charles B. Aycock, North Carolina State Archives, Raleigh, NC.

132. Charles Aycock, "The Disfranchisement of the Negro" for "The World Today," unpublished article, Aycock Papers, box 2; Jeffrey J. Crow, "An Apartheid for the South: Clarence Poe's Crusade for Rural Segregation," in *Race, Class, and Politics in Southern History: Essays in Honor of Robert F. Durden*, ed. Jeffrey J. Crow et al. (Baton Rouge: Louisiana State University Press, 1989), 221.

133. Ali, *In the Lion's Mouth*, 137.

134. "Senator Butler's Speech on Manhood Suffrage in North Carolina and the Proposed Constitutional Amendment," *Caucasian*, March 8, 1900, 1.

135. Daniels, *Editor in Politics*, 326.

136. "Senator Butler's Position," *Caucasian*, January 4, 1900, 2.

137. Letter to the editor from "A Populist" from Lenoir, NC, *Caucasian*, May 31, 1900, 3.

138. "White Voters in Danger; The Amendment More Dangerous If Constitutional to White Men," *Caucasian*, May 25, 1900, 1.

139. "White Men's Rights in Danger," *Caucasian*, May 17, 1900, 2.

140. Political cartoon, *Caucasian*, June 14, 1900, 1.

141. "As Fit as the White Man," *Carolina Mascot* (Statesville, NC), July 26, 1900, 2.

142. Beeby, "'[T]he Angels from Heaven Had Come Down and Wiped Their Names off the Registration Books,'" 171.

143. Postel, *Populist Vision*, 173.

144. T. B. Parker to J. Bryan Grimes, May 7, 1900, J. Bryan Grimes Papers, Southern Historical Collection, University of North Carolina, Chapel Hill. Quoted in Joseph A.

Coté, "Clarence Hamilton Poe: Crusading Editor, 1881–1964," Ph.D. diss., University of Georgia, 1976, 71.

145. Poe, "Suffrage Restriction in the South; Its Causes and Consequences," *North American Review* 175 (July 1902): 535–38.

146. Poe, *My First Eighty Years*, 66.

147. In his 1915 book *How Farmers Co-operate and Double Profits*, for example, Poe expressed many Populist ideas: "Heretofore the farmer too often has been only a hireling in his own house. He has been the laborer who did the hard work but received only such profits as were left him by his industrial masters—these masters being the men from whom he bought his supplies; the men who converted his products into secondary form; the men who marketed his products; and the men who lent him money to carry on his business or to buy food from other farmers while he worked. . . . The farmer has surrendered to other interests all the business side of agriculture apart from production, and . . . all these other interests have prospered in greater degree than has the farmer, who is the creator of all the basic wealth." In this passage, Poe, like the Populists before him, describes farmers as the true producers of wealth, the fruits of whose labors are taken from them by a greedy moneyed class. He goes on to decry the concentration of wealth into the hands of the few, arguing that if farmers cooperate in the buying and selling of goods, they will be able to hold onto some of the profits derived from the goods they produce, thus leading to a more equitable distribution of wealth. Instead of producing just a raw product (such as corn or cotton), farmers should "finish" the products (by, for example, grinding or ginning it); this would allow them to recapture the money taken from them by the product finishers. Cooperation would allow them to own and operate mills, gins, and the other equipment they would need. They ought also to market their products. Clarence Poe, *How Farmers Co-operate and Double Profits* (New York: Orange Judd, 1915), 22–27.

148. See Andrew C. Baker, "Race and Romantic Agrarianism: The Transnational Roots of Clarence Poe's Crusade for Rural Segregation in North Carolina," *Agricultural History* 87, no. 1 (Winter 2013): 93–114. See also Poe, *How Farmers Co-operate*, chaps. 18–20.

149. See Daniel Rodgers, *Atlantic Crossings: Social Politics in a Progressive Age* (Cambridge, MA: Harvard University Press, 1998), chap. 8.

150. Poe, *My First Eighty Years*, 60, 56. See also Coté, "Clarence Hamilton Poe"; Jack Temple Kirby, "Clarence Poe's Vision of a Segregated 'Great Rural Civilization,'" *South Atlantic Quarterly* 68 (1969): 28; Clarence Poe to Henry C. Taylor, April 11, 1940, Polk Papers, box 16, folder 227.

151. Goodwyn, *Populist Moment*, 33.

152. Among these white supremacists was Governor Locke Craig, who had worked while in the state legislature on the constitutional amendment that disfranchised black voters in the state. As governor, Craig appointed Poe to a committee on Agricultural Credit, Marketing, and Co-operation. "The North Carolina Election of 1898: Locke Craig (1860–1924)," http://www.lib.unc.edu/ncc/1898/bios/locke.html.

153. Poe, *My First Eighty Years*, 112–113; Escott, *Many Excellent People*, 173; Gilmore, *Gender and Jim Crow*, 66. Poe was president of the club between 1926 and 1950.

154. Charles Aycock, "A Message to the Negro (Address, opening the Negro State Fair, 1901)," in *Life and Speeches*, 250.

155. Crow, "Apartheid for the South," 219–22.

3. INSPIRATIONS FOR RESIDENTIAL SEGREGATION

1. "Poe Aycock Wedding: Prominent Couple Wed and Set Sail for Europe Saturday Morning," *Daily Argus* (Goldsboro), May 30, 1912, 1; "Poe-Aycock," *Mebane Leader*, June 6, 1912, 1; "Quiet Home Wedding," *Daily Sun* (Durham), May 21, 1912, 3.
2. R. H. Boyd, *The Separate or "Jim Crow" Car Laws or Legislative Enactments* (Nashville: National Baptist Pub. Board, 1909), 35–36; see also Gilbert Stephenson, "Racial Distinctions in Southern Law," *American Political Science Review* 1 (November 1906): 52–54.
3. C. Vann Woodward, *The Strange Career of Jim Crow*, 3rd rev. ed. (New York: Oxford University Press, 1974), 97–98.
4. Stephenson, "Racial Distinctions in Southern Law," 60–61.
5. Stephen A. Berrey, *The Jim Crow Routine: Everyday Performances of Race, Civil Rights, and Segregation in Mississippi* (Chapel Hill: University of North Carolina Press, 2015), 21.
6. Paul D. Escott, *Many Excellent People: Power and Privilege in North Carolina, 1850–1900* (Chapel Hill: University of North Carolina Press, 1985), 260.
7. Glenda Elizabeth Gilmore, *Gender and Jim Crow: Women and the Politics of White Supremacy in North Carolina, 1896–1920* (Chapel Hill: University of North Carolina Press, 1996), 21.
8. Berrey, *Jim Crow Routine*, 20–21, 3.
9. Grace Elizabeth Hale, *Making Whiteness: The Culture of Segregation in the South, 1890–1940* (New York: Vintage, 1998), 129); Cell also discusses segregation as a solution to modern problems in John W. Cell, *The Highest Stage of White Supremacy: The Origins of Segregation in South Africa and the American South* (New York: Cambridge University Press, 1982): "It was the economically necessary and irreversible movement of black and brown people into towns and industries, their increasingly effective political participation, their growing uppityness as they became educated or left their place on plantations or on tribal lands that created the crisis of white supremacy in the first place" (234).
10. Quoted in W. E. B. Du Bois, "The Last Word in Caste," *NAACP Fourth Annual Report, 1913*, 74.
11. Charles J. McClain, *In Search of Equality: The Chinese Struggle Against Discrimination in Nineteenth-Century America* (Berkeley: University of California Press, 1994), 92, 225, 224.
12. See Marilyn Lake and Henry Reynolds, *Drawing the Global Colour Line: White Men's Countries and the International Challenge of Racial Equality* (Cambridge: Cambridge University Press, 2008), 263–67; Mae M. Ngai, *Impossible Subjects: Illegal Aliens and the Making of Modern America* (Princeton, NJ: Princeton University Press, 2014), 39–40.
13. Clarence Poe, "Education, Co-Operation, Legislation," *Progressive Farmer*, June 14, 1913, 703.
14. Poe, "Education, Co-Operation, Legislation," 703.
15. Poe, "Education, Co-Operation, Legislation," *Progressive Farmer*, June 7, 1913, 681.
16. Don H. Doyle, *New Men, New Cities, New South: Atlanta, Nashville, Charleston, Mobile, 1860–1910* (Chapel Hill: University of North Carolina Press, 1990), 261–62, 264. See also Howard Rabinowitz, *Race Relations in the Urban South, 1865–1890* (New

York: Oxford University Press, 1978), 97. On the shift to urban segregation after the
Civil War, see also John Kellogg, "Negro Urban Clusters in the Post-Bellum South,"
Geographical Review 67 (July 1971): 287–303; John Kellogg, "The Formation of Black
Residential Areas in Lexington, Kentucky, 1865–1885," *Journal of Southern History* 4
(February 1982): 21–52; Paul Groves and Edward Muller, "The Evolution of Black Residential Areas in Late Nineteenth Century Cities," *Journal of Historical Geography* 1,
no. 2 (1975): 169–91; Howard Sumka, "Racial Segregation in Small North Carolina Cities," *Southeastern Geographer* 17, no. 1 (1977): 58–75; Earl Lewis, *In Their Own Interests: Race, Class, and Power in Twentieth-Century Norfolk, Virginia* (Berkeley: University of California Press, 1991), 8–28; Geraldine McTigue, "Patterns of Residence:
Housing Distribution by Color in Two Louisiana Towns, 1860–1880," *Louisiana Studies* 15 (Winter 1976): 345–88.

17. Garrett Power, "Apartheid Baltimore Style: The Residential Segregation Ordinances
of 1910–1913," *Maryland Law Review* 42, no. 2 (1983): 290.

18. Power, "Apartheid Baltimore Style," 293–94.

19. On segregation as a Progressive reform, see, for example, Jack Temple Kirby, *Darkness
at the Dawning: Race and Reform in the Progressive South* (Philadelphia: Lippincott,
1972), 4–25. On residential segregation as separate from this reform effort, see Gretchen
Boger, "The Meaning of Neighborhood in the Modern City: Baltimore's Residential
Segregation Ordinances, 1910–1913," *Journal of Urban History* 35 (January 2009):
236–58.

20. Fredrickson quoted in Power, "Apartheid Baltimore Style," 302. On the paternalism
and racism of white Progressive reformers, see Gilmore, *Gender and Jim Crow*; and
Clayton McClure Brooks, *The Uplift Generation: Cooperation Across the Color Line in
Early Twentieth-Century Virginia* (Charlottesville: University of Virginia Press, 2017).

21. See Doyle, *New Men, New Cities, New South*, 301–2.

22. Hale, *Making Whiteness*, 94, 105, 117–18, 118. On relations between white women and
their black cooks, see Rebecca Sharpless, *Cooking in Other Women's Kitchens: Domestic Workers in the South, 1865–1960* (Chapel Hill: University of North Carolina Press,
2010), esp. chap. 6. On how "black and white children of the Jim Crow era *learn[ed]*
race—both the racial roles they were expected to play in their society and a sense of
themselves as *being* 'black' or 'white,'" see Jennifer Ritterhouse, *Growing Up Jim Crow:
How Black and White Southern Children Learned Race* (Chapel Hill: University of
North Carolina Press, 2006), 2.

23. Stephen Grant Meyer, *As Long as They Don't Move Next Door: Segregation and Racial
Conflict in American Neighborhoods* (Lanham, MD: Rowman & Littlefield, 2000),
2–3; Kenneth T. Jackson, *Crabgrass Frontier: The Suburbanization of the United States*
(New York: Oxford University Press, 1985), 49–53. On changing conceptions of home,
see Margaret Garb, *City of American Dreams: A History of Home Ownership and Housing Reform in Chicago, 1871–1919* (Chicago: University of Chicago Press, 2005).

24. Jackson, *Crabgrass Frontier*, 53.

25. LeeAnn Lands, *The Culture of Property: Race, Class, and Housing Landscapes in
Atlanta, 1880–1950* (Athens: University of Georgia Press, 2009), 2–12, 5.

26. *Buchanan v. Warley*, Brief for the Plaintiff in Error, 19, NAACP Papers, reel 4, group
1, box G-76.

27. "Baltimore," *Crisis* 1, no. 1 (November 1910), 11; Boger, "Meaning of Neighborhood in
the Modern City," 245; "Segregate Negroes in East Winston: Would Prevent Negroes

from Living on East Fourth Street," *Winston-Salem Journal*, June 14, 1912, 1. According to T. J. Woofter Jr., sometimes property values depreciated *before* African Americans moved in, too, rather than afterward, as white residents believed, and "if one of these depreciating sections lies close to a Negro neighborhood, or if it has good transit service to places where Negroes work, the time finally comes when Negroes are willing to pay more for property there than the white occupants are, and the transition begins." T. J. Woofter, *Negro Problems in Cities* (New York: Doubleday, Doran & Co., 1928), 74–75. Kruse tells the story of why whites left interracial cities for suburbs in a later period in Kevin M. Kruse, *White Flight: Atlanta and the Making of Modern Conservatism* (Princeton, NJ: Princeton University Press, 2007). He locates the emergence of modern conservatism in white flight as whites "were forced to abandon their traditional, populist, and often starkly racist demagoguery and instead craft a new conservatism predicated on a language of rights, freedoms, and individualism" (6).

28. According to one contemporary report, "the high rentals paid, by the negroes for their town dwellings is a serious handicap to their economic progress as a race. It would seem that, on account of the undesirability and inconvenience of the localities in which these houses are located and the cheapness of the houses, a low scale of rents should prevail. But, generally speaking, negro rental property is looked on by the landlord class as one of the most lucrative investments for small amounts of money." "Dr. Chas. H. Brough on the Southern Race Question," *Arkansas Gazette*, January 3, 1915, 12.

29. Boger, "Meaning of Neighborhood in the Modern City," 252–53.

30. Case on appeal before the Superior Court of Forsyth County, North Carolina, January Term 1914, 7–10, in the original case file for *State v. Darnell*, North Carolina State Archives.

31. Meyer, *As Long as They Don't Move Next Door*, 3.

32. Power, "Apartheid Baltimore Style," 324–25.

33. "Negro Farmer Not a Menace: Secretary of International Y.M.C.A. Committee Opposes Segregation," *Topeka Plaindealer*, February 12, 1915, 3.

34. W. Ashbie Hawkins, "A Year of Segregation in Baltimore," *Crisis* 3, no. 1 (November 1911): 27, 28. See also Power, "Apartheid Baltimore Style," 298; Woofter, *Negro Problems in Cities*, 21, 73, 76–77.

35. A. Leon Higginbotham, F. Michael Higginbotham, and S. Sandile Ngcobo, "De Jure Housing Segregation in the United States and South Africa: The Difficult Pursuit for Racial Justice," *University of Illinois Law Review* (1990): 810–13; Power, "Apartheid Baltimore Style," 298–300, 302–6; Boger, "Meaning of Neighborhood in the Modern City," 246–52; "Race Segregation Ordinance Invalid," *Harvard Law Review* 31, no. 3 (January 1918): 475–79. The Winston ordinance would also go through a new iteration made to ensure its constitutionality. "Segregation in Whole City: Not Constitutional to Apply Only to Individual Sections," *Journal* (Winston-Salem), July 6, 1912, 1.

36. Higginbotham, Higginbotham, and Ngcobo, "De Jure Housing Segregation in the United States and South Africa," 809–10.

37. "Logic," *Crisis* 6, no. 2 (June 1913): 81.

38. Stephenson, "The Segregation of the White and Negro Races in Cities," 4.

39. Boger, "Meaning of Neighborhood in the Modern City," 237–38.

40. Boger, "Meaning of Neighborhood in the Modern City," 238.

41. Hawkins, "A Year of Segregation in Baltimore," 28, 30. See also Power, "Apartheid Baltimore Style," 295–96, 299, 313; Boger, "Meaning of Neighborhood in the Modern City," 243.

42. Hawkins, "A Year of Segregation in Baltimore," 28.
43. "Baltimore Not Satisfied with Segregation: St. Louis Newspaper Prints Misleading Information with Reference to Local Opinion," *Afro-American* (Baltimore), February 19, 1916, 1.
44. Boger, "Meaning of Neighborhood in the Modern City," 238–40, 244; *Sun*, quoted in *Crisis* 1, no. 3 (January 1911): 12; *Plessy* quotation from Higginbotham, Higginbotham, and Ngcobo, "De Jure Housing Segregation in the United States and South Africa," 809n198.
45. Boger, "Meaning of Neighborhood in the Modern City," 244–45.
46. "Louisville Segregation," newspaper clipping in folder "Newspaper Clippings: 1913," box 6, Storey Papers. An article from the Boston *Guardian* also reported that the agitation in favor of residential segregation there came from poor whites; cited in Roger L. Rice, "Residential Segregation by Law, 1910–1917," *Journal of Southern History* 34 (May 1968): 183–84, 197–98.
47. "Louisville Segregation Ordinance," *Crisis* 10, no. 4 (August 1915): 199.
48. Rice, "Residential Segregation by Law," 183–84, 197–98. The Louisville ordinance, declared unconstitutional by the Supreme Court in *Buchanan v. Warley*, is discussed further in chapter 4.
49. Lands, *Culture of Property*, 86.
50. Lands, *Culture of Property*, 92–95.
51. Higginbotham, Higginbotham, and Ngcobo, "De Jure Housing Segregation in the United States and South Africa," 814–17.
52. Mary White Ovington, "Segregation," *Crisis* 9, no. 3 (January 1915): 143.
53. "The Ghetto," *Crisis* 9, no. 5 (March 1915): 220.
54. Lake and Reynolds, *Drawing the Global Colour Line*, 2.
55. Carl H. Nightingale, *Segregation: A Global History of Divided Cities* (Chicago: University of Chicago Press, 2012), 3.
56. Clarence Poe, "What Is Justice Between White Man and Black?" *Progressive Farmer*, August 14, 1915, 9.
57. Andrew C. Baker, "Race and Romantic Agrarianism," *Agricultural History* 87, no. 1 (Winter 2013): 95, 100–1.
58. *The Natal Who's Who: An Illustrated Biographical Sketch Book of Natalians* (Durban: The Natal Who's Who Publishing Company, 1906), 65; George M. Fredrickson, introduction to Maurice S. Evans, *Black and White in the Southern States: A Study of the Race Problem in the United States from a South African Point of View* (Columbia: University of South Carolina Press, 2001), x–xi; Maurice S. Evans, "International Conference on the Negro: Report of the African Society's Representative, Mr. Maurice S. Evans, C.M.G.," *Journal of the Royal African Society* 11, no. 44 (July 1912): 418.
59. Robert M. Park, "Tuskegee International Conference on the Negro," *Journal of Race Development* 3 (July 1912): 118.
60. Park, "Tuskegee International Conference on the Negro," 119, 120.
61. Park, "Tuskegee International Conference on the Negro," 119.
62. Evans, "International Conference on the Negro," 423–24.
63. See Booker T. Washington, "My View of Segregation Laws," *New Republic* 5 (December 4, 1915): 113–14. This will be discussed in chapter 4.
64. Fredrickson, introduction to *Black and White in the Southern States*, x–xiii; Maurice S. Evans, "Present Position of Native Affairs in the Union of South Africa: A Plea for the

Scientific Study of Race Relations," *Journal of the Royal African Society* 12, no. 48 (July 1913): 343–47, 351–52.

65. Saul Debow, *Racial Segregation and the Origins of Apartheid in South Africa, 1919–36* (London: Macmillan, 1989), 6, 26.

66. David Welsh, *The Roots of Segregation: Native Policy in Colonial Natal, 1845–1910* (Cape Town: Oxford University Press, 1971), 7–30; Shula Marks, "Natal, the Zulu Royal Family and the Ideology of Segregation," in *Segregation and Apartheid in Twentieth-Century South Africa*, ed. William Beinart and Saul Dubow (London: Routledge, 1995), 94–96.

67. John Lambert, *Betrayed Trust: Africans and the State in Colonial Natal* (Pietermaritzburg: University of Natal Press, 1995), 1–3.

68. Evans, *Black and White in the Southern States*, xvi; George Fredrickson, *The Arrogance of Race: Historical Perspectives on Slavery, Racism, and Social Inequality* (Middletown, CT: Wesleyan University Press, 1988), 260; Cell, *Highest Stage*, 214–15, 220–24; Edgar H. Brookes, *White Rule in South Africa, 1830–1910: Varieties in Governmental Policies Affecting Africans* (Pietermaritzburg: University of Natal Press, 1974), 7.

69. Evans, *Black and White in the Southern States*, xxv, 4, 15; W. E. B. Du Bois, *The Souls of Black Folk* (New York: Oxford University Press, 2007), 8.

70. Maurice S. Evans, *Black and White in South East Africa: A Study in Sociology* (London: Longmans, Green & Co., 1911), 6–7.

71. Evans, *Black and White in South East Africa*, 15, 228; Thomas Jefferson, *Notes on the State of Virginia* (Chapel Hill: University of North Carolina Press, 1955), 162–63.

72. Evans, *Black and White in South East Africa*, 155.

73. Evans, *Black and White in South East Africa*, 160–61, 207.

74. Evans, *Black and White in South East Africa*, 207–8; Jefferson, *Notes*, 164–75.

75. Thomas Jefferson to John Holmes, April 22, 1820, in Paul Leicester Ford, ed., *The Works of Thomas Jefferson* (New York: G. P. Putnam's Sons, 1905), 12:159; Jefferson to Jared Sparks, February 4, 1824, in *Works*, 10:289–93; Evans, *Black and White in South East Africa*, 209–10. White South Africans worried how industrialization might transform the social order, fearing that a large black proletariat might become radicalized, as had happened in other industrializing nations. Dubow, *Racial Segregation*, 7–10.

76. Evans, *Black and White in South East Africa*, 202. See also 17, 151–53, 182, 200–1, 310, 325–26.

77. Evans, *Black and White in South East Africa*, 314–20, 318.

78. The South was indeed like South Africa in "racial make-up," though it may be that a comparison with the Indian reservation system would have been more appropriate, as it was American Indians—like blacks in South Africa—who were native to the nation and who were kept on reservations. Indeed, such a comparison might have allowed Evans to witness just how "beneficial" it was for native peoples to be kept on reservations.

79. Evans, *Southern States*, xxvi, 270. Evans's work recalled not only Jefferson but also the Englishman James Bryce, who depicted America's experiment with interracial democracy as a failure in *The American Commonwealth* (1888) and in "Thoughts on the Negro Problem," *North American Review* (December 1891). Bryce argued that African Americans were "unfit" for political rights. He believed that racial homogeneity was necessary for democracy to succeed, an argument used to justify segregation in the United States and South Africa. See the discussion of Bryce in Lake and Reynolds, *Drawing*, 49–74. Poe dedicated his book *Where Half the World Is Waking Up: The Old and the New in Japan, China, the Philippines, and India, Reported with Especial Reference to American Conditions* (New York: Doubleday, Page, 1911) to Bryce.

80. Evans, *Southern States*, 257–58, 270; Evans, "International Conference on the Negro," 423.

81. Cell, *Highest Stage*, 194–95.

82. Cell, *Highest Stage*, 192–93.

83. Harvey M. Feinberg, "The 1913 Natives Land Act in South Africa: Politics, Race, and Segregation in the Early 20th Century," *International Journal of African Historical Studies* 26, no. 1 (1993): 66.

84. P. L. Wickins, "The Natives Land Act of 1913: A Cautionary Essay on Simple Explanations of Complex Change," *South African Journal of Economics* 49, no. 2 (1981): 107; George M. Fredrickson, *White Supremacy: A Comparative Study in American and South African History* (Oxford: Oxford University Press, 1981), 242; Feinberg, "1913 Natives Land Act," 70.

85. Feinberg, "1913 Natives Land Act," 82–83, 105–7; Timothy J. Keegan, *Rural Transformations in Industrializing South Africa: The Southern Highveld to 1914* (London: Macmillan, 1987), 183–84; Harold Wolpe, "Capitalism and Cheap Labour Power in South Africa: From Segregation to Apartheid," in *Segregation and Apartheid in Twentieth-Century South Africa*, ed. William Beinart and Saul Dubow (London: Routledge, 1995), 60–90.

86. Feinberg, "1913 Natives Land Act," 82–3; Feinberg and Andre Horn, "South African Territorial Segregation: New Data on African Farm Purchases, 1913–1936," *Journal of African History* 50 (2009): 41; Kirby, *Darkness at the Dawning*, 117.

87. Maurice Evans to Edgar Gardner Murphy, July 25, 1912, Edgar Gardner Murphy Papers, folder 8, #1041, Southern Historical Collection, Wilson Library, University of North Carolina at Chapel Hill; Clarence Poe, "The Negro Problem in Two Continents," *Progressive Farmer*, July 6, 1912, 755–56. In October 1913, Poe announced the formation of the "North Carolina Committee on Rural Race Problems" to push forward the segregation idea. Participants included leaders from "State Farmers' Union, the State Farmers' Alliance, and the State Farmers' Convention"; Poe was president of the group. *Progressive Farmer*, October 11, 1913, 1066.

88. Poe, "Negro Problem in Two Continents," 755–56.

89. Poe, "Negro Problem in Two Continents," 756.

90. A. O. Murphey, "Segregation Necessary to Develop Good Farming and White Farmers," *Progressive Farmer*, December 6, 1913, 1277; Poe, "Editorial Comment," and W. M. Webster, "Wants to Go with the Negro," both in *Progressive Farmer*, November 8, 1913, 1171.

91. Clarence Poe, "A South-Wide Campaign for Racial Segregation," *Progressive Farmer*, August 2, 1913, 845.

92. Clarence Poe, "Which Is the Handicapped Race?" *Progressive Farmer*, August 7, 1915, 734.

93. Clarence Poe, "Suffrage Restriction in the South; Its Causes and Consequences," *North American Review* (1902): 543.

4. SEPARATING RESIDENCES IN THE CAMEL CITY

1. "Segregate Negroes in East Winston: Would Prevent Negroes from Living on East Fourth Street," *Winston-Salem Journal*, June 14, 1912, 1.

2. Special Meeting of the Board of Aldermen, June 13, 1912, *Alderman's Record*, City of Winston, 9:385–87. The original minute books from the Board of Aldermen's meetings are held in the City Secretary's Office, Winston-Salem.

3. "Segregate Negroes in East Winston," 1.
4. No doubt segregationists concerned with the legality of the Winston ordinance studied the Baltimore ordinance, which went through four versions. See Gretchen Boger, "The Meaning of Neighborhood in the Modern City: Baltimore's Residential Segregation Ordinances, 1910–1913," *Journal of Urban History* 35 (January 2009): 252; Garrett Power, "Apartheid Baltimore Style: The Residential Segregation Ordinances of 1910–1913," *Maryland Law Review* 42, no. 2 (1983): 298–99, 302–6; "Race Segregation Ordinance Invalid," *Harvard Law Review* 31 (January 1918): 478–79.
5. Special Meeting of the Board of Aldermen, June 13, 1912, *Alderman's Record*, City of Winston, 9:385–87; Regular Meeting of the Board of Aldermen, July 5, 1912, *Alderman's Record*, City of Winston, 9:388–91; "Segregation in Whole City: Not Constitutional to Apply Only to Individual Sections," *Winston-Salem Journal*, July 6, 1912, 1; John Wertheimer, *Law and Society in the South: A History of North Carolina Court Cases* (Lexington: University Press of Kentucky, 2009), 48–49.
6. "Segregate Negroes in East Winston," 1, 8; Wertheimer, *Law and Society in the South*, 43–46. It seems to have been a pattern that urban communities used restrictive covenants, then segregation ordinances, then (after *Buchanan*) restrictive covenants again to promote segregated neighborhoods. On this, see Jeffrey D. Gonda, *Unjust Deeds: The Restrictive Covenant Cases and the Making of the Civil Rights Movement* (Chapel Hill: University of North Carolina Press, 2015), 4–5. Bertha Hampton Miller explains the driving force behind the ordinance in Winston-Salem as "status anxiety" on the part of whites who felt left behind as African Americans gained property in the city and wealthy white industrialists continued to flourish. Some experienced the gains of others as a "reduc[tion of] the significance of the white workers['] position in society." Bertha Hampton Miller, "Blacks in Winston-Salem, North Carolina, 1895–1920: Community Development in an Era of Benevolent Paternalism," Ph.D. diss., Duke University, 1981, 126–27.
7. "S. J. Bennett for the State Legislature," *Winston-Salem Journal*, July 14, 1912, 2; "Mr. S. J. Bennett: Candidate for House of Representatives," *Winston-Salem Journal*, August 18, 1912, 7; "Local News," *Union Republican* (Winston-Salem), January 4, 1912, 6; "Wilson Man Buys Out S. J. Bennett & Co.," *Winston-Salem Journal*, August 20, 1911, 8; "Mr. S. J. Bennett Is Spending Sunday at Home," *Winston-Salem Journal*, July 2, 1911, 8; "Mr. Bennett Elected President of His Class," *Winston-Salem Journal*, June 14, 1911, 8; "County Ticket Named Today," *Winston-Salem Journal*, July 20, 1912, 1; "Strong County Ticket Named by Democrats in a Big Convention," *Winston-Salem Journal*, July 21, 1912, 1.
8. *Union Republican* (Winston-Salem), October 24, 1912, 6; obituary of J. B. Haley [Bennett's father-in-law], *Winston-Salem Journal*, May 10, 1910, 6; *Twin-City Daily Sentinel* (Winston-Salem), July 30, 1912, 8; "To Open Law Office at His Home Also," *Twin-City Daily Sentinel* (Winston-Salem), February 6, 1919, 6; "Attorney Bennett Moves to New Home," *Winston-Salem Journal*, August 6, 1912, 8; "Baptist Church in East Winston Is Organized," *Western Sentinel* (Winston-Salem), September 30, 1912, 5; "The Home Mutual Insurance Co. of Winston-Salem, N.C.: What Is It? Who Are Behind It?" *Winston-Salem Journal*, April 22, 1917, 17.
9. "The Ghetto," *Crisis* 4, no. 3 (July 1912): 115–16. The Mooresville ordinance also appears in "National Association for the Advancement of Colored People," *Crisis* 4, no. 4 (August 1912): 177.

10. Ordinance quoted in "The Ghetto," 116.

11. "The Deserted Negro," *Washington Bee*, August 24, 1912, 4.

12. Sanborn Fire Insurance Maps of Mooresville, NC, June 1908 and August 1914, North Carolina Collection, University of North Carolina Libraries, http://web.lib.unc.edu /nc-maps/sanborn.php.

13. Sixteenth Census of the United States: 1940, Mooresville, North Carolina, Ward 2, Iredell County, E.D. no. 49-9, sheet no. 14A.

14. "Richard Joshua Reynolds," *Sphinx: Emory and Henry College, Virginia* (1913): 9–10; and "Newspapers the Standard Form of Advertising: R. J. Reynolds Says They Are the Right Mediums to Reach the People," *Herald Courier* (Bristol, VA), May 23, 1915, esp. 1–2; both in "Biographical Information," Reynolds Family Papers, box 1, folder 10, Reynolda House Museum of American Art, Winston-Salem, NC. "Mr. R. J. Reynolds, Honored Citizen, Passes, Aged 68," *Twin City Sentinel* (Winston-Salem), July 29, 1918, 1; in "Biographical Information," Reynolds Papers, box 1, folder 11. Michele Gillespie, *Katharine and R. J. Reynolds: Partners of Fortune in the Making of the New South* (Athens: University of Georgia Press, 2012), 45–46, 77–79, 98–99, 180; "Reynolds Leads in Tobacco Production in North Carolina," *E.S.C. Quarterly* 9 (Summer–Fall 1951): esp. 76; in the Reynolds Papers, box 22, folder "R. J. Reynolds Tobacco Company Articles and Correspondence"; U.S. Census Bureau, *Negro Population, 1790–1915* (Washington, D.C., 1918), table 1, 772; Wertheimer, *Law and Society in the South*, 46.

15. Lenwood G. Davis, William J. Rice, and James H. McLaughlin, *African Americans in Winston-Salem/Forsyth County: A Pictorial History* (Virginia Beach: Donning Company, 1999), 17. Davis et al. note that the R. J. Reynolds Tobacco Company "was the largest employer of Blacks in the county," that "generation after generation of African American families worked for Reynolds Tobacco Company," and that Reynolds workers influenced black "businesses, churches, social organizations, etc." (17).

16. Of 419 African American men and women sampled (mostly men, as they were listed by head of household), 198 worked in tobacco factories, 85 worked as laborers, 17 as drivers, 6 as business proprietors, and 4 as grocers. Three or fewer worked in the other occupations mentioned. Ernest H. Miller, *The Winston-Salem, N.C. City Directory* (Asheville, NC, 1912), 13:343–55; Robert Rodgers Korstad, *Civil Rights Unionism* (Chapel Hill: University of North Carolina Press, 2003), 91. On black women's desire to live in their own homes rather than with their employers, see Tera Hunter, *To 'Joy My Freedom: Southern Black Women's Lives and Labors After the Civil War* (Cambridge, MA: Harvard University Press, 1997), 57–59.

17. Wertheimer, *Law and Society in the South*, 46–7.

18. "Segregation Up to the Legislature," *Winston-Salem Journal*, April 10, 1914, 12.

19. Twelfth Census of the United States: Population, 1900, Forsyth County, North Carolina, Winston Township, Winston City, Enumeration District 37, sheets 14A, 15B, 16B; and Enumeration District 39, sheets 3A and 4A; Thirteenth Census of the United States: 1910, Population, Forsyth County, North Carolina, Winston Township, City of Winston, Enumeration District 69, sheets 3A, 3B, 4A, 7A; and Enumeration District 71, sheets 13A, 16A, 16B, http://familysearch.org. Sanborn-Perris Map Co., *Insurance Maps of Winston-Salem, North Carolina* (May 1900), map 10; Sanborn Map Co., *Insurance Maps of Winston-Salem, North Carolina* (April 1912), maps 19, 20, North Carolina Collection, University of North Carolina Libraries, http://web.lib.unc.edu /nc-maps/sanborn.php.

20. Miller, "Blacks in Winston-Salem," 114–23; "Colored People and Law Enforcement: Address Delivered by Mr. Gilbert T. Stephenson Before the Colored People of Winston-Salem on the Occasion of Their School Closing," *Winston-Salem Journal*, May 10, 1913, 2.

21. "Atkins Outlines Negroes' Progress," *Winston-Salem Journal*, February 10, 1929, 21.

22. Miller, "Blacks in Winston-Salem," 123; Korstad, *Civil Rights Unionism*, 74; "Segregate Negroes in East Winston," 1, 8.

23. "Segregate Negroes in East Winston," 1, quoted in Wertheimer, *Law and Society in the South*, 49. Wertheimer does not discount this claim as empty rhetoric, suggesting that certain African Americans might have benefited from the ordinance. Simon G. Atkins, for example, the "Booker T. Washington" of Winston-Salem, founded a suburb of Winston for African Americans that might have declined in popularity if blacks had been welcomed into white neighborhoods in the city. Wertheimer, *Law and Society in the South*, 49–50.

24. "Favor Strict Enforcement of Segregation Law," *Winston-Salem Journal*, May 17, 1913, 1; Adjourned Meeting of the Board of Aldermen, May 16, 1913, *Alderman's Record*, City of Winston, 10:308–9; Wertheimer, *Law and Society in the South*, 50.

25. Warrant for Violating Segregation Ordinance, Municipal Court of the City of Winston, Forsyth County, in original case file for *State v. Darnell*, 1022, North Carolina State Archives; Petition in *Darnell* Original Case File, 1030; Testimony for the Defense—Examination of F. M. Sledge, in original case file for *Darnell*, 1041; Bond for Costs ($40), January 26, 1914, in original case file for *Darnell*, 1025; and Bond ($25), July 9, 1913, August 2, 1913, November 15, 1913, and December 13, 1913, in original case file for *Darnell*, 1026–29; Jeffrey J. Crow, "An Apartheid for the South: Clarence Poe's Crusade for Rural Segregation," in *Race, Class, and Politics in Southern History: Essays in Honor of Robert F. Durden*, ed. Jeffrey J. Crow et al. (Baton Rouge: Louisiana State University Press, 1989), 244–46; Wertheimer, *Law and Society in the South*, 50–54 (on Sledge, see 50–51).

26. "For Segregation of Races; Bill Before Assembly," *News and Observer* (Raleigh), September 30, 1913, 3; *Journal of the Senate of the General Assembly of the State of North Carolina: Extra Session, 1913* (Raleigh, 1913), 3, 17, 219. Unfortunately, neither the *News and Observer* article nor the *Senate Journal* recorded the debate on the bill (S.B. 50).

27. "Call Out the Troops?" *Greensboro Record*, December 19, 1913, 4; "Retirement of Negro Educator Announced . . . Windsor Now in Charge," *Greensboro Daily News*, September 21, 1916, 3; Deed Book 262, 141, and Book 246, 215 (Register of Deeds, Guilford County, North Carolina), http://rdlxweb.co.guilford.nc.us/guilfordNameSearch.php; "Buy Property to End the Strife: Citizens Purchase Negro's House and Ask Him to Move: The Segregation Muddle," *Greensboro Record*, February 20, 1914, 1; "Commissioners Pass Segregation Measure," *Greensboro Daily News*, February 17, 1914, 10; "The Ghetto," *Crisis* 7, no. 6 (April 1914): 271; William H. Chafe, *Civilities and Civil Rights: Greensboro, North Carolina, and the Black Struggle for Freedom* (Oxford: Oxford University Press, 1980), 14–17.

28. "Commissioners Pass Segregation Measure," *Greensboro Daily News*, February 17, 1914, 10.

29. "Commissioners Pass Segregation Measure," 10; "Notice to Delinquent Tax Payers of the City of Greensboro," *Greensboro Record*, June 2, 1913, 7; "Notice to Delinquent Tax

Payers of the City of Greensboro," *Greensboro Daily News*, May 16, 1918, 10; Guilford County Register of Deeds Online Records System, Grantor Index to Real Estate Conveyances to December 31, 1921, 37, and General Index to Real Estate Conveyances—Guilford County, NC—Grantees to December 31, 1921, 39, http://rdlxweb.co.guilford .nc.us/guilfordNameSearch.php; advertisement for Brooks Lumber Co., *Greensboro Daily News*, October 14, 1928, 6; "C. V. Clark Is Laid to His Final Rest," *Greensboro Record*, October 23, 1924, 11; "Danger from Flies Is Not Yet Passed," *Greensboro Daily News*, September 24, 1913, 5; "Wharton Rites Will Be Sunday," *Greensboro Record*, May 28, 1932, 3.

30. Sanborn Map Company, Insurance Maps of Greensboro, North Carolina (April 1913), Maps 21, 26, North Carolina Collection, University of North Carolina Libraries, http: //web.lib.unc.edu/nc-maps/sanborn.php; Thirteenth Census of the United States: 1910—Population, Greensboro, Ward 3, Enumeration District 105, sheets 5A-B, 6A-B, 7A, 8A-B, 9A-B, 10A, 11A, http://familysearch.org.

31. "Call Out the Troops?" *Greensboro Record*, December 19, 1913, 4.

32. "Buy Property to End the Strife," 1; "Citizens Purchased House from Windsor," *Greensboro Daily News*, February 20, 1914, 8; "Endorses Segregation: Yet He Cannot Endorse All the Acts of That Committee," *Greensboro Record*, February 23, 1914, 3.

33. *Greensboro Record*, February 18, 1914, 4.

34. "Commissioners Pass Segregation Measure," *Greensboro Daily News*, February 17, 1914, 10.

35. "Buy Property to End the Strife," 1.

36. "The Windsor Case," *Greensboro Record*, February 20, 1914, 4; *Greensboro Record*, February 23, 1914, 5.

37. *Greensboro Record*, April 9, 1914, 4; "Alderman Talks of Race Segregation Here," *Charlotte News*, September 16, 1913, 9.

38. On local interest in the case, see Wertheimer, *Law and Society in the South*, 54.

39. "City Segregation in Supreme Court: Question as to Colored Man's Right to Live in Certain Section," *News and Observer* (Raleigh), April 1, 1914, 5.

40. Wertheimer, *Law and Society in the South*, 52–56.

41. Clayton McClure Brooks, *The Uplift Generation: Cooperation Across the Color Line in Early Twentieth-Century Virginia* (Charlottesville: University of Virginia Press, 2017), 1–13, 2, 12. Around the 1920s, this generation was replaced in Virginia by one that dismissed paternalism (187).

42. Walter McKenzie Clark, "The Negro in North Carolina and the South: His Fifty-Five Years of Freedom and What He Has Done. Commencement Address at St. Augustine's School, Raleigh, N.C., May 26, 1920," 2, in Documenting the American South, UNC Libraries, http://docsouth.unc.edu/nc/staugust/clark.html. On Clark, see Wertheimer, *Law and Society in the South*, 55–56; David Clark and Charles W. Eagles, "Clark, Walter McKenzie," in *Dictionary of North Carolina Biography*, ed. William S. Powell (Chapel Hill: University of North Carolina Press, 1979–1996), 1:378–79; William G. Ross, "Walter Clark," in *Great American Judges: An Encyclopedia*, ed. John R. Vile (Santa Barbara, CA: ABC-CLIO, 2003), 1:162; and Aubrey Lee Brooks, *Walter Clark: Fighting Judge* (Chapel Hill: University of North Carolina Press, 1944).

43. Clark, "The Negro in North Carolina and the South," 4–5.

44. Clark, "The Negro in North Carolina and the South," 7, 6. Clark's paternalistic perspective on race relations fit well with that of his friend Charles Aycock. In a 1900

letter to Clark, Aycock asked Clark for feedback on his inaugural address, which he said would focus on "the subject of education and the change in the election law," and noted that "with the elimination of the negro," there would be room for different political perspectives in the state. Letter from Charles Aycock to Walter Clark, October 22, 1900, folder 1, Walter Clark Papers, #2751, Southern Historical Collection, Wilson Library, University of North Carolina at Chapel Hill, https://finding-aids.lib.unc.edu/02751/#.

45. *State v. Darnell*, 166 N.C. 300–6, 304 (1914); Clark, "The Negro in North Carolina and the South," 6–7.

46. *State v. Darnell*, 166 N.C. 300, 302; Wertheimer, *Law and Society in the South*, 43–56; A. Leon Higginbotham, F. Michael Higginbotham, and S. Sandile Ngcobo, "De Jure Housing Segregation in the United States and South Africa: The Difficult Pursuit for Racial Justice," *University of Illinois Law Review* (1990): 835; Ross, "Walter Clark," in Vile, ed., *Great American Judges*, 162.

47. *State v. Darnell*, 166 N.C. 306, 302; Wertheimer, *Law and Society in the South*, 55–57.

48. *State v. Darnell*, 166 N.C. 303–4.

49. *State v. Darnell*, 166 N.C. 304.

50. Gillespie, *Katharine and R. J. Reynolds*, 178–88. Michele Gillespie argues that through "behind-the-scenes tinkering" Reynolds worked against the residential segregation ordinance (186). Gillespie came to this conclusion by triangulating Reynolds's philanthropic efforts on behalf of black workers against Clark's argument about the need to retain workers and Wertheimer's claim that Watson and Buxton had reasons to oppose the ordinance—not through primary sources that showed a direct connection between Reynolds and the ordinance.

51. Generally, scholarship that examines southerners' concern about the region's "business climate" (meaning its appeal to corporations by offering cheap labor, weak support for unions, and limited corporate taxes) show this concern emerging in the 1940s. Katherine Rye Jewell, *Dollars for Dixie: Business and the Transformation of Conservatism in the Twentieth Century* (Cambridge: Cambridge University Press, 2017), 13. See also Bruce J. Schulman, *From Cotton Belt to Sunbelt: Federal Policy, Economic Development, and the Transformation of the South, 1938–1980* (Durham, NC: Duke University Press, 1994).

52. For example, Roscoe Conkling, one of the framers of the Fourteenth Amendment, argued before the Supreme Court in 1882 that the amendment granted corporations like the Southern Pacific Railroad Company equal rights. Corporations were a type of "person," according to Conkling. Adam Winkler, *We the Corporations: How American Businesses Won Their Civil Rights* (New York: Liveright, 2018), xxi–xxii.

53. Wertheimer, *Law and Society in the South*, 51–52. I estimated the number of properties bought and sold by Buxton by multiplying the number of entries per page (36) by the number of pages of listings under Buxton's name in the Forsyth County Register of Deeds index books.

54. "Atkins Outlines Negroes' Progress," *Winston-Salem Journal*, February 10, 1929, 21.

55. Walter Clark to Clarence Poe, May 7, 1913, in *The Papers of Walter Clark*, vol. 2: *1902–1924*, ed. Aubrey Lee Brooks and Hugh Talmage Lefler (Chapel Hill, 1950), 200; Brooks, *Walter Clark*, 177–91, esp. 188.

56. Wertheimer, *Law and Society*, 212n48. C. B. Watson, "Cyrus B. Watson for Judge Clark," *Advance* (Elizabeth City), May 17, 1912, reprinted from the *News and Observer* (Raleigh), 2.

57. See "Watson Portrait on Court Walls," *News and Observer* (Raleigh), May 13, 1914, 5; "Portrait of Hon. Cyrus B. Watson Is Presented to Supreme Court of State," *Western Sentinel* (Winston-Salem), May 15, 1914.

58. No biography has yet been written of Gilbert Stephenson. "Mr. Stephenson New Solicitor: Elected to Succeed Mr. Sams as Prosecuting Attorney in Municipal Court," *Winston-Salem Journal*, February 8, 1913, 1, pasted in Journal XVIII (December 12, 1912–April 23, 1913), 140, folder 27, box 2, Gilbert T. Stephenson Papers, Z. Smith Reynolds Library Special Collections and Archives, Wake Forest University, Winston-Salem, NC.

59. For example, in his journal entry for November 18, 1911, Stephenson wrote out notes for a speech he planned to give at a black church on "the Mutual Responsibilities of the Two Races," a topic he had also taken on at another church two months earlier. Stephenson planned to say that it was neither practical nor desirable for African Americans to leave the United States, and as a result, blacks and whites had to work together to their mutual benefit. Journal XIII (November 3, 1911–January 9, 1912), 51–76, folder 22, box 2, Stephenson Papers. See also Gilbert Thomas Stephenson, "Racial Distinctions in Southern Law," *American Political Science Review* 1 (November 1906): 44–61; Gilbert Thomas Stephenson, *Race Distinctions in American Law* (New York: D. Appleton and Co., 1910); Gilbert Thomas Stephenson, "The Separation of the Races in Public Conveyances," *American Political Science Review* 3 (May 1909): 180–204; Gilbert Thomas Stephenson, "The Segregation of the White and Negro Races in Cities," *South Atlantic Quarterly* 13 (January 1914): 1–18.

60. Notes for "Relation of the House to Crime Among Negroes," box 12, folder 175, Stephenson Papers; "Gilbert Stephenson Talked to Negroes; Gave Interesting Advice on Maintenance of Proper Social Relations Between Races," February 5, 1914, 5, clipping from the *Greensboro News* in Journal XX (October 4, 1913–February 9, 1914), 282, folder 29, box 2, Stephenson Papers. On black "crime" providing labor for mines and other industries, see Douglas A. Blackmon, *Slavery by Another Name: The Re-Enslavement of Black Americans from the Civil War to World War II* (New York: Doubleday, 2008), 6–9, 108–13, 124–33.

61. "Segregate Negroes in East Winston," *Winston-Salem Journal*, June 14, 1912, 1. There are other examples of the ties connecting these men: Stephenson invited Buxton and Watson to his 1912 wedding. Invitation List Stephenson-White Marriage, December 19, 1912, box 2, folder 257, Stephenson Papers. Stephenson wrote at length in his journal about Watson, whose offices were next to his in the Masonic Temple. He described Watson as "one of the greatest criminal lawyers in the history of the state"—great because Watson's understanding of human beings allowed him to pry "the truth" out of witnesses and "appeal to men in the jury box." See undated entry, Journal XVIII (December 12, 1912–April 23, 1913), 208, 209, folder 27, box 2, Stephenson Papers. On the lawyers' offices in the Masonic Temple, see Ernest H. Miller, comp., *Winston-Salem, N.C., City and Suburban Directory* (Asheville, N.C., 1913), 14:366, 397. Stephenson also spoke warmly about Reynolds in a tribute held shortly after Reynolds's death in July 1918. Stephenson told of how he had met with Reynolds when he was conducting

research for a publication on the connection between home life and criminality among African Americans, and he found remarkable "the genuineness of [Reynolds's] interest in the welfare of the people who were employed in his company." "Many Beautiful Expressions for Mr. R. J. Reynolds," *Winston-Salem Journal*, July 30, 1918, 6, in "Biographical Information," Reynolds Papers, box 1, folder 11.

62. "The Municipal Court broke all record[s] here yesterday when a total of 60 cases were disposed of in four hours," one of them about the theft of a cabbage. See "Record Broken in City Court Here Monday; Sixty Cases Proved to be Biggest Docket Ever Heard," *Winston-Salem Journal*, May 12, 1914, 8, pasted into Journal XXI (February 10, 1914–July 31, 1914), folder 30, box 3, Stephenson Papers.

63. "Urban Segregation (Outline of Argument Before Supreme Court in *State vs. Darnell*)," in Journal XXI (February 10, 1914–July 31, 1914), 97, 96, folder 30, box 3, Stephenson Papers.

64. Testimony of V. E. Barnes and J. D. Welch, *Darnell* Original Case File, 1036–40.

65. "City Segregation in Supreme Court," *News and Observer* (Raleigh), April 1, 1914, 5; "Segregation of Races in Court," *Winston-Salem Journal*, April 2, 1914, 8; "City Segregation," *Union Republican* (Winston-Salem), April 9, 1914, 3.

66. Stephenson, *Race Distinctions in American Law*, 2–4.

67. Stephenson, *Race Distinctions in American Law*, 361.

68. *Buchanan* Brief for the Plaintiff in Error, 19–23, NAACP Papers, reel 4, group 1, Box G-76.

69. Gilbert T. Stephenson, "The Segregation of the White and Negro Races in Rural Communities of North Carolina," *South Atlantic Quarterly* 13 (April 1914), 107–17.

70. Booker T. Washington to Gilbert Thomas Stephenson, October 7, 1913, in Louis R. Harlan and Raymond W. Smock, eds., *The Booker T. Washington Papers*, vol. 12: *1912–1914* (Urbana: University of Illinois Press, 1982), 308. See also Louis R. Harlan, *Booker T. Washington: The Wizard of Tuskegee, 1901–1915* (New York: Oxford University Press, 1983), 422–26.

71. "Richard Joshua Reynolds," 10; "Newspapers the Standard Form of Advertising," 2; "Mr. R. J. Reynolds, Honored Citizen, Passes, Aged 68."

72. Gillespie, *Katharine and R. J. Reynolds*, 86–87, 98. Reynolds's use of paternalism to help create a compliant work force is not unusual. See for example Beth Tompkins Bates, *Pullman Porters and the Rise of Protest Politics in Black America, 1925–1945* (Chapel Hill: University of North Carolina, 2001), which shows a similar approach on the part of the Pullman Company in Chicago.

73. "Mr. R. J. Reynolds: Our Esteemed Friend and Benefactor, Dead, Buried But Can Never Be Forgotten," *Twin City Advertiser* (Winston-Salem), August 16, 1918, 1, in "Biographical Information," Reynolds Papers, box 1, folder 11.

74. "Tentative Plans for Two New Hospitals," clipping labeled (inaccurately) Winston-Salem *Twin City Sentinel*, March 3, 1919, 2; "Plans for R. J. Reynolds Addition to City Hospital Are Complete and Contract for Work Will Be Let Soon," *Winston-Salem Journal*, August 28, 1919, 1–2, both in folder 546, box 20, Reynolds Papers.

75. Deed Book 95, 572–73 (Forsyth County Office of the Register of Deeds, Winston-Salem, N.C.), http://www.forsythdeeds.com/deedhold.php.

76. "A Dealer in Real Estate," *Crisis* 9, no. 5 (March 1915): 222.

77. Index Books 1849–1927, Forsyth County Register of Deeds, http://www.co.forsyth.nc.us/ROD/online_lookup.aspx.

78. Randal L. Hall and Ken Badgett, ed., "Robinson Newcomb and the Limits of Liberalism at UNC: Two Case Studies of Black Businessmen in the 1920s South," *North Carolina Historical Review* 86 (October 2009): 402; "For Rent—Eight Nice Rooms," *Winston-Salem Journal*, June 27, 1917, 9; *Walsh's Winston-Salem, North Carolina City Directory for 1908* (Charleston, SC: Walsh Directory Company, 1907), 95; J. S. Hill to the editor, "A Correction," *Winston-Salem Journal*, January 6, 1911, 4; Davis, Rice, and McLaughlin, *African Americans in Winston-Salem/Forsyth County*, 95–96.

79. "Segregation Up to the Legislature," *Winston-Salem Journal*, April 10, 1914, 12.

80. Quoted in Harlan, *Booker T. Washington*, 426.

81. "Segregation," *Crisis* 9, no. 1 (November 1914): 17–18.

82. Washington to Stephenson, October 7, 1913, in *Booker T. Washington Papers*, 12:308.

83. Booker T. Washington, "My View of Segregation Laws," *New Republic* 5 (December 4, 1915): 113–14. Reprinted in Louis R. Harlan and Raymond W. Smock, eds., *The Papers of Booker T. Washington*, vol. 13: *1914–1915* (Urbana: University of Illinois Press, 1984), 357.

84. Washington, "My View of Segregation Laws," 358.

85. Washington, "My View of Segregation Laws," 358.

86. Washington, "My View of Segregation Laws," 359.

87. "Segregation a Boon to Real Estate Sharps: Restricted Area Enables Them to Charge Exorbitant Rentals in Good Residential Sections," *Afro-American* (Baltimore), January 23, 1915, 1.

88. John Haley, *Charles N. Hunter and Race Relations in North Carolina* (Chapel Hill: University of North Carolina Press, 1987), 175.

89. Washington, "My View of Segregation Laws," 359.

90. On Atkins, see Elizabeth Anne Lundeen, "The Accommodation Strategies of African American Educational Leaders in North Carolina, 1890–1930," M.Phil. diss., University of Cambridge, 2008; and Elizabeth Anne Lundeen, "Simon G. Atkins: Race Leader," honors thesis, Wake Forest University, 2007.

91. "Slater Normal School Has Just Observed Its Tenth Annual Commencement Closing a Successful Year," *Winston-Salem Journal*, May 15, 1903, 1.

92. "Fine Editorial on Slater School; Search-Light Gives Interesting Facts About Great Institution," *Winston-Salem Journal*, July 26, 1914, 5.

93. Atkins is listed as president of both companies in *Walsh's Winston-Salem, North Carolina City Directory for 1908*, 95. He is listed as president only of the Twin City Building and Loan Company in the 1912 directory (Twin City Realty is no longer listed). Miller, *Winston-Salem, N.C. City Directory* (1912), 346.

94. Lundeen, "The Accommodation Strategies," 76–77.

95. Wertheimer, *Law and Society*, 49–50; Gillespie, *Katharine and R. J. Reynolds*, 91, 176.

96. "Advice to the Negro: President Atkins Tells Them What to Do to Become Good and Useful Citizens," *New York Times*, August 14, 1900, 1.

97. Atkins, "Special to the Observer," *Charlotte Observer*, August 12, 1900, 7.

98. Observer, "Columbian Heights, Its Reception and Growth," *Union Republican* (Winston-Salem), March 26, 1896, 1; Lundeen, "Simon G. Atkins," 42; Miller, "Blacks in Winston-Salem," 121–22.

99. Observer, "Columbian Heights, Its Reception and Growth," 1.

100. "For the Colored Race: Will Receive $460 from Peabody Fund," *Western Sentinel* (Winston-Salem), December 12, 1895, 1.

101. Lundeen, "The Accommodation Strategies," 83–84.

102. [no name given], President of the Board of Trustees of the Slater Industrial and State Normal School to the Honorable T. W. Bickett, Governor of North Carolina, March 5, 1918, box 2, Correspondence, Simon G. Atkins Papers, Winston-Salem State University Archives.

103. Lundeen, "The Accommodation Strategies," 48.

104. Tracy E. K'Meyer, *Civil Rights in the Gateway to the South: Louisville, Kentucky, 1945–1980* (Lexington: University Press of Kentucky, 2009), 1–10.

105. George C. Wright, "The NAACP and Residential Segregation in Louisville, Kentucky, 1914–1917," *Register of the Kentucky Historical Society* 78, no. 1 (Winter 1980): 39–41.

106. Wright, "The NAACP and Residential Segregation," 42; Patricia Hagler Minter, "Race, Property, and Negotiated Space in the American South: A Reconsideration of *Buchanan v. Warley*," in *Signposts: New Directions in Southern Legal History*, ed. Sally E. Hadden and Patricia Hagler Minter (Athens: University of Georgia Press, 2013), 345–68, see 347, 349 on Binford.

107. Patricia Hagler Minter, "William Warley: A Leader Ahead of His Time," in *One Hundred Americans Making Constitutional History: A Biographical History*, ed. Melvin I. Urofsky (Washington, DC: CQ, 2004), 200–2. Brooks discusses a generational change among black leaders in 1920s Virginia, where an older generation of people that "were experts at 'handling' whites, knowing when to compliment, when to beseech, and how to appeal to whites' sentimentality for 'their Negroes'" (like Booker T. Washington or Simon G. Atkins) was replaced by a younger generation more critical of accommodationism. Brooks, *Uplift Generation*, 34–38, 199–212.

108. Article in the *Louisville News* quoted in "Segregation," *Crisis* 9, no. 2 (December 1914): 71.

109. Rice, "Residential Segregation by Law," 182–88, Brinsmade quoted on 185.

110. Wright, "The NAACP and Residential Segregation," 47; Rice, "Residential Segregation by Law," 186.

111. Little is known about Buchanan. The literature generally describes him as sympathetic to the cause of civil rights, which seems correct, given that one of his lawyers was the president of the NAACP (Moorfield Storey).

112. S. S. Field, "The Constitutionality of Segregation Ordinances," *Virginia Law Review* 5, no. 2 (November 1917): 82; *Buchanan v. Warley*, Brief for the Plaintiff in Error, 12, 9.

113. *Buchanan v. Warley*, Brief for the Plaintiff in Error, 15–17.

114. Higginbotham, Higginbotham, and Ngcobo, "De Jure Housing Segregation in the United States and South Africa," 852–54; "Race Segregation Ordinance Invalid," 477–78.

115. Rice, "Residential Segregation by Law," 195–99; James W. Ely Jr., "Reflections on *Buchanan v. Warley*, Property Rights, and Race," *Vanderbilt Law Review* 51, no. 4 (May 1998): 955; Higginbotham, Higginbotham, and Ngcobo, "De Jure Housing Segregation in the United States and South Africa," 851–52, 768–70.

116. Field, "Constitutionality of Segregation Ordinances," 84–87.

117. Field, "Constitutionality of Segregation Ordinances," 87–88.

118. Eric Foner, *Reconstruction: America's Unfinished Revolution, 1863–1877* (New York: Harper & Row, 1988), 256–58.

119. Wertheimer notes that J. W. Carter sued James Timble (both of whom were white) for breaking a restrictive covenant in the deed of the property that Carter sold to Timble

by selling the property to a black person. Carter claimed the property should return to him because of the broken covenant. His suit was unsuccessful. Wertheimer also points to white residents of Winston complaining of whites breaching restrictive covenants. Wertheimer, *Law and Society in the South*, 47–48.

120. Thomas W. Hanchett, *Sorting Out the New South City: Race, Class, and Urban Development in Charlotte, 1876–1975* (Chapel Hill: University of North Carolina Press, 1998), 116.

121. Power, "Apartheid Baltimore Style," 315, 318.

122. "Atkins Outlines Negroes' Progress," *Winston-Salem Journal*, February 10, 1929, 21.

5. JIM CROW FOR THE COUNTRYSIDE

1. Letters to the editor published in the *Progressive Farmer*, December 6, 1913, 1277.

2. Clarence Poe, "What Is Justice Between White Man and Black? A Study of Conditions in the Rural South," address delivered at the University of Virginia, [April 1915], 8, North Carolina Collection, Wilson Library, University of North Carolina, Chapel Hill.

3. Clarence Poe, "Two Big Measures White Farmers Should Support," *Progressive Farmer*, January 2, 1915, 11.

4. Clarence Poe, "Great Rural Civilization in North Carolina," address at Mooresville, NC, July 31, 1913, Clarence H. Poe Papers, North Carolina State Archives; E. C. Branson, "Get Land and Hold to It Like Grim Death: That Is the Advice That Should Be Given Every White Tenant Farmer in the South—Danger of Great Estates, Absentee Landlordism, and a Dangerous Excess of Negro Tenants—Will the South Awake?" *Progressive Farmer*, May 28, 1910, 457; (Rev.) A. H. Shannon, "Segregation and Amalgamation," *Progressive Farmer*, February 21, 1914, 253.

5. Poe, "Great Rural Civilization in North Carolina"; Clarence Poe, "The General Plan for Segregation . . . General Compulsory Negro Segregation Not Sought by North Carolina Committee Whose Arguments Are Presented by Clarence Poe; The Real Argument," *News and Observer* (Raleigh), November 16, 1913, 1.

6. Kathryn Marie Dudley, *Debt and Dispossession: Farm Loss in America's Heartland* (Chicago: University of Chicago Press, 2000), examines competition of farmers over land and other resources. Ben Kiernan argues in *Blood and Soil: A World History of Genocide and Extermination from Sparta to Darfur* (New Haven, CT: Yale University Press, 2007) that agrarian thought has historically lent itself to evil actions, including genocide.

7. Mark Schultz, *The Rural Face of White Supremacy: Beyond Jim Crow* (Urbana: University of Illinois Press, 2005), 66–72. For histories of urban segregation, see, for example, C. Vann Woodward, *The Strange Career of Jim Crow*, 3rd rev. ed. (New York: Oxford University Press, 1974); Howard N. Rabinowitz, *Race Relations in the Urban South, 1865–1890* (New York: Oxford University Press, 1978); and Thomas W. Hanchett, *Sorting Out the New South City: Race, Class, and Urban Development in Charlotte, 1876–1975* (Chapel Hill: University of North Carolina Press, 1998).

8. "Hancock [County] was characterized by a stable, conservative, and wholly self-assured merchant-planter class that dominated the county from the antebellum period until World War II. These wealthy white men controlled some of the richest cotton estates in Georgia—and thousands of the poor, mostly black dependent farmers who tended them." Schultz, *Rural Face of White Supremacy*, 5–6.

9. Hugh MacRae, "Vitalizing the Nation and Conserving Human Units Through the Development of Agricultural Communities," *Annals of the American Academy of Political and Social Science* 63 (January 1916): 283–85; Hugh MacRae, "The Potential South: Its Youth and Its Call to Youth" (pamphlet), Wilmington, NC, n.d., Loeb Library, Harvard University, Vertical Files HD 1516. See also Paul Conkin, *Tomorrow a New World: The New Deal Community Program* (Ithaca, NY: Cornell University Press, 1959), 277–79; Marcia G. Synnott, "Hugh MacRae, Penderlea, and the Model Farm Communities Movement," *Proceedings of the South Carolina Historical Association* (1987): 54; David S. Cecelski and Timothy B. Tyson, "Hugh MacRae at Invershiel," blog for the University of North Carolina's site "A View to Hugh: Processing the Hugh Morton Photographs and Films," http://www.lib.unc.edu/blogs/morton/index.php/essays /hugh-macrae-at-invershiel/. In 1923, MacRae, along with the forester Gifford Pinchot, Elwood Mead (an irrigation engineer who served as director of the U.S. Bureau of Reclamation and supported government-funded farm colonies), and others, formed the Farm City Corporation of America, intended to design a "farm city" that would offer the best aspects of urban and rural living. Investors would fund the project, which would use eight thousand acres for a planned rural community, made up of a community center surrounded by subsistence homesteads, industry, and larger farms. Clarence Poe sat on the advisory committee of the Farm City project. The corporation did not attract enough private investment to reach fruition in the 1920s, but the government supported similar projects through the New Deal a decade later. MacRae won federal funding through the Division of Subsistence Homesteads in 1933 to set up a farm colony on land he owned in Pender County, North Carolina, about forty miles north of Wilmington. He meant for the Penderlea Homesteads, as the colony was named, to help tenant farmers become land owners. Farmers who received homesteads (which they were supposed to pay for over a course of years) were selected from a pool of poor farmers for their ability. In the 1920s, MacRae "tempered the racial dimensions of his agricultural program," according to the historian J. Vincent Lowery, and he considered including African Americans in his farm communities in the 1930s. J. Vincent Lowery, "The Transatlantic Dreams of the Port City Prophet: The Rural Reform Campaign of Hugh MacRae," *North Carolina Historical Review* 90, no. 3 (2013): 320. See also Conkin, *Tomorrow a New World*, 280–82; Daniel Rodgers, *Atlantic Crossings: Social Politics in a Progressive Age* (Cambridge, MA: Harvard University Press, 1998), 346.
10. Herbert Francis Sherwood, "Directing the Great Human River," *Outlook*, December 10, 1910, 827.
11. Sherwood, "Directing the Great Human River," 825.
12. Joseph F. Steelman, "The Progressive Democratic Convention of 1914 in North Carolina," *North Carolina Historical Review* 46, no. 2 (April 1969): 83–104 (the rural segregation plank is described on 95–97); "The Call for Democratic Mass Meeting in Raleigh," *News and Observer* (Raleigh), March 21, 1914, 1; Jack Temple Kirby, "Clarence Poe's Vision of a Segregated 'Great Rural Civilization,'" *South Atlantic Quarterly* 68 (1969): 31–34; Jeffrey J. Crow, "An Apartheid for the South: Clarence Poe's Crusade for Rural Segregation," in *Race, Class, and Politics in Southern History: Essays in Honor of Robert F. Durden*, ed. Jeffrey J. Crow et al. (Baton Rouge: Louisiana State University Press, 1989), 244–56.
13. W. E. Yelverton, "No Strings to Visit of Bryan," *News and Observer* (Raleigh), April 7, 1914, 1.

14. Parker R. Anderson, "Mr Bryan Demanded Elimination of the Segregation Plank," *Greensboro Daily News*, April 5, 1914, 1.

15. Parker R. Anderson, "Bryan Is Prevented from Attending the Democratic Meeting," *Greensboro Daily News*, April 8, 1914, 1.

16. "The Progressive Aims," *Daily Observer* (Charlotte), March 15, 1914, 4; "The Issues," *Daily Observer* (Charlotte), April 3, 1914, 4.

17. Clarence Poe, "The Segregation Plank," *Greensboro Daily News*, April 19, 1914, 4.

18. Clarence Poe, "Racial Segregation Necessary to Education and Co-operation," *Progressive Farmer*, August 9, 1913, 865.

19. Clarence Poe, "Suffrage Restriction in the South; Its Causes and Consequences," *North American Review* (1902): 534–43.

20. Clarence Poe, "Education, Co-Operation, Legislation," *Progressive Farmer*, October 4, 1913, 1043. See also Clarence Poe, "Education, Cooperation, Legislation," *Progressive Farmer*, March 6, 1915, 231; Clarence Poe, "Education, Cooperation, Legislation," *Progressive Farmer*, February 20, 1915, 177; Poe, "The General Plan for Segregation," 1.

21. Clarence Poe, "Education, Cooperation, Legislation," *Progressive Farmer*, February 20, 1915, 181.

22. Clarence Poe, "Education, Cooperation, Legislation" *Progressive Farmer*, February 20, 1915, 181, 177.

23. "Segregation of the Races," *Winston-Salem Journal*, September 5, 1913, 4.

24. Crow, "An Apartheid for the South," 247–253.

25. H. Q. Alexander, "A White Civilization for the Rural South," *Greensboro Daily News*, May 30, 1914, 4. See also "Farmers' Union in Session," *Charlotte Daily Observer*, October 20, 1909, 1; "Dr. Alexander Coming," *Robesonian* (Lumberton, NC), September 7, 1914, 1.

26. W. Fitzhugh Brundage, *Lynching in the New South: Georgia and Virginia, 1880–1930* (Urbana: University of Illinois Press, 1993), 24–28. On whitecapping, see William F. Holmes, "Whitecapping: Agrarian Violence in Mississippi, 1902–1906," *Journal of Southern History* 35, no. 2 (May 1969): 165–85; Kidada E. Williams, *They Left Great Marks on Me: African American Testimonies of Racial Violence from Emancipation to World War I* (New York: NYU Press, 2012), 1–2; James W. Loewen, *Sundown Towns: A Hidden Dimension of American Racism* (New York: Simon & Schuster, 2006); and Elliot Jaspin, *Buried in the Bitter Waters: The Hidden History of Racial Cleansing in America* (New York: Basic Books, 2007). *The Crisis* reported on this phenomenon, including an example of intimidation in a section of Cobb County, Georgia, in January 1913 in which "notices" were sent to farm owners telling them to "dismiss their Negro tenants" and to local African Americans with messages such as the following: "Hurry up Niggers and leve this town if you dont leve you will wish you hadder got out Get out of this town." The store of W. H. Bivens, who had been ordered to fire his black employees, was burned, also in this section. "The Place for the Negro Is On the Farm," *Crisis* 5, no. 5 (March 1913): 247.

27. Schultz, *Rural Face of White Supremacy*, 138, 95, 145–52.

28. Brundage, *Lynching in the New South*, 25–27.

29. William F. Holmes, "Moonshining and Collective Violence: Georgia, 1889–1895," *Journal of American History* 67, no. 3 (December 1980): 590, 597.

30. "The Land," *Crisis* 10, no. 1 (May 1915): 21.

31. "The Land," 22.

32. Clarence Poe, "A South-Wide Campaign for Segregation," *Progressive Farmer*, August 2, 1913, 845.

33. O., "Many Large Landowners Blind to Their Own Interests" (letter to the editor on the topic "Does the Negro Help or Hinder Southern Farm Progress?"), *Progressive Farmer*, December 6, 1913, 1277.

34. M. B. Forbes to the editor, "The Sort of Land-Owners Who Are to Blame," *Progressive Farmer*, September 20, 1913, 995; Harold D. Woodman, "Class, Race, Politics, and the Modernization of the Postbellum South," *Journal of Southern History* 63, no. 1 (February 1997): 21.

35. (Rev.) A. H. Shannon, "Segregation and Amalgamation," *Progressive Farmer*, February 21, 1914.

36. "J.C.W." to the editor, "Are These Facts Worth Considering?" *Progressive Farmer*, February 21, 1914, 253.

37. "E.S.W." to the editor, "Town Landlord Doesn't Care," *Progressive Farmer*, September 20, 1913, 995.

38. Senator B. R. Tillman (SC), article in *Trotwood's Magazine*, reprinted in the *Progressive Farmer*, February 21, 1914, 253, along with "Editorial Comment."

39. Reprinted in Clarence Poe, "Racial Segregation Necessary to Education and Co-Operation," *Progressive Farmer*, August 9, 1913, 865.

40. W. H. Gould to the editor, "Against Segregation," *Progressive Farmer*, December 6, 1913, 1277.

41. W. M. Webster to the editor, "Wants to Go with the Negro," *Progressive Farmer*, November 8, 1913, 1171.

42. Clarence Poe, "Editorial Comment" on "Wants to Go with the Negro," *Progressive Farmer*, Nov. 8, 1913, 1171.

43. "Land Segregation Bill Is Defeated," *News and Observer* (Raleigh), March 19, 1915, 6.

44. "Senate Against Land Segregation," *News and Observer* (Raleigh), March 6, 1915, 2.

45. Jack Temple Kirby, *Rural Worlds Lost: The American South, 1920–1960* (Baton Rouge: Louisiana State University Press, 1987), 236. Jeffrey Crow presents this vote as a big defeat for Poe, as he needed three-fifths of the senators present to approve the amendment for the amendment to pass; there were fifty state senators serving this session. I see it differently—that Poe's plan received real consideration and had backing from farmers in the Farmers' Union rather than from elites who attended the convention or sat in the state senate. Crow, "Apartheid for the South," 256.

46. Poe, "What Is Justice Between White Man and Black?"; *Journal of the Senate of the General Assembly of the State of North Carolina: Session 1915* (Raleigh, 1915), 3, 682.

47. Frank P. Cauble, "Efird, Joseph Bivens," in *Dictionary of North Carolina Biography*, ed. William S. Powell (Chapel Hill: University of North Carolina, 1986), 2:142–43; Mary A. Baker, "Jonas, Charles Andrew," in Powell, ed., *Dictionary of North Carolina Biography*, 3:311–12.

48. "Senate Against Land Segregation," *News and Observer* (Raleigh), March 6, 1915, 2. Also quoted in "Killed Segregation," *The Freeman: An Illustrated Colored Newspaper* 28, no. 12 (March 20, 1915): 4.

49. Nash quoted in "Land Segregation Bill Is Defeated," *News and Observer* (Raleigh), March 19, 1915, 6. See also Mary Claire Engstrom, "Nash, Francis (Frank)," in Powell, ed., *Dictionary of North Carolina Biography* 4 (1991), 358–59; "Senate Against Land Segregation," *News and Observer* (Raleigh), March 6, 1915, 2.

50. *Winston-Salem Journal*, October 8, 1913, 1.

51. "The Question of Constitutionality," *Greensboro Daily News*, May 30, 1914, 4.

52. See, for example, "Land Segregation," *Crisis* 9, no. 4 (February 1915): 181–82; "Ghetto," *Crisis* 9, no. 3 (January 1915): 115.

53. "Afro-American Cullings," *Gazette* (Cleveland, OH) 31, no. 28 (February 7, 1914): 1.

54. Booker T. Washington, "The Atlanta Exposition Address," reprinted in *Up from Slavery*, in *The Norton Anthology of African American Literature*, ed. Henry Louis Gates Jr. and Nellie Y. McKay (New York: Norton, 1997), 515.

55. "Afro-American Cullings," 1.

56. W. E. B. Du Bois, "The Last Word in Caste," *NAACP Fourth Annual Report, 1913*, 73.

57. Oswald Garrison Villard to Robert Russo Moton, March 9, 1914, in *The Booker T. Washington Papers*, vol. 12: *1912–1914*, ed. Louis R. Harlan and Raymond W. Smock (Urbana: University of Illinois Press, 1982), 472–73.

58. Booker T. Washington to Robert R. Moton, April 4, 1914, in *The Booker T. Washington Papers*, vol. 13: *1914–1915*, ed. Louis R. Harlan and Raymond W. Smock (Urbana: University of Illinois Press, 1984), 5–6.

59. Booker T. Washington to Robert R. Moton, April 4, 1914, in *Booker T. Washington Papers*, 13:6.

60. Booker T. Washington to James Edward McCulloch, March 11, 1914, in *Booker T. Washington Papers*, 13:474.

61. Crow, "Apartheid for the South," 241.

62. Booker T. Washington to James Edward McCulloch, June 3, 1914, in *Booker T. Washington Papers*, 13:40.

63. "Segregation," *Crisis*, November 1914, 17.

64. "Segregation," 18.

65. "Segregation," 17.

66. Washington, "The Atlanta Exposition Address," 515.

67. "It was one thing . . . for blacks to join together on terms that promoted group solidarity and quite another for the whites to herd them together on white terms and limits under laws imposed on the disfranchised blacks." Louis R. Harlan, *Booker T. Washington: The Wizard of Tuskegee, 1901–1915* (New York: Oxford University Press, 1983), 429.

68. Benjamin R. Justesen, *George Henry White: An Even Chance in the Race of Life* (Baton Rouge: Louisiana State University Press, 2001), 356–59, 371–75.

69. Mary G. Rolinson, *Grassroots Garveyism: The Universal Negro Improvement Association in the Rural South, 1920–1927* (Chapel Hill: University of North Carolina Press, 2007), 7, 60–61, 103. According to Rolinson, there was some overlap in black southerners' views on self-segregation and legally mandated segregation; as she puts it, "UNIA men and perhaps even women desired strictly enforced social separatism more than they opposed legally sanctioned segregation" (149).

70. Transcript of interview with Robert "Chick" Black by Robert Korstad, June 1, 1976 (E-0093), n.p., Southern Oral History Program Collection #4007, Southern Historical Collection, Wilson Library, University of North Carolina at Chapel Hill, https://dc.lib.unc.edu//utils/getfile/collection/sohp/id/17177/filename/17219.pdf.

71. Rolinson, *Grassroots Garveyism*, 39–45. "Newspaper Account of a Meeting Between Black Religious Leaders and Union Military Authorities," February 13, 1865, Freedmen & Southern Society Project, http://www.freedmen.umd.edu/savmtg.htm. Examples of

books that discuss black separatism include Kendra Taira Field, *Growing Up with the Country: Family, Race, and Nation After the Civil War* (New Haven, CT: Yale University Press, 2018); Steven Hahn, *A Nation Under Our Feet: Black Political Struggles in the Rural South from Slavery to the Great Migration* (Cambridge, MA: Harvard University Press, 2003), 454–57; Nell Irvin Painter, *Exodusters: Black Migration to Kansas After Reconstruction* (New York: Knopf, 1977); Thad Sitton and James H. Conrad, *Freedom Colonies: Independent Black Texans in the Time of Jim Crow* (Austin: University of Texas Press, 2005). North Carolina has at least one all-black town founded by former slaves that could be considered an example of separatism: Princeville, in Edgecombe County (part of the "Black Second"). On this, see J. A. Mobley, "In the Shadow of White Society: Princeville, a Black Town in North Carolina, 1865–1915," *North Carolina Historical Review* 63, no. 3 (1986): 340–84; and J. A. Mobley, *Princeville, A Black Town in North Carolina* (Raleigh: Division of Archives and History, 1981).

72. Rolinson, *Grassroots Garveyism*, 7, 143–46.

73. "New Form of Race Attack: Southern Editor Advocates Farm Segregation," *Washington Bee* 35, no. 11 (August 15, 1914): 1.

74. "Southerner Urges Equality for Negro: Noted Educator Says Social Repression of Blacks Is a Growing Menace to Whites," *New York Times*, January 31, 1915, 9.

75. "Dr. Chas. H. Brough on the Southern Race Question," *Arkansas Gazette*, January 3, 1915, 12. This article reprints much of the report.

76. T. S. Inborden, "A Negro Reader Protests," *Progressive Farmer*, September 20, 1913, 995.

77. Clarence Poe, "Education, Cooperation, Legislation," *Progressive Farmer*, January 30, 1915, 97.

78. Jas. B. Dudley, "Southern Oligarchy: Negroes Not Wanted Upon the Farm—President Dudley's Masterly Letter—An Appeal to Reason," *Washington Bee* 34, no. 26 (December 13, 1913): 1.

79. Dudley, "Southern Oligarchy," 1.

80. James L. Leloudis, *Schooling the New South: Pedagogy, Self, and Society in North Carolina, 1880–1920* (Chapel Hill: University of North Carolina Press, 1996), 215–17; Charles H. Moore to the editor, *News and Observer* (Raleigh), October 29, 1913, published November 5, 1913, 10; Poe, "General Plan for Segregation," 1.

81. "Dr. Poe's Segregation Scheme," *Washington Bee*, May 1, 1915, 4.

CONCLUSION: PLANNING FOR RESIDENTIAL SEGREGATION AFTER *BUCHANAN*

1. Karen Benjamin, "Suburbanizing Jim Crow: The Impact of School Policy on Residential Segregation in Raleigh," *Journal of Urban History* 38, no. 2 (March 2012): 232–33.

2. On *Shelley*, see Jeffrey D. Gonda, *Unjust Deeds: The Restrictive Covenant Cases and the Making of the Civil Rights Movement* (Chapel Hill: University of North Carolina Press, 2015).

3. Bertha Hampton Miller, "Blacks in Winston-Salem, North Carolina, 1895–1920: Community Development in an Era of Benevolent Paternalism," Ph.D. diss., Duke University, 1981, 198, 200.

4. Joanne Glenn, "The Winston-Salem Riot of 1918," MA thesis, University of North Carolina, Chapel Hill, 1979, 9–24, 37–40; Miller, "Blacks in Winston-Salem," 196, 206–11.

5. Miller, "Blacks in Winston-Salem," 200–1.

6. Miller, "Blacks in Winston-Salem," 210–13, 196.

7. Elizabeth Lundeen, "The Accommodation Strategies of African American Educational Leaders in North Carolina, 1890–1930," M.Phil. diss., University of Cambridge, June 2008, 80–81; Miller, "Blacks in Winston-Salem," 219.

8. "Sentiment of the Colored People in a Recent Race Riot—Committee Denounces the Element in the Race That Took Part in the Affair and Upholds the Officers," *Winston-Salem Journal*, November 26, 1918, 11.

9. "Thousand Dollar Game of Skin Staged on Vine St.: Amelia Smith Is Hostess to a Gambling Event Which Probably Sets a Record in This City's Colored Circles," *Winston-Salem Journal*, January 14, 1919, 7.

10. "Negro Cocaine Dealers Jailed: Have Novel Manner in Concealing Dope from the Searching Policemen," *Winston-Salem Journal*, June 29, 1922, 2.

11. "Whiskey Everywhere," *Winston-Salem Journal*, October 12, 1921, 9.

12. See, for example, *Twin-City Daily Sentinel*, May 18, 1914, 5; "In Municipal Court," *Winston-Salem Journal*, February 22, 1916, 6; "Municipal Court," *Winston-Salem Journal*, February 8, 1917, 5; "Municipal Court," *Winston-Salem Journal*, October 9, 1917, 8; "Cases Disposed of in Superior Court," *Winston-Salem Journal*, November 14, 1919, 6; "Municipal Court," *Winston-Salem Journal*, September 17, 1918, 10; "Special Criminal Term for County," *Winston-Salem Journal*, June 9, 1921, 9; "Cora and Pauline," *Winston-Salem Journal*, October 12, 1921, 9; *Winston-Salem Journal*, October 14, 1921, 8; *Winston-Salem Journal*, November 28, 1921, 6.

13. "Fined for Speeding," *Winston-Salem Journal*, September 18, 1920, 10; "Rollins Is Convicted and Given Two Years," *Winston-Salem Journal*, October 6, 1920, 12.

14. "Two Boys are Charged with Capital Crime . . . Cora Smart Must Leave State," *Winston-Salem Journal*, December 22, 1921, 1; "69 Cases Heard in the Superior Court During Term," *Winston-Salem Journal*, August 31, 1924, 13; "Lights and Shadows in Police Court," *Winston-Salem Journal*, July 15, 1924, 10.

15. "Federal Grand Jury; Cora Greer, Alias Cora Smart, Is Charged with Selling Narcotics Here," *Greensboro Daily News*, January 31, 1926, 9.

16. "Municipal Court," *Winston-Salem Journal*, January 23, 1919, 10; "Doub Given 14 Month Sentence," *Winston-Salem Journal*, December 23, 1921, 8; "Negro Held for Robbery," *Winston-Salem Journal*, June 21, 1927, 5; "Municipal Court," *Winston-Salem Journal*, January 26, 1915, 8.

17. "Colored People and Law Enforcement: Address Delivered by Mr. Gilbert T. Stephenson Before the Colored People of Winston-Salem on the Occasion of Their School Closing," *Winston-Salem Journal*, May 10, 1913, 2; Frank V. Tursi, *Winston-Salem: A History* (Winston-Salem, NC: John F. Blair, 1994), 236.

18. Answer to Plaintiffs' Complaint, in original case file for *D. Elwood Clinard, et al. v. City of Winston-Salem* (1939), North Carolina State Archives, 19, 20, 21.

19. Case on Appeal, in original case file for *Clinard*, 5, 7.

20. Case on Appeal, in original case file for *Clinard*, 7, 8.

21. Case on Appeal, in original case file for *Clinard*, 10–12; Temporary Restraining Order, in original case file for *Clinard*, 12–13; Judgment (of Alley, J.), in original case file for *Clinard*, 34, 35, 38, 39.

22. Defendant Appellees' Brief, in the original case file for *Clinard*, 8.

23. Plaintiff Appellants' Brief, in the original case file for *Clinard*, 8–12.

24. *Clinard v. Winston-Salem*, 217 N.C. 120–123 (1940), 121.

25. Robert K. Nelson, LaDale Winling, Richard Marciano, Nathan Connolly, et al., "Bibliographic Note," in "Mapping Inequality," in *American Panorama*, ed. Robert K. Nelson and Edward L. Ayers, https://dsl.richmond.edu/panorama/redlining/#loc=4/36.71/-96.93&opacity=0.8.

26. H. K. Ogburn, Real Estate Sales Broker and Property Management Broker, HOLC, Area Description of Winston-Salem, NC, Security Grade A, Area no. 1, July 23, 1937. In "Mapping Inequality."

27. H. K. Ogburn, Real Estate Sales Broker and Property Management Broker, HOLC, Area Description of Winston-Salem, NC, Security Grade B, Area no. 2, July 23, 1937. In "Mapping Inequality."

28. H. K. Ogburn, Real Estate Sales Broker and Property Management Broker, HOLC, Area Description of Winston-Salem, NC, Security Grade C, Area no. 5, July 23, 1937. In "Mapping Inequality."

29. H. K. Ogburn, Real Estate Sales Broker and Property Management Broker, HOLC, Area Description of Winston-Salem, NC, Security Grade C, Area no. 4, July 23, 1937. In "Mapping Inequality."

30. H. K. Ogburn, Real Estate Sales Broker and Property Management Broker, HOLC, Area Description of Winston-Salem, NC, Security Grade D, Area no. 1, July 23, 1937. In "Mapping Inequality."

31. H. K. Ogburn, Real Estate Sales Broker and Property Management Broker, HOLC, Area Description of Winston-Salem, NC, Security Grade D, Area no. 2, July 23, 1937; H. K. Ogburn, Real Estate Sales Broker and Property Management Broker, HOLC, Area Description of Winston-Salem, NC, Security Grade D, Area no. 3, July 23, 1937. Both in "Mapping Inequality."

32. H. K. Ogburn, Real Estate Sales Broker and Property Management Broker, HOLC, Area Description of Winston-Salem, NC, Security Grade D, Area no. 5, July 23, 1937. In "Mapping Inequality."

33. Thomas W. Hanchett, *Sorting Out the New South City: Race, Class, and Urban Development in Charlotte, 1875–1975* (Chapel Hill: University of North Carolina Press, 1998), 231.

34. Richard Rothstein, *The Color of Law: A Forgotten History of How Our Government Segregated America* (New York: Liveright, 2017), vii–xv, 63–67. Rothstein defines de jure segregation as put in place through law as well as "public policy" (viii).

35. Langdon E. Oppermann, *Winston-Salem's African-American Neighborhoods: 1870–1950: Architectural and Planning Report* (1994), 43, https://www.cityofws.org/portals/o/pdf/planning/publications/historic/WSAfAmNeighborhoods_20101209.pdf; Robert Rodgers Korstad, *Civil Rights Unionism* (Chapel Hill: University of North Carolina Press, 2003), 75.

36. Korstad, *Civil Rights Unionism*, 1–40.

37. Tursi, *Winston-Salem*, 225, 231–32, 236–37, 264; Oppermann, *Winston-Salem's African-American Neighborhoods*, 17.

38. Oppermann, *Winston-Salem's African-American Neighborhoods*, 16–18, 25–26, 31–35, 17; Tursi, *Winston-Salem*, 237.

39. Tursi, *Winston-Salem*, 264–65.

40. Robert Watson Winston, *It's a Far Cry* (New York: Henry Holt, 1937), 377; Robert Watson Winston, "Rebirth of the Southern States," *Current History* 22, no. 4 (July 1925): 545.

41. Winston, "Rebirth of the Southern States," 545.

42. Robert Watson Winston, "Should the Color Line Go?" *Current History* 18, no. 6 (September 1923): 950.

43. Winston, *It's a Far Cry*, 376–77.

44. Winston, *It's a Far Cry*, 377.

45. Winston, *It's a Far Cry*, 306–7.

46. Winston, "Should the Color Line Go?," 950.

47. Winston, *It's a Far Cry*, 376–77.

48. See Michael W. Fitzgerald, "'We Have Found a Moses': Theodore Bilbo, Black Nationalism, and the Greater Liberia Bill of 1939," *Journal of Southern History* 63, no. 2 (May 1997): 293–320.

49. Winston, *It's a Far Cry*, 317–18.

50. Winston, *It's a Far Cry*, 317–18.

51. Winston, *It's a Far Cry*, 347–48.

52. Robert Watson Winston, "The South in Transition," *Current History* 35, no. 2 (November 1931): 191–92; Winston, *It's a Far Cry*, 379.

53. W. O. Saunders, "The 'Dixie Plowboy': Remarkable Story of Clarence Poe—Friend of Roosevelt: His Rise to Fame," *Success: The Human Magazine*, May 1924, 117.

54. Clarence Poe to John D. Moore and Claude Justice, May 16, 1919, and January 16, 1918, Poe Papers, NCSA.

55. "W.D.S." (probably William D. Snider), "Faith in Longview," *Greensboro Daily News*, April 8, 1958, 8.

56. National Register of Historic Places Registration Form for Longview Gardens Historic District, section 8, 64–66; section 7, 2–3, http://www.hpo.ncdcr.gov/nr/WA4441.pdf.

57. Quoted in the National Register of Historic Places Registration Form for Longview Gardens Historic District, section 8, 67. Original article: "Poe Development Now on Market," *News and Observer* (Raleigh), May 7, 1939, O-4.

58. National Register of Historic Places Registration Form for Longview Gardens Historic District, section 8, 68.

59. See deed between Longview Gardens, Inc., and Julian M. Gregory, July 19, 1943, Wake County, NC, 000897-00173, 173, 175. Wake County Registry of Deeds, http://www.wakegov.com/rod/Pages/default.aspx.

60. It is worth noting—and the language of "racial stocks" is in keeping with this—that Poe embraced eugenics. Eugenics makes sense as a "reform" that Poe would like; the idea behind it is that the propagation of "desirable" peoples should be encouraged and that of undesirables should be discouraged. Overseen by the state Eugenics Board—which quickly approved most requests for sterilization—North Carolina operated a sterilization program for the "weak and defective." The state sterilized over 7,600 individuals, most involuntarily, through this program between 1929 and 1973 (enabled by a 1919 statute passed by the North Carolina General Assembly). As historians have pointed out, eugenic sterilization in the 1920s and 1930s was meant to improve the "white race," perceived as in the process of decline and at risk of losing its lofty position in the world—not to improve the genetic makeup of other groups. A 1935 editorial in the *News and Observer* presented sterilization as an economic necessity: the state could ill afford to use its funds supporting the children of "the lowest orders of humanity." Indeed, "we cannot make a better world," the editorial insisted, "if we deliberately give our substance to subsidizing the production of the least worthy stock among

men." Unlike other states, which turned away from sterilization after Hitler's policies became known, North Carolina even expanded its program after World War II. See Daniel J. Kevles, *In the Name of Eugenics: Genetics and the Uses of Human Heredity* (Berkeley: University of California Press, 1985); Edward J. Larson, *Sex, Race, and Science: Eugenics in the Deep South* (Baltimore, MD: Johns Hopkins University Press, 1995), esp. 2, 153–57; Karen Kruse Thomas, *Deluxe Jim Crow: Civil Rights and American Health Policy, 1935–1954* (Athens: University of Georgia Press, 2011), 144–45; R. Eugene Brown, Secretary of the Eugenics Board of North Carolina, *Eugenical Sterilization in North Carolina: A Brief Survey of the Growth of Eugenical Sterilization and a Report on the Work of the Eugenics Board of North Carolina Through June 30, 1935* (Raleigh: Eugenics Board of North Carolina, 1935), 5–8 (*News and Observer* quotation on 6), http://digital.ncdcr.gov/u?/p249901coll22,417354; Kevin Begos, "Lifting the Curtain on a Shameful Era," in *Against Their Will: North Carolina's Sterilization Program*, special report from the *Winston-Salem Journal* and Journalnow.com, http://againsttheirwill.journalnow.com/; Katherine Castles, "Quiet Eugenics: Sterilization in North Carolina's Institutions for the Mentally Retarded, 1945–1965," *Journal of Southern History* 68, no. 4 (November 2002), 864.

61. National Register of Historic Places Registration Form for Longview Gardens Historic District, section 8, 71; Benjamin, "Suburbanizing Jim Crow," 227, 234, 237.

62. National Register of Historic Places Registration Form for Longview Gardens Historic District, Section 8, 68–70.

63. Benjamin, "Suburbanizing Jim Crow," 231, 233–34.

64. Rather than integrating white neighborhoods, some middle-class African Americans chose to move to black developments outside of Raleigh such as Rochester Heights, Battery Heights, Madonna Acres, and Biltmore Hills. Margaret Ruth Little argues that homes in these neighborhoods were architecturally distinct from those in white neighborhoods, showing that blacks preferred modern architecture and avoided elements such as porticos and columns that were reminiscent of plantation days. Margaret Ruth Little, "Getting the American Dream for Themselves: Postwar Modern Subdivisions for African Americans in Raleigh, North Carolina," *Buildings and Landscapes* 19, no. 1 (Spring 2012): 74, 81–84.

65. Conversation with Ruth Little, March 1, 2017, on the neighborhood's history, strengths, and weaknesses. National Register of Historic Places Registration Form for Longview Gardens Historic District, section 8, 72; home values from Zillow.com; information on Enloe High School from Enloe Magnet High School, "About Our School," http://www.wcpss.net/Page/17504, http://enloehsstudentservices.weebly.com/uploads/3/0/7/0/30704513/2015-16_profile_update.pdf, and *U.S. News & World Report*, "High School Rankings," https://www.usnews.com/education/best-high-schools/north-carolina/districts/wake-county-schools/william-g-enloe-high-14753/student-body.

66. Pierre Bourdieu, "The Forms of Capital" (1986), https://www.marxists.org/reference/subject/philosophy/works/fr/bourdieu-forms-capital.htm.

Bibliography

Portions of this book were published previously as Elizabeth A. Herbin-Triant, "Southern Segregation, South Africa-Style: Maurice Evans, Clarence Poe, and the Ideology of Rural Segregation," *Agricultural History* 87, no. 2 (Spring 2013): 170–93; and Elizabeth A. Herbin-Triant, "Race and Class Friction in North Carolina Neighborhoods: How Campaigns for Residential Segregation Law Divided Middling and Elite Whites in Winston-Salem and North Carolina's Countryside, 1912–1915," *Journal of Southern History* 83, no. 3 (August 2017): 531–72.

ABBREVIATIONS

LOC Library of Congress
NCSA North Carolina State Archives, Division of Archives and History
RLDU David M. Rubenstein Rare Book and Manuscript Library, Duke University
SHC Southern Historical Collection, Wilson Library, University of North Carolina at Chapel Hill

MANUSCRIPTS

Alderman's Record. City of Winston-Salem, City Secretary's Office, Winston-Salem, NC.
Atkins, Simon G. Papers. Winston-Salem State University Archives, NC.
Aycock, Charles. Papers. NCSA.
Behind the Veil: Documenting African-American Life in the Jim Crow South Records, 1940–1997. RLDU.
Bryan, William Jennings. Papers. LOC.
Butler, Marion. Papers. 1862–1938. SHC.

Clark, Walter. Papers. SHC.

D. Elwood Clinard, et al. v. City of Winston-Salem. Original Case File. NCSA.

Daniels, Josephus. Papers. LOC.

MacRae Family Papers. 1817–1943. RLDU.

Murphy, Edgar Gardner. Papers. 1893–1913. SHC.

North Carolina Collection. Wilson Library, University of North Carolina at Chapel Hill.

Papers of the NAACP, Part 5 (Campaign Against Residential Segregation, 1914–1955). Microfilm.

Poe, Clarence. Papers. NCSA.

Polk, L. L. Papers. 1857–1919. SHC.

Records of the Extension Service, RG 33. National Archives II, College Park, MD.

Reynolds Family Papers. Reynolda House Museum of Art Archives, Winston-Salem, NC.

Simmons, Roscoe Conkling. Papers. Pusey Library, Harvard University.

Simmons, Roscoe Conkling. Papers. RLDU.

Spingarn, Arthur. Papers. LOC.

State v. Darnell. Original Case File. NCSA.

Stephenson, Gilbert T. Papers. Special Collections and Archives. Wake Forest University.

Storey, Moorfield. Papers. LOC.

Waddell, Alfred M. Papers. 1768–1935. SHC.

Watson and Morris Family Papers. 1830–1933. SHC.

Williams, Anne Jackson. Papers. 1880–1950. SHC.

Wilson, Woodrow. Papers. Princeton University.

Winston, Francis Donnell. Papers. 1787, 1828–1943. SHC.

Winston, Robert W. Papers. 1826–1944. SHC.

NEWSPAPERS AND PERIODICALS

Advance (Elizabeth City, NC)

Afro-American (Baltimore)

Arkansas Gazette (Little Rock)

Bee (Washington, DC)

Bristol (VA) Herald Courier

Caucasian (Clinton, NC, then Raleigh, NC)

Charlotte (NC) Observer

Charlotte (NC) Daily Observer

Chatham Record (Pittsboro, NC)

Congressional Record

Crisis (Baltimore)

Daily Argus (Goldsboro, NC)

Daily News (Greensboro, NC)

Daily Sun (Durham, NC)

E.S.C. Quarterly (Raleigh, NC)

Freeman: An Illustrated Colored Newspaper (Indianapolis, IN)

Gazette (Cleveland, OH)

Gazette (Raleigh, NC)

Greensboro (NC) Daily News

Greensboro (NC) Record
Harvard Law Review
Journal of the Senate of the General Assembly of the State of North Carolina (Raleigh)
Louisville (KY) Courier-Journal
Louisville (KY) Leader
Mebane (NC) Leader
Outlook
Progressive Farmer (Raleigh, NC)
New York Times
News and Observer (Raleigh, NC)
South Atlantic Quarterly (Durham, NC)
Sphinx Yearbook (Emory and Henry College, Emory, VA)
Topeka (KS) Plaindealer
Twin City Advertiser (Winston-Salem, NC)
Twin-City Daily Sentinel (Winston-Salem, NC)
Union Republican (Winston-Salem, NC)
Virginia Law Review
Western Sentinel (Winston, NC)
Winston-Salem Journal (NC)
World To-Day

LEGAL CASES

Buchanan v. Warley, 245 U.S. 60 (1917)
Clinard v. Winston-Salem, 217 N.C. 119 (1940)
Curtis v. Cash, 84 N.C. 41 (1881)
Harrison v. Ricks, 71 N.C. 7, 22 (1874)
Haskins v. Royster, 70 N.C. 600, 486 (1874)
State v. Copeland, 86 N.C. 691 (1882)
State v. Darnell, 166 N.C. 300 (1914)

DIGITAL COLLECTIONS

Against Their Will: North Carolina's Sterilization Program. https://www.journalnow.com/specialreports/againsttheirwill/.
American Life Histories: Manuscripts from the Federal Writers' Project, 1936–1940. Library of Congress, American Memory. https://www.loc.gov/collections/federal-writers-project/.
Broadsides and Ephemera Collection, David M. Rubenstein Rare Book & Manuscript Library. Duke University. https://repository.duke.edu/dc/broadsides.
Digital Forsyth. Forsyth County, NC. http://www.digitalforsyth.org/.
Documenting the American South. University Library, University of North Carolina, Chapel Hill. http://docsouth.unc.edu/.
East North Carolina Digital Library, East Carolina University. Greenville, NC. http://digital.lib.ecu.edu/historyfiction/.
Forsyth County Register of Deeds. Winston-Salem, NC. http://www.co.forsyth.nc.us/ROD/online_lookup.aspx.

Historical Census Browser. Geospatial and Statistical Data Center, University of Virginia. Website no longer in operation.

Mapping Inequality: Redlining in New Deal America, 1905–2016. Digital Scholarship Lab, University of Richmond, VA. http://dsl.richmond.edu/mappinginequality.html.

Manuscript Census. Family Search. Church of Jesus Christ of Latter-Day Saints. https://www.familysearch.org/.

North Carolina Maps. Carolina Digital Library and Archives, University of North Carolina, Chapel Hill. https://web.lib.unc.edu/nc-maps/.

Sanborn Fire Insurance Company Maps. Washington, DC: Library of Congress, 1867. https://loc.gov/collections/sanborn-maps.

Southern Oral History Program Collection, Southern Historical Collection, Wilson Library, University of North Carolina at Chapel Hill. https://sohp.org/.

United States Census. Social Explorer. Bronxville, NY. http://www.socialexplorer.com.

A View to Hugh: Processing the Hugh Morton Photographs and Films. University Library, University of North Carolina, Chapel Hill. http://www.lib.unc.edu/blogs/morton/index.php/essays/hugh-macrae-at-invershiel/.

Woodrow Wilson Presidential Library. Digital Archive. http://presidentwilson.org/items/search.

BOOKS, ARTICLES, REPORTS, AND DISSERTATIONS

Primary

Bailey, Liberty Hyde. *The Country-Life Movement in the United States*. New York: Macmillan, 1911.

——. *The Holy Earth*. Ithaca: New York State College of Agriculture and Life Sciences, 1980.

Belden, Henry M., and Arthur Palmer Hudson, eds. *The Frank C. Brown Collection of North Carolina Folklore*. Vol. 3: *Folk Songs from North Carolina*. Durham, NC: Duke University Press, 1952.

Boyd, R. H. *The Separate or "Jim Crow" Car Laws or Legislative Enactments*. Nashville, TN: National Baptist Publishing Board, 1909.

Brooks, Aubrey Lee, and Hugh Talmage Lefler, eds. *The Papers of Walter Clark*. Vol. 2: *1902–1924*. Chapel Hill: University of North Carolina Press, 1950.

Brown, R. Eugene. *Eugenical Sterilization in North Carolina: A Brief Survey of the Growth of Eugenical Sterilization and a Report on the Work of the Eugenics Board of North Carolina Through June 30, 1935*. Raleigh: Eugenics Board of North Carolina, 1935.

Bryan, William Jennings. "Cross of Gold." Speech. In *Official Proceedings of the Democratic National Convention Held in Chicago, Ill., July 7th, 8th, 9th, 10th and 11th, 1896*. Logansport, IN: Wilson, Humphreys, 1896.

Bryce, James. *The American Commonwealth*. New York: Commonwealth, 1888.

——. "Thoughts on the Negro Problem." *North American Review* 153, no. 421 (December 1891): 641–60.

Butler, Marion. "The Address of President Marion Butler, to the North Carolina Farmers' State Alliance at Greensboro, N.C." In *Addresses of Marion Butler, President, and Cyrus Thompson, Lecturer, to the North Carolina Farmers' State Alliance, at Greensboro, N.C., Aug. 8, 9, and 10, 1893, at Its Seventh Annual Session*. Raleigh, NC: Barnes Bros., 1893.

Cauley, Troy J. *Agrarianism: A Program for Farmers.* Chapel Hill: University of North Carolina Press, 1935.

Clark, Walter McKenzie. "The Negro in North Carolina and the South: His Fifty-Five Years of Freedom and What He Has Done." Commencement Address, St. Augustine's School, Raleigh, NC, May 26, 1920.

Clark, Wm. Bullock, et al. *Reports of the North Carolina Geological and Economic Survey.* Vol. 3: *The Coastal Plain of North Carolina.* Raleigh, NC: E. M. Uzzell, 1912.

Collins & Goodwin. *Biographical Sketches of the Members of the General Assembly of North Carolina, 1895.* Raleigh, NC: Edwards & Broughton, 1895.

Committee on Agriculture, House of Representatives. *Men and Milestones in American Agriculture.* 89th Congress, 2nd Session. Washington, DC: U.S. Government Printing Office, 1966.

Connor, R. D. W., and Clarence Poe, eds. *The Life and Speeches of Charles Brantley Aycock.* Garden City, NY: Doubleday, Page, 1912.

Daniels, Josephus. *Editor in Politics.* Chapel Hill: University of North Carolina Press, 1941.

Du Bois, W. E. B. *Black Reconstruction in America: Toward a History of the Part Which Black Folk Played in the Attempt to Reconstruct Democracy in America, 1860–1880.* New York: Harcourt, Brace, 1935.

——. *Darkwater: Voices from Within the Veil.* New York: Harcourt, Brace and Howe, 1920.

——. *The Souls of Black Folk: Essays and Sketches.* Chicago: A. C. McClurg, 1903.

——. "The Upbuilding of Black Durham. The Success of the Negroes and Their Value to a Tolerant and Helpful Southern City." *World's Work* 23 (January 1912): 334–38.

Evans, Maurice S. *Black and White in South East Africa: A Study in Sociology.* London: Longmans, Green, 1911.

——. *Black and White in the Southern States: A Study of the Race Problem in the United States from a South African Point of View.* Columbia: University of South Carolina Press, 2001.

——. "International Conference on the Negro: Report of the African Society's Representative, Mr. Maurice S. Evans, C.M.G." *Journal of the Royal African Society* 11, no. 44 (July 1912): 416–29.

——. "Present Position of Native Affairs in the Union of South Africa: A Plea for the Scientific Study of Race Relations." *Journal of the Royal African Society* 12, no. 48 (July 1913): 343–53.

Federal Writers' Project. *North Carolina: A Guide to the Old North State.* Columbia: University of South Carolina Press, 1939.

Helper, Hinton Rowan. *Compendium of the Impending Crisis of the South.* New York: A. B. Burdick, 1860.

——. *The Impending Crisis of the South: How to Meet It.* New York: Burdick Brothers, 1857.

Jefferson, Thomas. *Notes on the State of Virginia.* Chapel Hill: University of North Carolina Press, 1955.

——. *The Works of Thomas Jefferson.* 12 vols. Ed. Paul Leicester Ford. New York: G. P. Putnam's Sons, 1905.

MacRae, Hugh. "The Potential South: Its Youth and Its Call to Youth." Pamphlet. N.d.

——. "Vitalizing the Nation and Conserving Human Units Through the Development of Agricultural Communities." *Annals of the American Academy of Political and Social Science* 63 (January 1916): 278–86.

Mead, Elwood. "How California Is Helping People Own Farm and Rural Homes." University of California College of Agriculture, Agricultural Experiment Station, Circular 221 (August 1920).

——. "What Should Be the Next Step in Rural Development." In *Colonization and Rural Development in California*. University of California College of Agriculture, Agricultural Experiment Station Circular 247 (June 1922): 5–30.

Miller, Ernest H. *The Winston-Salem, N.C. City Directory*. Vol. 13. Asheville, NC: Palala, 1912.

——. *Winston-Salem, N.C., City and Suburban Directory*. Vol. 14. Asheville, NC: Palala, 1913.

Murphy, Edgar Gardner. *The Basis of Ascendancy*. New York: Longmans, Green, 1910.

Natal Who's Who: An Illustrated Biographical Sketch Book of Natalians. Durban: Natal Who's Who Publishing Company, 1906.

National Association for the Advancement of Colored People. *NAACP Fourth Annual Report, 1913*. New York, 1914.

North Carolina Board of Agriculture. *North Carolina and Its Resources Illustrated*. Winston, NC: M. I. & J. C. Stewart, 1896.

Odum, Howard. *Southern Regions of the United States*. Chapel Hill: University of North Carolina Press, 1936.

Park, Robert M. "Tuskegee International Conference on the Negro." *Journal of Race Development* 3 (July 1912): 117–20.

Parliament of South Africa. Natives Land Act, 1913.

Plaatje, Solomon T. *Native Life in South Africa*. Middlesex: Echo Library, 1916.

Poe, Clarence H. *How Farmers Co-operate and Double Profits*. New York: Orange Judd, 1915.

——. "Lynching: A Southern View." *Atlantic Monthly* 93 (February 1904): 155–65.

——. *My First Eighty Years*. Chapel Hill: University of North Carolina Press, 1963.

——. "Suffrage Restriction in the South; Its Causes and Consequences." *North American Review* 175, no. 551 (October 1902): 534–43.

——. *Where Half the World Is Waking Up: The Old and the New in Japan, China, the Philippines, and India, Reported with Especial Reference to American Conditions*. New York: Doubleday, Page, 1911.

Polk, L. L. "The Protest of the Farmer: Address of President L. L. Polk to Citizens Alliance No. 4 of Washington, D.C. at Concordia Hall." April 14, 1891.

Raper, Arthur F. *Preface to Peasantry: A Tale of Two Black Belt Counties*. Chapel Hill: University of North Carolina Press, 1936.

——. *The Tragedy of Lynching*. Chapel Hill: University of North Carolina Press, 1933.

Raper, Arthur F., and Ira De A. Reid. *Sharecroppers All*. Chapel Hill: University of North Carolina Press, 1941.

Richardson, Clement, ed. *National Cyclopedia of the Colored Race*. Vol. 1. Montgomery, AL: National Publishing Company, 1919.

Rosengarten, Theodore. *All God's Dangers: The Life of Nate Shaw*. Chicago: University of Chicago Press, 1974.

Simmons, Furnifold. *Memoirs*. In *F. M. Simmons: Statesman of the New South: Memoirs and Addresses*. Ed. J. Fred Rippy. Durham, NC: Duke University Press, 1936.

Stephenson, Gilbert Thomas. *Race Distinctions in American Law*. New York: Appleton, 1910.

——. "Racial Distinctions in Southern Law." *American Political Science Review* 1 (November 1906): 44–61.

——. "The Segregation of the White and Negro Races in Cities." *South Atlantic Quarterly* 13, no. 1 (January 1914): 1–18.

——. "The Segregation of the White and Negro Races in Rural Communities of North Carolina." *South Atlantic Quarterly* 13, no. 2 (April 1914): 107–17.

——. "The Separation of the Races in Public Conveyances." *American Political Science Review* 3, no. 2 (May 1909): 180–204.

Taylor, Carl C., and C. C. Zimmerman. *Economic and Social Conditions of North Carolina Farmers: Based on a Survey of One Thousand North Carolina Farmers in Three Typical Counties of the State*. Raleigh: North Carolina Department of Agriculture, Tenancy Commission, 1923.

U.S. Works Progress Administration, North Carolina. *These Are Our Lives: As Told by the People and Written by Members of the Federal Writers' Project of the Works Progress Administration in North Carolina, Tennessee, and Georgia*. Chapel Hill: University of North Carolina Press, 1939.

Vance, Rupert B., and Nicholas J. Demerath, eds. *The Urban South*. Chapel Hill: University of North Carolina Press, 1954.

Waddell, Alfred Moore. *Some Memories of My Life*. Raleigh: Edwards & Broughton, 1908.

Walsh's Winston-Salem, North Carolina City Directory for 1908. Charleston, SC: Walsh Directory Company, 1907.

Washington, Booker T. *The Booker T. Washington Papers*. Vol. 12: *1912–1914*, and vol. 13: *1914–1915*. Ed. Louis R. Harlan and Raymond W. Smock. Urbana: University of Illinois Press, 1982, 1984.

——. "My View of Segregation Laws." *New Republic* 5 (December 4, 1915).

——. *Up from Slavery*. In *The Norton Anthology of African American Literature*, ed. Henry Louis Gates Jr. and Nellie Y. McKay, 490–521. New York: Norton, 1997.

Wells, Ida B. *Southern Horrors: Lynch Law in All Its Phases*. New York: New York Age Print, 1892.

Winston, Robert Watson. *It's a Far Cry*. New York: Holt, 1937.

——. "Should the Color Line Go?" *Current History* 18, no. 6 (September 1923), 945–51.

——. "The South in Transition." *Current History* 35, no. 2 (November 1931): 189–92.

Woofter Jr., T. J. *Landlord and Tenant on the Cotton Plantation*. New York: Negro Universities Press, 1936.

——. *Negro Problems in Cities*. New York: Doubleday, Doran, 1928.

Wright Jr., Richard R. "The Economic Condition of Negroes in the North III: Negro Communities in New Jersey." *Southern Workman* 37, no. 7 (July 1908): 385–93.

Secondary

Ali, Omar H. *In the Lion's Mouth: Black Populism in the New South*. Jackson: University Press of Mississippi, 2010.

Anderson, Eric. *Race and Politics in North Carolina, 1872–1901: The Black Second*. Baton Rouge: Louisiana State University Press, 1981.

Applewhite, Marjorie Mendenhall. "Sharecropper and Tenant in the Courts of North Carolina." *North Carolina Historical Review* 31, no. 2 (April 1954): 134–49.

Arnesen, Eric. "Whiteness and the Historians' Imagination." *International Labor and Working Class History* 60 (2001): 3–32.

Baker, Andrew C. "Race and Romantic Agrarianism: The Transnational Roots of Clarence Poe's Crusade for Rural Segregation in North Carolina." *Agricultural History* 87, no. 1 (Winter 2013): 93–114.

Baker, Bruce E. *This Mob Will Surely Take My Life: Lynchings in the Carolinas, 1871–1947.* London: Continuum, 2008.

Baptist, Edward E. *The Half Has Never Been Told: Slavery and the Making of American Capitalism.* New York: Basic Books, 2014.

Bates, Beth Tompkins. *Pullman Porters and the Rise of Protest Politics in Black America, 1925–1945.* Chapel Hill: University of North Carolina Press, 2001.

Bauerlein, Mark. "The Tactical Life of Booker T. Washington." *Chronicle of Higher Education* November 28, 2003, B12–B13.

Beckel, Deborah. *Radical Reform: Interracial Politics in Post-Emancipation North Carolina.* Charlottesville: University of Virginia Press, 2011.

Beeby, James M., ed. *Populism in the South Revisited: New Interpretations and New Departures.* Jackson: University Press of Mississippi, 2012.

——. "Red Shirt Violence, Election Fraud, and the Demise of the Populist Party in North Carolina's Third Congressional District, 1900." *North Carolina Historical Review* 85, no. 1 (January 2008): 1–28.

——. *Revolt of the Tar Heels: The North Carolina Populist Movement, 1890–1901.* Jackson: University Press of Mississippi, 2008.

Benjamin, Karen. "Suburbanizing Jim Crow: The Impact of School Policy on Residential Segregation in Raleigh." *Journal of Urban History* 38, no. 2 (March 2012): 225–46.

Bennett, Evan P. *When Tobacco Was King: Families, Farm Labor, and Federal Policy in the Piedmont.* Gainesville: University Press of Florida, 2014.

Berrey, Stephen A. *The Jim Crow Routine: Everyday Performances of Race, Civil Rights, and Segregation in Mississippi.* Chapel Hill: University of North Carolina Press, 2015.

Billings, Dwight B. *Planters and the Making of a "New South": Class, Politics, and Development in North Carolina, 1865–1900.* Chapel Hill: University of North Carolina Press, 1979.

Bishir, Catherine W., and Lawrence S. Earley, eds. *Early Twentieth-Century Suburbs in North Carolina: Essays on History, Architecture, and Planning.* Raleigh: Archaeology and Historic Preservation Section, Division of Archives and History, North Carolina Department of Cultural Resources, 1985.

Blackmon, Douglas A. *Slavery by Another Name: The Re-Enslavement of Black Americans from the Civil War to World War II.* New York: Doubleday, 2008.

Boger, Gretchen. "The Meaning of Neighborhood in the Modern City: Baltimore's Residential Segregation Ordinances, 1910–1913." *Journal of Urban History* 35 (January 2009): 236–58.

Bolton, Charles C. *Poor Whites of the Antebellum South: Tenants and Laborers in Central North Carolina and Northeast Mississippi.* Durham, NC: Duke University Press, 1994.

Bourdieu, Pierre. "The Forms of Capital." In *Handbook of Theory and Research for the Sociology of Education*, ed. J. Richardson, 241–58. New York: Greenwood, 1986. https://www.marxists.org/reference/subject/philosophy/works/fr/bourdieu-forms-capital.htm.

Bowers, William L. *The Country Life Movement in America, 1900–1920.* Port Washington, NY: Kennikat, 1974.

Brookes, Edgar H. *White Rule in South Africa, 1830–1910: Varieties in Governmental Policies Affecting Africans*. Pietermaritzburg: University of Natal Press, 1974.

Brooks, Aubrey Lee. *Walter Clark: Fighting Judge*. Chapel Hill: University of North Carolina Press, 1944.

Brooks, Clayton McClure. *The Uplift Generation: Cooperation Across the Color Line in Early Twentieth-Century Virginia*. Charlottesville: University of Virginia Press, 2017.

Brown, David. *Southern Outcast: Hinton Rowan Helper and* The Impending Crisis of the South. Baton Rouge: Louisiana State University Press, 2006.

Brundage, W. Fitzhugh. *Lynching in the New South: Georgia and Virginia, 1880–1930*. Urbana: University of Illinois Press, 1993.

Canaday, Neil. "The Accumulation of Property by Southern Blacks and Whites: Individual-Level Evidence from a South Carolina Cotton County." *Explorations in Economic History* 45, no. 1 (2008): 51–75.

Canaday, Neil, and Charles Reback, "Race, Literacy, and Real Estate Transactions in the Postbellum South." *Journal of Economic History* 70, no. 2 (June 2010): 428–45.

Castles, Katherine. "Quiet Eugenics: Sterilization in North Carolina's Institutions for the Mentally Retarded, 1945–1965." *Journal of Southern History* 68, no. 4 (November 2002): 849–78.

Cecelski, David S., and Timothy B. Tyson, eds. *Democracy Betrayed*. Chapel Hill: University of North Carolina Press, 1998.

Cecil-Fronsman, Bill. *Common Whites: Class and Culture in Antebellum North Carolina*. Lexington: University Press of Kentucky, 1992.

Cell, John W. *The Highest Stage of White Supremacy: The Origins of Segregation in South Africa and the American South*. New York: Cambridge University Press, 1982.

Chafe, William H. *Civilities and Civil Rights: Greensboro, North Carolina, and the Black Struggle for Freedom*. Oxford: Oxford University Press, 1980.

Coates, Ta-Nehisi. "The Case for Reparations." *Atlantic*, June 2014. https://www.theatlantic.com/magazine/archive/2014/06/the-case-for-reparations/361631/.

——. Keynote address. Conference on Universities and Slavery: Bound by History. Radcliffe Institute for Advanced Study, March 3, 2017. Cambridge, MA.

Cobb, James C. *Industrialization and Southern Society, 1877–1984*. Lexington: University Press of Kentucky, 1984.

Cohen, William. *At Freedom's Edge: Black Mobility and the Southern White Quest for Racial Control, 1861–1915*. Baton Rouge: Louisiana State University Press, 1991.

Conkin, Paul. *Tomorrow a New World: The New Deal Community Program*. Ithaca, NY: Cornell University Press, 1959.

Connolly, N. D. B. *A World More Concrete: Real Estate and the Remaking of Jim Crow South Florida*. Chicago: University of Chicago Press, 2014.

Coté, Joseph A. "Clarence Hamilton Poe: Crusading Editor, 1881–1964." Ph.D. diss., University of Georgia, 1976.

——. "Clarence Hamilton Poe: The Farmer's Voice, 1899–1964." *Agricultural History* 53, no. 1 (January 1979): 30–41.

Cottle, Ann S. *The Roots of Penderlea: A Memory of a New Deal Homestead Community*. Wilmington: Publishing Laboratory, University of North Carolina Wilmington, 2008.

Creech, Joe. *Righteous Indignation: Religion and the Populist Revolution*. Urbana: University of Illinois Press, 2016.

Crespino, Joseph. *In Search of Another Country: Mississippi and the Conservative Counterrevolution*. Princeton, NJ: Princeton University Press, 2007.

Crow, Jeffrey J. "An Apartheid for the South: Clarence Poe's Crusade for Rural Segregation." In *Race, Class, and Politics in Southern History: Essays in Honor of Robert F. Durden*, ed. Jeffrey J. Crow et al., 216–59. Baton Rouge: Louisiana State University Press, 1989.

——. "Cracking the Solid South: Populism and the Fusionist Interlude." In *The North Carolina Experience: An Interpretive and Documentary History*, ed. Lindley S. Butler and Alan D. Watson, 335–71. Chapel Hill: University of North Carolina Press, 1984.

Crow, Jeffrey J., and Robert F. Durden. *Maverick Republican in the Old North State: A Political Biography of Daniel L. Russell*. Baton Rouge: Louisiana State University Press, 1977.

Dailey, Jane, Glenda Elizabeth Gilmore, and Bryant Simon. *Jumpin' Jim Crow: Southern Politics from Civil War to Civil Rights*. Princeton, NJ: Princeton University Press, 2000.

Daniel, Pete. *Breaking the Land: The Transformation of Cotton, Tobacco, and Rice Cultures Since 1880*. Urbana: University of Illinois Press, 1985.

Davis, Lenwood G., William J. Rice, and James H. McLaughlin. *African Americans in Winston-Salem/Forsyth County: A Pictorial History*. Virginia Beach, VA: Donning, 1999.

Debow, Saul. *Racial Segregation and the Origins of Apartheid in South Africa, 1919–36*. London: Macmillan, 1989.

Downs, Gregory P. *Declarations of Dependence: The Long Reconstruction of Popular Politics in the South, 1861–1908*. Chapel Hill: University of North Carolina Press, 2011.

Doyle, Don H. *New Men, New Cities, New South: Atlanta, Nashville, Charleston, Mobile, 1860–1910*. Chapel Hill: University of North Carolina Press, 1990.

Dudley, Kathryn Marie. *Debt and Dispossession: Farm Loss in America's Heartland*. Chicago: University of Chicago Press, 2000.

Durden, Robert F. "North Carolina in the New South." In *The North Carolina Experience: An Interpretive and Documentary History*, ed. Lindley S. Butler and Alan D. Watson. Chapel Hill: University of North Carolina Press, 1984.

Edmonds, Helen G. *The Negro and Fusion Politics in North Carolina, 1894–1901*. Chapel Hill: University of North Carolina Press, 1951.

Ely Jr., James W. "Homestead Exemption and Southern Legal Culture." In *Signposts: New Directions in Southern Legal History*, ed. Sally E. Hadden and Patricia Hagler Minter, 289–314. Athens: University of Georgia Press, 2013.

——. "Reflections on *Buchanan v. Warley*, Property Rights, and Race." *Vanderbilt Law Review* 51, no. 4 (May 1998): 953–1058.

Escott, Paul. *Many Excellent People: Power and Privilege in North Carolina, 1850–1900*. Chapel Hill: University of North Carolina Press, 1985.

Feimster, Crystal N. *Southern Horrors: Women and the Politics of Rape and Lynching*. Cambridge, MA: Harvard University Press, 2009.

Feinberg, Harvey M. "The 1913 Natives Land Act in South Africa: Politics, Race, and Segregation in the Early Twentieth Century." *International Journal of African Historical Studies* 26, no. 1 (1993): 65–109.

Feinberg, Harvey M., and Andre Horn. "South African Territorial Segregation: New Data on African Farm Purchases, 1913–1936." *Journal of African History* 50, no. 1 (2009): 41–60.

Field, Kendra Taira. *Growing Up with the Country: Family, Race, and Nation After the Civil War*. New Haven, CT: Yale University Press, 2018.

Fields, Barbara J. *"Origins of the New South* and the Negro Question." *Journal of Southern History* 67, no. 4 (November 2001): 811–26.

——. "Slavery, Race and Ideology in the United States of America." In *Racecraft: The Soul of Inequality in American Life*, ed. Karen E. Fields and Barbara J. Fields, 111–48. New York: Verso, 2012.

Finley, Keith M. *Delaying the Dream: Southern Senators and the Fight Against Civil Rights, 1938–1965*. Baton Rouge: Louisiana State University, 2008.

Fite, Gilbert C. *Cotton Fields No More: Southern Agriculture, 1865–1980*. Lexington: University Press of Kentucky, 1984.

Fitzgerald, Michael W. " 'We Have Found a Moses': Theodore Bilbo, Black Nationalism, and the Greater Liberia Bill of 1939." *Journal of Southern History* 63, no. 2 (May 1997): 293–320.

Foley, Neil. *The White Scourge: Mexicans, Blacks, and Poor Whites in Texas Cotton Culture*. Berkeley: University of California Press, 1997.

Foner, Eric. *Reconstruction: America's Unfinished Revolution, 1863–1877*. New York: Harper & Row, 1988.

Fredrickson, George M. *The Arrogance of Race: Historical Perspectives on Slavery, Racism, and Social Inequality*. Hanover, NH: Wesleyan University Press, 1988.

——. *The Black Image in the White Mind: The Debate on Afro-American Character and Destiny, 1817–1914*. Hanover, NH: Wesleyan University Press, 1987.

——. *White Supremacy: A Comparative Study in American and South African History*. Oxford: Oxford University Press, 1981.

Freund, David M. P. *Colored Property: State Policy and White Racial Politics in Suburban America*. Chicago: University of Chicago Press, 2007.

Gaither, Gerald H. *Blacks and the Populist Revolt: Ballots and Bigotry in the "New South."* Tuscaloosa: University of Alabama Press, 1977.

Garb, Margaret. *City of American Dreams: A History of Home Ownership and Housing Reform in Chicago, 1871–1919*. Chicago: University of Chicago Press, 2005.

Genovese, Eugene D. "Yeomen Farmers in a Slaveholders' Democracy." *Agricultural History* 49, no. 2 (Spring 1975): 331–42.

Gillespie, Michele. *Katharine and R. J. Reynolds: Partners of Fortune in the Making of the New South*. Athens: University of Georgia Press, 2012.

Gilmore, Glenda Elizabeth. *Gender and Jim Crow: Women and the Politics of White Supremacy in North Carolina, 1896–1920*. Chapel Hill: University of North Carolina Press, 1996.

Glenn, Joanne. "The Winston-Salem Riot of 1918." MA thesis, University of North Carolina, Chapel Hill, 1979.

Gonda, Jeffrey. "Litigating Racial Justice at the Grassroots: The Shelley Family, Black Realtors, and *Shelley v. Kraemer* (1948)." *Journal of Supreme Court History* 39 (November 2014): 329–46.

——. *Unjust Deeds: The Restrictive Covenant Cases and the Making of the Civil Rights Movement*. Chapel Hill: University of North Carolina Press, 2015.

Goodwyn, Lawrence. *Democratic Promise: The Populist Moment in America*. New York: Oxford University Press, 1976.

——. *The Populist Moment: A Short History of the Agrarian Revolt in America*. New York: Oxford University Press, 1978.

Gordon, Colin. *Mapping Decline: St. Louis and the Fate of the American City*. Philadelphia: University of Pennsylvania Press, 2008.

Grantham, Dewey W. *The Life and Death of the Solid South: A Political History.* Lexington: University Press of Kentucky, 1988.

——. *Southern Progressivism: The Reconciliation of Progress and Tradition.* Knoxville: University of Tennessee Press, 1983.

Gregory, James N. *The Southern Diaspora: How the Great Migrations of Black and White Southerners Transformed America.* Chapel Hill: University of North Carolina Press, 2005.

Groves, Paul, and Edward Muller. "The Evolution of Black Residential Areas in Late-Nineteenth-Century Cities." *Journal of Historical Geography* 1, no. 2 (1975): 169–91.

Hackney, Sheldon. *Populism to Progressivism in Alabama.* Princeton, NJ: Princeton University Press, 1969.

Hahn, Steven. *A Nation Under Our Feet: Black Political Struggles in the Rural South from Slavery to the Great Migration.* Cambridge, MA: Harvard University Press, 2003.

——. *The Roots of Southern Populism: Yeoman Farmers and the Transformation of the Georgia Upcountry, 1850–1890.* New York: Oxford University Press, 1983.

Hale, Grace Elizabeth. *Making Whiteness: The Culture of Segregation in the South, 1890–1940.* New York: Vintage, 1998.

Haley, John. *Charles N. Hunter and Race Relations in North Carolina.* Chapel Hill: University of North Carolina Press, 1987.

Haley, Sarah. *No Mercy Here: Gender, Punishment, and the Making of Jim Crow Modernity.* Chapel Hill: University of North Carolina Press, 2016.

Hall, Jacquelyn Dowd, et al. *Like a Family: The Making of a Southern Cotton Mill World.* New York: Norton, 1987.

Hall, Randal L., and Ken Badgett. "Robinson Newcomb and the Limits of Liberalism at UNC: Two Case Studies of Black Businessmen in the 1920s South." *North Carolina Historical Review* 86 (October 2009): 373–403.

Hanchett, Thomas W. *Sorting Out the New South City: Race, Class, and Urban Development in Charlotte, 1876–1975.* Chapel Hill: University of North Carolina Press, 1998.

Harlan, Louis. *Booker T. Washington: The Wizard of Tuskegee, 1901–1915.* New York: Oxford University Press, 1983.

——. "Booker T. Washington and the White Man's Burden." *American Historical Review* 71 (January 1966): 441–67.

——. "The Secret Life of Booker T. Washington." *Journal of Southern History* 37 (August 1971): 393–416.

Harris, Cheryl I. "Whiteness as Property." *Harvard Law Review* 106, no. 8 (June 1993): 1709–91.

Herbin-Triant, Elizabeth A. "Race and Class Friction in North Carolina Neighborhoods: How Campaigns for Residential Segregation Law Divided Middling and Elite Whites in Winston-Salem and North Carolina's Countryside, 1912–1915." *Journal of Southern History* 83, no. 3 (August 2017): 531–72.

——. "Southern Segregation, South Africa-Style: Maurice Evans, Clarence Poe, and the Ideology of Rural Segregation." *Agricultural History* 87, no. 2 (Spring 2013): 170–93.

Hicks, John D. "The Farmers' Alliance in North Carolina." *North Carolina Historical Review* 2 (April 1925): 162–87.

Higginbotham, A. Leon, F. Michael Higginbotham, and S. Sandile Ngcobo. "De Jure Housing Segregation in the United States and South Africa: The Difficult Pursuit for Racial Justice." *University of Illinois Law Review* 1990, no. 4 (1990): 763–877.

Higgs, Robert. "Accumulation of Property by Southern Blacks Before World War I." *American Economic Review* 72, no. 4 (1982): 725–37.

Higuchi, Hayumi. "White Supremacy on the Cape Fear: The Wilmington Affair of 1898." MA thesis, University of North Carolina at Chapel Hill, 1980.

Hobbs Jr., S. Huntington. *North Carolina: An Economic and Social Profile*. Chapel Hill: University of North Carolina Press, 1958.

Hofstadter, Richard. *The Age of Reform: From Bryan to FDR*. New York: Knopf, 1965.

Holmes, William F. "Moonshining and Collective Violence: Georgia, 1889–1895." *Journal of American History* 67, no. 3 (December 1980): 589–611.

——. "Whitecapping: Agrarian Violence in Mississippi, 1902–1906." *Journal of Southern History* 35, no. 2 (May 1969): 165–85.

Holt, Sharon Ann. *Making Freedom Pay: North Carolina Freedpeople Working for Themselves, 1865–1900*. Athens: University of Georgia Press, 2000.

Holt, Thomas C. *The Problem of Race in the Twenty-First Century*. Cambridge, MA: Harvard University Press, 2002.

Hunt, James L. *Marion Butler and American Populism*. Chapel Hill: University of North Carolina Press, 2003.

Hunter, Tera. *To 'Joy My Freedom: Southern Black Women's Lives and Labors After the Civil War*. Cambridge, MA: Harvard University Press, 1997.

Jackson, Kenneth T. *Crabgrass Frontier: The Suburbanization of the United States*. New York: Oxford University Press, 1985.

Jaspin, Elliot. *Buried in the Bitter Waters: The Hidden History of Racial Cleansing in America*. New York: Basic Books, 2007.

Jewell, Katherine Rye. *Dollars for Dixie: Business and the Transformation of Conservatism in the Twentieth Century*. Cambridge: Cambridge University Press, 2017.

Johnson, Walter. *River of Dark Dreams: Slavery and Empire in the Cotton Kingdom*. Cambridge, MA: Harvard University Press, 2013.

Justesen, Benjamin R. *George Henry White: An Even Chance in the Race of Life*. Baton Rouge: Louisiana State University Press, 2001.

——. *In His Own Words: The Writings, Speeches, and Letters of George Henry White*. Lincoln, NE: iUniverse, 2004.

Kahrl, Andrew W. *The Land Was Ours: How Black Beaches Became White Wealth in the Coastal South*. Chapel Hill: University of North Carolina Press, 2012.

Kantrowitz, Stephen. *Ben Tillman and the Reconstruction of White Supremacy*. Chapel Hill: University of North Carolina Press, 2000.

Keegan, Timothy J. *Rural Transformations in Industrializing South Africa: The Southern Highveld to 1914*. London: Macmillan, 1987.

Kellogg, John. "The Formation of Black Residential Areas in Lexington, Kentucky, 1865–1885." *Journal of Southern History* 4 (February 1982): 21–52.

——. "Negro Urban Clusters in the Post-Bellum South." *Geographical Review* 67 (July 1971): 287–303.

Kelly, Brian. "Sentinels for New South Industry: Booker T. Washington, Industrial Accommodation, and Black Workers in the Jim Crow South." *Labor History* 44, no. 3 (2003): 337–57.

Kenzer, Robert C. *Enterprising Southerners: Black Economic Success in North Carolina, 1865–1915*. Charlottesville: University Press of Virginia, 1997.

Kevles, Daniel J. *In the Name of Eugenics: Genetics and the Uses of Human Heredity*. Berkeley: University of California Press, 1985.

Key Jr., V. O. *Southern Politics: In State and Nation*. New York: Vintage, 1949.

Kiernan, Ben. *Blood and Soil: A World History of Genocide and Extermination from Sparta to Darfur*. New Haven, CT: Yale University Press, 2007.

Kirby, Jack Temple. "Clarence Poe's Vision of a Segregated 'Great Rural Civilization.'" *South Atlantic Quarterly* 68 (1969): 27–38.

——. *Darkness at the Dawning: Race and Reform in the Progressive South*. Philadelphia: Lippincott, 1972.

——. *Rural Worlds Lost: The American South, 1920–1960*. Baton Rouge: Louisiana State University Press, 1987.

K'Meyer, Tracy E. *Civil Rights in the Gateway to the South: Louisville, Kentucky, 1945–1980*. Lexington: University Press of Kentucky, 2009.

Korstad, Robert Rodgers. *Civil Rights Unionism*. Chapel Hill: University of North Carolina Press, 2003.

Kousser, J. Morgan. *The Shaping of Southern Politics: Suffrage Restriction and the Establishment of the One-Party South, 1880–1910*. New Haven, CT: Yale University Press, 1974.

Kruse, Kevin M. *White Flight: Atlanta and the Making of Modern Conservatism*. Princeton, NJ: Princeton University Press, 2007.

Kulikoff, Allan. *The Agrarian Origins of American Capitalism*. Charlottesville: University Press of Virginia, 1992.

Kyriakoudes, Louis M. *Social Origins of the Urban South: Race, Gender, and Migration in Nashville and Middle Tennessee, 1890–1930*. Chapel Hill: University of North Carolina Press, 2003.

Lake, Marilyn, and Henry Reynolds. *Drawing the Global Colour Line: White Men's Countries and the International Challenge of Racial Equality*. Cambridge: Cambridge University Press, 2008.

Lambert, John. *Betrayed Trust: Africans and the State in Colonial Natal*. Pietermaritzburg: University of Natal Press, 1995.

Lands, LeeAnn. *The Culture of Property: Race, Class, and Housing Landscapes in Atlanta, 1880–1950*. Athens: University of Georgia Press, 2009.

Larson, Edward J. *Sex, Race, and Science: Eugenics in the Deep South*. Baltimore, MD: Johns Hopkins University Press, 1995.

Lassiter, Matthew D. "De Jure/De Facto Segregation: The Long Shadow of a National Myth." In *The Myth of Southern Exceptionalism*, ed. Matthew D. Lassiter and Joseph Crespino, 25–48. New York: Oxford University Press, 2009.

——. *The Silent Majority: Suburban Politics in the Sunbelt South*. Princeton, NJ: Princeton University Press, 2007.

Leloudis, James L. *Schooling the New South: Pedagogy, Self, and Society in North Carolina, 1880–1920*. Chapel Hill: University of North Carolina Press, 1996.

Leong, Nancy. "Racial Capitalism." *Harvard Law Review* 126, no. 8 (June 2013): 2152–2226.

Lester, Connie. *Up from the Mudsills of Hell: The Farmers' Alliance, Populism, and Progressive Agriculture in Tennessee, 1870–1915*. Athens: University of Georgia Press, 2006.

Lewis, Earl. *In Their Own Interests: Race, Class, and Power in Twentieth-Century Norfolk, Virginia*. Berkeley: University of California Press, 1991.

Link, William A. *The Paradox of Southern Progressivism, 1880–1930*. Chapel Hill: University of North Carolina Press, 1992.

Little, Margaret Ruth. "Getting the American Dream for Themselves: Postwar Modern Subdivisions for African Americans in Raleigh, North Carolina." *Buildings & Landscapes* 19, no. 1 (Spring 2012): 73–86.

Loewen, James W. *Sundown Towns: A Hidden Dimension of American Racism*. New York: Simon & Schuster, 2006.

Logan, Trevon D., and John M. Parman. "The National Rise in Residential Segregation." *Journal of Economic History* 77, no. 1 (March 2017): 127–70.

"Longview Gardens Historic District." *Living Places*. http://www.livingplaces.com/NC /Wake_County/Raleigh_City/Longview_Gardens_Historic_District.html.

Lowery, J. Vincent. "'Another Species of Race Discord': Race, Desirability, and the North Carolina Immigration Movement of the Early Twentieth Century." *Journal of American Ethnic History* 35, no. 2 (Winter 2016): 32–59.

——. "The Transatlantic Dreams of the Port City Prophet: The Rural Reform Campaign of Hugh MacRae." *North Carolina Historical Review* 90, no. 3 (2013): 288–324.

Lundeen, Elizabeth Anne. "The Accommodation Strategies of African American Educational Leaders in North Carolina, 1890–1930." M.Phil. diss., University of Cambridge, 2008.

——. "Simon G. Atkins: Race Leader." Honors thesis, Wake Forest University, 2007.

MacPherson, C. B., ed. *Property: Mainstream and Critical Positions*. Toronto: University of Toronto Press, 1978.

Magdol, Edward. *A Right to the Land: Essays on the Freedmen's Community*. Westport, CT: Greenwood, 1977.

Marable, Manning. *How Capitalism Underdeveloped Black America: Problems in Race, Political Economy, and Society*. Chicago: Haymarket, 2015.

Margo, Robert A. "Accumulation of Property by Southern Blacks Before World War I: Comment and Further Evidence." *American Economic Review* 74, no. 4 (1984): 768–76.

Marks, Shula. "Natal, the Zulu Royal Family and the Ideology of Segregation." In *Segregation and Apartheid in Twentieth-Century South Africa*, ed. William Beinart and Saul Dubow, 91–117. London: Routledge, 1995.

Massey, Douglas A., and Nancy A. Denton. *American Apartheid: Segregation and the Making of the Underclass*. Cambridge, MA: Harvard University Press, 1993.

McClain, Charles J. *In Search of Equality: The Chinese Struggle Against Discrimination in Nineteenth-Century America*. Berkeley: University of California Press, 1994.

McCoy, Drew R. *The Elusive Republic: Political Economy in Jeffersonian America*. Chapel Hill: University of North Carolina Press, 1980.

McCurry, Stephanie. *Masters of Small Worlds: Yeoman Households, Gender Relations, and the Political Culture of the Antebellum South Carolina Low Country*. New York: Oxford University Press, 1995.

McMath Jr., Robert C. *American Populism: A Social History, 1877–1898*. New York: Hill and Wang, 1993.

McTigue, Geraldine. "Patterns of Residence: Housing Distribution by Color in Two Louisiana Towns, 1860–1880." *Louisiana Studies* 15 (Winter 1976): 345–88.

Merritt, Keri Leigh. *Masterless Men: Poor Whites and Slavery in the Antebellum South*. Cambridge: Cambridge University Press, 2017.

Meyer, Stephen Grant. *As Long as They Don't Move Next Door: Segregation and Racial Conflict in American Neighborhoods*. Lanham, MD: Rowman & Littlefield, 2000.

Michney, Todd M. *Surrogate Suburbs: Black Upward Mobility and Neighborhood Change in Cleveland, 1900–1980*. Chapel Hill: University of North Carolina Press, 2017.

Miller, Bertha Hampton. "Blacks in Winston-Salem, North Carolina, 1895–1920: Community Development in an Era of Benevolent Paternalism." Ph.D. diss., Duke University, 1981.

Minter, Patricia Hagler. "Race, Property, and Negotiated Space in the American South: A Reconsideration of *Buchanan v. Warley*." In *Signposts: New Directions in Southern Legal History*, ed. Sally E. Hadden and Patricia Hagler Minter, 345–68. Athens: University of Georgia Press, 2013.

——. "William Warley: A Leader Ahead of His Time." In *One Hundred Americans Making Constitutional History: A Biographical History*, ed. Melvin I. Urofsky, 200–202. Washington, DC: CQ, 2004.

Mobley, J. A. "In the Shadow of White Society: Princeville, a Black Town in North Carolina, 1865–1915." *North Carolina Historical Review* 63, no. 3 (1986): 340–84.

——. *Princeville, a Black Town in North Carolina*. Raleigh, NC: Division of Archives and History, 1981.

National Register of Historic Places. Registration Form for Longview Gardens Historic District. http://www.hpo.ncdcr.gov/nr/WA4441.pdf.

Ngai, Mae M. *Impossible Subjects: Illegal Aliens and the Making of Modern America*. Princeton, NJ: Princeton University Press, 2014.

Nightingale, Carl H. *Segregation: A Global History of Divided Cities*. Chicago: University of Chicago Press, 2012.

Oppermann, Langdon E. *Winston-Salem's African-American Neighborhoods: 1870–1950: Architectural and Planning Report*. City of Winston-Salem, NC, 1994. https://www.scribd.com/document/385779331/Winston-Salem-s-African-American-Neighborhoods-1870-1950.

Orr Jr., Oliver H. *Charles Brantley Aycock*. Chapel Hill: University of North Carolina Press, 1961.

Painter, Nell Irvin. *Exodusters: Black Migration to Kansas After Reconstruction*. New York: Knopf, 1977.

Palmer, Bruce. *"Man Over Money": The Southern Populist Critique of American Capitalism*. Chapel Hill: University of North Carolina Press, 1980.

Perman, Michael. *Struggle for Mastery: Disfranchisement in the South, 1888–1908*. Chapel Hill: University of North Carolina Press, 2001.

Peterson, Merrill D., ed. *The Portable Thomas Jefferson*. New York: Penguin, 1975.

Petty, Adrienne Monteith. *Standing Their Ground: Small Farmers in North Carolina Since the Civil War*. New York: Oxford University Press, 2013.

Postel, Charles. *The Populist Vision*. Oxford: Oxford University Press, 2007.

Powell, William S., ed. *Dictionary of North Carolina Biography*. 6 vols. Chapel Hill: University of North Carolina Press, 1979–1996.

——. *North Carolina Through Four Centuries*. Chapel Hill: University of North Carolina Press, 1989.

Power, Garrett. "Apartheid Baltimore Style: The Residential Segregation Ordinances of 1910–1913." *Maryland Law Review* 42, no. 2 (1983): 289–328.

Rabinowitz, Howard. *Race Relations in the Urban South, 1865–1890*. New York: Oxford University Press, 1978.

Reid, Debra A., and Evan P. Bennett, eds. *Beyond Forty Acres and a Mule: African American Landowning Families Since Reconstruction*. Gainesville: University Press of Florida, 2012.

Rice, Roger L. "Residential Segregation by Law, 1910–1917." *Journal of Southern History* 34 (May 1968): 179–99.

Ring, Natalie J. "The 'New Race Question': The Problem of Poor Whites and the Color Line." In *The Folly of Jim Crow: Rethinking the Segregated South*, ed. Stephanie Cole and Natalie J. Ring, 91–123. Arlington: University of Texas at Arlington, 2012.

Ritterhouse, Jennifer. *Growing Up Jim Crow: How Black and White Southern Children Learned Race*. Chapel Hill: University of North Carolina Press, 2006.

Robinson, Cedric. *Black Marxism: The Making of the Black Radical Tradition*. London: Zed, 1983.

Rodgers, Daniel. *Atlantic Crossings: Social Politics in a Progressive Age*. Cambridge, MA: Harvard University Press, 1998.

Roediger, David R. *The Wages of Whiteness: Race and the Making of the American Working Class*. London: Verso, 2007.

Rolinson, Mary G. *Grassroots Garveyism: The Universal Negro Improvement Association in the Rural South, 1920–1927*. Chapel Hill: University of North Carolina Press, 2007.

Rothstein, Richard. *The Color of Law: A Forgotten History of How Our Government Segregated America*. New York: Liveright, 2017.

Schulman, Bruce J. *From Cotton Belt to Sunbelt: Federal Policy, Economic Development, and the Transformation of the South, 1938–1980*. Durham, NC: Duke University Press, 1994.

Schultz, Mark R. "Interracial Kinship Ties and the Emergence of a Rural Black Middle Class: Hancock County, Georgia, 1865–1920." In *Georgia in Black and White: Explorations in the Race Relations of a Southern State, 1865–1950*, ed. John C. Inscoe, 141–72. Athens: University of Georgia Press, 1994.

——. *The Rural Face of White Supremacy: Beyond Jim Crow*. Urbana: University of Illinois Press, 2005.

Schweninger, Loren. *Black Property Owners in the South, 1790–1915*. Urbana: University of Illinois Press, 1990.

Sharpless, Rebecca. *Cooking in Other Women's Kitchens: Domestic Workers in the South, 1865–1960*. Chapel Hill: University of North Carolina Press, 2010.

Shirley, Michael. *From Congregation Town to Industrial City: Culture and Social Change in a Southern Community*. New York: NYU Press, 1994.

Sitton, Thad, and James H. Conrad. *Freedom Colonies: Independent Black Texans in the Time of Jim Crow*. Austin: University of Texas Press, 2005.

Smith, John David, ed. *When Did Southern Segregation Begin?* Boston: Bedford/St. Martin's, 2002.

Sokol, Jason. *There Goes My Everything: White Southerners in the Age of Civil Rights, 1945–1975*. New York: Knopf, 2006.

Steelman, Joseph F. "The Progressive Democratic Convention of 1914 in North Carolina." *North Carolina Historical Review* 46, no. 2 (April 1969): 83–104.

Steelman, Lala Carr. *The North Carolina Farmers' Alliance: A Political History, 1887–1893*. Greenville, NC: East Carolina University Publications, 1985.

——. "The Role of Elias Carr in the North Carolina Farmers' Alliance." *North Carolina Historical Review* 57, no. 2 (April 1980): 133–58.

Strom, Claire. *Making Catfish Bait Out of Government Boys: The Fight Against Cattle Ticks and the Transformation of the Yeoman South*. Athens: University of Georgia Press, 2009.

Sumka, Howard. "Racial Segregation in Small North Carolina Cities." *Southeastern Geographer* 17, no. 1 (May 1977): 58–75.

Synnott, Marcia G. "Hugh MacRae, Penderlea, and the Model Farm Communities Movement." In *Proceedings of the South Carolina Historical Association*, ed. William S. Brockington, 53–66. Aiken: University of South Carolina at Aiken, 1987.

Thomas, Karen Kruse. *Deluxe Jim Crow: Civil Rights and American Health Policy, 1935–1954*. Athens: University of Georgia Press, 2011.

Tolnay, Stewart E., and E. M. Beck. *A Festival of Violence: An Analysis of Southern Lynchings, 1882–1930*. Urbana: University of Illinois Press, 1995.

Tursi, Frank V. *Winston-Salem: A History*. Winston-Salem, NC: John F. Blair, 1994.

Tushnet, Mark V. *Making Civil Rights Law: Thurgood Marshall and the Supreme Court, 1936–1961*. New York: Oxford University Press, 1994.

Umfleet, LeRae. "1898 Wilmington Race Riot Report." Wilmington Race Riot Commission and the North Carolina Office of Cultural Resources, May 31, 2006. http://www.ah.dcr.state.nc.us/1898-wrrc/report/report.htm.

Vile, John R., ed. *Great American Judges: An Encyclopedia*. Vol. 1. Santa Barbara, CA: ABC-CLIO, 2003.

Ward, Jason Morgan. *Defending White Democracy: The Making of a Segregationist Movement and the Remaking of Racial Politics, 1936–1965*. Chapel Hill: University of North Carolina Press, 2011.

Welsh, David. *The Roots of Segregation: Native Policy in Colonial Natal, 1845–1910*. Cape Town: Oxford University Press, 1971.

Wertheimer, John. *Law and Society in the South: A History of North Carolina Court Cases*. Lexington: University Press of Kentucky, 2009.

West, Michael Rudolph. *The Education of Booker T. Washington: American Democracy and the Idea of Race Relations*. New York: Columbia University Press, 2006.

West, Stephen A. *From Yeoman to Redneck in the South Carolina Upcountry, 1850–1915*. Charlottesville: University of Virginia Press, 2008.

Wickins, P. L. "The Natives Land Act of 1913: A Cautionary Essay on Simple Explanations of Complex Change." *South African Journal of Economics* 49, no. 2 (June 1981): 65–89.

Wiebe, Robert. *The Search for Order, 1877–1920*. New York: Hill and Wang, 1967.

Wiese, Andrew. *Places of Their Own: African American Suburbanization in the Twentieth Century*. Chicago: University of Chicago Press, 2004.

Wigginton, Russell. "'But He Did What He Could': William Warley Leads Louisville's Fight for Justice, 1902–1946." *Filson Club History Quarterly* 76, no. 4 (Fall 2002): 427–58.

Williams, Kidada E. *They Left Great Marks on Me: African American Testimonies of Racial Violence from Emancipation to World War I*. New York: NYU Press, 2012.

Williamson, Joel. *After Slavery: The Negro in South Carolina During Reconstruction, 1861–1877*. Chapel Hill: University of North Carolina Press, 1965.

——. *The Crucible of Race: Black-White Relations in the American South Since Emancipation*. New York: Oxford University Press, 1984.

Winkler, Adam. *We the Corporations: How American Businesses Won Their Civil Rights*. New York: Liveright, 2018.

Wolkoff, Adam Jacob. "Possession and Power: The Legal Culture of Tenancy in the United States, 1800–1920." Ph.D. diss., Rutgers University, 2015.

Wolpe, Harold. "Capitalism and Cheap Labour Power in South Africa: From Segregation to Apartheid." In *Segregation and Apartheid in Twentieth-Century South Africa*, ed. William Beinart and Saul Dubow, 60–90. London: Routledge, 1995.

Woodman, Harold D. "Class, Race, Politics, and the Modernization of the Postbellum South." *Journal of Southern History* 63, no. 1 (February 1997): 3–22.

——. *New South, New Law: The Legal Foundations of Credit and Labor Relations in the Postbellum Agricultural South*. Baton Rouge: Louisiana State University Press, 1995.

——. "Post–Civil War Southern Agriculture and the Law." *Agricultural History* 53, no. 1 (January 1979): 319–37.

Woodward, C. Vann. *Origins of the New South, 1877–1913* [1951]. Rev. ed. Baton Rouge: Louisiana State University Press, 1971.

——. *The Strange Career of Jim Crow* [1955]. 3rd rev. ed. New York: Oxford University Press, 1974.

——. *Tom Watson: Agrarian Rebel*. New York: Oxford University Press, 1938.

Woofter, T. J. *Negro Problems in Cities*. New York: Doubleday, Doran, 1928.

Wooley, Robert H. "Race and Politics: The Evolution of the White Supremacy Campaign of 1898 in North Carolina." Ph.D. diss., University of North Carolina at Chapel Hill, 1977.

Wright, Gavin. *Old South, New South: Revolutions in the Southern Economy Since the Civil War*. Baton Rouge: Louisiana State University Press, 1996.

Wright, George C. "The NAACP and Residential Segregation in Louisville, Kentucky, 1914–1917." *Register of the Kentucky Historical Society* 78, no. 1 (Winter 1980): 39–54.

Yeargin, Billy. *North Carolina Tobacco: A History*. Charleston, SC: History Press, 2008.

Index

CPSIA information can be obtained
at www.ICGtesting.com
Printed in the USA
LVHW031917290419
616004LV00003B/3